The British Navy's Victualling Board, 1793–1815

The British Navy's Victualling Board, 1793–1815

Management Competence and Incompetence

Janet Macdonald

THE BOYDELL PRESS

First published 2010
The Boydell Press, Woodbridge

ISBN 978 1 84383 553 0

The Boydell Press is an imprint of Boydell & Brewer Ltd
PO Box 9, Woodbridge, Suffolk IP12 3DF, UK
and of Boydell & Brewer Inc.
668 Mount Hope Ave, Rochester, NY 14604, USA
website: www.boydellandbrewer.com

A CIP catalogue record for this book is available
from the British Library

The publisher has no responsibility for the continued existence or accuracy of URLs for
external or third-party internet websites referred to in this book, and does not guarantee that any content on such websites is, or will remain, accurate or appropriate.

This publication is printed on acid-free paper
Edited and typeset by
Frances Hackeson Freelance Publishing Services, Brinscall, Lancs
Printed in Great Britain by
CPI Antony Rowe, Chippenham and Eastbourne

Contents

Author's notes   *page* vi
Acknowledgements   vii
Abbreviations   viii
Tables and Maps   ix

1   Introduction: Historiography and Early History of   1
Victualling
2   The Core Tasks: Obtaining and Distributing Bulk   16
Supplies of Food, Drink and Victualling Stores
3   Delivery at Home: Issuing Victuals to Warships   41
and Managing the Victualling Yards
4   Delivery Abroad for Warships, Army Garrisons   64
and Military Expeditions
5   Non-Core and Ad Hoc Tasks   86
6   Head Office Staff   108
7   Yard Staff   135
8   Theft, Fraud and Other Misdemeanours   160
9   Parliamentary Inquiries   187
10   Conclusions   213

Appendices

A   Substitute Provisions   225
B   An Account of the Expense of Victualling 110,000 Men   226
for 13 Lunar Months
C   Victualling Commissioners: Biographic Details   227
D   Staff numbers at Somerset Place   235
E   Head Office Staff Salaries   236
F   Establishment of Officers and Clerks at the Victualling   239
Yard at Deptford, as Proposed by the Board of Revision
G   Victualling Board Purchases of Cattle from Smithfield   240
Market

Glossary   241
Bibliography   245
Index   255

Author's note

All ADM C, G, D, DP and 110 series references are letters between the Admiralty and the Victualling Board unless otherwise stated.

All figures of naval manpower and numbers of ships are taken from N A M Rodger's *Command of the Ocean* pp. 606–9, 636–9.

The seeming inconsistency of non-italicisation of the word 'Instructions' is because those which are not in italics are handwritten copy documents, as opposed to published versions, which are italicised.

Figures given in the appendices of cost and weights/measurements are rounded and sometimes converted to a larger measure (e.g. pounds avoirdupois are converted to hundredweights).

St Catherine's was spelled with a 'C' or a 'K' at different periods; because the Victualling Board documents in the 1793–1815 period use the 'C', that spelling is used in this study.

Acknowledgements

I am grateful to the staff of the Admiralty Library, the National Archives, the National Maritime Museum, the Wellcome Trust, the British Library and the Intellectual Property Office; Pamela Clark, Registrar of The Royal Archives and Diane Clements of The United Grand Lodge of England for their generous assistance in finding research material and information; to my supervisors Professor Andrew Lambert and Dr Andrew James; to Professors David McLean and Richard Harding; to Professor Lewis Fischer of *The International Journal of Maritime History*; to John Day, Hugh Lyon, Dr Tim Voelcker, Rif Winfield and various student acquaintances who have suggested sources to investigate, and to my husband Ken Maxwell-Jones, who has not only tolerantly lived with naval victualling for many years, but who bravely duplicated my work with the Victualling Board's contract ledgers and other documents to check my figures.

Abbreviations

Board of Revision	The Board of Commissioners for Revising and Digesting the Civil Affairs of His Majesty's Navy
BOR 10	10th Report of the Board of Revision
BOR 11	11th Report of the Board of Revision
BOR 12	12th Report of the Board of Revision
BOR 13	13th Report of the Board of Revision
DNB	Dictionary of National Biography
Fees 8	8th Report of the Commissioners appointed to inquire into the fees, gratuities, perquisites and emoluments ...
Fees 9	9th Report of the Commissioners appointed to inquire into the fees, gratuities, perquisites and emoluments ...
NMM	National Maritime Museum, Greenwich, London
Regulations ... Home	Regulations for the Guidance of the Officers of the Several Victualling Establishments at Home
Regulations ... Abroad	Instructions for the Agents of the Victualling Establishments Abroad
R&I	Regulations and Instructions Relating to His Majesty's Service at Sea
SCF 32	32nd Report of the Select Committee on Finance
TNA	The National Archives, Kew, London

Tables and Maps

Tables

1 The ration for seamen   *page* 18
2 Periods of service of commissioners   115
3 Pension rates   131
4 Salaries proposed for the officers of the yards   142
5 Average total income of clerks at the yards before 1800   143
6 Annual salaries of clerks at the yards from 1800   143

Maps

1 The world   x
2 Western Mediterranean   xi
3 The Caribbean   xii
4 The Windward and Leeward Islands   xiii
5 The British Isles and northern Europe   xiv
6 London in the eighteenth century   xv
7 Plymouth Sound   xvi
8 Portsmouth, Isle of Wight and Spithead   xviii

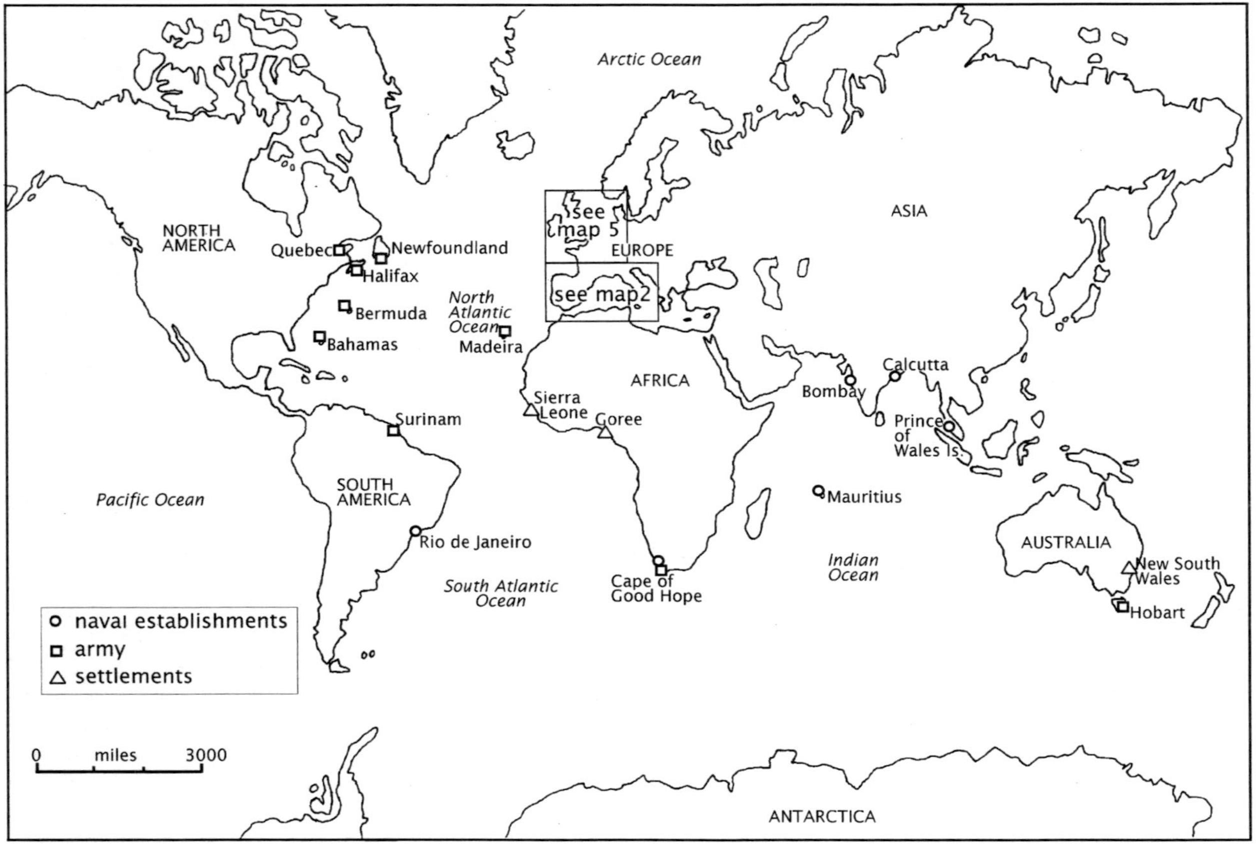

Map 1: The world

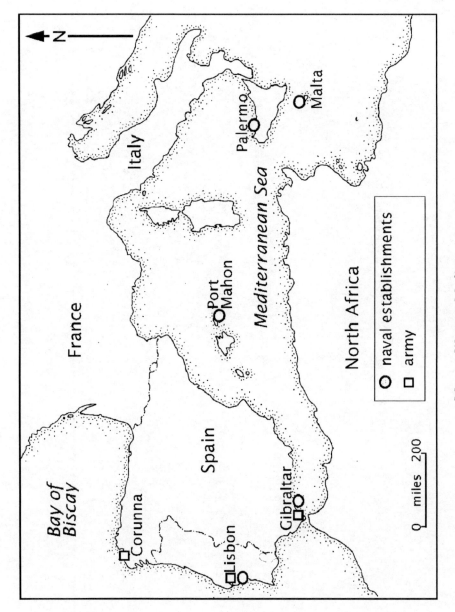

Map 2: Western Mediterranean

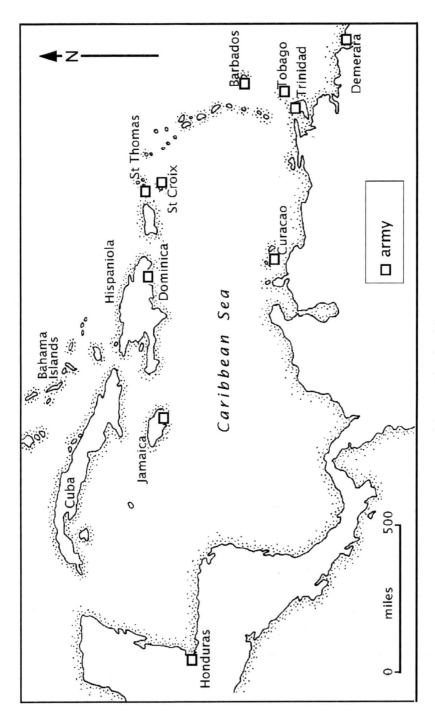

Map 3: The Caribbean

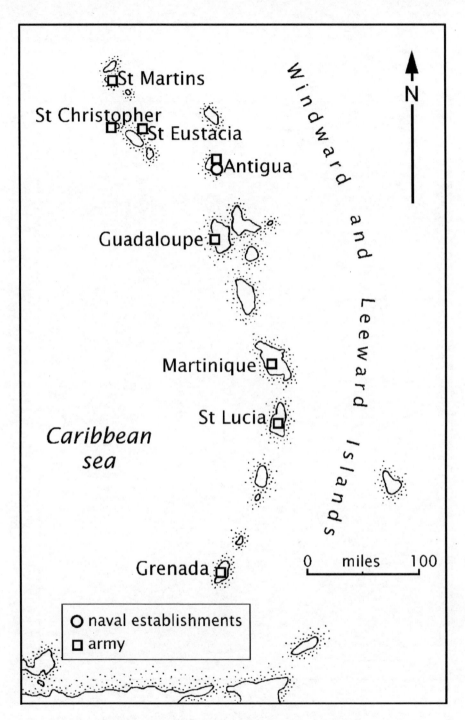

Map 4: The Windward and Leeward Islands

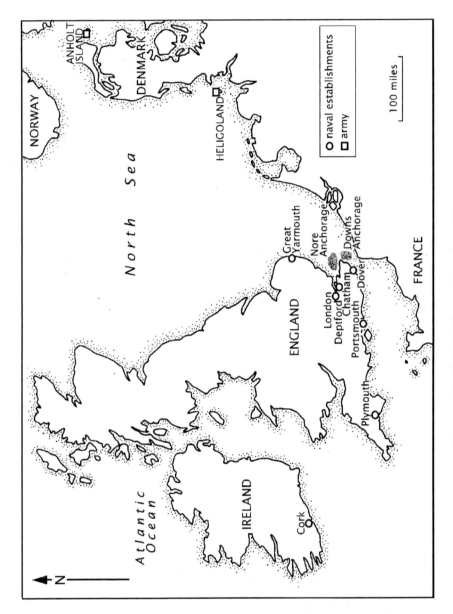

Map 5: The British Isles and northern Europe

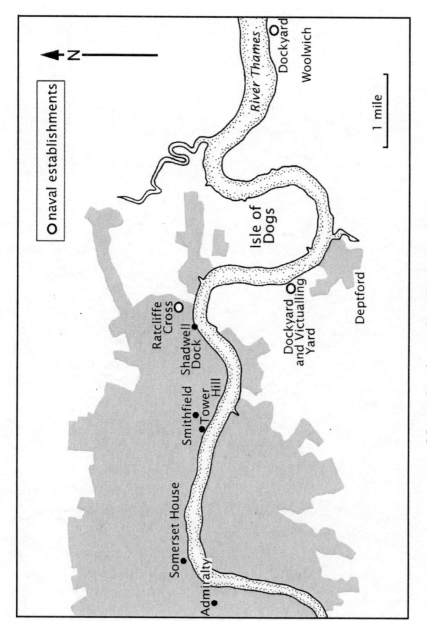

Map 6: London in the eighteenth century

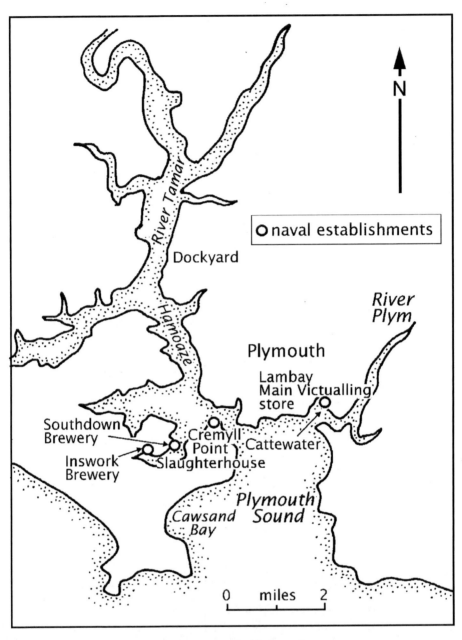

Map 7: Plymouth Sound

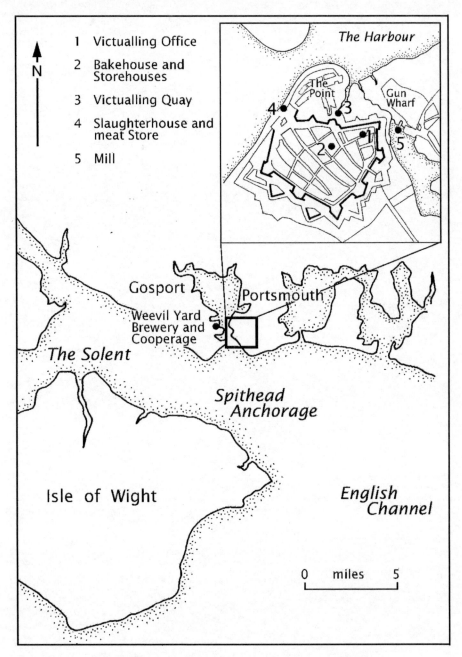

Map 8: Portsmouth, Isle of Wight and Spithead

1

Introduction, Historiography and Early History of Victualling

B RITISH NAVAL HISTORY has a history of its own. According to the social and political agendas of the day, it has been told as the story of a sequence of important battles which led to British naval supremacy, a sequence of hagiographies intended to offer the subjects as role models to the coming generation of naval officers, studies of battle tactics made at a time when a new outbreak of war seemed inevitable, studies of developing technologies and studies of the social history of the navy and life at sea. A few historians have recognised the importance of naval administration but they have tended to concentrate on the building and repairing of ships, the economic aspects of running a navy and the political personalities involved at high levels.

One aspect of British naval history which has received little attention is that of logistics and the art of keeping ships and their crews supplied with equipment and, perhaps more importantly, the victuals which fuelled their efforts. These victuals were supplied by the Board of Admiralty's subsidiary, the Victualling Board, which commenced its work in 1683 and continued, with only one brief pause, until 1832, when, with the other subsidiary boards, it was disbanded and its functions taken over by the newly created Victualling Department of the Admiralty. During this long period, the Victualling Board and its staff at the Victualling Office and yards had ample opportunity during numerous wars to improve its administrative systems, but it was during the twenty-three years of the great French wars that the Board was put to its greatest test: that of feeding over 147,000 men in over 800 ships deployed on stations around the world, and being given formal responsibility for feeding many people besides British naval personnel and occasionally soldiers on transports: soldiers in overseas garrisons, British settlements overseas, convicts en route to New South Wales, the men of other navies, and at various periods, distressed civilians in places such as the Shetland Islands. Taken all together, although accurate figures cannot be obtained, the number of men fed by the Victualling Board was probably well in excess of 250,000 at the high point between 1810 and 1815.

The Victualling Board and its staff in the Victualling Office performed many tasks relating to feeding the British Navy, Army and other dependants: these included arranging contracts for supplies of provisions, manufacturing some of these at several British locations, maintaining and improving their many properties, auditing pursers' accounts and maintaining a watch against fraud. During the course of the French Revolutionary and Napoleonic wars the manner in which these tasks were handled changed in a number of ways: the duration and number of supply contracts changed gradually from a system dominated by a few open-ended contracts with a small number of buying agents and contractors to one with more numerous short-term contracts using a larger pool of contractors and fewer agents; the staff remuneration changed from a system based on fees, gratuities and perquisites, to one of established salaries with regular long-service increases; and the accounting system for pursers and agents victualler changed from one of non-standardised paperwork to one of standard pre-printed forms which had to be completed in a specific way.

Although we know that most of these changes were prompted by the four major Parliamentary enquiries, some were prompted by other situations. These changes raise some questions: to what extent were the changes instigated by the commissioners themselves? Of the changes which came from outside, to what extent were these prompted by an adverse view of the management competence of the Victualling Board commissioners? Were the changes resisted by the Board's commissioners and staff? Did the process of feeding the navy improve as a result of these changes? The final question is perhaps the most important: given that the changes were deemed necessary, did the Victualling Board and its staff perform their jobs as competently as they might throughout the period, and if not, why not?

In order to answer these questions, it is necessary to ask several others: how much autonomy did the Victualling Board enjoy? What were the reporting chains within the Victualling Board, the Victualling Office and its external departments? Who were the commissioners who made up the Board and how were they and their staff selected? Were their political affiliations important? How effective were the mechanisms by which the Victualling Board dealt with the changing locations of naval operations? Did the changes of system have a marked effect on the quality of the foodstuffs delivered to the navy? To what extent did the Victualling Board concern itself with health issues? And one final but related question: did the Victualling Board's purchasing requirements have any effect on the country's agricultural output and marketing?

Before we attempt to assess competence of the commissioners of the Victualling Board as a management unit we need first to define the term 'management competence'. In any context, it has to mean the ability to get the *whole* job done promptly and properly, without allowing deep-seated problems to develop or remain without remedial action; it requires attention to detail, understanding of the processes and a willingness to instigate change when necessary. It is comparatively easy to assess this competence using twenty-first century hindsight; however, this risks an anachronistic judgement. It is therefore necessary to consider whether the concepts of competence and management per se were recognised at the time and whether they were deemed more important than the social and political requirements of the patronage system which were more likely to be utilised when seeking appointees for vacant posts. Although one cannot state that the latter was exclusively the case, as it is the actuality of appointments rather than the reasons for them which feature in the surviving correspondence and minutes, it has become accepted by naval historians that this was so. There is, in evidence of this, a revealing exchange of acrimonious correspondence between Charles Middleton (as Comptroller of the Navy Board) and Lord Sandwich (as First Lord of the Admiralty) over Navy Board appointments.[1] While this argument centred on who had the right to make such appointments, it highlights the fact that Sandwich was convinced that his political reasons for appointee choice were more valid than Middleton's practical requirement for experience and professional merit.

Whether the concept of management competence existed generally at the time is less certain and unfortunately the existing literature, which can be divided into general and naval history, is not particularly helpful on this aspect. Political and economic historians have written much about gradual changes in the bureaucratic culture and the shift from office holding and sinecures to what is now known as the civil service, but much of this literature, especially that of O MacDonagh, H Parris, and other writings which grew out of appraisals of A V Dicey's work, deals largely with post-Napoleonic War periods, usually after 1830 and many after 1850, when government departments were proliferating to administer sociologically inspired legislation such as the Factory Acts.[2] Of this literature which does relate to our period, that of G E Aylmer, Emmeline Cohen and Philip Harling are most useful. Aylmer suggests six principal features of 'the old

1   Sir John Knox Laughton (ed.), *Letters and Papers of Charles, Lord Barham*, Vol. 2 (London, 1910), pp. 2–36.
2   O MacDonagh, 'The nineteenth century revolution in government: A reappraisal', *Historical Journal* 1 (1958), pp. 52–67; H Parris, *Constitutional Bureaucracy: The Development of the British Central Administration since the Eighteenth Century* (London, 1969); H Parris, 'The nineteenth century revolution in government: A reappraisal reappraised', *Historical Journal* 3 (1960), pp. 17–37; A V Dicey, *Lectures on the Relation between Law and Order and Public Opinion in England during the Nineteenth Century* (London, 1905). See also Gillian Sutherland (ed.), *Studies in the Growth of Nineteenth Century Government* (London, 1972).

administrative system' which include entry to an office through purchase or patronage, lifetime tenure, the concept of offices as personal property and the associated right to appoint deputies to do the actual work, with the remuneration for these offices coming from fees and perquisites rather than fixed salaries.[3] Harling applies the label 'old corruption' to these practices, believing them to have lingered until the 1850s.[4]

Cohen points out, as do other writers, that the combination of the cost of the war with America and the disorderly state of the organization of public business had attracted attention; as Burke pointed out in his famous speech on economical reform 'neither the present, nor any other First Lord of the Treasury, has ever been able to … even make a tolerable guess of the expenses of government of any one year …' This led to the first of a series of commissions of enquiry into the public accounts and conditions in public offices which was followed by a select committee investigation into finance.[5] However, despite Aylmer's comment that 'one test of any administration is a functional one: how effectively did it do what it set out to do, or what contemporary society expected of it?', the writings of both Cohen and Aylmer and those who followed them tend to concentrate on the shift away from the principle of offices as property, the sale of positions within departments, and remuneration by fees and perquisites, and do not discuss the competence of those who were running those departments. Even those naval historians who answer the first of Aylmer's questions by stating that the administration was effective, judging this by the fact that fleets were able to remain operationally effective, only discuss the expectations of contemporary society in those terms.

One of the early manifestations of the shift to better practice was the appointment, in many government departments, of a second secretary to assist the 'first' secretary. The first secretary was the senior administrator of the department, but was a political appointee who departed when there was a change of government; many of them considered that they were personal employees of the minister, rather than of the department. The second secretary was appointed on a permanent basis, and many of them served for decades, which gave them invaluable experience of the workings of their department. But with only a few exceptions, these departments dealt with little more than correspondence and consisted of a small staff. This applied to the Board of Admiralty, where the secretariat, although swelling

3   G E Aylmer, 'From office-holding to civil service: The genesis of modern bureaucracy', *Transactions of the Royal Historical Society*, 5th series, part 30 (1980), pp. 91–108.

4   Philip Harling, *The Waning of 'Old Corruption': The Politics of Economical Reform in Britain, 1779–1846* (Oxford, 1996), passim.

5   Emmeline W Cohen, *The Growth of the British Civil Service 1780–1939* (London, 1941, 2nd edition 1965), p. 22. The results of these enquiries are discussed in Chapter 9.

in wartime, rarely exceeded twenty persons.[6] The abilities and efficiency of the members of such a small staff were well within the purview of the permanent secretary; it was the subordinate organisations of the Admiralty, especially the Navy Board and the Victualling Board, which had large numbers of clerical staff in numerous departments, in many cases more than could be known as anything other than faces in a dimly-lit office by the commissioner who was nominally responsible for them.

Although these general debates, especially the few which do mention the concept of efficiency (usually in the form of reports of personnel who were clearly incompetent, either from congenital or attitudinal inability when appointed or from approaching senility) do not do so with regard to the senior management, except in the person of the permanent secretary. These men are generally reported by modern historians to have been extremely competent; their length of service strongly suggests that this was also the contemporary view. In several cases, these men are referred to as 'men of business'. This term does not mean, as it does now, a man with experience of commercial business, but one who was a good administrator; Nelson used it as a description of Admiral Jervis (later Earl St Vincent) as commander-in-chief in the Mediterranean in 1796.[7] Another term which has been applied to such men is 'professional' but this tends to mean men in law, medicine or the Church, with the term coming into use for civil servants only after the 1854 Northcote and Trevelyan report. W J Reader, in his book on professional men in nineteenth century England, does mention accountants, engineers, architects and civil servants, but the latter is in connection with the period after that report.[8] Again, there is no discussion here, nor in any of the histories of government departments, of management competence. Even in Daniel Wren's *History of Management Thought*, the concentration is on the specific techniques for managing industrial workforces, with only brief mention of government administration (and that only in the twentieth century); there is no discussion on the qualities required of managers.[9]

With two exceptions, Daniel Baugh's *Naval Administration in the Age of Walpole*, and his *Naval Administration*, the literature on naval administration centres on the running of the royal dockyards, to such an extent that one might be forgiven for thinking these establishments were the

---

6   J C Sainty, *Admiralty Officials 1660–1870* (London, 1975), passim.

7   G B P Naish (ed.), *Nelson's Letters to his Wife* (London, 1958).

8   W J Reader, *Professional Men: The Rise of the Professional Classes in Nineteenth Century England* (London, 1966), passim.

9   For instance, Kenneth Ellis, *The Post Office in the Eighteenth Century: A Study in Administration History* (Oxford, 1958); R R Nelson, *The Home Office 1782–1800* (Durham, NC, 1969); Daniel A Wren, *The History of Management Thought* (Hoboken, NJ, 2005), passim.

totality of naval administration.[10] There is no significant writing on the other, non-dockyard, work of the Navy Board or any of the other boards, although Roger Morriss does bring the Victualling Board into his reports on fraud and of the grading and salaries of staff. Even within the context of the dockyards, these two aspects predominate: theft, wages and working conditions of the dockyard artisans and other manual workers; fees, salaries and pension arrangements for the middle management and clerical staff, and corrupt activities by those persons and the associated agents and supply contractors. Where inefficiency is discussed it is mainly in the context of resistance to new ideas from entrenched elderly middle managers of the dockyards. Dockyard inefficiency, together with the high levels of corruption upon which Earl St Vincent focused when he was First Lord of the Admiralty, are discussed in these writings, together with the publicly reported fraudulent practices which led to the Parliamentary inquiry into 'Irregularities, Frauds and Abuses',[11] as well as the much reported Atkinson affair.[12] But as with the general debates, these naval debates (although they are not so much debates as consensual reporting), concentrate on lower-level inefficiency, and have little to say on the management competence of the individuals who made up the Navy Board.[13]

The exception to this is J M Haas, who states in his *A Management Odyssey* that the royal dockyards were not well managed, 'as concluded by every official enquiry between the late eighteenth and early nineteenth century', but as with the rest of the literature, much of his analysis relates to post-Napoleonic War periods and to dockyard management, not Navy Board commissioners. Haas's book was received with mixed reactions, none of them unequivocally approving.[14]

Roger Morriss, in his *Naval Power and British Culture* 'aims to relocate the beginnings of the revolution in government to the late 1790s and to attach it to … Samuel Bentham.' Arising from this, he has much to say on the topic of collective (or joint) responsibility as opposed to individual responsibility. The idea behind collective responsibility was that it was a form of cross-checking by work colleagues; however, as Morriss points out, it had three weaknesses: it diluted responsibility of individuals who could rely on others

10   Daniel A Baugh, *British Naval Administration in the Age of Walpole* (Princeton, NJ, 1965); Daniel A Baugh (ed.), *Naval Administration 1715–1750* (London, 1977).
11   See Bibliography for the full title of this inquiry.
12   See page 12 below.
13   R J B Knight, 'The Royal Dockyards in England at the Time of the War of American Independence' (Unpublished Ph.D. thesis, London, 1972); Roger Morriss, *Royal Dockyards during the Revolutionary and Napoleonic Wars* (Leicester, 1983).
14   These reviews are summarised in Ann Coats, 'Efficiency in Dockyard Administration 1660–1800: A Reassessment', in N Tracey (ed.), *The Age of Sail*, Vol. 2 (London, 2004), p. 127.

to correct mistakes, it lulled superiors into a false sense of security, and it made individuals prey to the prejudices and conservatism of colleagues and also to personal rivalries and jealousies.[15] To all intents and purposes it worked well enough while everyone had time for such checking, but did not work when the workload increased, typically in wartime. The answer, as devised by Samuel Bentham and taken up by his brother Jeremy was for responsibility to rest with the individual. There are, however, some major flaws in this latter concept which Morriss did not mention: firstly that it assumes that all individuals are competent and conscientious, secondly that no one (other than the named individual in charge of the department where they occur) will be aware of problems until something serious eventuates, and thirdly that there is little point in knowing who is responsible for problems if, as tends to be the case, they are not replaced when such problems recur. In the event, the idea of individual responsibility was not taken up in the naval administration until after 1832 when the subordinate boards were abolished and a single superintendent was placed in charge of each of the subordinate departments, this superintendent reporting to a single member of the Board of Admiralty. But despite all his arguments about the merits of individual responsibility, and reports of Samuel Bentham's roving brief to consider improvements (most of which related to practical matters) Morriss does not discuss the actual competence of those individuals, either as a modern comment or reporting contemporary opinion, except in the case of Charles Middleton.

As Comptroller of the Navy Board, and later as First Lord of the Admiralty (when he became Lord Barham) Middleton, who was himself extremely competent, suffered much frustration over the quality of the people with whom he had to work. He complained that the matters brought before the Board were produced in the order in which they arrived in the post, with no attempt to sort them into topics. and he was constantly frustrated about the lack of order in the Navy Board records, to the extent that he started his own 'digest' of these. He was the guiding light behind the setting up of the Board of Revision and its investigations, and it is here that we finally encounter a contemporary view of what qualities department commissioners should possess. Middleton, and the two other commissioners who investigated the workings of the Victualling Board, made it quite clear in their reports that this Board's performance as managers was unsatisfactory; thus, in at least one key area the Victualling Board's contemporaries publicly expressed the need for those serving on the naval boards to be competent managers. Given that these reports are so comprehensive on the systems by which the

15   Roger Morriss, *Naval Power and British Culture 1760–1850* (London, 2004), pp. 3, 66–7.

Royal Navy was administered, it is unfortunate that they have received less attention from naval historians than they merit.

Since feeding a fleet spread throughout most of the world comes into the category of military logistics, one might expect that writing on that topic would cover both food and the navy, but as with the management competence of government administrators, the literature on any form of historical military logistics is, although growing in the last decade, still sparse and although occasionally to be found as detailed papers in journals, generally found only as sections, or mere passing mentions, in material on specific wars or campaigns. Even so, both journal papers and books tend, to a very large degree, to concentrate on twentieth-century conflicts. There is some literature on army supply in the mid-eighteenth century, and some on the Peninsular War, but as far as victualling is concerned the concentration is on merchant contractors and army commissaries, neither dealing extensively with the organisation at home.

The history of naval victualling in Britain

With the exception of Buchet's *Marine, économie et société;* this author's *Feeding Nelson's Navy* and 'The Victualling Board 1793–1815: A Study of Management Competence', and a few papers in journals, the historiography of British naval victualling consists almost entirely of chapters (or less) in books on more general aspects of specific periods of naval history.[16]

Little is known about victualling arrangements before the reign of Henry VIII but between his reign and the seventeenth century it was dealt with under arrangements that included purchase through purveyance by members of the royal household; management by formally appointed officials; by handing the whole situation over to contractors, and by a victualling department under the aegis of the Navy Board. This last method was no more successful than any of the others and complaints about the victuals continued: 'full of maggots, and so rotten no dog would eat it' said Captain Thomas Penrose, when refusing to name the men from his ship who demolished the victualling office in Rochester in 1658.[17]

In 1665 Samuel Pepys was appointed Surveyor-General of Victualling. He made some useful improvements to the systems, including a reform of pursery. He could, however, do nothing about the money shortage,

---

16 Christian Buchet, *Marine, économie et société* (Paris, 1999); Janet Macdonald, *Feeding Nelson's Navy: The True Story of Food at Sea in the Georgian era* (London, 2004); 'The Victualling Board 1793–1815: A Study of Management Competence' (Unpublished Ph.D. thesis, London, 2009).

17 N A M Rodger, *The Command of the Ocean: A Naval History of Britain, Vol. Two 1649–1815* (London, 2004), p. 54.

a problem which was not tackled for another 50 years. In October 1683, during the period when Pepys was out of office, the Admiralty created a separate board of Victualling Commissioners, to replace contractors.

This new board was provided with a detailed set of 'Instructions to the Commissioners of the Victualling' on how to perform their duties. The early decades of the Victualling Board were somewhat turbulent, with frequent alterations to the system; the original Instructions to the Commissioners of the Victualling of 1684 were expanded in 1700, 1711 and 1715.[18] There were also several changes to the Board itself, the first in 1689 after a Parliamentary inquiry led to the arrest and dismissal of all four members of the Board (Nicholas Fenn, Sir Richard Haddock, John Parsons and Anthony Sturt).[19] This was portrayed at the time as neglect of duty leading to victualling shortages, which in turn led to fleet failures, although in fact the problem was caused by a combination of inadequate finance and bad timing: by the time the requisite money for victualling was voted the season was too far advanced for proper food production.[20]

Following this situation, the number of commissioners was increased to five, and in April 1704 to seven. In June 1706, three of these departed (Samuel Hunter, Henry Lee and Abraham Tilghman). The specific reason for this has not emerged, but R D Merriman offers a clue in remarking on 'shortages of provisions which in 1703 and 1706 reduced the Mediterranean fleet to the point of starvation'.[21] Even so, Hunter and Lee were reappointed in November 1711, so these shortages may have been a convenient excuse for what was actually a politically motivated dismissal.

At that time five of the seven commissioners were replaced, and in December 1714 five more were replaced. In the first of these cases, an inquiry into 'abuses in the victualling office' uncovered what appeared to be major abuses throughout the system, centring on the brewing operations. However, with the exception of what does appear to have been embezzlement at the Hartshorne Brewery, the apparent collusion between victualling yard staff and outside brewers turned out to be a device to alleviate a problem with beer which had gone off.[22] This may be part of the reason Onslow and Reynolds, who had been dismissed in 1711, were reinstated in 1714.

Another complaint at this time, considered sufficiently serious to form part of the revised 'Instructions to [named] commissioners for victualling'

18 TNA T 52/9; TNA ADM/645–8. Instructions to the Commissioners of the Victualling (1684, 1700, 1711, 1715).
19 The new board was not appointed until May 1690. TNA C66/3334.
20 Rodger, *Command* (London, 2004), pp. 192–3.
21 R D Merriman (ed.), *Documents concerning the Administration of Queen Anne's Navy* (London, 1961), p. 250.
22 For the details of this situation, see *Cobbetts Parliamentary History of England*, Vol. VI, cols. 996–1001, 3 January 1711.

which were issued in 1715, was that various accounts had not been final-ised, despite, in many cases, the account holders having long left their posts (or died). The previous set of Instructions, issued in 1711, had also required the commissioners, although still operating as a board, to divide the depart-ments of the office between themselves so that each branch was in the care of a specific commissioner. The 1715 Instructions not only repeated this requirement, but allocated separate branches to individual commissioners by name. [23]

Meanwhile, on 14 December 1714, a further embezzlement, over boat hire, had been discovered at Plymouth.[24] This must have been one of the things which led to the change of commissioners later that month, again on the basis of failure of the commissioners to do their job properly. This is made clear in the 1715 Instructions issued to the new board. These state that following a review in 1710, the then commissioners had been instructed to 'do their utmost towards the stating and ballancing'[sic] of the accounts in arrears, but despite this,

> we have too much reason to believe from a return not long since made by the late [Board of Victualling] upon their being required to give an account of their proceedings therein, that very little has been done towards the performance of so necessary a work …

Whilst there is a strong possibility that some of the dismissals during the first decades of the Victualling Board's existence were politically motivated from faction loyalties (in these early years many of the commissioners were also sitting MPs), it is equally possible that the victualling commissioners were being used as scapegoats for government failures; there undoubtedly were shortages of victuals but most of these were not from the victual-ling commissioners' failure to do their job but from their inability to do it due to inadequate funding. Thomas Papillon, who headed the new Board appointed in 1690, complained about this in 1691, and in September 1711 the Victualling Board wrote to the Treasury explaining that their difficulties in providing provisions and the very high prices demanded by their usual suppliers were grounded 'on the present uncertainty of the payment'; all the merchants wanted to know how and when they would be paid before submitting tenders. However, although these and previous commissioners laboured under those difficulties, they were clearly, as the brewery and boat hire situations demonstrate, unaware of what was going on at the yards, and as repeated demands from the Admiralty and Treasury demonstrate, failing to finalise accounts amounting to large sums of money. As we shall

23 TNA ADM 7/646, 10 April 1711; ADM 7/648, 13 January 1714/15.
24 TNA ADM 3/29, 14 December 1714.

see later, these failings continued to mar the performance of the Victualling Board.

In 1747, when the 'Place' Act (which forbade MPs to hold public offices) came into force, three commissioners (Thomas Brereton, William Hay and Thomas Revell) resigned, preferring a seat in Parliament to one on the Victualling Board.[25]

Between 1683 and 1747 the Victualling Board's establishment had grown from 23 people to 122.[26] Some of this increase in staff was due to the greater volume of clerical work required to service a fleet which had approximately quadrupled, but 52 people were involved in the new activity of processing and packing of victuals.[27] Since its formation, the Board had extended its premises in London several times to allow manufacturing activities as well as increasing their storage capacity; eventually moving all this to larger premises at the Red House Estate at Deptford in the 1740s. The head office remained at Tower Hill until 1787 when it moved to Somerset Place.[28] By the beginning of the 1790s, the other yards at Chatham, Dover, Portsmouth and Plymouth, which had previously been little more than storage depots, gradually acquired slaughterhouses, meat processing premises, breweries and finally bakeries, as the emphasis of operations shifted from the North Sea during the Dutch Wars down the Channel and out into the Western Approaches when the French became the main enemy. One new procedure was to supply ships with fresh beef when in port; this developed later into sending live beasts out to the blockading squadrons off the French coast.[29] In 1759, this tactic changed to a close blockade just a few miles off Brest, where the French fleet would either have to remain in port or face immediate action on emerging. To maintain this close blockade all available ships were needed constantly on station, and it was to allow this that the practice of sending out fresh vegetables and live cattle and sheep was introduced. The practice continued and was still in operation during the French Revolutionary and Napoleonic wars at various locations, notably the Mediterranean where

---

25   15 Geo II c22; TNA ADM 111/33, Victualling Board minute, 24 June 1747.
26   John B Hattendorf, R J B Knight, A W H Pearsall, N A M Rodger & G Till (eds), *British Naval Documents 1204–1960* (London, 1993) pp. 244–5, quoting TNA ADM 3/278, pp 126–7, 5 October 1683; Baugh, *Walpole*, p. 55, quoting TNA ADM 110/15, 28 January 1747.
27   Rodger, *Command*, pp. 636–8.
28   David Elvin, 'The Founding and Development of the Victualling Yard at Deptford in the 1740s' (MA dissertation, Greenwich Maritime Institute, 2005).
29   Baugh, *Walpole*, pp. 433, 436–7; Rodger, *Command*, pp. 194, 281, 306; Hattendorf *et al.*, *British Naval Documents*, pp. 442–3.

blockading squadrons off Toulon were a minimum of one week's sail from the victualling yards at Gibraltar, Malta or Port Mahon.[30]

Although much has been written about naval victualling in the Seven Years' War, particularly the situation in the West Indies, there is a paucity of general information about naval victualling in the American War of Independence. It seems that all went comparatively smoothly for the navy, less so for the army in North America.[31] However, there were two major problems during that period, the first concerning allegations of large-scale fraud against the Navy Board, the Victualling Board and the Board of Ordnance in the West Indies which is discussed in Chapter 8; the second was the case of Christopher Atkinson, the Victualling Board's corn supplier. This case hinged on the precise nature of Atkinson's relationship with the Board: from a contract granted following public tendering, Atkinson gradually acquired a monopoly of supplying wheat, flour, oats, barley and pease. As far as the Victualling Board was concerned, these arrangements were on an agency basis, with Atkinson receiving a commission based on quantities plus his expenses for delivery as well as reimbursement of the market price of the grains. Atkinson clearly saw his position in a different light, and after some time he was accused of inflating the price he had paid for these commodities, effectively acting as both agent and merchant. This situation degenerated into a major public scandal, with a Parliamentary commission of enquiry, and Atkinson being convicted for perjury, and expelled from the House of Commons (although he was later exonerated, received a royal pardon and reelected). All this, however, could have been avoided had the Victualling Board clarified, at the outset, Atkinson's status as the servant of the Crown, not the private contractor he considered himself to be.[32]

Financing naval victualling

One aspect of early naval administration, which throws considerable light on the seeming incompetence of the Victualling Board in its early decades,

30 Janet Macdonald, 'Victualling the British Mediterranean Fleet, May 1803 to June 1804' (MA dissertation, Greenwich Maritime Institute, 2003).

31 There are three studies which cover this situation and offer some insights into the competence of government administration: Norman Baker, *Government and Contractors: The British Treasury and War Supplies 1775–1783* (London, 1971); R Arthur Bowler, *Logistics and the Failure of the British Army in America 1775–1783* (London, 1975); David Syrett, *Shipping and the American War 1775–1783: A Study of British Transport Organization* (London, 1970).

32 David Syrett, 'Christopher Atkinson and the Victualling Board, 1775–1782', *Historical Research* 69 (1996), pp. 129–42.

is the chaotic nature of public finance. This topic is discussed in several of the studies mentioned above (particularly Ehrman, Rodger and Watson) but perhaps the most important writer on military finance is John Brewer.[33] Quoting Cicero's dictum 'The sinews of war are infinite money', Brewer coins the phrase 'fiscal-military state' to describe the condition of Britain by the middle of the eighteenth century, when the increasing cost of war had led to a national debt of almost £243 million by 1784.[34] It was the need to manage and, hopefully, to reduce this debt that drove the financial reforms which, amongst other benefits, eased the task of the Victualling Board and improved the lot of the British sailor.

Although seemingly sound on government finance, Brewer is less so on naval victualling. Apart from making one of the classic errors (assuming that 'bisket' is a mis-spelling of 'brisket')[35] he uses as his main source of figures Rodger's *Wooden World*, which is itself flawed in several ways.[36] Nor are his conclusions all sound; he suggests that the fiscal-military state was instrumental in creating 'the City'. This is unlikely: although war certainly created greater opportunities for the money brokers and lenders of 'the City', they had been there for several centuries; government departments, including the subsidiary boards of the Admiralty merely utilised the existing financial establishments to meet their needs.[37]

These boards paid their suppliers by issuing 'in course' bills of exchange. 'In course' meant that although payment would be delayed, these bills would be paid (i.e. exchanged for cash) in strict order of acceptance. If payment was delayed beyond a certain time, say six months, interest at a stated rate was payable. Announcements on the dates when tranches of bills would be paid were published in the newspapers so the bankers and investors who specialised in buying these 'Navy bills' could calculate how long they would have to wait to realise their investment and thus the appropriate discounts to apply when buying or selling. The suppliers, who stood at the bottom of the discount ladder, could also calculate the potential cash value they would receive when encashing their bills and adjust their prices

---

33 John Brewer, *Sinews of Power: War, Money and the English State* (London, 1989).

34 Ibid., pp. 29–30. All figures given here are rounded up from those in Brewer's table.

35 Brewer *Sinews*, p. 37; the effects of this mistake on calorie counts (which have been much cited) are detailed in Macdonald, *Feeding*, p. 177.

36 N A M Rodger, *Wooden World: An Anatomy of the Georgian Navy* (London, 1996), pp. 83–4. There is a sequence of garbled information which runs from Gradish through *Wooden World* into Brewer and finally Buchet. For details of this see J Macdonald, 'A New Myth of Naval History', *International Journal of Maritime History*, 27:2 (December 1999), pp. 159–88.

37 Brewer, *Sinews*, pp. 250–1.

accordingly when tendering for Victualling Board contracts.[38] Most contractors, particularly those supplying wholesale items to the Victualling Board's yards, received early partial payments in the form of imprest accounts, but even these were in the form of post-dated bills and thus not instant cash.

For the Victualling Board, it meant supplies cost more than they would have done on the open market for immediate cash but given that the cash was not available, this situation was tolerable. It did, at least, mean that there would be no more incidents like that in 1696 when the cheese suppliers announced that they could no longer give credit and required an immediate cash payment before resuming deliveries.[39] A further advantage of having an orderly credit system in place was that it increased the number of suppliers willing to deal with the Victualling Board and thus introduced a greater element of competition which allowed the Board to exercise greater control over both quality and reliability of delivery.

It can be seen from the foregoing that a number of general themes emerge in the existing literature when dealing with naval victualling: lack of money, fraudulent contractors and officials, administrative inefficiency and what is often described as the 'inadequate technology' of food preservation, although examination of specific complaints shows that it was in fact faulty execution of the processes rather than the processes themselves which caused problems.[40] Almost all this literature approaches the topic of victualling as a problem area, concentrating on the visible results (i.e. the perceived successes and failures of the delivery systems), rather than the processes underlying the victualling administration, how this administration performed and the causes of any poor performance. It seems that the main problem with all the existing literature is that because no thorough analysis has been performed to date, the authors of this literature have had no starting point from which to judge what is important and thus worthy of deeper study for their period. Many have used only a limited range of primary source documents, and many have completely ignored the available copious detail of purchases and accounting practices. This narrowness of sources, and a generally uncritical repetition of what on closer examination often turn out to be flawed secondary sources, has provided an unbalanced picture of both the victualling task and the individuals who performed it.

Some historians have also accepted without investigation the picture of appalling food presented by a couple of lower-deck men, and this, with the

---

38 Paula K Watson, 'The Commission for Victualling the Navy, the Commission for Sick and Wounded Seamen and Prisoners of War and the Commission for Transport 1702–1714' (Unpublished Ph.D. thesis, London, 1965), pp. 111, 149; Rodger, *Command*, pp. 292–3.

39 John Ehrman, *The Navy in the War of William III: 1689–1697* (Cambridge, 1953), p. 588.

40 Rodger, *Command*, p. 193.

conflation of a few isolated and early incidents of failures of the system, has produced a false picture.[41] Close reading of these books indicates that the prose and opinions expressed are typically those of middle-class Victorians; this gives rise to the suspicion that these books were heavily rewritten by their publishers' editors to conform to the mores of the time of publication. Common sense should dictate that prolonged periods of hard physical work cannot be sustained on poor food, a view which is endorsed by Carl von Clausewitz: 'Anyone who tries to maintain that wretched food makes no difference to an army … is not taking a dispassionate view of the subject. … privation … is bound to sap the physical and moral strength of every man.'[42]

This study attempts to correct those pictures for one very important period of naval history, and in the process to open a debate not only on the place of victualling and logistics in the study of naval history but also on the matter of management competence throughout public administration.

41 For instance William Robinson, *Jack Nastyface: Memoirs of an English Seaman* (London, 1836, reprint 1973).
42 Carl von Clausewitz, *On War*, translated and edited by Michael Howard and Peter Parrel (Princeton, NJ, 1976), p. 331.

2

The Core Tasks: Obtaining and Distributing Bulk Supplies of Food, Drink and Victualling Stores

Although it is not stated in these terms in their formal instructions, it is clear that, to use a modern term, the core work of the Victualling Board was to ensure that 'His Majesty's Ships and Vessels' both at home and abroad, and soldiers abroad, were provided with food and beverages. In performing this aspect of its work, as in all others, the levels of autonomy and the areas of high and low competence can be seen.

The task was performed by utilising a combination of three strategies. Firstly, the purchase of bulk supplies of victuals which were then issued from stores operated by their own staff, manufacturing some of these items on their own premises (salt meat, biscuit and beer). Secondly, at locations where the first type of operation was not feasible, they arranged for contractors to operate stores in which to stock and issue victuals of an agreed type and quality. Thirdly, on a single ship level, they reimbursed pursers for items purchased at locations where neither of the other options was available, and on a fleet level, in some locations they employed a peripatetic agent victualler to purchase some perishable items from local merchants for the whole fleet.

In previous wars the tasks of providing victuals to army garrisons and settlements abroad had been carried out by other bodies, mainly the Treasury. There is a body of opinion that believes the Treasury's woeful performance of that task during the American War of Independence was one of the major factors contributing to the loss of that war.[1] Although not specifically stated to be for that reason in the Victualling Board records, these tasks, and that of feeding convicts en route to New South Wales, were passed to the Victualling Board.[2] For these additional tasks, the Victualling Board used three strategies similar to those for the navy: bulk supplies were

---

1 See Chapter 1, note 13.
2 TNA ADM 109/102, 24 Oct 1793, order from Treasury to Victualling Board.

sent to the army abroad from the store premises at St Catherine's dock. Contractor-run depots were set up close to garrison towns abroad, so that supplies could be delivered direct to the army's local commissaries; this was dealt with in much the same way, and frequently by the same firms, as those for naval provisions. In some cases, the commissaries made their own purchasing arrangements in which the Victualling Board had no involvement. Victuals for troops on transports were supplied from the victualling yard at the relevant port, with the costs being recovered via the Treasury as an exercise separate from the accounting for navy victualling.[3]

Until 1803, most bulk supplies for the navy were delivered initially to Deptford, and were sent from there to the British outports and the yards abroad. After that date, much of the bulk deliveries for the outports were delivered straight to those ports by the suppliers, but most supplies for the yards and garrisons abroad continued to be despatched from Deptford with the exception of some salt meat which was sent direct from Ireland to the Peninsula.

The ration for seamen and soldiers

In addition to as much water as he cared to drink, every member of naval personnel on board a naval ship, regardless of rank, was entitled to a set ration of food and drink.[4] This was long-established and apart from the substitution of six ounces of sugar per week in lieu of half the oatmeal, the ration, which was laid down in the official *Regulations and Instructions* (Table 1), remained the same throughout this period.[5]

The official ration for soldiers on expeditions was much simpler, consisting of no more than meat, bread or flour, and spirits; but when on warships or troop transports they received the same items as seamen, but at two-thirds the quantity. Women received three-quarters of the soldier's allowance and children half of that.[6] Convicts en route to New South Wales had a much more varied diet, sometimes including sugar, plums and stockfish as well as the usual salt meat and flour/biscuit.[7]

3 Instructions for victualling troop transports were sent to the agents victualler in the same way as those for warships (NMM ADM C series, passim).
4 The terms 'naval personnel' and 'seamen' includes marines, as do references to naval manpower.
5 J R Tanner (ed.), *Catalogue of the Pepysian Manuscripts, Vol. 1* (London, 1903), pp. 167–9; *Regulations and Instructions Relating to His Majesty's Service at Sea* (hereafter *R&I*) in all editions since the first in 1731 (in which see p. 61). Pepys's ration had included stock-fish (dried or salted) but this proved too difficult to keep in good condition at sea and was removed from the ration before 1731.
6 *BOR 13*, appendix 6: Instructions for [transport agents].
7 As shown in TNA ADM 109/103.

Table 1: The ration for seamen

	Biscuit pounds aver- dupois [sic]	Beer gallons wine measure	Beef pounds aver- dupois	Pork pounds aver- dupois	Pease pint Winchester measure	Oatmeal pint Winchester measure	Butter ounces	Cheese ounces
Sunday	1	1		1	1 half			
Monday	1	1				1	2	4
Tuesday	1	1	2					
Wednesday	1	1			1 half	1	2	4
Thursday	1	1		1	1 half			
Friday	1	1			1 half	1	2	4
Saturday	1	1	2					
Total	7	7	4	2	2	3	6	12

Together with an allowance of vinegar, not exceeding half a pint to each man per week.

The basic ration appears, to the modern eye, to be a rather restricted diet, but its component parts were based on what could be preserved for long periods using the preservation techniques available at the time. Sailors could add to their ration by fishing when circumstances permitted, and war-ships were supplied with trawling equipment for this purpose. Both sailors and soldiers could, of course, supplement their rations by purchasing 'personal choice' items when the opportunity arose; for seamen there was also an official set of substitutes when any basic ration items were not available, and these too were laid down, as shown in Appendix A. In general, these substitutes were issued to ships either when the basics had run out, on foreign stations in hot climates where items such as butter would not keep, or, in some cases, when the men requested them.[8] However, they were some-times used as part of the Victualling Board's purchasing strategy when the basics were too expensive or when there were widespread shortages.

The 'ration' system made it easy to organise bulk supplies of victuals: since a stated number of men were to be fed a stated ration for a stated period, all that was required was a little arithmetic to arrive at the amounts to be ordered. With the additional information of where these men were to be located, delivery details could also be calculated.

Once a year, usually in September or October, the Victualling Board received a letter from the Navy Board (which had the task of gathering together all the naval costs), asking for the cost of victualling a certain number of men, dividing this number roughly into those to be victualled

8 This is discussed in Macdonald, *Feeding*, pp. 18–19.

at the two main outports of Portsmouth and Plymouth and those to be victualled through London, this latter number covering those on stations abroad.[9] The Victualling Office produced a detailed estimate, as shown in Appendix B, based on the amount of each species of victual for that number of men, plus other necessary costs and sent this back to the Navy Board who added it to the full navy estimate made up of their own and other Admiralty departments' costs; this was passed up the line until it arrived at the House of Commons where it was voted on. In the due course of time, the Navy Board wrote again instructing the Victualling Board to make the necessary arrangements to supply the provisions for the stated number of men.

To a certain extent these calculations included some aspects which were more in the spirit of lip service than the true facts, especially the assumption that all the victuals were supplied through either the outports or Deptford. As will be seen below, much of the revictualling done both at home and abroad was dealt with by contractors and never touched the Victualling Board-run yards. Nor did the estimate include any substitute items; however, the correspondence suggests that the substitutes were chosen more for their cost equivalent than for food value, for instance the substitution of tea for cheese.[10]

For some items where production was a seasonal matter, it was necessary to know numbers well in advance of the usual estimating season. To a certain extent this applied to butter and cheese, which were made in summer, but the most important items were salt beef and pork. Since the salting process had to be carried out in the cool weather of late autumn and winter the contractors would have needed sufficient notice of requirements to arrange for the purchase and processing of livestock, so the Victualling Board usually wrote to the Admiralty in late August or early September to mention this necessity and ask for manpower numbers.[11] The timing for other products was less important and thus the tendering and contracting process continued throughout the year.

So the Victualling Board did have the comparatively simple situation of knowing, well in advance, approximately how many seamen were to be fed for the coming year. These numbers rose from a pre-war 17,000 to a high point of 147,000 in 1813, with a dip to 67,000 during the Peace of Amiens, and dropped back to 79,000 at the end of the war in 1815 and 33,000 in 1816.[12]

---

9 For example, NMM ADM C/681, 24 January 1794.

10 NMM ADM DP/17, 19 October 1797.

11 For example, TNA ADM 110/64 f. 154, 9 August 1811.

12 Rodger, *Command*, pp. 636–9, these figures coming from his first list of men borne. These do not extend beyond 1815, but TNA ADM 110/71, ff. 245–6, 5 December 1815, Victualling Board to Navy Board, gives the estimated figure for 1816 as 33,000 men.

The situation with numbers of land-based soldiers to be fed and the locations at which they were stationed was far more complex and rarely static: the correspondence from the Treasury to the Victualling Board is notable for the constant changes.[13] There were attempts to give the Victualling Board advance warning for the provisions required at the garrisons abroad, but even these were subject to constant change. For instance, on 8 October 1794 a letter lists the amounts of victuals to be sent to troops overseas in 1795, showing numbers of men at six locations (Gibraltar, West Indies, Canada, Nova Scotia, New Brunswick and Newfoundland). On 4 November, another letter instructs that one-third of the amount for the West Indies is to be sent immediately with the rest following as soon as possible. On 24 December, the quantities listed in the first letter are changed, and there is an endorsement that mentions difficulties in obtaining rice, while a further note dated 20 March 1795 states that the order to send rice to Canada and Nova Scotia has been countermanded as it will now be procured abroad; on 16 May 1795 a further order states that certain quantities of flour, meat, butter and rice are to be sent to the governor of Newfoundland for a regiment which is to be raised there.[14] This set of correspondence is typical, but minor in comparison with later years when there were more locations to be supplied: by 1814 there were eighteen garrisons and settlements.[15] Although most of these were spread around the Caribbean and Spanish Main, North America and the island groups in the Western Atlantic (Bahamas and Bermuda) there were also orders for the West African coast, Madeira, New South Wales and the North Sea (Anholt and Heligoland).

The situation with victualling for military expeditions was equally volatile. Not only did requirements change constantly and at very short notice, it was not unusual for a letter to arrive reporting quantities of unwanted foodstuffs at certain locations and requesting the Victualling Board to either take these into the local navy stores or sell them at the best price obtainable. For instance, in June 1809, there was an order to send, without delay, 1,500,000 lbs of bread to Portugal; this was changed to half bread and half flour and it went from the victualling stores at Portsmouth. In October, a further 1,000 barrels of flour was to be sent to Lisbon from Plymouth, but by the end of December a letter stated that since there were now plenty of provisions in store in Portugal, the shiploads waiting to sail from Portsmouth and Plymouth should be diverted to navy use. This letter is endorsed to the effect that these shipments should be sent to Gibraltar, or elsewhere if the commander-in-chief preferred.[16]

13 This correspondence is at TNA ADM 109/102–10.
14 All these letters are in TNA ADM 109/102.
15 TNA ADM 109/102–9, passim.
16 TNA ADM 109/106, passim. The content weight of a barrel of flour was 196 lbs.

The origins of victualling stores and victuals, and some difficulties in supply

Most of the basic species of provisions and some of the substitutes were items grown in the British Isles; it was the Victualling Board's policy to specify 'English' products in contracts, other than in exceptional circumstances such as the corn shortages of 1795 and 1800. The non-comestible items known as victualling stores came from both the British Isles and abroad. There is nothing in the correspondence to indicate that any problems were experienced in obtaining the British-produced coals or hoop iron for casks. It was the items from the countries around the Baltic known as 'the East Country' which were the most problematical, although this does not appear to have applied to the hemp used to make biscuit bags.

The major source of difficulties was in the supply of staves for making casks. There do not appear to have been any problems with the availability of these at the point of origin; the difficulties arose from the political affiliations of the supplying countries. For instance, in 1800 the Emperor of Russia issued a ukase against the export of staves; the supply was never completely cut off, as the contractor, Isaac Solly, took to using neutral ships to disguise the destination, but he did write to ask that British cruisers in the Baltic be instructed to stop harrassing his ships. Because of their activities, which included pressing the ships' crews, he was having difficulty in hiring shipping; he also requested protections for the crews.[17] Later, starting in 1807, and largely prompted by the Board of Trade and Plantations, there was an attempt to introduce staves from Canada, but this was not successful. The greatest requirement was for large casks for beer and water, and the Canadian staves were prone to miniscule insect holes and thus leaked. This resulted in a great deal of correspondence between the Victualling Board and the Admiralty, with reports from the master coopers outlining the unsuitability of these staves, and then some abortive contracts on which the contractors reneged when the prices shifted dramatically. The problem, at least as far as water storage was concerned, was largely alleviated by the introduction of iron tanks in 1809, which (presumably on the logic that since the Victualling Board was responsible for water casks, they were automatically responsible for any alternative to those casks) remained the responsibility of the Victualling Board until 1816 when it was handed over to the Navy Board.[18]

---

17 TNA ADM 110/46, ff. 99–100, 31 March 1800, ff. 580–1, 23 March 1801.
18 This situation is encapsulated in Roger Morriss, 'The supply of casks and staves to the Royal Navy, 1779–1815', *Mariner's Mirror*, vol. 93, no. 1 (February 2007), pp. 43–50. See also page 102 below.

Other kinds of victualling stores included tobacco and candles, the latter supplied through a contract made by the Navy Board with a manufacturer who had invented a green dye which solved the problem of permanently marking candles as His Majesty's property.[19] The unit of measurement for candles was per dozen pounds, and over the twenty-three years 177,788 dozen pounds were purchased, over half of these being delivered to Deptford. Tobacco was available through the purser: there was a set 'ration' amount which the men had to pay for by a deduction from their wages; if they wanted any more it was available from the purser's private stock. The Victualling Board took over the responsibility for tobacco in 1799, having suggested themselves that they should do so after inflation made it difficult for pursers to buy it ad hoc.[20]

The final item was bavins, the bundles of wood used for firing the bread ovens in the victualling yards; according to a contract of 1805, a bavin was 4' 6" long and 2' 6" in girth.[21] These were bought in large quantities, usually priced in multiples of 100 or 1,000; however, it is not possible to state the total amounts bought as those supplied to Portsmouth and Plymouth were on the basis of the amount of biscuit baked. There is nothing in the documents to indicate the origin of bavins, but at a price between 10s 6d and 22s 8d for 100 and given that they could be produced in British woodland, it is unlikely that they would have been imported other than as packing material; there is no indication of any difficulties in obtaining a regular supply.

With the exception of beer, most of which was brewed in the Victualling Board's own breweries, beverages were imported. Tea came via the East India Company and does not appear in the contract ledgers. Cocoa, which was not purchased in bulk at all until 1804, and not consistently until 1809, came from the West Indies, much of it through J Fry & Co. There were no difficulties in obtaining either of these commodities, nor in wine and spirits, despite much of the latter two items originating in Mediterranean countries which were, at various times, under enemy control. Curiously, given the large British production of gin, this was rarely used: once when a quantity of 'Holland' was sent to the Cape of Good Hope, and once when the Commissioners of Excise wished to dispose of quantities they had seized.[22]

The spirits, with the occasional exception of arrack purchased locally on the East Indies station, were rum or brandy,[23] but in 1806, prompted by the lobbying of West Indies merchants, the Treasury ordered that unless brandy

19 NMM ADM C/682, 9 January 1795.
20 NMM ADM C/680, 21 August and 14 November 1798.
21 TNA ADM 112/111, 31 December 1805.
22 NMM ADM C/691, 15 February 1799; TNA ADM 110/56, f. 83, 18 July 1807.
23 Proportions varied from year to year: in 1804 the proportion was 367,000 gallons of rum and 268,000 gallons of brandy, in 1805 it was 250,000 gallons of rum and 625,000 gallons of brandy.

could be obtained at least one shilling per gallon more cheaply than rum, rum only was to be bought. Given that the price of brandy at that time was just under 2s per gallon, compared with 2s 9d for rum, this is an indication of the power of the West Indies lobby: that a normally thrifty government department was prepared to pay up to half as much again for a product which they bought in hundreds of thousands of gallons.[24]

The Treasury's interest in all this rumbled on for some time: in July 1807 the chairman of the West Indies Trade committee requested a return of the quantities bought for the army and navy over the previous three years and a few months later the Treasury instructed that only rum should be bought.[25] The Treasury continued to monitor the situation, asking first how much rum had been contracted for, how much was in store and how long this would last, then two months later wanting to know why the Victualling Board had advertised for a large quantity of spirits when there was already so much in store and when the new supply was more expensive. The Victualling Board replied that the supply for which they had advertised was not to be delivered until the point at which the old stock would have been used, and that despite the higher price, they felt it was better to pay this than run out.[26] They did not comment on the likelihood of brandy being cheaper; an indication, perhaps, of their subordinate position in such matters.

Later that year, the Treasury suggested that a further supply of spirits (134,272 gallons of brandy and 26,159 gallons of rum) should be bought from the Commissioners of Excise; the Victualling Board, having checked the quality, duly accepted most of it; the rest was at Bristol, and the Excise officers there, not having been told of the arrangement, refused to let the Victualling Board's representative check it.[27] This was not untypical of the generally unhelpful attitude of Excise officials; in addition to a tendency to hold cargoes destined for the Victualling Board on the suspicion of smuggling by the ships' crews, they insisted that wine which had gone sour should be 'started' instead of being converted to vinegar: a waste which clearly offended the Victualling Board's thrifty souls.[28]

Most of the Victualling Board's cheese came from the counties of Warwickshire, Gloucestershire, Derbyshire and Cheshire;[29] the fresh beef for the ships at the outports (with the exception of Plymouth) and the

24 NMM ADM C/709, 19 March 1806, C/710, 17 & 27 June 1806; TNA ADM 110/54, f. 300, 10 June 1806; 110/55, ff. 125–7, 17 November 1806.
25 NMM ADM C/715, 13 July 1807; C/716, 19 October 1807.
26 NMM ADM C/717, 3 March and 27 April 1808; TNA ADM 110/57, ff. 361–6, 17 May 1808.
27 TNA ADM 110/59, ff. 2–4, 22 December 1808.
28 See, for instance, NMM ADM C/698, 9 September 1802.
29 TNA ADM 110/45, ff. 137–9, 23 May 1799; George Edwin Fussell, 'The London cheesemongers of the eighteenth century', *Economic History*, vol. 3 (January 1928)

live oxen for slaughter and packing at Deptford came through Smithfield market in London. Of the grain products it is only possible to say that much of these would have come from East Anglia,[30] and were probably delivered by coastal vessels. Before the practice of delivering to the out-ports became widespread, bulk supplies to replenish the outports were sent from Deptford with all the difficulties which that entailed; these being partly predators and partly adverse winds, as the Board of Revision's eleventh report remarks.[31] The Select Committee on Finance also pointed out the illogicality of sailing products from Ireland and the Mediterranean up the Channel to London, unloading them, reloading them and sailing them back down the Channel to the very ports which they had passed on the way up; the Victualling Board's response to this comment was that they used the casks of meat as the bottom tier for mixed cargoes, thus avoiding the necessity of paying extra costs for dunnage.[32] It is not easy to tell whether this argument is valid or just an example of a failure to monitor and change long-established procedures, but the amounts of Irish meat which had begun to be delivered straight to Portsmouth and Plymouth in 1803 increased markedly after 1806. The Board of Revision also remarked about the lack of foresight in failing to send additional supplies down to Portsmouth and Plymouth before the winter (with its contrary winds and bad weather) set in, thus causing shortages at those yards.[33]

With very few exceptions, butter and the salt meats came from Ireland: the latter were actually referred to as 'Irish Beef' or 'Irish Pork' and they came mainly from Cork or Waterford. There seem to have been two main reasons for buying butter and salt meat from Ireland: because it was of reliable quality, in both meat and packaging, and because the lack of import duty on salt into Ireland allowed lower prices.[34]

It was with the grain-based foodstuffs that external events, such as Bonaparte's embargoes, caused problems of rising prices and market availability. However, these events were more likely to be natural than political, especially those associated with the weather and its effect on agriculture; the most obvious being poor harvests. There were many of these. Lord Ernle

pp. 394–8; G E Fussell and C Goodwin, 'Eighteenth century traffic in milk products', *Economic History*, vol. XII (Feb. 1937), pp. 380–7.

30 Baker, *Government and Contractors*, p. 80.

31 *BOR 11*, pp. 35–6, 44.

32 *32nd Report of the Select Committee on Finance, June 1798*; (hereafter shown to as *SCF 32*) (printed 1798), pp. 4, 66–7; nothing was done about this and it was raised again in *BOR 11*, p. 36.

33 *BOR 11*, p. 6.

34 J O'Donovan, *The Economic History of Livestock in Ireland* (Dublin, 1940), pp. 128–9, 133–136, 151; William O'Sullivan, *The Economic History of Cork City from the Earliest Times to the Act of Union* (Cork, 1937), p. 143.

remarks that fourteen out of twenty-two wheat harvests between 1793 and 1814 were deficient and that in seven of those fourteen years (1795, 1797, 1799, 1800, 1810, 1811 and 1812) 'the crops failed to a remarkable extent'.[35] These bad years followed others in a sequence that ran from about 1750 to 1840; H H Lamb attributes this yo-yo sequence of good and bad years to 'the extraordinary frequency of explosive volcanic eruptions, which maintained dust veils high up in the atmosphere'.[36]

E L Jones gives a full list of annual conditions, from which it is possible to track the bad harvests by consulting the listings of grain prices in various sources. William Beveridge, for instance, shows that the price of wheat rose from an annual average of 69.01s per quarter in 1794 to 90.86s in 1795, with a high point of 113.83s in March, and from an annual average of 62.78s per quarter in 1798 to 125.65s in 1800, with a high point of 148.08s in January 1800.[37] These years also provoked some of the more rigorous corn laws, especially those which followed the disastrous harvests of 1794 and 1799.[38] These Acts were attempts to ensure that such grain as was available went into bread rather than being used for starch, hair powder or distilling; there was also what came to be known as 'the Stale Bread Act', which forbade the sale of bread less than twenty-four hours old on the assumption that since people tended to eat most of their bread when it was fresh, they would eat less overall if fresh bread was not available; there were also various attempts to persuade the working public to eat loaves made with a percentage of wholemeal flour or flour from other grains, none of which succeeded.[39] At this time the Board of Agriculture experimented with a whole range of substitute ingredients, from other grains to flour made from beans, pease, chestnuts, potatoes or turnips.[40] The Victualling Board also experimented,

35 Lord Ernle, *English Farming Past and Present* (6th edition, London, 1961), pp. 267–9.
36 H H Lamb, *Climate, History and the Modern World* (2nd edition, London, 1995), pp. 246–7.
37 E L Jones, *Seasons and Prices: The Role of the Weather in English Agricultural History* (London, 1964), pp. 136–60 and passim; William Henry Beveridge (with the collaboration of L Liepmann, F J Nicolas, M E Rayner, M Wretts-Smith, and others), *Prices & Wages in England, from the Twelfth to the Nineteenth century, Vol. 1, Mercantile Era* (London, 1939, reprint 1965), pp. 568–9.
38 The results of this bad harvest were exacerbated in 1800 by the trade embargoes imposed by the Russian Czar Paul, which hampered the import of grain from the Baltic area. Mancur Olson Jnr, *The Economics of the Wartime Shortage: A History of British Food Supplies in the Napoleonic War and in World Wars I and II* (Durham, NC, 1963), p. 52.
39 W F Galpin, *The Grain Supply of England during the Napoleonic Period* (London, 1925), p. 7; Donald Grove Barnes, *A History of the English Corn Laws* (New York, 1930, reprinted 1965), pp. 38, 74–8.
40 A Edlin, *A Treatise on the Art of Bread-Making Wherein the Mealing Trade, Assize Laws, and every Curcumstance [sic] Connected with the Art, is Particularly Examined*

at this time and during the later crises of 1800 and 1809, using wheat mixed with other grains, pease, potato, turnip or molasses, and passing quantities of the result out to several ships to try. The captains duly reported back that although some of these mixtures were acceptable they did not feel they could recommend them for general use. There is no indication that these mixtures were ever used on anything other than an experimental scale.[41]

Ernle, W F Galpin and Donald Grove Barnes all believe that the corn laws had little effect on prices before 1815.[42] Barnes reports that he examined numerous eighteenth- and nineteenth-century pamphlets which proposed many reasons for increased prices, ranging from merchant profiteering to a rather charming suggestion that shortages of wheat were caused by the fashion for tea-drinking and its consequent requirement for milk which had encouraged farmers to abandon arable farming for dairy farming, but none of these pamphleteers appear to have blamed the navy or army for using excessive amounts.[43]

The Victualling Board was obviously concerned about prices but does not seem to have experienced any major difficulties in obtaining supplies, although in 1800 there was a potential problem of defending what supplies they did have: the Mayor of Portsmouth wrote that there was considerable unrest in the town over the large stocks of wheat and flour in the various bakeries which supplied the navy and remarked that he feared riots might follow.[44]

The government's reaction to the grain shortages, as well as passing the various Corn Laws, was to encourage additional imports of grain. In 1795 they persuaded the East India Company to bring large quantities of rice back from India, encouraged merchants to buy grain in the Mediterranean and also used the corn factor, Claude Scott, to stockpile wheat on their behalf.[45] In early 1796 the Victualling Board were instructed to buy 50,000 quarters of Polish wheat through Scott; and in 1802 they were instructed to buy substantial quantities of rice from the East India Company.[46] The Victualling

   (London, 1805, reprinted privately with introduction by Tom Jaine, Devon, 1992), pp. 47–57.
41 NMM ADM DP/29A, 27 February 1809, DP/29B, 4 September 1809. J Macdonald, *Feeding*, p. 16; Edlin, *A Treatise*, passim.
42 Ernle, *English Farming*, pp. 210, 253–4; Galpin, *Grain Supply*, p. 8; Barnes, *English Corn Laws*, passim.
43 Barnes, *English Corn Laws*, pp. 32–3.
44 TNA ADM 109/104, 11 June 1800, letter from Mayor of Portsmouth to Duke of Portland, passed to Victualling Board via the Treasury.
45 Huw Bowen, *The Business of Empire: the East India Company and Imperial Britain 1756–1833* (Cambridge, 2006), p. 51; Privy Council papers on 1795 grain crisis TNA PC 29/64–73, 30–71.
46 The precise quantity of rice is not recorded; there were several instructions to buy specific quantities adding up to 43,000 bags, then a final instruction which just said

Board were also peripherally involved in some of the wheat imports from the Mediterranean, being asked to direct the masters of returning transports to bring back wheat rather than return empty. Several cargoes are reported as arriving from Alexandria and Sicily in 1795, and again from Sicily in 1800; it is not clear whether any of this wheat was purchased by the Victualling Board.[47]

Other strategies used by the Victualling Board to combat the national wheat shortages, as well as the use of substitutes (rice or pearl barley), were to issue the full fresh meat ration to ships in port or in Ordinary instead of the more usual substitution of part of this by flour and suet;[48] to reduce the period for which ships on Channel service were victualled (from four to three months);[49] and to increase the amount paid to seamen as short allowance money to encourage them to 'save' more biscuit and take cash instead.[50]

One other point of interest about the first of these wheat crises is that when a Parliamentary committee was set up to investigate the high price of provisions, despite numerous people being consulted in the course of this enquiry, the committee did not consult the commissioners of the Victualling Board. This does not speak well of Parliament's opinion of the one set of people in government employ who might be thought to have some expertise in the matter.[51]

There was also, in the two exceptional years of 1795 and 1800, some difficulty in obtaining supplies of other products. In 1795/96 the severity of the winter made it almost impossible to move cattle; this made it necessary to reduce issues of fresh beef to ships in port;[52] at one point the ice was so bad on the river Medway that the supply boats couldn't reach the ships anchored off Sheerness.[53] It was not just bad winters which affected the availability of animal products: in 1803 there was a drought which affected milk production and the annual round of tenders for butter and cheese were for abnormally high prices. It transpired that a group of merchants

'a further quantity': NMM ADM C697, 24 March, 6, 21, 22 & 29 April, 6 May, 2 June, all 1802.

47 The correspondence does not report who purchased this grain. NMM ADM D/39, 26 December 1795; D/42, 20 December 1800; C/694, 17, 24 & 21 December 1800; C/696, 15 & 25 July 1801.

48 NMM ADM C/699, 10 March 1803; C/701, 16 February 1804; C/720, 1 November 1808; C/722, 4 May 1809.

49 NMM ADM C/683, 15 July 1795 & C/684, 19 September 1795.

50 NMM ADM C/683, 27 February 1795, C/693, 15 April 1800.

51 *Reports of the Committee Appointed to Consider of the Present High Price of Provisions*: HC 174 of 1800–1801.

52 NMM ADM C/683, 27 February 1795; C/686, 31 July 1796.

53 NMM ADM C/683, 23 January and 27 February 1795.

had advance-purchased almost all the coming season's production, on the assumption that this would allow them to set the prices they wished. The Victualling Board, with Admiralty approval, simply refused to purchase any butter or cheese for that year, issuing the substitutes of tea, cocoa and sugar instead; in the following year they issued half of the ration in butter and cheese and the rest in the substitutes, only reverting to the full ration two years later, thus demonstrating the flexibility which the substitute system allowed.[54]

Obtaining stock – agents, contractors and the tendering process

Once the numbers of men to be fed were established, and after checking stocks at the various victualling yards at home,[55] the amounts actually needed were calculated and the buying process commenced. Although occasionally letters arrived from people wishing to be employed to buy at the livestock markets, this strategy was never adopted. However, commission agents were used and this practice was continued despite the Atkinson scandal. There are no surviving agreements with these agents, but the minutes suggest that they included a clause to prevent this: William Mellish, the agent for fresh beef and live oxen, was required to produce receipts showing the seller and the price paid, and instructed not to mix his private purchases with those for the Victualling Board.[56] It is not always possible to tell whether purchases of other foodstuffs came through agents or from contractors, as the contract records are incomplete and the contract ledgers, where most information of purchases is to be found, do not indicate any difference. However, other sources show that Irish meat, cheese, wheat, pease, malt, hops, molasses, rice and sugar were purchased by agents.[57]

The financial arrangement with these purchases was that the agent paid for supplies by issuing bills of exchange drawn on the Victualling Board; the Victualling Board kept control by means of an imprest account with a fixed upper limit, rather like a modern overdraft limit. For their trouble these agents received a commission of a set amount per unit of weight (for instance Mellish received 7½d per hundredweight of meat) rather than a percentage of the purchase price, thus eliminating any temptation to

---

54 NMM ADM D/45, 13 October 1803 and D/46, 2 August 1804. The prices quoted were 10½d per pound for butter and more than 7½d per pound for cheese, compared with the maximum 9¼d and 6½d paid in 1802.

55 TNA ADM 224/17, passim. As with all other information which passed up or down the chain of command, this was done by letter and reported in the board minutes.

56 *BOR 10*, pp. 47–8.

57 Parliamentary Papers 1823 (417) *Navy and Victualling Contracts*, pp. 8–12; SCF 32, pp. 4, 58, 63–5.

neglect their duty of seeking the best price. The Victualling Board only paid for the carcase meat issued fresh to ships and used for salting, the suet and tongues; the beasts were slaughtered by Mellish at his expense (although in the Board's yards), and he retained the rest of the carcase.[58]

Apart from the commodities purchased through agents, most of the rest was purchased through a system of tendering. This started by placing advertisements in the major newspapers and various locations where the contractors were known to visit regularly (such as the Customs offices) stating what was needed, that the Victualling Office 'will be ready to receive tenders in writing' on a certain date, stating the payment terms and that details of requirements could be seen at the Victualling Office in Somerset House.[59] One major exception to this routine was at the beginning of the French Revolutionary War in January 1793, when the urgent necessity to buy quantities of meat did not allow the usual leisurely process of advertising and waiting for tenders to arrive. On Friday 13 January, the Board decided that thirteen of the major meat suppliers should be contacted, asking them to tender for deliveries to be made both immediately and in a month or six weeks, and for these tenders to be in the Victualling Office by midday the following day (Saturday), marked 'Tenders for flesh'. Twelve contractors did this, and by the following Monday, ten of them had been awarded contracts.[60] The decision to make these purchases must have been driven by the necessity for immediate delivery which could only be achieved by buying from firms which held stocks in England; it would have taken the usual suppliers a considerable time to organise delivery, especially in January when most of the Irish production would already have been spoken for. There were other occasions when this method was used: as remarked on by the Victualling Board itself, and later by the Board of Revision, this was sometimes for political expediency, or 'to prevent an alarm in the market which might enhance the price and create a combination amongst the merchants and dealers'.[61]

There was another exception to the tendering process, although most examples of this took place at the beginning of the war: during the first months of 1793, both the board minutes and the copy letters to Portsmouth record numerous offers of bulk items from various merchants, many of which were accepted. Later on, the volume of these offers was considerably reduced and in general these offers were refused on the basis that there was no need for the offered items. However, sometimes the offer was clearly too good to refuse (for instance a cargo of 370 tons of Spanish salt, considered

---

58 *BOR 10*, pp. 47–8.
59 For instance, an advertisement in the *Gazette*, 25 June 1793, TNA ZJ1/89, p. 544.
60 Minuted in TNA ADM 111/126, 13 to 16 January 1793.
61 *SCF 32*, pp. 508, 533; *BOR 10*, p. 44.

the best sort for meat packing) and then the Victualling Board would report the offer to the Admiralty, remark on the desirability of accepting, and the Admiralty would duly send back an order to make the purchase.[62]

The normal situation with tenders was to give three or four weeks notice, stating a day by which the tenders, in sealed envelopes, should be received. They were put into a locked box; originally this had a single key which was held by the board secretary, but later this was changed to two different locks, the second key being held by the chairman. In neither the Board of Revision report which recommends the second lock, nor in that of the Fees commissioners, is the box described but it is reasonable to assume that to avoid the need for the keyholders to be present every time a tender was delivered, it would have been something like a ballot box with a slot.[63] On the stated day, at 1 p.m., the secretary took the box into the board room where it was opened and the contents examined and listed, and decisions were made. The lowest price was usually accepted, unless there was 'substantial ground to doubt [the tenderer's] competency' or 'he was unable to procure the customary security', in which case the next lowest tender was accepted.[64]

This simple tendering system was of long standing. Until 1809, when the Board of Revision insisted on it, the bidders were not required to attend the meeting when the tenders were opened.[65] Another change which occurred a little earlier than this was that instead of advertising for a specific quantity of a commodity, they invited bids for 'such quantities [as the contractor] saw fit to offer', doing this several times a year instead of only once. This appears to have been in response to a volatile market of rapidly fluctuating prices where neither side wanted a long-term commitment to a single price; there were many occasions when the prices offered were not to the Victualling Board's taste and they did not buy at all.

In any given tendering situation the individual bids would not necessarily be for the full amount required and in this case several contracts would be awarded. One might surmise that these bids came from merchants who actually held a stock of the commodity, as opposed to the larger firms of middlemen who held no stock but merely made their 'turn' by buying on the market when they had a sale arranged.[66] Many of the fixed quantity contracts involved deliveries staggered over several months; it is not known whether the contractors bespoke the whole amount at once from their suppliers, or bought each tranche as the delivery date approached. The imprest

62 NMM ADM D/37, 9 July 1790.
63 *Fees 8*, p. 612; *BOR 10*, pp. 44–5.
64 *SCF 32*, p. 58.
65 *BOR 10*, p. 44.
66 R B Westerfield, *Middlemen in English business, particularly between 1660–1760* (2nd edition, Newton Abbott, 1968), passim.

system, with its numerous payments and 'overdraft limits', strongly suggests the latter, a point which is important when considering the Victualling Board's influence on the market.[67]

Another type of contract was the 'standing' contract, where instead of a fixed amount of the commodity, the contract was for whatever quantities were demanded for an indefinite period. They were usually stated as being for 'twelve months certain' (i.e. the minimum period) with a 'warning' period of termination to be given by either party. This was usually six months. The Navy Board also used these standing contracts, but lacked a procedure for monitoring prices against market prices;[68] it seems that the Victualling Board did not do so either, although they had often approved (or rather the Admiralty had approved at the Victualling Board's prompting) price increases in line with the market. It is well-known that St Vincent, as First Lord of the Admiralty, forced the Navy Board to change their ways in this regard; he did the same with the Victualling Board when the Peace of Amiens caused a drop in prices, requiring them to make the holders of standing contracts revert to their original prices or face termination.[69]

With all contracts, other than for small amounts for immediate delivery, the contractors were required to provide sureties in case of non-performance, so they were given a simple agreement immediately and once the sureties had been produced and registered, a formal contract was drawn up and signed. These contracts were originally handwritten, but during 1807 a set of printed pro forma contracts, one for each specific item, came into use. This was probably triggered by the Board of Revision, who recommended that the form of contracts in use should be revised by the Victualling Board's solicitor.[70]

Although the general principle of all the contracts was more or less the same (including, for relevant items, an insistence on English produce), different clauses were used for different items: for instance a contract for pease requires that they should be 'sound, dry, hard and sweet, free from any bad mixture whatever, prime good boilers' and that they should be kiln dried and should be of the year of growth immediately prior to the date of the contract; while a contract for biscuit states that the meal from which is it

---

67 This system, which allowed bills to be drawn on the principal's account, seems to have been common practice amongst merchants as well as government departments: Baker, *Government and Contractors*, p. 79.
68 Bernard Pool, *Navy Board Contracts 1660–1832* (London, 1966), pp. 101–3.
69 Beveridge, *Prices and Wages*, pp. 565–82 (for prices); TNA ADM 111/163, 28 September 1802; TNA ADM 112/140, undated list. All the contracts on this list were for contractor-run depots.
70 *BOR 10*, pp. 44–5. Although their report on the victualling office was not printed and distributed until April 1809, the Commissioners of the Board of Revision had completed this report in August 1807.

made must be 'good, sound, sweet and dry wheat without any mixture of middlings, or any other mixture or adulteration whatsoever, but consisting wholly of the entire produce, as it came from the mill'.[71]

One requirement which appeared in all contracts after the payment structure for the Victualling Office staff changed from one which included fees and gratuities to one which consisted of pure salaries and nothing else, was that the contractor had to swear an affidavit to the effect that no one had received 'any money or any other thing, as a gratuity, fee, or reward' connected with the contract.[72]

Other clauses which appeared in all contracts were those relating to sub-standard products, those imposing financial penalties for non-delivery and those relating to size, timing and location of deliveries. In general the rule on sub-standard products was that they should be replaced at the supplier's expense; where the deficiency was detected at the point of delivery into one of the victualling yards the whole of that delivery was to be replaced, but where individual packages of provisions were found to be faulty when opened on board ship, it was only those specific quantities that were to be replaced. A system of cask marking enabled each package to be traced back to the supplier, and those marks form part of the formal survey documents produced by ships' officers on these occasions. Where possible in such circumstances the packages were resealed and returned to the contractor via the victualling yards, but if they were in the offensive condition described in surveys as 'rotten, stinking and a nuisance to the ship' they were often dumped overboard. Even so, the contractors were not always meekly accepting of this situation: Thomas Bell, the cheese contractor, complained that he had suffered an unnecessary loss of £950.5.2 on some butter and cheese which had been dumped, because he could have sold the offending products if they had been returned to him (although it is hard to imagine for what purpose).[73]

This loss was, however, minor compared to that suffered by Messrs Bogle French on their 1806 contract for 35,000 tierces of Irish beef and 45,000 tierces of Irish pork. Despite the long-standing Victualling Board insistence that all beef for the navy should be from oxen (i.e. castrated males), and the fact that this was also specifically stated in the contract, when it was discovered after an anonymous tipoff that some 10,000 tierces of meat (over 1,400 tons) contained a mixture of ox and cow beef, the Victualling Board rejected the whole amount.[74] Stating that this was likely to bring about not only their own bankruptcy, but also that of the various merchants to whom

71 Both these contracts are in TNA ADM 112/84, together with others for other items.
72 TNA ADM 112/84, passim.
73 NMM ADM C/686, 14 November 1796; D/40, 14 February 1797.
74 The difference would have been visibly obvious, in the amounts of fat and the musculature around the back, shoulders and hind-quarters.

they had issued Bills to a total of £250,000, Bogle French first begged the Victualling Board to accept the offending beef for a reduced price, and then suggested that the Victualling Board should sort out the cow beef, repack the whole and retain the ox-beef, a suggestion which was rejected as being impracticable.[75]

The penalties for non-delivery were often substantial; they seem to reflect the difficulty and extra cost of finding an alternative supply, as well as being intended as a punitive discouragement for such contractors who thought they might abandon their obligations. On most occasions when contractors found themselves in difficulties they wrote to explain why, and when, as was often the case, it was due to circumstances beyond their control, the Victualling Board recommended a sympathetic response to the Admiralty. For instance, in early 1797, when Jordaine and Shaw were trying to fulfill their contract for Irish meat just after the failed French invasion attempt, they found that Irish confidence in English bills was shaken to the point where suppliers would accept no more than twenty-one day payment terms (the norm in Ireland was sixty days). Jordaine and Shaw did not ask for a higher price, they just asked for an extension to their imprest limit, which was freely granted.[76]

None of the extant contracts included a condition on the format of delivery notes/invoices, or if they did, it appears to have been ignored, as can be seen from some of the entries in the contract ledgers. These may, even on a single page, show different forms of measurement (for instance salt meat may be shown in the number of pieces of different weights, or in the number of different sizes of casks). One would have expected, for consistency, that the clerks making entries in these ledgers would have converted these measurements to a single type, but as with other signs of haste in these ledgers, such as the poor addition, this suggests that the department heads did not check this work.[77]

The contractors

Information on individual contractors is hard to find, and what can be found is spread over numerous sources; however, a certain amount can be gleaned from the Victualling Board's documentation and some parallels can

75 NMM ADM C/710, 3 & 14 May 1806; TNA ADM 110/53 f. 272, 7 May 1806 & f. 296, 19 May 1806. The end of this story does not appear in the correspondence, but it is noticeable that Bogle French do not appear again in the contract ledgers as supplying Irish meat until 1811: TNA ADM 112/197.
76 NMM ADM D/40, 15 March 1797, endorsed on the reverse in agreement.
77 Copy contracts are at TNA ADM 112/84, the contract ledgers are in the series 112/162–212.

be seen in Baker when he discusses the contractors used to victual the army in North America in the American War of Independence.[78] He describes a set of

> individuals who were, almost without exception, London businessmen with strong financial and commercial connections with the City. However, most of these were not dealing, in the normal course of their business, in the commodities to be supplied under the provisioning contracts, and in both England and Ireland they acted through agents or sub-contractors – men more closely connected with the actual sources of supply.

During the French Revolutionary and Napoleonic wars although the documents offer little information on such a heavy use of agents, in many cases a similar situation is likely to have occurred, as some of the contractors appear to be specialists and others generalists. For some of the small contracts, they are clearly specialists; the Board rarely bought straight from the producer, but did so when the contract was small and for immediate delivery, for instance William Patton to supply vegetables to Chatham, John Rigden to brew and deliver beer to the ships at Faversham and Whitstable Bay, and John Hughes to provide fresh beef to the ships in Whitstable Bay.[79] Some of the small biscuit contracts seem to be with individual bakers and one, at the beginning of the war, makes this clear by stating the quantity as 'as much as you can bake'.[80]

The Mellish brothers, Peter junior and William, were by no means a 'small' firm, but they were clearly specialists, providing all the fresh beef and live oxen for the area from Yarmouth round to Portsmouth including London, and providing nothing else other than suet and some salt beef and pork, despite being listed in the London trade directories by no more than the general term 'merchant'.[81] The Mellish brothers owned considerable real estate: a slaughterhouse and dwelling house at Shadwell Dock, another house at Woodford, an estate at Chingford and numerous pieces of land on the Isle of Dogs, some of which was used to build the West India Docks. After Peter died in 1803, William continued on his own beyond the end of the Napoleonic war; Samuel and Peter senior had provided meat to the

78 Baker, *Government and Contractors*, pp. 64–5. Many of these contractors dealt with numerous agents (eight in one case) and the individual agents dealt with numerous contractors.
79 TNA ADM 112/160, 25 June 1803 and 25 June 1804 (Patton); 2 April 1804 (Rigden); 17 December 1803 (Hughes).
80 TNA ADM 112/179.
81 *Kent's Directory*, 62nd edition, 1794, 69th edition, 1801, 76th edition, 1808; *Lowndes or A London Directory*, 33rd edition, 1794; *Wakefield's Merchants and Tradesman's General Directory*, Vol. 94 (1794); *The Post Office New Annual Directory* 2nd edition, 1801 and 9th edition, 1808; TNA ADM 68/500, Greenwich Hospital Household accounts.

navy since the Seven Years' War and continued to do so into the American War of Independence.[82] The Victualling Board often asked William's advice on meat handling and in 1798, when they did not want to alarm the market by his purchases of live oxen for the yard at Deptford, arranged for him to slaughter and pack these beasts in his own yard.[83] They referred to William as 'a considerable merchant and ship-owner'; these ships including several shares in East Indiamen and several whalers.[84]

Charles Flower handled several products, mainly salt meat, butter and cheese. He was a member of the Framework Knitters Guild, which indicates wider business interests; in 1808 he became Lord Mayor of London, an 'honour' which traditionally requires considerable wealth, and was also made a baronet in 1809. Four other of the large contractors were aldermen, and these were also members of trade guilds outside the provision trades; one other of these was also Lord Mayor.[85]

Several other contractors appear regularly over a long period, including the firm of Jordaine and Shaw, who were supplying both the Victualling Board and the Treasury (for the army in America) in the American War of Independence; they had been in business together since 1768.[86] Like Flower (with whom they sometimes acted as partners) they supplied butter and cheese, and also salt meat from Ireland, which they provided to the Victualling Board as agents until 1802 and under contract after this.

Edward Knight, Abraham de Horne, Christopher Dunkin and Aaron Moody provided various of the cereals and cereal products (oatmeal, biscuit meal, flour, malt and pease) which were normally handled through corn exchanges.[87] These names rarely appear connected to other products and one can surmise that these contractors were members of one or more corn exchanges and confined their business activities to these products.

---

82 Samuel was an uncle, described as a 'butcher', Peter senior was the father of Peter junior and William. Their wills are at TNA PROB 11/1122 (Samuel); 11/1033 (Peter senior); 11/1403 (Peter junior); 11/1831 (William); Buchet, *Marine*, pp. 227 et sequae; contract ledgers from 1776.

83 TNA ADM 111/148, minutes 9 August & 24 September 1798.

84 I am grateful to Hugh Lyon for the information on William's ship ownership; information on his land ownership is to be found at the Tower Hamlets Library. This William Mellish should not be confused with the synonymous director of the Bank of England.

85 Sir James Shaw (Bt) was a member of the Scriveners Guild; William Newman was a member of the Curriers Guild; Sir William Curtis (Bt) was a member of the Drapers Guild, and was Lord Mayor 1795–96; Charles Flower was Lord Mayor 1808–09; Thomas Rowcroft was a member of the Patten Makers Guild: Alfred B Beaven, *The Aldermen of the City of London, vol II* (London, 1913), pp. 137–40.

86 Baker, *Government and Contractors*, p. 233; *BOR 9*, p. 10; contract ledgers.

87 It is likely that Aaron Moody was related to Robert Sadleir Moody, one of the victualling commissioners: see Appendix C.

Cheese, but nothing else other than a little butter, was also supplied for several years through Thomas Bell who was obviously a cheese specialist, as the Victualling Board accepted and acted upon his suggestions for improving the cheese storage at Portsmouth.[88]

Then there were other contractors who seemed willing to handle anything in large quantities, including Charles Flower, and it is with these that some complex relationships emerge, as sets of names come together in various combinations; these combinations were not static, but changed as time progressed (a pattern which is also shown in the Seven Years' War).[89] For instance, Messrs Jordaine and Shaw held many contracts in this name, but they, or either of the two partners, also held some jointly with Charles Flower and/or J W Green; in the American War of Independence they had been in partnership with Christopher Potter and John Dearman.[90] Such shifting groupings seem to be a common feature of Georgian commerce, as seen in David Hancock's study of a group of London merchants, or T M Devine's study of Glasgow tobacco merchants.[91] The reason for this is not explained, but we can surmise that it was to spread risk, in the same way that individuals owned shares of numerous ships rather than owning a few ships outright.

With the exception of Mellish, Flower and Curtis, we have no information on the wealth of these merchants, but the frequency with which the same names occur as the suppliers of a particular commodity strongly suggests that they operated substantial businesses. There are occasional comments in the documents on reliability, and it is clear that there were practical advantages in using a few firms instead of many: fewer contracts to be negotiated and drawn up, fewer sets of sureties to be checked and accepted, fewer imprest accounts to be maintained, fewer bills of exchange to be accounted for; all this compared with the multiplication of these tasks required when awarding numerous small contracts to equally numerous small contractors. Certainly one can see how a firm of middlemen could afford to bid at a lower price than one which had money tied up in a stock of goods; for a large firm economy of scale allows an even smaller profit ratio per unit. This can be seen with the commission agents; the usual commission for agencies was 2½ per cent,[92] but a rough calculation on the amount Mellish received on cattle shows this to be about 1¾ per cent. On

---

88 TNA ADM 224/17, 28 July 1793.

89 Buchet, *Marine*, p. 233.

90 Baker, pp. 233–4.

91 David Hancock, *Citizens of the World: London Merchants and the Integration of the British Atlantic Community 1735–1785* (Cambridge, 1995); T M Devine, *The Tobacco Lords: A study of the Tobacco Merchants of Glasgow and their Trading Activities c 1740–90* (Edinburgh, 1975).

92 Baker, *Government and Contractors*, p. 89.

this basis however, he was receiving in the region of £70,000 a year from the Victualling Board; the amounts he earned from the sale of the beef 'offal' from the beasts he slaughtered for them cannot be calculated, but must have been considerable.[93]

After about 1803, for most of the major products, there was a shift from a single supplier for the whole year to several; rather than splitting a single large annual contract into multiple deliveries, these were multiple small contracts awarded throughout the year. There does not appear to have been a formal instruction to do this, but the timing suggests that it might have been a dictat from St Vincent. Alternatively, it could have been a result of high inflation; in such difficult trading conditions, few firms would have been willing to make a long-term commitment on a single price. It is at this time that the numerous syndicates of merchants start to appear, which tends to confirm this possibility.

The merchants also assigned contracts between them: in the years of 1806 to 1808, the three firms of Jordaine, Shaw & J Green, Flower & Rowcroft, and Atkins French & Canning, were amongst those tendering for the annual supply of Irish beef and pork; in each of these years, the contract was awarded to one of the three firms, but a few days later they wrote and asked to assign two-thirds of the contract to the other two firms (one third each). This suggests a level of pre-arranged collusion (in one case the request for assignment was only two days after the contract had been awarded) but the Victualling Board agreed to these arrangements without demur.[94]

It is obvious that the central core of the more frequently seen names in the Victualling Board records for 1793–1815 were all well acquainted with each other; in addition to the above, they can be seen in newspaper lists of subscribers to loyal addresses or advertisements offering rewards for information against criminals; several were freemasons; and many of them appear regularly in the London shipping registers as joint owners of numerous ships.[95]

Just as there is a paucity of information on the individual contractors, so there is a paucity of information on the relationships between the contractors and the victualling commissioners and the victualling office staff. We do know that Peter Mellish left £500 to 'Richard Harman of the victualling office' in his will, and that William Mellish invited a number of the clerks to his annual beef dinner.[96] Some of the contractors gave presents of wine, game and lottery tickets to the clerks at Christmas and other times; although there

---

93 This calculation is based on information in the contract ledgers.

94 TNA ADM 111/180, 12 & 19 September 1806, 111/184, 16 & 18 September 1807, 111/188, 15 & 20 September 1808.

95 I am indebted to Hugh Lyon for this last piece of information.

96 TNA PROB 11/1403; Richard Harman was at that time the second clerk in the office for 'keeping a charge on the Treasurer for assigning bills and for collecting old and

is no evidence of similar gifts to the commissioners, it would be strange if they had not received them. On at least one occasion some of the clerks worked out of hours for one of the contractors to bring his accounts up to the stage where they could be presented to the Board for approval; this may not have been an isolated occurrence.[97]

The larger contractors providing bulk supplies delivered these to the outports as well as to London. Most of the merchants handling goods for London and the outports of Chatham, Dover and Portsmouth appear to have been based in the City. For those with unusual names this can be verified in the London directories; but for those with more common names one cannot be sure that these are the right people, since they are often described as nothing more than 'merchant' and give no more detailed address than 'London' in the contracts. However, the contract ledgers show that Plymouth seems to have been supplied by a different set of wholesale merchants from those supplying London and the closer outports, and although we lack copy contracts with contractors' addresses for specific confirmation of this, it seems reasonable to assume that those supplying Plymouth were not only located in, but also buying their wares from, that part of the country, a situation which is relevant when considering the Victualling Board's influence on the London markets.

The Victualling Board's influence on food marketing and national agricultural production

An idea which has been aired by several naval historians within recent years is that because the Victualling Board was a very large (possibly the largest single) purchaser of foodstuffs in Britain, or sometimes more specifically on the London markets, this must have had a profound effect on national agriculture and food marketing. Despite the opinion of a near-contemporary, Tooke, who dismissed it as a fallacy, the theory that war must stimulate a higher demand for food has persisted.[98] The most recent advocates of this theory are John Brewer and N A M Rodger.[99]

recent debts': *The Royal Kalendar* (London, 1803). This sum was equivalent to two years' salary for Harman.

97 This, and some other inappropriate behaviour from the clerks, is detailed in Chapter 8.

98 Thomas Tooke, *History of Prices and Circulation from 1793 to the Present Day*, Vol. 1 (London, 1838), pp. 90–2. Some other advocates include Barnes, *English Corn Laws*, p. 12; and A H John, 'Farming in Wartime 1793–1815', in E L Jones and G E Mingay (eds), *Land, Labour and Population in the Industrial Revolution* (London, 1967), p. 28. However, all these are discussing the whole of the military, not just the navy.

99 Brewer, *Sinews*, p. 37; Rodger, *Wooden World*, p. 84.

However, Brewer, who stated 'The navy required extraordinarily large quantities of foodstuffs' bases this on a dubious set of figures for 1760 taken from Rodger's *Wooden World*, then goes on to remark 'what impact this requirement had on civilian prices, or what effect the navy's demand for such foodstuffs had on their production and marketing is still a little-understood but undoubtedly important subject'.

This remark is echoed and enlarged upon by Rodger, who cites part of Buchet's conclusions as a basis for his assertions that the Victualling Board 'was the largest single purchaser on the London markets for agricultural products', that it had a policy of encouraging the growth of firms of suppliers, and that it was fundamental in pushing forward the growth of a national agricultural market.[100]

The facts, when examined in detail, do not support these assertions. These facts fall into two categories, those relating to the national production and consumption of the relevant commodities, and those relating to the activities of the Victualling Board. Firstly it must be pointed out that there is no consistent data on either national agricultural production during 'our' period, or, with the exception of the Smithfield cattle market, on the quantities purchased in any markets.[101] Secondly, most of the fluctuations in commodity prices can be linked either to the effect of weather conditions on production, the effects of enemy embargoes on trade, or the availability of money. Thirdly, the number of men in the navy, when compared with the whole population, is so small (less than 1 per cent) that it cannot have had any influence, especially given that these people would have been fed anyway, whether or not in the navy.

As far as Victualling Board purchases are concerned, only two-thirds of these went through the London markets, and the Board based its purchasing on a system of competitive tendering, which negates both the idea of their having an effect on civilian prices, and of their manipulating the size of supplying firms. Examination of the contract ledgers demonstrates that in fact they purchased large quantities of essential victuals, such as biscuit, through hundreds of small firms.[102]

There are many factors in the way in which the Victualling Board performed the core tasks of obtaining and distributing bulk supplies of victuals which indicate the government's philosophy behind the Admiralty's system of using subordinate boards to handle the minutiae of naval logistics. The Victualling Board operated under a system of long-established and detailed instructions beyond which the victualling commissioners could not stray without consulting their masters on the Board of Admiralty; even then,

---

100 Rodger, *Command*, p. 307, citing Buchet, *Marine*, pp. 337–8.
101 A short run of figures for Smithfield is available, and reproduced in Appendix G.
102 For a more detailed discussion of this topic, see J. Macdonald, 'Myth'.

such recommendations as they did make, or responses which they gave to Admiralty queries in such situations, were usually based on precedents which might go back decades. The lack of autonomy suggested by this necessity indicates a comparatively lowly position which is borne out by the way other government departments forced actions on the Board which fell outside their normal practice (and often economic sense), as evidenced by the directives to buy rice, foreign wheat and rum.

However, within the parameters of this established system, the Victualling Board performed well in situations requiring an immediate decision; these include all the day-to-day activities associated with maintaining stock, such as deciding to advertise for a commodity, deciding which bid to accept, deciding it was time to send supplies to one of the outports when their regular stock reports showed a need, or deciding what course of action to recommend to the Admiralty when they could not make the actual decision themselves.

It was on the matters which fell outside this 'immediate decision' situation where their performance was poor: those situations which should have been, but were not, monitored, such as the need to reduce prices paid under standing contracts when market prices fell; those where a long-standing practice should have been changed, such as requiring the attendance of tenderers at contract awarding meetings; those where a practice such as using casks of meat as dunnage for dry provisions was continued beyond the point where it became uneconomical; and those where a little foresight, such as sending additional stocks before the weather made it difficult to sail down the Channel, would have prevented winter shortages at the outports west of the Thames.

These two different levels of competence might be likened to a doctor who provides rapid and effective treatment to a patient who presents with an 'acute' condition but fails to notice that another patient is suffering from a 'chronic' condition.[103] As will be seen, this malaise existed throughout all the Victualling Board's activities.

---

103 '"Acute": of rapid onset and generally of short duration; "chronic": of long duration and often gradual onset.' P. Wingate (ed.), *The Penguin Medical Encyclopedia* (London, 2nd edition 1972), pp. 8, 103.

3

Delivery at Home: Issuing Victuals to Warships and Managing the Victualling Yards

THE SECOND PART of the Victualling Board's core task of supplying the Royal Navy and the army abroad with victuals and victualling stores was the delivery of bulk supplies to army garrisons abroad, the delivery of those items to warships on stations at home and abroad, and to troopships leaving Britain. Although the general principles of performing this task were the same regardless of location, each had their own types of difficulty to overcome. Abroad, there were problems relating to distance and communication times, with occasional clashes of personality; at home problems tended to arise from shortages and delays caused by the weather or the arrival of unusually large numbers of ships for revictualling.

With very few exceptions, the arrangements for delivery of victuals to warships at home through contractor depots worked without requiring major Victualling Board intervention; apart from a few minor cases of fraud so did the third strategy of ad hoc purser purchases. Delivery by the first strategy via the victualling yards at the outports produced no 'acute' problems beyond those created by adverse weather conditions and occasional complaints from commissioned officers about shortages or delays; nor were there any at Deptford. However, the 11th Report of the Board of Revision made it clear that the administration of operations at all these yards had degenerated over the years into a state so chronic that major reorganisations of procedures, management and personnel had to be instigated.[1]

Secondary source material on the delivery of victuals to warships from yards and contractor depots is somewhat sparse. There is, however, copious primary source material in the correspondence and board minutes which enables a fairly detailed picture to emerge, despite an unfortunate paucity of surviving correspondence between the victualling office in London and the individual yards.

---

1 An outline of the findings of the Board of Revision on this topic is given in this chapter. For full details, see Chapter 9.

Second and third strategies: contractor depots and ad hoc purser purchases at home

Of the three strategies described in Chapter 2, acquisition of victuals for warships at home by individual pursers was, in terms of magnitude, the least of them. Very few warships in home waters, and these mostly the smallest, operated so far from either yard or contractors' depot that they had to rely on pursers' ad hoc purchases. Apart from a few small-scale incidents of dishonest pursers (or lieutenants acting as their own purser) the strategy of purser-buying at home seems to have been problem-free. The number of purser purchases diminished during the course of the two wars as more contractor depots were arranged; in 1793 there were twenty-two of these, in 1804 the number had risen to thirty, the greatest concentration of these being along the south and east coasts, as the threat of invasion from France increased and the North Sea and Baltic fleets were enlarged. By 1813, the number had dropped back to twenty-five after some of the shore locations were replaced by depot ships. As with the merchants who wrote promiscuously to offer a quantity of bulk foodstuffs, occasional letters arrived at the victualling office offering victualling facilities at a particular location but these were usually refused on the basis of insufficient need.[2]

If for no other reason than to warn contractors of major increases or decreases of manpower in their catchment area, there must have been considerable correspondence between the Victualling Board and the contractors running depots but this has not survived.[3] Correspondence between the Victualling Board and the Admiralty contains very few items on these contractor depots round the British Isles: merely some queries on what the arrangements were at certain places and a few complaints about insufficient stocks, which were usually due to adverse winds preventing restocking. Given the number of depots and the length of time involved, such a minimal level of problems serious enough to come to the Admiralty's attention indicates a system that worked extremely well.

These depots were operated on standing contracts, running for a minimum of twelve months and usually with six months notice of termination to be given by either side. The contracts were of two sorts, the first being for individual perishable items such as beer, water, fresh beef and vegetables; of all the depots, ten supplied only these items, all being on the south coast and thus within comparatively easy reach of the outport yards for 'sea provisions' (i.e. the basic ration and substitutes). Other depots supplied both

---

2   For instance, for the north Devon coast, which was refused as there was only one sloop operating in that area: NMM ADM C/686, 12 November 1796.

3   For instance, there was an instruction from the Admiralty to tell the contractor at Falmouth how many ships would be wintering there: NMM ADM C/712, 24 October 1806.

sea provisions and perishable items; at these depots the perishable items were usually the subject of separate contracts, although often supplied by the same contractor. Regardless of the type of victual, the contracts required that all items be supplied within forty-eight hours of being requested (winds and weather permitting), of stated quality, at the listed prices and without any charges for delivery or new packaging (casks, biscuit bags, etc.). Like the bulk supply contracts, these were awarded by competitive tender, but with the contracts for sea provisions, where numerous individually priced items were involved, a little arithmetic was required before a decision could be made. The accountant for cash calculated the cost per man per day for each bid, from which it could be seen whose aggregate price was best.[4] Anything up to seven bids might be received, although more than five was rare. The bids for each location could vary considerably; for instance in 1799 there were six bids for Liverpool, the lowest at 9.26 pence per man per day, the highest at 12.44 pence. One might speculate that many of those who failed to get contracts were small businessmen who lived at the named port and who did not enjoy the economies of scale available to the larger London-based firms. Of all the contractors supplying sea provisions through these depots, three names predominate, with two holding by far the greatest number of contracts.

Of the total 354 'location-years',[5] of British depot sea provision contracts during this period, 57.1 per cent were held by three contractors: John Grant held 113 (31.9 per cent) across 17 locations, Thomas Pinkerton held 64 (18.1 per cent) across 15 locations, and Alexander Donaldson held 25 (7.1 per cent) across 9 locations. One other contractor, Quintin Blackburn, held a further thirteen (3.7 per cent), all these being for Newcastle or Tynemouth. No other contractor exceeded ten location-years.[6]

It can be seen in the contract ledgers that there was considerable crossover for certain locations; these were the busiest and thus potentially the most lucrative; unfortunately it is impossible to calculate the total amounts earned by these four contractors. There was tremendous variation in the volume of business at these depots; the smallest charged less than a few hundred pounds a year, the largest charged many tens of thousands of pounds each year (e.g. over £1.9m at Yarmouth over the twenty-three year period).[7]

---

4 These calculations were made in a bound book and certified and signed by the accountant: TNA ADM 112/160–1.
5 This term has been invented by the author, meaning the number of locations, multiplied by the number of calendar years in which the named contractors featured in the contact ledgers. Without a complete set of contracts, it is not possible to calculate the exact calendar time involved.
6 See Macdonald, 'Victualling Board', Appendices E & F for detail, and page 78 below for equivalent data for foreign depots.
7 See *Ibid.*, Appendix G for details.

Pinkerton and Donaldson also held contracts for depots abroad, Grant and Blackburn did not. Donaldson and Blackburn did not supply bulk items to the Victualling Board's stores, Grant and Pinkerton did so occasionally, mainly rum and some oatmeal, but also a little Irish beef and pork. However, it would seem that this form of naval victualling business was more precarious than providing bulk supplies: both Grant and Pinkerton went bankrupt before the end of the Napoleonic war. It is interesting that the creditors and trustees of both these men include several other sea-provision contractors and bulk product suppliers mentioned in Chapter 2, another indication of the close-knit world of the provisions trade.[8]

For most of the home depots where Grant, Pinkerton and Donaldson supplied sea provisions, they also supplied fresh beef; this and the widely spread locations involved indicates that they must have had a network of local agents.

The sheer volume of information available on the items supplied at these depots (the quantity of each item supplied at each collection by each ship is listed) gives an indication of the task involved in checking both contractors' and pursers' accounts at the victualling office. At busy locations such as Yarmouth and Torbay, the entries in the contract ledgers run to many pages for the fresh beef, let alone other items.[9] It has not been possible to calculate what percentage of all victuals supplied to ships came from these depots, but it is possible, using the (admittedly crude) method of money claimed by the contractors, to apportion the money spent on this form of victualling between home and foreign locations: of the whole £13.9m spent on these depots, £5.2m (37.7 per cent) was spent at home-based depots.[10]

The Victualling Board-run yards: the outports

Throughout this period, the Victualling Board ran five main establishments: the main yard at Deptford and the outport yards of Chatham, Dover, Portsmouth and Plymouth. The smallest of the outports were those at Chatham and Dover, Dover being the smaller of the two. These yards served ships anchored at The Downs and The Nore and those ships operating at the eastern end of the Channel and in the North Sea off the Low Countries

---

8   TNA B3/1903 (Pinkerton); B3/3906 (Grant).
9   For further detail on the content of these ledgers, see J Macdonald, 'Documentary sources relating to the work of the British Royal Navy's Victualling Board during the French Revolutionary and Napoleonic wars', *International Journal of Maritime History*, 21.1 (June 2009), pp. 239–62.
10 Including those round Ireland and on the Channel Islands. Unfortunately the amounts charged for fresh beef and other single items (as opposed to sea provisions) are not not shown separately in the contract ledgers.

and up into the Baltic. There were also victualling facilities at Yarmouth and Cork; the latter consisted only of storehouses, but this was extended in 1809 to provide victuals for the Peninsula and then North America after 1812.[11] There were also some small stores and manned watering places at strategic points on land, and after 1800, several depot ships located at the main anchorages at The Downs, The Nore, Spithead, Yarmouth and Torbay/Brixham.

The largest of the outport yards, in terms of the quantity of victuals supplied, was Portsmouth. As well as serving part of the fleets operating in the Channel and the North Sea, it supplied most of the warships leaving Britain for foreign service (which received a larger proportion of victuals than ships on home service) and most of the troop transports. Despite its importance, unlike Deptford, Chatham and Dover, the premises at Portsmouth were not in a single location but spread round the town, with the offices in St Mary's Street, the bakery and its store in King Street, both at some distance from the victualling wharf to the west of the town, the slaughterhouse and meat store further to the west (outside the main harbour entrance and south of the Sally Port), and the mill across a bridge by the gun wharf, all of which caused delays in both unloading victualling transports and loading delivery craft as victuals had to be moved round the town on drays and wagons.[12] This was particularly tiresome in the winter months with their shorter days, and even more when they coincided with low tide.[13] The brewery and its stores were across the harbour at Weevil (Gosport). The inconvenience of this was well-known but was not remedied until 1828 when the new Royal Clarence yard was completed.

Plymouth was the main victualling place for that part of the Channel fleet which protected trade in the Western Approaches and the Channel Soundings, and the Western Squadron which had the crucial task of blockading Brest and the other western French ports. However, there was insufficient space for the whole of the Channel fleet to anchor at Plymouth, so when the winds permitted, the Western Squadron used Torbay, east of Plymouth. Because of the difficulties with adverse winds (Torbay was sheltered from westerlies but dangerously exposed in easterlies), the demand for victuals there was too spasmodic to maintain a full-time victualling yard; instead, hired vessels full of victuals, with clerks to supervise the issues, were sent round from Plymouth when the squadron was expected;

11 NMM ADM C/683, 24 January 1795; C/722, 20 May 1809; TNA ADM 110/62, f. 211, 19 July 1810; f. 528, 20 November 1810. I am grateful to Dr Roger Knight for clarification of the Yarmouth situation.
12 Matthew Sheldon, 'A tale of two cities: The facilities, work and impact of the victualling office in Portsmouth, 1793–1815', *Transactions of the Naval Dockyards Society*, vol. I (July 2006), pp. 35–45.
13 NMM ADM DP/19, 25 November 1799.

later this evolved into a semi-permanent depot of several ships at Brixham. Although fresh provisions were available at both Plymouth and Torbay, the demands of a close blockade on Brest kept the squadron at sea and then, as in previous wars, several vessels operated a shuttle service' with live cattle, fresh vegetables and water.[14] During the worst of the winter, the fleet sheltered at Falmouth.[15]

At Plymouth, the stores were located at various points round the Tamar estuary, with the main store at Lamhay on the Plym estuary, the slaughterhouse at Cremyll Point and the brewery at Insworke with its store at Southdown. Ships were victualled either at the anchorage at Cawsand Bay or at the dockyard further up the Hamoaze.[16] As at Portsmouth, the inconvenient situation at Plymouth was not remedied until the new Royal William yard was completed in 1834.

The work of the yards

As well as receiving and storing bulk supplies of items either sent from Deptford or arranged by the victualling office to be delivered to the yards by supply contractors, the agents victualler who ran the yards were also responsible for arranging their own contracts for certain items, mainly biscuit and soft bread but also some wheat, malt, coals, candles and 'sundry species of small stores', restricting such decisions to the normal precedents.[17] As with the bulk supply contracts dealt with by the victualling office in London, these local contracts had to go through the standard processes of advertising for tenders and comparing the responses, with the agent victualler, storekeeper, and clerk of the check standing in for the commissioners.[18] One small variation in the procedure here was the Board of Revision's recommendation that the box for holding the tenders was to have three locks instead of the two recommended for the boxes in the victualling office and the yards abroad.[19]

Agents victualler also had responsibility for any manufacturing activities in their yards. All the larger yards baked biscuit and some had their own mills for grinding corn into biscuit meal; all brewed beer and made casks, as well as repairing them. The outports did not pack meat on a regular basis, although they did salt occasional amounts of fresh beef that had not been

---

14 Emma Laird, 'The Victualling of the Channel Fleet in 1800' (MA Dissertation, Greenwich Maritime Institute, 2001), pp. 21, 50, 53–6, 61.
15 NMM ADM C/712, 24 October 1806.
16 Laird, 'Channel Fleet', p. 20.
17 *Fees 8*, p. 563. For detailed lists of items contracted for in this way, see TNA ADM 112/87–114.
18 *Fees 8*, p. 563.
19 BOR 11, p. 65, clause 85.

issued promptly and were thus in danger of spoiling, and, in one case at Plymouth, a number of beasts intended for delivery to the Channel Fleet as fresh meat which turned out to be surplus to that requirement.[20] Although the contract ledgers show the quantities of commodities delivered direct to the home yards by suppliers, there is no consistent record of provisions sent to the outport yards from Deptford; we therefore cannot know the full quantities of provisions which passed through these yards.

Issuing victuals

The final part of the agent victualler's job was to oversee the issuing, and sometimes delivery, of victuals and victualling stores to warships, other naval vessels and troop transports. The instructions for these issues, known as warrants, came from the Admiralty, via the Navy Board until July 1808, and then, 'for the purposes of celerity' direct either as an Admiralty Order or a letter from the Admiralty Secretary; in February 1812 the Victualling Board suggested that it would save time for everyone if, instead of these orders being sent every time a ship came into port to restock, they were only sent when each ship was first commissioned, a suggestion which the Admiralty accepted.[21] Given that replenishment orders had first passed from the port admiral to the Admiralty, and that a formal set of paperwork had long been in use to deal with replenishment, it is surprising that it took so long to think of this time-saving measure. The saving was consider-able: of the total 9,815 victualling warrants received 1793–1815, 7,774 came before July 1808, 1,590 between that date and February 1812, and only 451 between that date and the end of the war. These instructions were passed to the agent victualler in charge of the stated location so that, in order to pre-vent fraud, they could be matched up with the documentation produced by the pursers when they went to collect their provisions.[22]

These warrants (originally handwritten and then as printed pro-formas with spaces for the relevant information) stated the name of the ship, where she was to be victualled, for how many months, and for what sort of serv-ice. This latter was usually either 'Channel' or 'foreign' but occasionally 'for a particular service' (i.e. secret). With the exception of occasional special situations, such as 'a voyage to Newfoundland', the location of foreign service was not specified.[23] The type of service was differentiated because it

---

20   TNA ADM 113/232–241, pay-books Portsmouth; 113/199–208, pay-books Plymouth; Laird, 'Channel Fleet', p. 58.

21   NMM ADM C/719, 12 July 1808; TNA ADM 110/65, 14 February 1812.

22   TNA ADM 224/17 & 18 are letter books, from the Victualling Office to the agent victualler at Portsmouth, covering the period 1790 to 1799. These contain some examples of these instructions.

23   NMM ADM G/790, 9 February 1793, *Stately* at Portsmouth, six months' provisions.

meant different items and different quantities: for Channel service (except in summer months when it was likely to go off quickly)[24] the major amount of beverage was beer, and the full amount of butter and cheese was issued; the total amount was for three or four months.[25] For foreign service, the ship received sufficient sea provisions for six months, only sufficient butter and cheese for three months, sufficient beer for three months and a larger proportion of wine and spirits but was forbidden to broach the latter whilst in reach of the British coast, in case of collusion with smugglers.[26]

In both cases it was assumed that the ship would have her full complement of men; only rarely was the number of men mentioned. Although not specifically mentioned in the correspondence it can be deduced that the victualling office kept a record of each ship's rating and complement: letters frequently arrived from the Navy Board stating that a certain ship's complement was increased or decreased by x men; less frequently a letter arrived stating that the complements of a whole class of ships had changed, for instance in June 1796 a letter listed the new complements for all classes of frigates, the numbers being differentiated by the number of guns.[27]

Troop transports were dealt with in a slightly different way. Although what was issued was still a multiple of the ration for the stated period, because the transports were hired and thus could be of various sizes, the instructions stated either the number of men or the modifier 'at the rate of x tons per man'.[28] This did not mean that the weight of victuals was to be a multiple of the stated weight and the number of men, but that the tonnage of the ship should be divided by the stated weight to arrive at the number of men she could carry. Thus a 600-ton ship could carry 300 men at 'two tons per man' or 400 at 'one and a half tons per man'. This situation was supervised at the port by the regiments' agents; sometimes when a large armament was at its height (such as during the armament for the West Indies in 1793) the instructions were more general: 'as requested by [the regiment's] agent'.[29] As above, these instructions were for sea provisions, not to be consumed whilst in port. Transporting troops involved the Victualling Office in more than just providing food: one letter enquired whether troops should be supplied with pudding bags and if so, could they be sent immediately as the troops were destroying their pillow cases for

24 For example, NMM ADM C/697, 1 May 1812.
25 Other variations were for so many months of some items and a lesser number of months for others.
26 *R&I*, 13th edition, p. 64 (butter and cheese); *R&I*, 14th edition, p. 302.
27 NMM ADM C/685, 25 June 1796.
28 For example, NMM ADM G/791, passim.
29 NMM ADM G/790 and C/678–682, passim. There was a total of 185 such instructions during August and September 1793, when the norm for the rest of the year was between 40 and 50 each month.

pudding bags; another asks for empty biscuit bags to carry oats for cavalry horses.[30]

For newly commissioned ships, a full amount of provisions for the stated period would be issued; for replenishment, a requisition was submitted to the agent victualler by the ship's officers and here the items and amounts requested were to complete (top-up) the ship's stock for the stated number of months. Ships did not wait until they were running out before seeking replenishment, but topped-up their supplies whenever the opportunity allowed, on the assumption that they might be prevented from getting into port by some event such as bad weather or pursuing the enemy. This topping-up situation was orchestrated by the commander-in-chief of the squadron, who received regular situation reports from all his captains and wrote to the Admiralty to prompt the required warrants.[31] As above, these were sea provisions, not to be used while in port. When in port, a different victualling situation applied, known as 'extra petty warrant'.[32] In this situation, the purser put in a requisition for no more than three days at a time, stating the exact number of men on board. The actual form of the provisions was also different: biscuit was often replaced by 'soft' bread (i.e. loaves) and the salt meat and dried pease were replaced (in varying proportions relating to availability and price) by fresh meat and fresh vegetables.

These constituent items of 'port' provisions also applied to those ships which were semi-permanently in port or in the Thames or Medway: those in ordinary or guard ships, or the crews of prison ships (although for these a warrant continued to be issued by the Navy Board, even after the issue of other warrants was taken over by the Admiralty).[33] For these ships, the bulk of provisions was issued on a monthly basis, with the fresh items delivered more frequently.[34] For ships in ordinary, and possibly the others (though there is no mention of this in the correspondence), the long-term storable items were often supplied from the returned stocks which were too close to their 'use by' date to be issued to ships expected to be at sea for any length of time. For all parties concerned, whether victualling yard personnel or ships' pursers, the rule for issuing and using victuals was 'oldest first'; for pursers this was enforced by refusing the credit for returns of dated items which had not been used in the requisite time (unless of course they had been designated unusable by survey).[35]

30 NMM ADM G/790, 7 October 1793; 9 January 1794 and 26 February 1794.
31 Laird, 'Channel Fleet', pp. 25–6 (gives a chart showing the sequence of actions required).
32 *R&I*, 13th edition, p. 115.
33 NMM ADM C/719 et seq. passim. This was for the naval personnel only, not the prisoners who were victualled by a different method.
34 *BOR 11*, p. 18.
35 TNA ADM 49/59.

The victualling yards had an ongoing problem with water, requiring large amounts needed for brewing beer as well as supplying ships;[36] at Deptford the problem was compounded by the tides which brought salt water not only up the Thames but also into its tributaries; there were constant complaints about this water which was not only frequently brackish but also had an offensive smell and taste (hardly surprising given that all the domestic and commercial effluent of the city ended up in the river); at Dover the cistern and pump-house backed on to a slaughterhouse and pig yard.[37] The solution, in the yards which did not have their own reliable wells, seems to have come in 1810–11, when a number of water companies were founded and offered supplies, for example, the Ravensbourne River Water Company which offered to supply Deptford, the Portsea Island Water Works Company which offered to supply Portsmouth, and 'the water works about to be erected for the inhabitants of Deal' which offered to supply the dockyard at Deal for the ships at The Downs.[38] Earlier, under the direction of Samuel Bentham, several of the yards installed their own systems of iron pipes, with steam-driven pumps to raise the water; some watering places also had large reservoirs with pipes and cocks to facilitate filling ships' casks and, later, tanks.[39]

In addition to issuing victuals and victualling stores, the officers at the yards and on the depot ships were responsible for returns of unused items, unusable items condemned by survey, and empty containers. The unused victuals, which would have come from ships paying off at the end of a commission or being stripped for major repairs in the dockyards, were returned to store and reissued in the normal way; the paperwork required for items returned to store was much like that required for issues.[40] The system of cask marking showed packing dates as well as the supplier. Given the frequent replenishment of stock as well as the regular returns, the agents victualler and storekeepers must have had some system of ensuring a proper rotation; there is no indication of what this was, but equally there were few complaints about old stock being issued; there are some records of small quantities of old stock being sold, mostly after 1815.

---

36 See Macdonald, *Feeding*, pp. 78–9 for a discussion of the amounts of water used by warships.

37 NMM ADM C/700, 24 August & 29 December 1803; TNA ADM 110/64, ff. 396–7, 22 November 1811; NMM ADM D/45, 17 November 1803.

38 TNA ADM 110/63, f. 254, 6 March 1811; 110/63 f. 234, 27 February 1811; and 110/65, ff. 99–100, 25 February 1811.

39 NMM ADM C/700, 10 September & 28 December 1803, C/706, 26 June 1805; TNA ADM 110/53, ff. 202–205, 4 September 1805.

40 Examples of all these forms can be found in the appendices of the *R&I*, 14th edition.

Condemned returned victuals were either returned to their supplier or sold off at intervals for whatever they would fetch.[41] Empty containers were cleaned, repaired and reused. Some of the yard paylists include people employed to wash and repair biscuit bags; all the yards employed coopers who would rebuild casks which had been shaken.[42] This seems to have been an ongoing problem, despite the Victualling Board's opposition to the practice. They were particularly anxious that it should be avoided with beer and water casks, unless in the utmost emergency. This rule was incorporated in the fourteenth edition of the *Regulations and Instructions*, but an Admiralty Order to all ships' commanders to that effect was issued at regular intervals, the reason for this being the high cost of rebuilding shaken casks, especially those which had to be liquid-tight.[43] This task was rendered especially difficult if the component parts of each cask had not been kept together; for this reason the Admiralty order stated that when casks were shaken, the components should be marked and that the iron hoops should not be bent.

Moving victuals from the yards to warships

Since ships in port spent most of their time at anchor or moorings away from the land, the physical process of moving victuals from stores to ships (and the returns and empties back to store) was usually done by boats or hoys. The correspondence contains some indirect mentions of ships' boats being sent in for collections (often of fresh beef or water) and many mentions of boats and vessels either hired or belonging to the yards; but beyond this there seems to have been no specific ruling on whether yard or ships' boats were to be used for particular items.[44] One might surmise that for small collections, ships' boats would be used even if this involved several trips, but large amounts for one ship would be loaded onto one of the yard's hoys and delivered to the ship, with a clerk in attendance to sign off the vouchers.[45]

An exchange of letters between Vice Admiral Graves at Spithead, the Victualling Board and the agent at Portsmouth gives a useful insight into procedures and some of the difficulties involved: the admiral complained that since the previous method of delivering fresh beef to ships by the yard's hoy had been stopped, having to send ships' boats in to fetch the beef was

---

41 *SCF* 32, p. 74.
42 For example, the pay lists for Deptford show seven men employed for 'sack mending, bag washing' in 1796, TNA ADM 113/62.
43 For instance, on 18 July 1803. (A copy of this order is at TNA PC1/3578.)
44 For instance TNA ADM 110/58, f. 298 6 October 1808 is a request to the Navy Board to supply a cutter at Portsmouth.
45 However, NMM ADM C/679, 8 January 1793, is an Admiralty Order to send water out to ships at Spithead in the Portsmouth yard boats.

'attended with much inconvenience'. The allocation to each ship's boat was in order of its arrival at the landing place near the slaughterhouse; in order to get a good place in the queue the boats were sent off as early as 4 a.m. but the clerk who attended the issuing did not start work until 7.30 a.m. This was not a problem in mild weather, but with the wind in certain directions there was so much sea at the usual landing place that the boats had to move round the Point to a smaller landing place and the meat then had to be carried through the narrow gates and across the beach. The number of people on the beach created confusion and impeded the men, already hampered with quarters of meat on their backs, from getting to the boats. This made it difficult for the officer in charge of the boat to keep an eye on his own crew and prevent their being encouraged to desert or given drink by the gathered civilians:

> The confusion and tumult occasioned by fifty or sixty boats with nine persons to each boat busied in carrying meat to their respective boats and the passing and repassing of so many through a narrow gateway with meat upon their backs … occasions a struggle and contention not easily described.

Then, having become overheated, the men had to row back to their ships, which chilled them. Sometimes, if the boats were overloaded and the sea was rough, boats would overturn (and some lives had been lost through this); some were damaged by being crowded into such a small landing place. Could they not, the admiral asked, go back to the old system of sending the meat out in hoys?

This letter had been passed to the agent victualler at Portsmouth for his comments, and these are shown on the back: they had used hoys in the past, but it required three, and the boats were likely to be stove alongside them in windy weather, not to mention the damage to the hoys themselves and the beef lost overboard in the process. Equally, because of the tides, sometimes the meat had to be put on the hoys overnight and if the weather was warm it went off ('musty and putrid from such a large quantity lying together'); this then had to go back to the yard and although they tried salting it this was rarely successful and 'caused muttering, and the victualling department unjustly got the blame'. Also, the meat hoys could not be used for anything else, they cost £20 each per month to hire, plus the cost of the three clerks to issue the meat, who also had to see it loaded at night and thus could do no other work during the day. However, he finished, they were aware of the problem and were in process of rebuilding the stage and installing more cranes.[46] This final comment seems to indicate that the Board might not have been aware of this work, but perhaps he was merely

46   NMM ADM C/683, 25 February 1795.

giving a detailed draft of a letter that the Victualling Board could copy and send to the Admiralty.

Some problems faced by the agents victualler

The propensity of sailors to get drunk described above was not only a problem for their ships' officers, it could also create problems for the victualling yard staff. For instance, in 1800, associated with the cask depot at Brixham, the crews from the Brest blockade fleet treated the locals to 'scenes of drunkenness, obscenity, blasphemy and consequent casualties from the men fighting and falling over precipices'. This problem was not solved until Samuel Bentham hired a guardhouse for officers to oversee the watering.[47] There were other problems associated with this fleet: when St Vincent took over the command, he immediately gave orders designed to prevent ships lingering in port, where many officers' wives were staying; one of the ruses employed by their captains to circumvent this was to leave large gaps when stowing water casks so they would run out sooner and thus have to return in order to fill up again. They also delayed putting their provision orders in to the victualling office; St Vincent made a further sequence of orders to prevent this. He also wrote to the agent at Plymouth requiring him to complete a form for each ship, showing when it arrived, when it placed its order and when the order was filled, with reasons for any delays, a requirement which was approved by the Admiralty, but which obviously increased the work of the yard staff.[48]

It was not only Plymouth which suffered from admirals complaining about delays, and in most cases such delays were not the agent's fault. There were two main reasons for such delays. The first was the sheer volume of provisions demanded by the arrival of a whole fleet or group of transports, sometimes both together; the second was bad weather, either keeping delivery vessels in port or delaying their arrival from Deptford. Sometimes both these situations coincided, as happened in Portsmouth in 1808, when one hundred transports had arrived from the Baltic with sixteen ships of the line, several frigates and sloops; this, combined with a 'long continuance of westerly winds attended with tempestuous weather having prevented the arrival of scarcely any supplies from the eastwards ...' explained why stocks were low.[49] There had been an order issued to the agents victualler at Portsmouth and Plymouth in 1795, on the precedence to be given in victualling groups of ships which arrived together (Channel fleet, cruising frigates and then ships on particular services to be served before others) but

---

47 Laird, 'Channel Fleet', p. 62; TNA ADM 1/3526, 28 September 1800, letter from Bentham to Admiralty.
48 Laird, 'Channel Fleet', pp. 51, 54–5.
49 TNA ADM 110/57 ff. 12–15, 1 February 1808.

of course this would not have helped if these arrived after a large fleet of transports had been and gone.[50]

Normally the Victualling Board had advance warning that a large fleet was expected, and were then able to make immediate arrangements to send the necessary supplies from Deptford. Often the problem was insufficient forethought being given to the potential difficulties caused by the normal seasonal weather; it was the ports to the west of Deptford which were affected by strong winds from the west which prevented shipping getting down the Channel. It took the Board of Revision to point out that this problem would be alleviated by ensuring that the yards at Portsmouth and Plymouth were well stocked before winter set in, something which the victualling commissioners should have seen for themselves.[51]

There were also problems with the personnel of the two revenue boards, Customs and Excise. It must have been irritating enough for yard officers to have to obtain their permission, and physical presence with keys, whenever dutiable items needed to be received into stores or issued; there were other occasions when they must have been positively infuriating. In 1801, the Customs officers in Cork insisted on adding a new layer of requirements to those normal in England, including a new set of paperwork to be completed, fees to be paid to their staff, and on one occasion insisting that the cargo of a victualling transport (which had been loaded at Portsmouth and was exclusively for the warships in the harbour) should be unloaded onto the quay to be gauged and inspected, and bonds posted for the duty on the goods, which no one local was prepared to give. Although the delays this caused were not the making of the agent there, he found himself receiving veiled threats of complaints to higher authority from the captain of *Galatea* who wanted provisions immediately.[52]

The job of the agent victualler was one of great responsibility and must also have been one of considerable stress, especially at the two larger yards. Without a full set of correspondence it is not possible to judge the extent to which the Board oversaw the day-to-day running of the yards, but from the correspondence between the Victualling Board and the Admiralty it appears that other than requiring explanations of the background to complaints from naval officers (and these averaged less than one a year) the victualling commissioners allowed the agents victualler a great deal of autonomy until the Board of Revision reported. What should have been regular yard visitations from the commissioners for stock- and accounting-checks were rare; the Board of Revision, although recommending unannounced annual visits in peacetime, merely stated that in wartime they should be 'as often as

50   NMM ADM C/684, 17 July 1795.
51   *BOR 10*, p. 36.
52   TNA ADM 110/46, ff. 687–90, 16 June 1801; 110/47, ff. 14–16, 14 July 1801.

practicable'. However, the report did lay down the aspects of the yard work to be inspected: not only that 'the business in every department be properly carried on [and] to see that the Instructions under which the officers act are duly observed ...' but also to ensure that the office and yard personnel were physically capable of doing their jobs, to the extent of having the workmen mustered for their inspection, and to list in their report those who should be discharged or retired.[53]

Certainly, such visits as were made prior to the Board of Revision enquiry were somewhat ineffectual. The visitations made in 1803 by commissioners Towry and Moody to Portsmouth and Plymouth are notable for their naivety: at Plymouth, attended by their own two clerks and three from the yard, the commissioners started in the granary where they were immediately daunted by the sheer volume of wheat and malt which confronted them. This grain was kept loose because it had to be turned and screened regularly to prevent it heating up, and to screen out insects;[54] this created an immediate problem: how to measure it accurately. The most accurate method of doing this is not mentioned; we can only surmise that it involved bagging it and weighing the bags, but this would 'take more time than we thought proper to devote' and would also require the assistance of numerous labourers who would have to abandon their other work. So, remembering that malt was sometimes gauged to assess duty, they decided to try that, and employed two Customs officers to do it. The results of the first attempt were so different from the running balances kept by the yard officers (2,875 quarters of wheat gauged against 3,245 balance, 3,715 quarters of malt gauged against 4,041 balance) that the commissioners immediately concluded 'that no reliance could be placed on a method so apparently erroneous'. Then they wondered if this 'erroneous' result might have been caused by the uneven surface of the floor and the irregular shape of the piles, so they weighed sixty quarters of wheat and laid it out in a rectangle on a level surface and had this gauged, the result being fifty-eight quarters. They may have been right about the inaccuracy of the gauging, but it is their response which is noteworthy: instead of biting the bullet and weighing the rest to get a proper figure, they decided to accept the figures from the yard's books. It just does not seem to have occured to them that the amorphous heaps of wheat and malt might have concealed a pile of rocks placed there to conceal a major theft or even that such a shapeless pile would not show steady pilfering performed on the 'they'll never notice it' principle.

With the other items of stock, they happily accepted the proferred explanations for the differences between the count and the books: a deficiency of 94,751 lbs of biscuit was said to be due to a combination of some being

53   *BOR 10*, p. 30.
54   *BOR 11*, proposed new regulations, article 83.

shown as flour, some having been baked but not yet entered in the receipt books and some (24,639 lbs) which would be accounted for when the quarterly accounts were made up to the survey date; a 10,103 lb surplus of cheese was 'a casting error'; almost forty gallons of wine had been used to top up casks and not shown in the books; a beer surplus of 10,507 gallons was because the brewer had been stating less than he actually brewed but now he intended to brew less and state more until he'd caught up; the various deficiencies and surpluses of casks, hoops, staves and headings were because the count was not made until the quarter end and even then did not include the foreign contract puncheons; and other assorted differences which the storekeeper said 'must have been occasioned by unavoidable errors in the weekly accounts'.

The 'findings' at Portsmouth were much the same: rather than stop the mill to measure the wheat properly, the commissioners accepted the figure in the accounts; they accepted a 'wastage' loss of some 7,500 lbs of cheese, and a loss of 3,370 biscuit bags used as bung cloths; and for various other deficiencies and surpluses they just accepted the book figures as accurate. They had also been to Dover and Chatham, as part of the 'annual visitation' a few weeks previously. As before the 'surveys' were cursory as the commissioners did not want to disturb the stocks or stop the work to make a proper measurement of the wheat and malt. At these yards they were, however, concerned that the weekly account was 'considered of less consequence than its importance had claim to' (at Chatham these accounts hadn't been balanced for eight months) and they did duly reprimand the officers for this.[55]

To issue a reprimand on only one aspect of inadequate record-keeping and reporting, when they had encountered so many similar examples; to fail to insist on performing proper stock counts; to accept as reasonable the oxymoron 'unavoidable errors'; and to fail to see that the chaotic situations they had met were a clear indication to the dishonest that theft would go unnoticed and were thus an open invitation to dishonesty (if not actual evidence of its concealment), speaks of an unforgivable level of naivety in senior managers responsible for the care of large quantities of essential wartime supplies. This series of visitations were so ineffectual that in terms of obtaining accurate figures they might as well not have bothered, and worse, that they had demonstrated their weakness to any interested parties who might have been contemplating a little income enhancement.

The next visit by the same two commissioners, two years later, to Chatham and Dover, were, they reported, carried out in the same manner as their previous visits to Portsmouth and Plymouth (those reported above).[56] These

55   NMM ADM D/48 22 January 1805; DP/28, 25 & 29 June & 2 July 1808.
56   NMM ADM D/48, 22 November 1805.

two small yards did have bakeries but did not operate their own mills, so there was not the problem to be faced of trying to count vast stocks of loose material; when they proceeded on to Portsmouth and Plymouth, they did not remark on how the surveys of wheat and malt were carried out, but seemed happy to accept the reasons for discrepancies offered by the officers (at Plymouth, a discrepancy of 47 quarters of malt was explained as being the result of the survey being carried out the day after brewing, when the books were made up to the day before brewing). There were as many items with a count above the book figure as below it, and in each case what the commissioners accepted as plausible explanations were made.

Detailed reports of other inspection visits to the outports by commissioners are rare, although the minutes indicate that these were made. However, there were some for special purposes: commissioner Rodney spent several days at Plymouth in May/June 1800 to report on the cause of delays in replenishing St Vincent's Brest blockade fleet, as a result of which procedures for delivery to warships were tightened up and a system of depot ships at Brixham was instigated; the Admiralty also ordered St Vincent to avoid sending in the whole fleet together.[57] In September 1802 two commissioners went to Chatham to investigate the personal behaviour of the agent victualler Matthews, this being serious enough to result in his dismissal.[58] And in 1808, commissioner Searle paid a visit to Cork to investigate allegations that the agent there, John Dunsterville, was favouring one particular biscuit contractor.[59] There had been three letters signed by 'John Wilson', who turned out to be a man called Walter Lane; Searle had several meetings with Lane, meeting the agent and the commander-in-chief (Admiral Whitshed) in between. It transpired that the biscuit contractor, Callaghan, a substantial local businessman of impeccable reputation, operated his own mill and also twice as many ovens as all the other local bakers put together. This allowed him to produce biscuit at a lower price, which was how he was consistently awarded the contracts; the decision on which was taken in London, not by Dunsterville. Lane, on being questioned, said that he did not actually have any evidence to support his allegations, he just thought something was going on. Lane further alleged that Callaghan had all the contracts to supply the victualling in Cork, again obtained through collusion with Dunsterville (he was actually merely the local agent for the London-based firms who held the contracts). Lane then suggested that someone should be appointed to compare the price of meal with that of biscuit to come at a reasonable price, remarking that he had experience in

57 Laird, 'Channel Fleet', pp. 44–6.
58 This was the visit from commissioners Towry and Moody in 1802 to Chatham to investigate the lease for use of a well: NMM ADM C/698, 18 September 1802, and see pp. 168–70.
59 NMM ADM C/719, 13 July 1808.

these trades. Searle remarked in his report 'I conjectured who he wished to be appointed to this situation' and when asked, Lane agreed that he had been thinking of applying for that position through Lord Hawkesbury, with whom he had 'some acquaintance'.[60] Lane remarked that he deemed it his public duty to keep a watchful eye on all public business, then made a further allegation that Dunsterville's standard of living was 'many thousands' above his salary. Searle found that in fact Dunsterville and his family were living in modest lodgings with a shared kitchen. Although he suggested that it would be wise to make a survey of stock at Cork, a task which the commander-in-chief would carry out when the stores had emptied a little, his questions of the mayor of Cork and several prominent businessmen, as well as the commander-in-chief and some of the naval captains on the station, showed that Dunsterville was well thought of. Searle cannot have been pleased at having had to spend many days on a wild goose chase, although his visit did also allow him to investigate and report on the inadequacy of the storage space there.[61] He also paid a visit to Plymouth on his way; his only report on this seems to be a minuted comment praising the work of the master miller.[62]

Clearly the victualling commissioners did not see the normal operations of the outport yards as a cause for concern. Whether those operations were as efficient as they might have been is another matter. Morriss describes how each of the dockyards had evolved their own procedures; from the findings of the Board of Revision, while it would be an exaggeration to say the same had happened on a grand scale at the victualling yards there were certainly some aspects which varied from yard to yard, notably who had the responsibility for checking stores in and out.[63] Equally, there were many office procedures which were pointlessly repetitive, to the extent that the Board of Revision recommended these activities be abandoned and staff numbers reduced.[64]

Deptford and St Catherine's

The operation at Deptford had originated on the other side of the river at St Catherine's Dock, adjacent to the victualling office at Tower Hill. After the acquisition of premises at Deptford in the 1740s, much of the work had gradually moved across the river; how the premises at St Catherine's were used before 1793 when they were converted to the army victualling store is

60 This would have been Robert Banks Jenkinson, who became 2nd Earl of Liverpool in December 1808. At this time he headed the Home Office. *DNB*, Vol. X (Oxford, 1917), pp. 748–52.
61 NMM D/51, 15 July 1808.
62 TNA ADM 111/187, 25 June 1808.
63 Morriss, *Naval Power*, p. 29; *BOR 11*, pp. 6–7.
64 These are discussed in Chapter 9.

not known. After this they were used for army victuals, which were delivered there in bulk and sent off as required to the various garrisons. These premises remained in Victualling Board ownership throughout, finally being sold in 1816.[65]

Deptford yard did issue supplies to a few warships in the Thames and some troop transports at Woolwich, but in general its activities are better likened to those of a wholesaler than a retailer; its main function was to receive and, to a certain extent manufacture, bulk victuals, and to distribute them to the other yards round Britain and overseas. Apart from the times when it had been forewarned by the Admiralty that a large fleet was to return to one of the yards to replenish, or when a large armament was to take place (in which case the commissioners arranged immediate shipments to be sent to the relevant port), sending replenishments to the yards was prompted by the regular stock reports from the agents victualler.[66] There are no surviving instructions to the yard at Deptford until 1809,[67] but the minute books report that this was done and the letter book to the agent victualler at Portsmouth has several letters stating that such bulk supplies had been despatched.[68]

The vessels used to move these bulk replenishments to the outports were hired by the hoytaker, although there were occasional requests to the Transport Board to find vessels, or if that failed, send quantities of victuals on freight terms; these could sometimes be substantial quantities. There is no surviving consistent record in the Victualling Board correspondence or minutes of the ships hired by the hoytaker, or requests to the Transport Board for transports to carry victuals abroad, only some minuted lists, requests in the out-letters for depot ships and a few letters asking for coal to be purchased and sent straight to the outports on colliers.[69]

From 1808 on, the Admiralty asked for monthly reports of the vessels loaded and ready to leave for yards and garrisons abroad, so that they could arrange convoys; the Victualling Board tried to evade this task on the grounds that once loading was complete, the responsibility for each ship passed to the Transport Board, but the Admiralty insisted and these reports were sent on the first of each month.[70] From January 1808 to July 1815, a total of 1,481 ships were listed, 658 for the navy and 823 for the army. Transports bound for the outports are not listed, nor are there any requests

65 NMM ADM DP/35B, 15 December 1815; TNA ADM 114/40 (poster for the sale of St Catherine's on 18 October 1816).

66 *Fees 8*, p. 563.

67 TNA ADM 114/69, passim.

68 TNA ADM 224/17, passim.

69 TNA ADM 110/62, ff. 491–7 & 510, 8 November 1810 (depot ships); 110/62, ff. 132 & 145, 6 & 15 June 1810 (coal).

70 TNA ADM 110/57–70, passim.

for these to be convoyed; the lack of records on these subjects suggests that these were kept in separate letter books which have not survived.

There was, however, a major problem with the management structure at Deptford: an anarchical reporting structure, with the superintendant who was supposed to be in charge unable to enforce his authority because the layer of management below him insisted that they report direct to the commissioner nominally responsible for their department. That this situation, at the largest and most important of the yards, had been allowed to continue for so long may have been due to apathy, a failure to notice the problem, or inter-commissioner jealousy in preserving 'their' departments, or all three, and is another major failing of the Board, which required the Board of Revision to point it out and force a change in the system.[71]

Manufacturing activities

Deptford was the only yard where cattle and hogs were slaughtered and packed; one might wonder why the Victualling Board continued to pack their own meat when it was so freely available from Ireland at a reasonable price. Apart from a few exceptional years when they packed enough beef for about 35,000 men, the amounts of beef and pork which they did pack during most of the twenty-three-year period would have been barely sufficient to feed the navy even in peacetime. The Fees commissioners were convinced that it was, in view of recent frauds by contractors, wise to manufacture as much as possible at Deptford, although they did admit that the quality of the meat packed there (and the quantities in each cask) was not as good as that obtained from Ireland; but this, they thought, would improve as practice developed better skills.[72] Twenty years later, the Board of Revision remarked that it had been suggested to them that the meat-packing operation should be abandoned, and that consideration should be given to this; if it was considered, nothing was done, as the meat-packing operation continued throughout the war, as evidenced by the pay books.[73]

The cattle were all oxen, theoretically all producing over five hundredweight of meat, but the contract ledgers do show some smaller beasts, for which a slightly lower price per hundredweight was paid.[74] The cutting-house only operated in the cool autumn and winter months of October to April. The instructions for killing the oxen and hogs, and salting and

---

71 See Chapter 9.

72 *Fees 8*, pp. 571–2. This is a strange comment, unless there was a completely new set of workers at Deptford who were inexperienced.

73 *BOR 11*, pp. 37–8. Unfortunately, the report does not say who made this suggestion. The pay books are at TNA ADM 113/58–83.

74 Contract ledgers are at TNA ADM 112/162–212 (1776 to 1826), passim.

packing the meat, were originally issued in 1715, and reissued in 1808.[75] These instructions specified that the marrow bones and shins of oxen should be removed before the rest of the meat was cut up; these were offered to the Sick and Hurt Board to make portable soup.[76] This product, which is essentially a strong stock tablet, was made by simmering beef and mutton until all the goodness had passed into the liquid, adding seasoning, reducing this by further simmering to a thick jelly and then drying it in small cakes.[77] There was an ongoing effort by the Sick and Hurt Board and then the Transport Board, when it took over the Sick and Hurt Board's functions in 1806, to get the Victualling Board to take over this task at Deptford. The Victualling Board clearly did not want to do this, although they did not actually say so, just making excuses as to why they could not: first they said they had no space at Deptford, then when Samuel Bentham had found an empty building and proposed converting it into a soup house, they announced that they intended moving the army victualling function to Deptford and needed the building for that purpose.[78] Quite why they were so reluctant to take on this task is a mystery; they appear to have had sufficient space, they had most of the ingredients to hand and would, presumably, have taken on the experienced workers from the Sick and Hurt Board's premises at Ratcliffe Cross; perhaps it was due to the reluctance to disturb the status quo which they had displayed in other areas.

As at the other yards, biscuit was baked at Deptford; there they originally ground their own flour and meal in two adjacent mills, but on discovering that it was cheaper to have corn ground at private mills than to use its own windmill, that mill was dismantled in 1797; the other mill at Rotherhithe was sold off in 1802 rather than pay for some expensive essential repairs.[79] As with the instructions for processing meat, the instructions for baking biscuit were given in the 1715 instructions and again in 1808, although the former concentrates on the processes of firing the ovens and does not mention the processing of the dough. At both dates the production level was twelve 'shutes'[80] per oven per day, each shute resulting in 100 pounds of biscuit. The pay records for Deptford show twelve teams of bakers and thus

75 Originally TNA ADM 49/59, but printed in Baugh, *Naval Administration*, pp. 413–14; *Regulations …Home*, pp. 64–8, 171–9.

76 For example, TNA ADM 110/55, 11 & 20 October 1806.

77 The seasoning was black pepper, garlic, celery seed and essence of thyme. The recipe for this can be found in NMM ADM D/46, 16 January 1804.

78 NMM ADM C/685 8 March 1796; C/700 29 December 1803; C/701 20 & 24 March 1804; C/707 21 August 1805; C/711 12 July 1806; TNA ADM 110/50, ff. 349–50. 23 March 1804; 110/54, ff. 390–2, 11 July 1806; 110/56, f. 50, 3 July 1807.

79 NMM ADM C/688, 14 September 1797; D/44, 14 July 1802; C/698, 15 July 1802.

80 This word appears with several different spellings: 'suites' and 'suits' as well as shutes. The etymology of this word is unclear, but may stem from the way the

twelve ovens; working at full production this would produce enough biscuit for 12,310 men per year.

The Board of Revision felt that the production of biscuit at Deptford was excessive, and suggested that this activity should be diminished at Deptford and increased at the other yards.[81] This does not appear to have happened, as the numbers of men employed in the bakeries remains more or less static throughout the period. There were, judging by the number of men employed, six ovens at Portsmouth, eight at Plymouth, six at Dover and one at Chatham, totalling thirty-three with the twelve at Deptford. With all ovens working at standard capacity, this would produce 13.4m pounds of biscuit per annum, enough for 33,850 men, or more than enough for peacetime. Although some increased production would have been possible by working overtime, this would only have been possible during the long days of summer; any sustained major increase in production would have required the building of additional ovens. This was not done, nor does there seem to have been any suggestion from the Victualling Board that it should be. As with the salt meat, the Victualling Board made up the shortfall of their biscuit requirements for the home yards by purchasing ready-made biscuit.

The Board of Revision also thought that most of the cooperage operation at Deptford should be gradually transferred to the other yards. It is impossible to tell whether this happened, as there were no consistent reports of the number of casks made and repaired at any of the yards, and the methods by which the coopers were paid and staves accounted for are so complex that they do not throw any light on production levels. There were, however, no major purchases of pre-made casks during this period, so production must have been adequate. Equally, there were no major complaints about beer brewed at the Victualling Board's yards during this period, so this operation also appears to have gone smoothly.

Overall, the delivery of victuals to warships in home waters through the outports, contractor depots and ad hoc purser purchases created very few problems for either ships' commanders or the Victualling Board. There were problems related to the tardiness of checking accounts, but this did not affect the efficiency of the actual deliveries.[82] Nor do there seem to have been major problems with the manufacturing operations (other than some over wage levels) although there were occasional difficulties with the water for warships and for brewing. The Board of Revision did suggest a shift in the magnitude of production from Deptford to the outports, declaring it 'an

bakers shot the uncooked biscuits onto the oven shelves from a peel (a tool with a wide flat blade).

81   BOR 11, pp. 35–6.
82   See Chapter 5.

obvious absurdity to keep Deptford on so extensive and the outports on so small a scale' but no action was taken on these suggestions.

These problems aside, and the smaller difficulties such as the temporary disruptions caused by such things as the need to repair a wharf or provide more cranes, the actual delivery from yard to ship worked quite well. It was the other side of the task, that of accounting for stores as they moved in and out of the yards, which was woefully neglected. Either the victualling commissioners did not consider this to be particularly important (and one of them did remark to the Select Committee on Finance that they did not feel they could be expected to take a 'clerk-like interest' in such matters)[83] or they had lost sight of the fact that what their staff did, and the way in which they did it, was also an essential part of management.

As before, 'acute' problems were dealt with promptly and efficiently, but 'chronic' problems were left to fester undetected.

83   *SCF* 32, p. 105.

4

Delivery Abroad for Warships, Army Garrisons and Military Expeditions

Delivery of victuals to warships on stations outside home waters, although catering for a much smaller proportion of men than those operating in home waters, seem, if the volume of correspondence to and from the Admiralty is a true indicator, to have created an equal volume of work for the Victualling Board and its staff at Somerset House. The whole of the work of feeding the army was, with the exception of supplying troopships leaving Britain, for troops abroad.

The actual delivery system for warships abroad, although conducted on the same basis, was weighted almost diametrically opposite to that at home: less from the Victualling Board's own yards and more from the second and third strategies of contractor depots and ad hoc purchases by pursers. Two variations of these strategies, those of peripatetic agents victualler and the use of senior pursers as buying agents for a whole squadron, which were not used at home, played an important part in the victualling of fleets operating far from other sources of supply. Problems also tended to be of different sorts from those at home. In most cases, for the Victualling Board in London, problems arose or were exacerbated by the difficulties of communication over vast distances, with a simple exchange of letters taking many weeks, and often many months. Other ever-present difficulties were those of a shortage of specie to pay for purchases abroad, the effects of epidemic diseases and seasonally tempestuous weather; finding suitable personnel to run the yards, and the need for subsequent monitoring of their activities. For the agents themselves, particularly those round the Mediterranean, there were constant difficulties caused by shifting political alliances and the intransigence of local rulers; this was especially prevalent in the countries of North Africa. As far as dealings with contractors were concerned, apart from the ever-present (and as it turned out in this period, exaggerated) worry about fraudulent activities, the principal effect on the victualling office in London was that of delayed accounts; this did not, however, affect the actual delivery of victuals to warships.

Victualling Board yards

At the beginning of the French Revolutionary war, the only permanent yard abroad was at Gibraltar; other yards were opened as wartime operations required: at Antigua, Lisbon, Port Mahon, the Cape of Good Hope, Malta and Rio de Janeiro. Other facilities, which were little more than stores, operated at various times at Newfoundland, Heligoland and Anholt Island. The people in charge of the latter were often referred to, especially by commissioned officers, as 'agents', but they were basically just storekeepers; when the Victualling Board was asked to provide a list of agents victualler abroad for Parliament in April 1809, it only listed five: those at Gibraltar, Lisbon, Malta, Cape of Good Hope and Rio (Mahon had been vacated when Minorca was returned to Spain in the Peace of Amiens, and the yard at Antigua had reverted to a contractor depot in 1804).[1]

The opening of new yards can be seen to be directly related to the shifting theatres of war; many were instigated by the station's commander-in-chief. The 'yard' at Gibraltar (which consisted of two separate storehouses, one at the Waterport by the Old Mole, and another at the White Convent) with the rest of the town, had suffered badly during the 'Great Siege' of 1779 to 1783;[2] and as early as 1799 Admiral Earl St Vincent was recommending that it should be sold and a new facility be built.[3] The first store, although it had been rebuilt after the Great Siege, was within range of enemy fire and the wharf was, according to St Vincent, 'the vilest wharf in the universe'; it lacked a crane, and 'the facing stones of the wharf [were] crumbled away and lying under water, to the ruin and destruction of all our boats, none of which can approach until three-quarters flood'.[4]

In view of this, St Vincent took the agent victualler, Benjamin Tucker, with him when he left Gibraltar for the Mediterranean, setting him up in what was to become the official yard at Port Mahon. Earlier, in 1793, when operations centred on the area off Toulon and north-west Italy, David Heatley was employed as a peripatetic agent victualler, then when the British fleet abandoned the Mediterranean in 1797, he set up the yard at Lisbon.[5] This

1   Although not specifically stated as such by the Victualling Board, one might define an agent victualler as an officer who purchased items as well as handling them, while a storekeeper only handled those items sent out from Britain.
2   Tito Benady, 'The Role of Gibraltar as a Base during the Campaign Against the French and Spanish Fleets 1796–1808' (MA Dissertation, Greenwich Maritime Institute, 2006), p. 6.
3   TNA ADM 1/399, 10 March 1799. This new facility was not completed until 1812: Tito Benady, *The Royal Navy at Gibraltar* (Gibraltar, 1992), p. 12.
4   Julian S Corbett (ed.) *The Private Papers of George, 2nd Earl Spencer 1794–1801, Vol. II* (London, 1914), pp. 484–5.
5   NMM ADM C/687 11 March 1797.

yard, like that at the Cape of Good Hope and Port Mahon, was closed during the Peace of Amiens; the latter did not reopen until the Spanish withdrew their support for Napoleon. The yard at Malta was started in November 1800; this yard, with Gibraltar, remained operational after 1815. The facility at Rio de Janeiro was started in 1808, when the Portuguese royal family were evacuated to Brazil, and was closed in 1815.

During the American War of Independence, there had been two yards in the West Indies, one at Jamaica and one at Antigua. Both these yards, with the associated dockyards, had been involved in major frauds in the 1780s, as a result of which both were closed. The facility at Antigua was reopened in 1794 but Jamaica was dealt with by a contractor throughout the period. That such a large friendly island did not have a Victualling Board-run facility might seem strange; Vice-Admiral Hyde Parker certainly thought so when he complained about difficulties in obtaining provisions from the contractor's stores, and asked why this could not be organised. The Victualling Board's explanation was quite simple: they had not been able to find a sufficiently trustworthy person who was prepared to take the job at the normal salary; the agent at Antigua, George Desborough, was only prepared to take the job at 'the most exhorbitant terms'.[6]

Duties of agents victualler abroad

The duties of agents victualler running yards abroad were rather different from those of agents running yards at home. Although the agent victualler abroad generally dealt with a smaller volume of stock and a smaller number of warships than those at home, he had a much smaller office staff and a range of additional duties, despite the eighth report of the Fees commissioners, which says that when the Victualling Board was asked about the duties of the staff at Gibraltar, they had replied that there was an agent victualler, a clerk and a store clerk 'whose duty respectively is nearly similar to that of the same officers at Portsmouth, Plymouth, etc.'[7] This report, and the ninth report which covers both victualling and naval yards abroad have little else to say about victualling yards, other than expressing concern over the scope for fraud afforded by the lack of senior personnel to oversee the agents victualler.[8] The Board of Revision, however, in their twelfth

---

6 TNA ADM 110/43, ff. 51–4, 21 April 1797. Desborough's annual salary and table money totalled £673.15.0: NMM ADM C/681, 24 February 1794. At this time, the agent at Gibraltar received an annual total of £250: TNA ADM 110/72 (no folio nos), 17 May 1816.

7 *Fees 8*, p. 565.

8 This was occasioned by the recent fraud which had taken place in the West Indies. *Fees 9th Report*, pp. 729–31. See page 165 below.

report (on victualling yards abroad) had two things to say: that an agent victualler abroad 'combines in his own person the duties of storekeeper, clerk of the cheque and agent' (each of these being a separate officer at home); and that the greater part of the existing instructions, being almost a century old, were 'entirely obsolete' and that no officer would be able to learn his job from them.[9] They proposed a new set of instructions, consisting of 100 clauses and fifty-two forms; this became the new printed and bound *Regulations ... Abroad*, which is discussed in Chapter 7.[10]

The other major way in which the work of the yards abroad differed from those at home was the extent of the geographical area the station covered. At home, ships needing to complete their provisions were never far from a yard or contractor's depot, but abroad their area of operation could extend for many hundreds or even thousands of miles, which often meant the agent victualler had to send bulk supplies to meet the squadron at a remote rendezvous.[11] For instance, Nelson frequently wrote to the agent at Gibraltar with instructions to send victualling transports from England straight on without unloading at Gibraltar, or to send a transport filled with a proportionate load of provisions.[12]

Agents victualler abroad received a substantial proportion of their stock from England, but they also had to purchase locally. Most of those local purchases were fresh food or substitutes for items which were either not available on the station or would not keep well in warm conditions, such as butter. In the Mediterranean they also bought wine and brandy. The new instructions included a clause stating that they should keep an eye on local prices with a view to purchasing instead of importing; this led Patrick Wilkie in Malta first to buy local biscuit and then, when he realised he could produce his own biscuit more economically than the Victualling Board could send it, to build ovens and employ bakers.[13] Such local purchases, as well as having to go through the usual advertising and tendering process with the resident naval commissioner and commander-in-chief taking the place of the victualling commissioners, often also involved local consuls.[14]

9   *BOR* 12, pp. 3–4.

10   Ibid., pp. 5–25.

11   Unlike the items carried on the shuttle service for the Brest blockade, these were the items which made up the basic ration.

12   Sir Nicholas Harris Nicolas, *The Dispatches and Letters of Lord Nelson*, Vol. V (London, 1844, repr. 1997–98), pp. 124, 331, 418.

13   *BOR* 12, p. 7, Clauses 17–19; TNA ADM 111/166, 3 February 1803 (minute on Wilkie's purchase); ADM 113/176, paylist for Malta, showing bricklayers employed to build ovens.

14   TNA CO 173/5. In-letters to Commonwealth Office from consuls: for example 26 March 1807, on the export of sheep and poultry; 7 April 1806, on livestock sent to Malta; NMM ADM C/689, 18 May 1798, on cattle, sheep and poultry from Tangiers.

Problems encountered by agents victualler abroad

As well as a range of problems similar to those encountered by agents at home, agents abroad had a different set of problems with which to contend. In addition to the physical constraints of the location's geomorphology, the climate, epidemic diseases, and the attitudes of the local inhabitants, these could include naval commissioners exerting their authority in a heavy-handed way.[15] As far as climate was concerned most of it was a regular pattern that was expected and could thus be worked round, such as the monsoon in the eastern seas and the winter in the Baltic or Canada; it was the sudden onset of violent events such as hurricanes which could do serious damage. None of any magnitude seem to have happened during the 1793–1815 period, but Jamaica had been struck by two major hurricanes in 1780, followed by another in 1784.[16]

Equally, epidemic diseases such as malaria or typhoid in the West Indies were a known hazard, and the local population did develop some immunity; the problems came when a fiercely contagious disease struck an area which was unprepared. A major outbreak of yellow fever struck southern Spain in 1804 and inevitably also affected the naval and victualling yards at Gibraltar; it killed thirty-seven people in the dockyard and twenty-seven in the victualling yard.[17] The deputy naval commissioner ordered what amounted to a quarantine of the yard: directing the agent victualler to supply new beds for the yard workers, who were forbidden to bring their own beds into the yard, and who were to be washed and examined by the surgeon before admission.[18] There was a further outbreak of yellow fever at Gibraltar in 1813; although by this time some stocks were held on a floating depot ship, most were on shore and thus unobtainable by warships.[19] Another outbreak, this time of plague, effectively closed the ports of Malta in 1814, delaying the replacement agent victualler who was about to leave

15   See pages 146–7 below for more on this problem.
16   For the 1780 hurricanes, see Lowell Joseph Ragatz, *The Fall of the Planter Classes in the British Caribbean 1763–1833* (New York, 1963), p. 158. For the effects of the hurricane in 1784, see DP/4, 11 October 1784.
17   Dockyard figures from TNA ADM 106/2022, victualling yard figures taken from the paylists at TNA ADM 113/118. These show the workers as 'D' in the 'discharged' column, which is taken to mean 'dead' as it does in ships' muster books. The workers with a 'D' disappear from the paylists after that entry. See also: Tito Benady, 'The Role of Gibraltar', pp. 39–40; J Macdonald, 'The victualling yard at Gibraltar and its role in feeding the Royal Navy in the Mediterranean during the Revolutionary and Napoleonic wars', in *Transactions of the Naval Dockyards Society*, Vol. 2 (December 2006), pp. 55–64.
18   Macdonald, 'The victualling yard at Gibraltar', p. 59.
19   TNA ADM 110/66, ff. 34–6, 17 September 1812; NMM ADM C/740, 23 October and 24 November 1813.

Britain to take up his post.[20] At that time, plague was quite common in North Africa and as well as strict quarantine regulations at all Mediterranean ports which could delay the unloading of transports, actual outbreaks of the disease affected the availability of cattle and other provisions. In such situations there was little the Victualling Board in London could do other than send loaded victualling transports to serve as floating depots.

Local politics in what were nominally friendly counties could also prove troublesome. In 1798, the Emperor of Morocco withdrew the right to buy cattle and sheep, and the following year the Spanish ambassador in Lisbon tried to prevent the agent victualler David Heatley buying foodstuffs in the markets.[21] Other problems included the inhabitants of parts of Sardinia who made a practice of plying watering parties with drink to facilitate theft of casks,[22] and the murderous propensities of the populace elsewhere. As part of his excuses for failing to produce his accounts on time, Heatley said that the clerk in his office who should have been working on the accounts had had an argument with a co-worker and was then too frightened to go to work.[23] This is of interest as an example of what may have been a common failing of persons who performed well in 'acute' situations (as Heatley did when acting as a peripatetic agent before taking on the job at Lisbon) but not in situations where the requirement was for regular attention to the more mundane (and thus 'chronic') tasks of running a yard and an office.

Smaller stores abroad

The smaller version of official victualling yards was the storehouses or depot ships; like those situated round Britain, these were for squadrons operating in locations deemed unsuitable for (or by) contractors. There were few of these abroad, most appearing in the later stages of the Napoleonic War, such as the depot ships at Wingo Sound, Gibraltar and Messina, and the depot at St Johns (Newfoundland) for which a prefabricated store had to be manufactured by the Navy Board and shipped out.[24] The most problematic of these depots was at Heligoland, the small island in the North Sea off Bremerhaven; with steep cliffs round most of the island, it had appalling weather in the winter and, as one transport agent complained, a bad anchorage with foul ground and heavy surf.[25] Its launch was first damaged, then

20 TNA ADM 110/67, f. 392, 12 August 1813.
21 NMM C/689, 18 May 1798; DP/19, 20 July 1799.
22 Macdonald, *Feeding*, p. 86.
23 NMM ADM DP/21, 7 May 1801.
24 TNA ADM 110/65, f. 309, 19 May 1812; 110/66, ff. 34–6 & 291–2, 17 September & 16 December 1812.
25 NMM ADM DP/29B, 13 October 1809.

lost and had to be replaced, and a transport full of provisions was wrecked there; it continued to be used as a depot in the summer, but was effectively abandoned in the winter, with ships either returning to Yarmouth for their victuals or spending the whole winter there.[26]

Peripatetic agents victualler

Elsewhere, the 'far from a yard' problem was handled by appointing an 'agent victualler afloat' to a particular fleet or squadron. This long-established solution to the problem seems to have been used most frequently in the Mediterranean during this period, especially before the yard at Malta was established.[27] Part of Jervis's problem when operating in the area off Toulon, Corsica and Italy was solved by appointing David Heatley to travel through the region arranging for food to await collection at various locations. At Naples, Heatley arranged for Joseph Littledale to operate nineteen bread ovens to bake biscuit, instructed him to salt down meat, and to purchase sufficient flour, calavances and rice for 20,000 men for three months. He had also dealt with the Pope through the British consul at Rome, General Graves, and arranged to ship provisions out from Civitia Vecchia, although the Pope, concerned about his position with the French, insisted that this be done in 'foreign' (i.e. not British) ships. More biscuit was available in Sardinia, but since no samples were forthcoming, Heatley only ordered a small quantity; he had also arranged for the use of five biscuit ovens on Elba; due to British troops having taken possession of Piombino, he anticipated easy purchases of live cattle.[28] Heatley also liased with John Udney, the consul at Leghorn, to purchase live oxen, Udney paying for these by writing bills on the Victualling Board, either on his own, or jointly with Heatley and/or Jervis.[29]

Having seen how well this arrangement worked with Heatley, when Nelson became commander-in-chief in the Mediterranean in 1803 he requested similar assistance and was sent two clerks from the victualling office: Richard Ford as agent victualler afloat and John Geoghegan as his assistant; Ford already had experience of this work, having taken over from

---

26 TNA ADM 110/63, f. 5, 22 November 1810, ff. 298–9, 15 March 1811; NMM ADM C/724, 2 January 1810.
27 The earliest letter appointing one of these agents was for Richard Bosswell, in 1744: TNA ADM 49/59.
28 NMM DM DP/16, 20 December 1796 (covering letter) and 14 November 1796 (the enclosed letter from Heatley). Heatley's accounts are at TNA ADM 112/45.
29 During this period there are numerous Admiralty orders to the Victualling Board to accept these bills. e.g. in NMM ADM G/790–1.

Heatley as agent victualler at Lisbon.[30] Heatley had spent most of his time as agent victualler afloat away from the fleet; Ford spent most of his first two years on *Victory* and various other of the fleet's ships and this enabled him, as well as organising provisions, to take charge of the cash which was supplied by James Cutforth, the agent victualler at Gibraltar. Ford issued this money to the individual ships in amounts relating to their size to be used as necessary money; he also visited each ship soon after he arrived in the Mediterranean, to pay the backlog of short allowance money.

When Ford bulk-bought such items as live oxen or lemons, he paid for them either in cash, or with bills drawn on the Victualling Board, then charged each ship for them in his accounts, as he did with the necessary money. As with items supplied by victualling stores, vouchers must have been prepared and exchanged, but none have been found. Until the Spanish declared war against Britain in late 1804, Ford did a considerable amount of business with the Rosas-based Quaker merchant Edward Gaynor, buying cattle and sheep, fruit and vegetables and wine, and arranging for casks to be repaired; he also arranged for cattle to be assembled near the anchorage at the Madalena Islands at the northern tip of Sardinia, one of Nelson's favourite rendezvous. After Trafalgar, when the emphasis of the war shifted to the Eastern end of the Mediterranean, Ford was based on shore in Sicily, where he opened a victualling store at Palermo; by this time he was referred to as 'agent victualler Mediterranean', as were his successors.[31]

Ford remained in the Mediterranean until the end of 1808, when he was recalled to London to take over the job of Accountant for Cash; he had barely settled into his new job before he was sent to run a depot at Flushing in 1809. He had been sent out to do this on an emergency basis as no one else was available, but due to the Admiralty's reluctance to appoint someone else, he stayed there for several months, despite repeated pleas from the Victualling Board to have him back at his desk in London where he was urgently needed. As well as this period as a temporary agent victualler at Flushing, Ford was sent to Corunna in 1811 to investigate a suspected fraud, and he also spent many weeks in the Peninsula in 1814 dealing with the remaining stocks in the army depots after Wellington had moved up into France.[32] There was even a suggestion that he should go out to North America to handle cash and purchases of meat in November 1814; all that prevented this was that he had not yet returned from the Peninsula.[33]

As accountant for cash, Ford was one of only three second-level managers in the victualling office (taking the commissioners as the first level) and

---

30 Geoghegan became agent victualler at Rio in 1807: NMM ADM C/716, 29 December 1807.
31 Ford's accounts are at TNA ADM 112/46, his letter book is at TNA ADM 114/55.
32 TNA ADM 1/4601, 28 January 1822.
33 TNA ADM 110/69, ff. 238–41, 3 November 1814.

it is strange that the Victualling Board should have been prepared to send such an important staff member abroad as a troubleshooter. Whilst it can be accepted that these tasks required someone with experience of dealing with the accounting procedures for provisions, that part of the task could have been done by a senior clerk and the rest by a local Spanish-speaking consul. The victualling commissioners cannot necessarily be blamed for Ford's long absences: they did protest to the Admiralty several times, asking for replacements, but to no avail, and when explaining that he could not go to North America they did comment that he was needed in the office. It seems that it was the Admiralty which was profligate in this use of a crucial staff member; perhaps the Admiralty board did not see the necessity for continuity of management, or perhaps the Victualling Board's habit of deference prevented them from making a strong enough case.

Other agents

Most of the arrangements made by commanders-in-chief for purchases by consuls were trouble-free, but a few were not, these being where the consul proved opportunistic but basically incompetent. Nelson had the misfortune to encounter several of these, including J B Gibert and Archibald MacNeill. Gibert was the deputy consul at Barcelona, and when a message was sent to the consul (who was away) saying that wine, lemons and onions would be 'very acceptable' to the fleet, Gibert took it on himself to send some in a Spanish vessel which, through what seems to have been pure incompetence on the part of the ship's master, failed to find the fleet, resulting in the total loss of the lemons and onions and deterioration of the wine.

MacNeill had been the consul at Leghorn before moving to Naples, where he offered to produce a monthly supply of cattle; the offer was accepted and transports arranged, but having heard no more these were cancelled. After several months, a letter arrived from MacNeill saying that arrangements were proceeding; it was nearly a year after the initial approach before a second letter arrived saying that the first batch was ready for collection, by which time Ford had arrived and further dealings with MacNeill were abandoned.[34]

The Victualling Board also occasionally found other agents wished on it by higher authority; one such was William Eton. After prolonged travels in southern Russia and the area round Odessa, Eton had obtained a commission from the Treasury to find a regular source of army provisions for

---

34   J Macdonald, 'Two years off Provence: The victualling and health of Nelson's fleet in the Mediterranean, 1803 to 1805', *Mariner's Mirror*, vol. 92, no. 4 (November 2006), pp. 443–54.

Malta, and cordage and timber for the Navy Board. Eton was already in the Black Sea area when St Vincent (then First Lord of the Admiralty) added a commission to make a bulk purchase of wheat, pease and salt meat for the navy.[35] The Victualling Board had already rejected an offer to supply victuals from the Black Sea by the firm of Forrester and Yeames, on the basis that the quality would not be adequate.[36] Eton interpreted his meat-buying commission as allowing him to set up a meat-packing operation, and purchased the broken-down Great Bath at Caffa. His attempts to pro-duce good-quality meat were a miserable failure, and when the first batch arrived at Malta, samples were cooked and tasted; these were rejected as being unsuitable for naval use and were sold off cheaply. The Victualling Board concluded that Eton's efforts had 'not been attached with any advan-tages to the service of this department'; but Eton continued to badger not only the Victualling Board but everyone else he could think of in an attempt to renew his commission, including Sir John Borlase Warren, then the British ambassador at St Petersburg. Henry Lavage Yeames, who had been sub-contracted to handle the purchases by Eton (and who was later appointed British Consul General of the Black Sea), also wrote to Warren pleading for him to intervene: Eton's conduct, he said 'has been uniformly as if he intended to destroy the British credit here', this conduct involv-ing flying into a violent temper whenever crossed.[37] Further evidence of Eton's unsuitability for this task comes in a long letter which his secretary, John Dawson, wrote to the Navy Board; this tells the story of Eton's general incompetence, cupidity and dishonesty, which latter included attempting to get the Navy Board to fund a further trip to Russia to recover documents which he had personally destroyed many months before.[38]

Eton's attempts to purchase naval supplies had proved equally unsuccess-ful. His character had been well known for some years; in a letter to William Otway in 1804, Nelson remarked 'I never saw Mr Eaton [sic] but my opin-ion of him was formed some years ago; and from all I hear I have no reason to alter it. He is, as Burke said of a noble Marquis, "a giant in promises, a pigmy in performance"'.[39] Quite how such a person had managed to get the commission in the first place is not evident, but it may have been due to his friendship with Samuel Bentham, who had accompanied him on a trip through Russia several years before. Equally, it may have been seen as a method to get Eton away from Malta, where he was fomenting trouble with a group of disaffected natives and was conducting a slanderous campaign

---

35   NMM C/699, 10 March 1803.
36   NMM ADM C/699, 24 May 1803; TNA ADM 110/50 ff. 110–115, 2 January 1804.
37   NMM WAR/73, passim.
38   NMM ADM C/714, 21 April 1807.
39   Nicolas, *Dispatches*, Vol. V, pp. 265–7.

against Sir Alexander Ball, the governor.[40] This is a further demonstration of the way external authorities were able to over-rule the Victualling Board's judgement and normal procedures.

Pursers acting as agents

Ford and his successors were salaried employees of the Victualling Board, sent out from London. In other situations far from a yard, the senior commissioned officer could appoint a purser to act as an agent. Although this was done on other stations as well, the best evidence of the activities of these gentlemen is in the Mediterranean. Captain Samuel Hood used Thomas Alldridge (purser of *Lion*) to buy for his squadron blockading Alexandria between October 1798 and June 1799. Alldridge bought bullocks, flour, raisins, sugar, rice, pease, onions and lemons, mainly from St Jean d'Acre but also a little from Cyprus and Syria, for which he received a commission of 2½ per cent.[41]

During the Egyptian campaign of 1800 to 1801, Vice-Admiral Lord Keith used two senior pursers to find provisions for his voyage across the Mediterranean from Cadiz to Marmaris and then at Alexandria. Nicholas Brown, who was also paid a 2½ per cent commission, bought from various places from Tetuan to the eastwards, William Wills bought from the hinterland behind Alexandria.[42] This was not the easiest of tasks: when Wills wrote to the Victualling Board asking for a proper salary for his efforts, he explained that his duties had put him at risk from 'the Bedouin and vagrant Turks who infest the desert' and that he was exposed to the plague and other diseases, so that he was put to great expense by being quarantined at Malta when he was trying to get home. He had also had nearly £600 of the expedition's money stolen from his house by a soldier; although the culprit was seen and subsequently court-martialled, the money was not recovered, but since there were no banking facilities Wills was absolved of responsibility for the money. After some time, the Victualling Board agreed that he should be paid a back-dated salary of £400 p.a. pro rata from the time he

---

40 Macdonald, *Feeding*, pp. 23–5; NMM ADM DP/24, 25 June 1804, DP/26, 8 August 1806, DP/30a, 26 April 1810; Anthony Cross, *By the Banks of the Neva: Chapters from the Lives and Careers of the British in Eighteenth Century Russia* (Cambridge, 1997), passim; William Hardman, *A History of Malta during the Period of the French and British Occupation 1798–1815* (London, 1909), pp. 494–503.

41 Alldridge's accounts are at TNA ADM 112/40.

42 This is the Nicholas Brown who later became Keith's secretary and eventually a victualling commissioner. Brown's accounts are at TNA ADM 112/41, those for Wills are 112/42.

started the job until his arrival back in England.[43] In all such cases, the pursers-agent had to submit a full set of accounts for their efforts, supported by vouchers and with details of the currency used and the exchange rates.

Apart from that theft, these were relatively trouble-free situations; two others which were not demonstrate more of the problems the victualling office had to deal with when pursers employed by admirals to carry out such tasks turned out to be less experienced in dealing with the commercial world abroad. The first of these was in the Baltic in 1801; Richard Booth was appointed by Nelson to buy fresh meat from Dantzic (modern Gdansk) for the fleet off Bornholm, an instruction which he interpreted to mean he could also buy live cattle. He thought he had organised a purchase of 600 head of cattle but then realised that the local butchers had got together to push up the price. Unable to cope with this, he handed the task over to a local firm, Solly & Gibson, asking them to buy the cattle for him, but by the time they had purchased cattle and had them driven to the pick-up point, the cost had risen far beyond what Booth had told Nelson they would cost: 5½d per pound instead of the 4¾d which Booth had expected to pay. However, Booth still expected to receive a 2½ per cent commission on this purchase, but so did Solly & Gibson; Nelson thought Booth should have it, the Victualling Board thought Solly & Gibson should, on the grounds that Booth had handed the task over to them. After much correspondence, the Victualling Board prevailed and the merchants had their money.[44] One might speculate that this was because the Victualling Board already had a long-term relationship with the Solly family, whose name appears over many years in the contract ledgers as suppliers of staves from the Baltic.

The second of these cases involved William Fitzgerald, who was sent by Admiral Edward Pellew to buy bread, flour, wine and cattle in the hinterland behind Ferrol and Corunna. It was originally thought that he had taken advantage of the situation, and after a preliminary investigation he was accused of a variety of overcharging practices: 66 pipes of wine charged as 164, cattle costing 4½d a pound charged at 8d, falsification of certificates of market prices by filling them in with invented names and persuading local farmers to sign receipts when they could not read English. The Victualling Board passed their file to the Admiralty solicitor to commence a prosecution, but this was delayed because the ships' officers needed as witnesses had moved on and were difficult to assemble in one place and Spanish witnesses could not be questioned as Spain was then at war with Britain.[45] Meanwhile, Fitzgerald protested his innocence, but it was not until 1811

43   TNA ADM 112/42.
44   Macdonald, *Feeding*, p. 64.
45   NMM ADM DP/25, 28 January, 3 May & 13 December 1805.

that the case was resurrected, originally with a suggestion that a commissioner and two other staff members should be sent out to investigate. This was deemed impossible, as none of the commissioners could be spared, and eventually Richard Ford went out with another clerk and a naval captain.[46] Their report showed a complex situation indicating that Fitzgerald, rather than setting out to defraud the Victualling Board, had merely been very naive, having entrusted the task of buying to the local vice-consul, Francisco Fernandez, who had in turn entrusted it to Angel Garcia Fernandez; it was the latter (who we may surmise was a relative) who had persuaded local sellers to sign blank receipts. Although concluding that Fitzgerald's conduct had been negligent and irregular, it was finally decided to deduct the costs from his pursery account and pay him the balance. Having been more or less exonerated, Fitzgerald was allowed an appointment as purser to another ship.[47]

Individual pursers' promiscuous purchases

Under the third strategy outlined in Chapter 3, pursers could use their necessary money, or bills of exchange, to buy in the markets of a convenient port. In this situation, the *Regulations and Instructions* required them to obtain a signature from the local governor or consul to the effect that the price they had paid was the current market rate for those items; where there was no formal market and no such dignitaries, and they had to buy from local farmers, they had to be accompanied by two officers from their (or better still, another) ship who would then certify the actual price paid.[48] As always, these certificates had to be attached to their accounts for checking. These transactions are recorded in the contract ledgers in a single section headed 'promiscuous supplies'; the location of the purchase is shown in a separate column and in these, as with the sections for contractor depots, the volume of entries reflects the volume of activity on the station. These entries in any individual year's ledger cover several years' transactions; this suggests that, as above, they were not recorded until the purser's ship was paid off and he settled his accounts. The sheer volume of these purchases, each of which involved an entry in the contract ledger, a bill of exchange to be dealt with (and entered in a separate ledger) and cross-checking of vouchers against the purser's accounts, must have occupied a substantial proportion of clerical time in the victualling office. This would have played

---

46   NMM ADM C/729, 19 January 1811; TNA ADM 110/63, ff. 166–8, 191–6, 22 January 1811.
47   NMM ADM C/730, 25 April & 30 May 1811; TNA ADM 110/64, ff. 539–540, 20 January 1812.
48   *R&I*, 13th edition, pp. 122–3.

its part in the build-up of arrears of accounts, but in general the strategy of pursers' ad hoc purchases abroad did not cause any acute problems.

Ship to ship transfers

One other method of maintaining stocks of provisions on individual ships in fleets far from victualling stores can be seen from some documents in the private papers of both Keith and Nelson, and in the log books of the ships themselves.[49] Both these commanders-in-chief (and from the similarity of the documents used, probably other commanders-in-chief, although none have yet come to light) received weekly statements of stocks of victuals held by each ship in their immediate squadron. Shown as the number of weeks' supply of each item remaining, these statements allowed the commander-in-chief to instruct a ship with plenty of a certain item to send some to another ship which was running short (and also alerted him to the need for a letter to the nearest agent victualler to send a bulk supply). The log books of the ships frequently show quantities of victuals being sent to, or received from, other ships; in this situation, another set of vouchers would be exchanged by the relevant pursers.[50] This was another reason for long delays in settling pursers' accounts, as the Victualling Office would not pass a set of accounts until they had cross-checked every item with the other side of the transaction. Since no attempt was made to deal with such accounts until each ship reached the end of its commission and was paid off, a complex set of exchanges between numerous ships could, and often did, take many years to check.

Contractor-run depots

Whilst, with the exception of Yarmouth and the fresh meat and vegetables at Torbay, the contractor-run depots at home generally dealt with provisions on a small scale, those abroad tended to be much busier. They were in three main geographical regions: North America, the West Indies, and the East Atlantic and Mediterranean.[51] However, it is not certain that those in the Mediterranean were actually contractor depots rather than local consuls

---

49 NMM KEI 23/24–30 (Keith papers); Wellcome Trust Library, Western MSS 3667–3681 (Nelson papers).

50 For a list of logbooks from over 30 of the ships in Nelson's Mediterranean fleet showing these exchanges of provisions, see Macdonald, 'Victualling', pp. 73–6; *R&I*, 13th edition, p. 67.

51 These divisions have been chosen by the author for convenience and were not descriptions applied by the Victualling Board.

supplying the peripatetic agent victualler David Heatley between 1794 and 1798; there were also two locations in the North Sea and off Denmark in the same category.[52] In addition, the East Indies was handled by a combination of agent victualler and contractor; in several respects this station was a special case and thus is dealt with separately below. The number of these contractor-supplied depots increased from nine in 1793 to sixteen in 1813.

During the French Revolutionary war, almost all these depots were dealt with by standing contracts on 'twelve months certain and six months warning' terms; the exception was Jamaica, where the contract term was for the duration of the war plus six months.[53] When St Vincent discovered that these standing contracts had not had their prices adjusted at the Peace of Amiens and insisted that this should be done or notice given, although the prices changed, there was little change in the named contract holders at most locations. Although there were quite frequent changes in the firms providing fresh beef and other perishable products, the contracts for sea provisions tended to stay with the same firm for many years. There was some regional specialisation: for instance the contracts for the locations on the north-west Atlantic and Canadian interior were mostly held by John Brymer until 1810, then most of these passed to Andrew Belcher, with a few held jointly by Belcher and Brymer. This firm also held a few contracts at home (Bristol and Yarmouth) but with the exception of Bermuda, none before 1810. Brymer did not hold any contracts at home. The West Indies were dominated by Thomas Pinkerton, Alexander Donaldson and Alexander Thomson, and much of the fresh beef was supplied by J Cruden.

Overall, of the total 187 location-years for naval sea provisions abroad, 60.9 per cent were held by three contractors: J Brymer held 50 (26.7 per cent) across 4 locations, Thomas Pinkerton held 40 (21.4 per cent) across 6 locations, and A Donaldson held 24 (12.8 per cent) across 2 locations.

Taking all sea provisions depots both at home and abroad, of the total 541 location-years, Grant held 266, Pinkerton held 104, Brymer held 50 and Donaldson held 49, adding up to 58.4 per cent of the whole.[54] These four contractors also handled some of the items for the army garrisons.[55] Clearly the Victualling Board preferred to deal with firms of known ability and integrity.

---

52 The 'contractor' in the contract ledgers is shown as John Udney, who was the British Consul at Leghorn.
53 TNA ADM 110/43, ff. 51–4, 21 April 1797.
54 These figures are only for those locations where sea provisions were provided and do not include those which only provided perishable products.
55 Army garrison provisions are dealt with on page 82 below.

East Indies

Unlike other stations remote from home, where each separate location had separate contracts, the East Indies station was supplied under a single contract which covered all the British bases east of the Cape of Good Hope: Bombay, Calcutta, Madras, Prince of Wales Island (modern Penang), and later Java, Canton and Trincomalee.[56]

Under its charter, the East India Company was obliged to provide free carriage of British military supplies; any victuals sent out from Britain would have been under that category. This was the case with the salt provisions (beef, pork and suet) which were sent out from Deptford, and for these items, and the handling and repairing of casks, the contractor acted as an agent of the Victualling Board.[57] There were periodic offers to cure meat in India, but the general quality of this was unsatisfactory; finally, in 1811, a set of instructions on the proper method was sent out to the naval commissioner, Peter Puget, in the hope that this would produce a better product.[58]

The Hon. Basil Cochrane, who held the contract for other items from 1796 to 1806 (having taken it over from his brother John who held it from 1790), built flour mills and bakeries at Calcutta and Madras, to supply flour and biscuit.[59] Cochrane was followed by the firm of Madras merchants Messrs James Balfour and Joseph Baker; they held the contract from 1806 to 1815 and beyond, first jointly and then by Balfour on his own.[60]

The first of these contracts lists not only all the items to be supplied and their prices at the different locations but also a list of prices for moving provisions from 'European' (i.e. East India Company) ships to the contractor's godowns (storehouses) and from godown to warships, for rent of godown space, care and attention including cooperage work, and transporting provisions from one location to another. All these charges were per cask (per cask per month in the case of storage and attention) and some seem exhorbitant: for instance between one and two shillings per cask for moving them from ship to godown and vice versa, and as much as £2.5.0 per cask for transporting them from Bombay to the Bay of Bengal. There was also a clause in the original contract (made in 1790) which automatically increased all prices by 35 per cent in the event of war, this being defined as 'immediately from the time the first intelligence shall be received of an Enemy's

---

56 TNA ADM 112/118–120.
57 Syrett, *Shipping and the American Wars*, pp. 62–3; (NMM ADM C/684, 1 November 1795 is an example of an instruction to inform the East India Company directors of the amounts of tonnage needed for this purpose).
58 TNA ADM 110/57, ff. 112–5, 7 March 1808; 110/65, ff. 537–8, 26 August 1812; NMM ADM C/735, 25 August 1812.
59 TNA ADM 112/118 & 119, 7 June 1803.
60 TNA ADM 112/120.

fleet or ships or ships of war being in the Indian seas'.[61] This contract was terminated in 1804 (St Vincent ordered this, thinking the prices too high) and replaced with a new one which gave fixed prices per item regardless of location of delivery,[62] and reduced the wartime surcharge to 16 per cent; only two tenders were received and as his was the lowest Basil Cochrane was awarded the contract again.[63]

From 1810, separate contracts were awarded to local merchants for fruit, vegetables and tobacco; these, unlike the main contracts which were priced in sterling, were priced in the local currency. Unfortunately, neither these nor the main contracts are entered in the contract ledgers, so there is no record of what quantities were supplied.

The delivery of victuals from contractor/agent to ships on this station does not seem to have been a source of problems, and this part of the system operated well. It is likely that any problems which did arise would have been settled locally by the commander-in-chief rather than by complaint to the Victualling Board; the journey times between London and India (a minimum of four months by sea and three months overland) and the operational constraints of the monsoon winds made complaining to London impractical. However, this does not mean that the victualling on this station did not create difficulties for the Victualling Board, although these difficulties were of the Board's own making.

In 1806, Basil Cochrane returned home and his contract was passed by indenture to Balfour and Baker. It took nearly fourteen years and much acrimony before Cochrane was able to get his accounts passed. Part of the problem was the magnitude of the task: twelve years' worth of transactions over numerous locations, partly as a contractor and partly as an agent. The Board of Revision had remarked on the size of Cochrane's imprest account (standing at £1,418,236.6.9) and queried why it had not been dealt with earlier, only to be told loftily 'in the case of an agent abroad [the passing of the final accounts] is never done until the close of his agency'. Towry, the commissioner who made this statement, then went on to remark that the amount of Cochrane's imprest account had arisen from payment of bills which had been approved by the commander-in-chief; and that since this was the case, Towry felt that the expenditure must have been proper. The Board of Revision was not impressed by this comment; if this were a valid argument, they said, then there would be no need to check any accounts

---

61   This seemingly repetitive wording would have been to cover the French privateers which were active in that area.

62   In the first contract, to give two examples, biscuit cost £1.0.6 per cwt at 'River Houghly' and £2.14.6 at Prince of Wales Island; rice cost £0.9.6 per cask at River Houghly and £0.14.3 at Prince of Wales Island. The only item which was the same price at all locations was fresh beef, at 3½d per pound.

63   TNA ADM 112/119.

which had been approved by a commander-in-chief, 'an omission that would lead to the introduction of the greatest abuses'.[64] At this point, it was stated that Basil Cochrane's actual debt to the Victualling Board was £13,908.6.7. Cochrane disputed this and after some time a new debt figure of £9,129.0.1 was declared. Cochrane disputed this again and the Victualling Board started legal procedings against him for that sum; these moved through an arbitration stage before the whole exercise was done again, and eventually it was agreed that far from Basil Cochrane owing them money, they owed him £928.15.6, which they paid in 1819.[65] Cochrane published a sequence of 'pamphlets' detailing his grievances against the Victualling Board: not least of these was that the victualling office had managed to lose not only all the original but also a duplicate set of vouchers by splitting them up among numerous clerks.[66]

Whether this was all gross incompetence or whether there was also some personal antagonism involved in the delays cannot be known, but the latter possibility cannot be discounted: the commissioner in charge of the department which was responsible for this work was Towry, whose son-in-law, Lord Ellenborough, tried the famous stock exchange fraud case against Basil Cochrane's nephew, Captain Thomas Cochrane, which took place while Basil Cochrane's account 'saga' was in process.[67] This may well have coloured Towry's opinion of the Cochrane family which was notorious for their aggressive attitude; as well as the incidents above, Basil's brother, Admiral Alexander Cochrane, had been involved in a running feud between Admiral Keith and several of his captains over an alleged embezzlement in the price of sailors' shoes in the Mediterranean in 1800.[68] Nor did Basil hesitate to express his low opinion of the Victualling Board and its activities in his pamphlets, singling out commissioners Cherry and Towry for especial criticism.

Whatever the cause, this sorry saga, which dragged on for thirteen years after the Board of Revision's recommendations should have put things right, serves to demonstrate that whilst the accounting systems in operation prior to 1808 may have been faulty, the new systems were little better, and suggest that it was the personnel, as much as the systems, which were inadequate.

---

64 *BOR 10*, p. 17.
65 Records of Arbitration between Basil Cochrane and Victualling Board, TNA ADM 114/3–4.
66 These are printed bound books, each of more than 300 pages: see the bibliography for the full titles.
67 This trial has been included in numerous books about Thomas Cochrane, the most recent of which is Brian Vale, *The Audacious Admiral* (London, 2004).
68 See page 181 below.

Army garrisons

Until 1808, these were supplied by bulk items sent out from England to the local army commissaries, with other items purchased by those commissaries; after that date the other items were supplied by contracts arranged in London by the Victualling Board, following the findings of a Parliamentary inquiry into corruption in army purchasing in the West Indies.[69] This inquiry had found Valentine Jones, the Commissary General in the West Indies, guilty of various frauds, and recommended that 'the rum, wine, flour, provisions and etc. … should be contracted for in London' and in due course the Treasury instructed the Victualling Board to advertise for tenders and award contracts in the usual way.[70]

These contracts commenced in 1808; those for individual items such as flour, rum and wine were made with various contractors, some of whom were also supplying items to warships. The fresh beef/oxen were, with the exception of Martinique and Trinidad, all supplied by J Cruden, either on his own or with partners: a total of 94 location-years (88 per cent of the whole). Those for Martinique were supplied by Alex Worswell (for 6 of the 8 years); and those for Trinidad by Messrs Inglis Ellice or James Inglis (6 years) and Thomas Pinkerton (2 years). These garrisons were located, with a few exceptions, on the Windward and Leeward Islands, or on the Spanish Main. The exceptions were a few items occasionally supplied to Quebec, Heligoland, Madeira, Gibraltar and Minorca, over only 6 location-years.

The Victualling Board's only involvement with these provisions was to arrange the contracts and handle the accounting task of collecting the cost from the relevant regiments. This should not, however, be taken to mean that the Victualling Board's involvement with army victualling was insignificant. It did supply great quantities of victuals to the army, to expeditionary forces as well as the smaller static garrisons, for instance Wellington's Peninsular army. In this case it can be seen that the Victualling Board's work was for the war effort as a whole, not just that of the navy.

Problems of, and with, contractors abroad

Such problems as emanated from contractor depots abroad during the French Revolutionary and Napoleonic wars tended to be those *suffered* by the contractors rather than those *caused* by the contractors. However,

69 *Ninth Report of the Commissioners of Military Enquiry for the more effectual examination of Accounts of Public Expenditure for His Majesty's Forces in the West Indies*: HC 141 of 1809.
70 *The Times*, 19 May 1809; *9th Report of the Military Inquiry*, p. 300; TNA ADM 109/105, 19 April 1806 – 28 December 1807, passim.

whatever the cause, the Victualling Board became involved in two ways: dealing with complaints from fleet commanders on station, and interceding with the Admiralty or other government organisations when events put the contractors' businesses at risk.

The complaints were usually of shortages at depots, particularly of biscuit; as with similar complaints about victualling yards at home, the problems were sometimes caused by the weather delaying supply ships. This could be contrary winds keeping ships for the West Indies and North America in British ports, but there was also the hurricane season to be considered. Other delays arose when the contractors' ships had to wait for convoy: in 1798 the contractor for Jamaica, Donaldson, had four ships detained at Portsmouth for fifteen weeks waiting for a convoy. The ships finally arrived at Jamaica on 1 February, but Vice Admiral Hyde Parker, who had raised the original complaint, complained again in a letter dated 10 February, alleging that the lack of biscuit was the cause of the death of 160 men. Donaldson's London partner, Glenny, was puzzled by this, remarking that he didn't see how this could have been so, unless their deaths could be blamed on a diet of soft bread and fresh beef while in port. This was, presumably, a case of poor communications between the admiral and his fleet, but it was yet another of the situations which had to be sorted out with an investigation. Hyde Parker seemed to be suffering an outbreak of irrascibility on the matter; not only did he continue complaining after the problem was solved, the tone of his letter was such that the Victualling Board felt obliged to protest to the Admiralty about his 'unpleasant manner', commenting 'we are confident that you will not let this Board be insulted or its character to be wantonly traduced'.[71] Later that year, Glenny reported that in order to avoid further delays caused by a shortage of shipping, he had purchased a ship to send victuals out to Jamaica.[72]

The West Indies was the most problematic of the stations; as well as the weather and endemic diseases, some victuallers were seized by the enemy, and American embargoes sometimes prevented the contractors obtaining products from North America, hence the need to import from Britain.[73] There were also difficulties over exporting certain products, especially grain products from Ireland, and the Victualling Board had to obtain special permission for this.[74]

The provision of convoys for contractors' supply ships was another ongoing difficulty: typical of this is the sequence of correspondence with the

71   NMM ADM C/691, 4 April 1799; DP19, 30 January 1799; TNA ADM 110/45, f. 58, 9 April 1799.
72   NMM ADM C/692, 26 October 1799.
73   NMM ADM C/680, 5 September 1793; TNA ADM 110/57, ff. 358–360, 16 May 1808.
74   NMM ADM C/705, 21 January 1805.

Admiralty in 1814. The contractor for the North America station, Andrew Belcher, wrote in May asking for a special convoy for five vessels which were waiting at Spithead; he was anxious for convoy because he had just lost two vessels to a privateer, and because his agent was concerned about stocks running low. The Admiralty were not pleased to be asked, and stated in no uncertain terms that they did not wish to provide any more special convoys for contractors' vessels; the Victualling Board's response was extremely apologetic: they had, they said, only asked because they thought it was important, but they would not do so again, and they had told Belcher not to write direct to the Admiralty. Three days later, the Victualling Board again wrote to the Admiralty, apologetically enquiring when the next convoy would be going to America so that they could inform Belcher. The tone of these letters reinforces the subordinate relationship of the Victualling Board to the Admiralty, as does the request for the Admiralty to tell Hyde Parker to mind his manners rather than doing this themselves.[75] However, this was not the end of Belcher's requests for convoy: he asked again in November 1814 and January 1815 to add his ships to a convoy of transports going to Bermuda, a request which the Victualling Board endorsed, as the commander-in-chief, Vice Admiral Alexander Cochrane was once again complaining about a bread shortage there and it was felt that it would be better to send it from Cork than attempt to ship it down from Halifax in mid-winter.[76]

Another difficulty suffered by the contractors was sudden and unexpected changes of manpower on station; Pinkerton, when asked why there was a shortage of provisions at the Leeward Islands replied that he had not been told that four more sail of the line were arriving; he had, however, already sent several shiploads from London and Liverpool.[77] Worse though, was a sudden reduction in force when a contractor had large stocks which he could not easily dispose of elsewhere. This also happened to Pinkerton, whose Leeward Islands contract had been extended in 1809 to include the newly captured Martinique. The following year, Cochrane wrote to express his concern about the effect the current reduction of naval manpower (from 10,000 to 4,500) would have on Pinkerton, due to the removal of the embargo against trading with America. This had lowered the prices of provisions in the West Indies, and Pinkerton would thus be left with excess stock which he could not sell for the high prices he had been obliged to pay for it when the embargo was in force. Cochrane's concern was not for Pinkerton himself, but for a lack of provisions if the squadron returned to the West Indies after

75 TNA ADM 110/68, ff. 513, 518–9, 525–7 & 528, 31 May, 2, 6 & 9 June 1814, 110/69 ff. 29–30, 5 July 1814.
76 TNA ADM 110/69, ff. 281 & 424–5, 11 November 1814, 14 January 1815.
77 TNA ADM 110/57, ff. 417–21, 2 June 1808. He had also suffered a fire in his store at Trinidad, but only mentioned this in passing.

the hurricane season and found Pinkerton had 'failed' (gone bankrupt).[78] Pinkerton estimated his losses at £36,648.10.1; the Victualling Board, after some deliberation, suggested to the Admiralty that they should allow him compensation totalling £30,538.14.3.

They were rather more sympathetic in 1815 with Belcher and Brymer who were left with large stocks when most of the naval force left the Halifax and Quebec area for New Orleans. In April the Treasury was asked to direct the army commissariats at Halifax, Bermuda and Quebec to take some of the salt meat and rum, and in August it was decided that more of these provisions should be transferred to settlers moving to Canada.[79] All these situations involved the Victualling Board in a great deal of correspondence, and although they seem to have been inclined to pinch pennies when they suspected a contractor was exaggerating the scale of his losses, they did go out of their way to help those who were in genuine difficulties through unexpected changes in the size of the force they had to feed. Sometimes this sympathy was met with serious disapproval by the Admiralty, and the tone of some of the exchanges of letters on these situations demonstrates, once again, the Victualling Board's lowly position in the naval administration hierarchy.

Overall, deliveries to warships abroad created fewer problems than might have been expected given the communication difficulties inherent in the distances involved. The large-scale problems of corrupt agents or contractors which were anticipated by the commissioners as a result of earlier experiences, did not occur during this period. Such problems as did occur with agents were with those who were appointed by commanders-in-chief; these were mainly from inexperience rather than deliberate misbehaviour.

Also as before, there were problems with checking and finalising accounts which did not affect the actual deliveries but did create some long-term difficulties for the Victualling Office in London; in the case of Basil Cochrane, that these dragged on for over a decade after the Board of Revision's recommendations had been accepted and acted upon indicates that people as well as systems should have been replaced.

78   TNA ADM 110/59, ff. 416 & 506–9, 28 & 29 April 1809; NMM ADM C/727, 28 July
       1810. Pinkerton did go bankrupt at the end of 1812: TNA B3/3906.
79   TNA ADM 110/69, ff. 519–23, 2 March 1815; 110/70, ff. 42–8, 70–71, 479–81, 3 & 7
       April, 17 August 1815.

5

Non-core and ad hoc Tasks

IN ADDITION TO THE CORE TASKS of obtaining and dispensing food and drink to the Royal Navy and parts of the army, the Victualling Board had numerous other tasks to perform. Some of these were of a regular nature, such as accounting, reporting to other government departments, property management, and staff management; others were of an ad hoc nature, although they tended to fall into certain categories such as feeding various groups of people who did not belong to the Royal Navy or British army, investigating complaints from commissioned officers, and investigating, and sometimes incorporating, innovations in food preparation, storage and preservation. There were a few other ad hoc tasks which involved the Victualling Board in considerable extra work, often to little or no useful effect, such as dealing with the edible cargoes destined for enemy countries on neutral ships which were seized at the beginning of the French Revolutionary war.

Accountancy

This aspect of the Victualling Board's work is dealt with here, as a 'non-core' task, because it is clear from copious evidence (including two of the Parliamentary reports) that the commissioners of the Victualling Board regarded it in that light and gave it a lower priority in their daily deliberations than the tasks of obtaining and delivering victuals and victualling stores to the fleet; this despite the fact that by far the greater part of the staff at Somerset Place was in the two accounting departments, with only a small secretariat to deal with everything else.

The commissioners may have taken their lead from the original Instructions to the Commissioners of the Victualling, most of which fall into three categories: accounting for stocks of provisions, detailing the paperwork required from pursers, and ensuring that all bills were paid in course. The penultimate instruction, almost an afterthought, requires an annual account to be made up and passed to the Admiralty by the end of the following March. The first three sets of these Instructions are much the same, but the fourth is in a different format and commences with a warning statement about the performance of the two previous boards. Their failings, as well as 'great negligence' included allowing large arrears of accounts to build up; the new commissioners were told in no uncertain terms to ensure that the arrears were dealt with and were not allowed to build up again.

However, the matter continued to be given a low priority and vast arrears of accounts had been allowed to build up. The magnitude of these arrears included not only the amounts involved but also the numbers of individual accounts involved. These sums came in three categories: actual proven debts, accounts which had not been examined or not finalised in the accounting department, and those which had been finalised in the accounting department but not passed by the Board.

It was the Victualling Board's responsibility to collect the proven debts from either the debtor or his sureties. At the end of 1786, this consisted of 329 accounts totalling £175,274. During the ten months while the Fees Commissioners were working on the victualling office, £31,606 was collected, leaving £143,668 outstanding. Once those commissioners had departed, the effort lapsed and by the time the Board of Revision reported twenty years later, only another £13,525 had been recovered, leaving a balance due of £130,142. Despite the Board of Revision having written to the Victualling Board to enquire what was being done to recover this sum, no proper answer had been forthcoming after two months, and rather than delay their report any further, the Board of Revision sadly remarked that they suspected that the money would never be recovered. Since 1786, additional debts totalling £221,185 had become due, making a grand total of £351,328, much of this relating to victualling troops prior to June 1798. There had been a change of system at that point, but under the old system the army paymasters wanted detailed information of how many men from each regiment had been victualled and for how long, so that they could stop the money from individual soldiers' pay.[1] This not only involved the victualling office staff in considerable work to compile this information, but was a major cause of delay in payment.

Of the accounts in arrears, the Fees commissioners gave no specifics, merely remarking that these 'had been disregarded, as well from neglect, as for other causes which no longer exist; we have now every reason to be satisfied, from the proofs laid before us, of the diligence lately exerted in that branch of the service.'[2] As with the effort to collect proven debts, this

---

1 *BOR 10*, pp. 9–10.
2 *Fees 8*, p. 570. These commissioners appear to have had the wool pulled over their eyes on this, as at least one of the larger accounts listed by the Board of Revision dated back to 1785.

diligence must have lapsed, since the Board of Revision found a rather different situation: arrears totalling some £10,985,100, made up of £2,740,885 in thirteen commission agents' accounts, £6,554,923 in forty-two foreign agents' accounts, £989,295 in fourteen home agents' and storekeepers' accounts and approximately £700,000 in 177 of the promiscuous accounts of pursers, correspondents and others.

These were the figures given in December 1806; between that date and August 1807, when the Board of Revision reported, six of the foreign agents' accounts had been passed, including the oldest (that of Cuthbert, the agent for the East Indies station, which amounted to £1,024,526). Fifteen other foreign agents' accounts had been prepared and were awaiting a board decision (four of them since 1791), as were those of ten home agents/storekeepers and six of the commission agents.

As far as the arrears of pursers' accounts were concerned, the Board of Revision recommended that any pursers' accounts relating to periods earlier than 1803 were to be treated as part of the exercise to deal with arrears which had started in October 1804 (some two years before the Board of Revision started its detailed work on the Victualling Board). It seems that this exercise was prompted by a complaint to the Admiralty from Admiral Lord Keith about delays in clearing his accounts (which depended to a certain extent on the accounts of his fleet's officers); prompting the Admiralty to ask the Victualling Board for its comments and suggestions.[3] The reason for the build-up, said the Victualling Board, was the long duration of the French Revolutionary war and the short period of the peace between that and the Napoleonic War; an 'unexampled magnitude' of accounts in the office; and additional work required on these accounts due to the fact that ships' companies were now obliged to 'sell' their savings of provisions to the government (i.e. the ships' pursers), all of which left little time to investigate the accounts of commanders-in-chief or those who purchased provisions under their authority. They had, they said, concluded that the only answer was 'a liberal encouragement' of the victualling office staff by allowing them to work paid overtime (which had previously been forbidden), and which they thought might also help to stem the flood of people leaving for better-paid jobs.[4]

This latter aspect could well have been prominent in the Victualling Board's thinking, as the real answer to the problem of an 'unexampled magnitude' of work would have been a substantial increase in the number

---

3 Keith was not only one of the better regarded senior admirals, but a fellow Scotsman on good terms with Lord Melville, who was First Lord of the Admiralty at that time. His daughter, Miss Mercer Elphinstone, was a very close friend of Princess Charlotte. I am grateful to Pamela Clark, Registrar of The Royal Archives, for this latter detail.

4 TNA ADM 110/51, ff. 371–7, 15 October 1804.

of staff; this was not mentioned. Although the Victualling Board would have been aware that such a suggestion would normally meet with resistance, such resistance would have been against permanent increases in staff, not the temporary increase which such a situation required. The Board of Revision recommended this approach with the other arrears of accounts in its 10th report.[5]

The Admiralty approved the overtime plan, and requested quarterly progress reports, which were duly sent. However, the report in November 1805, whilst commenting that the backlog of pursers' accounts had been reduced from eighteen to eight months, remarked that the recent increase in the number of ships in service had also increased the volume of pursers' accounts to be dealt with. Lists of outstanding amounts due from pursers were to be compiled regularly, and where pursers had failed to send in the proper vouchers after six months, their sureties were to be prosecuted for payment; however, this extreme situation should be avoided by notifying the Navy Board that the individual's wages should be withheld.

Progress was also being made on the cash and store accounts of foreign and home agents, storekeepers and commission agents.[6] It took more than seven years of this overtime work to eliminate the worst of these arrears; part of the problem was the numerous queries raised when dealing with accounts. The task was basically one of auditing the books of the account holder, checking the vouchers against the claimed expenditure and deciding the permissibility of various items. There are no surviving examples of pursers' accounts, but there are a few for agents; that for Henry Papps, the acting agent victualler for the Leeward Islands, shows the process: a book was created for each account, with the agent's original accounts pasted into the front, then for each type of entry, a separate listing was created. Papps' accounts book shows thirty-four such listings, including bills of exchange drawn, cash received by Papps from the previous agent victualler George Desborough, cost of freight, horse hire, purchases of provisions at six of the Leeward Islands, rent and salaries. For each of these, there are columns headed 'Remarks' (comments or queries), 'Replies thereto' (responses from the agent), 'The Board's Resolution' (whether or not the item is to be allowed, and sometimes a complaint such as 'want of signature on [specified] receipt'). Some of these last are irrationally concluded: for instance in Papps' accounts, against horse hire, the Board's remark was 'These charges appear objectionable, but as no explanation can be had, they are allowed'; the very situation where one would expect the item to be disallowed.[7] This was a

---

5   BOR *10*, p. 41.
6   For instance the progress reports Victualling Board to Admiralty, TNA ADM 110/53, ff 395–406 & 430–33, 6 & 25 November 1805.
7   TNA ADM 112/9, Papps' accounts.

comparatively small set of accounts covering only a few years; where the account was large and complex and covered many years, as did those from the East Indies station, the whole task was magnified, and one can see the temptation to put it aside to deal with it later.

That the Victualling Board did eventually learn its lesson on this type of work can be seen in 1817, when it took over the medical department of the disbanded Transport Board. This included another tranche of ancient arrears of Sick and Hurt Board accounts dating back as far as 1738.[8] The Victualling Board commented 'The confused state of these accounts and vouchers, the immense mass of books and papers, old and recent [was such that it would be] impossible to find room to arrange and select them …' They had thought at first that they might retain the best of the Transport Board's medical department clerks to try and sort out the mess, but concluded that they should abandon the effort and write off all the old accounts up to the end of 1802, and thus save the cost of the clerks; they would also be able to send all the old documentation to Deptford for storage. The Admiralty agreed and these arrears were written off.[9]

The Victualling Board's situation with their own arrears is, however, another example of their inability to deal with the 'chronic' type of work, where, until pressure from outside turned it into an 'acute' situation, the necessity to attend to the day-to-day routine work of accounting was given a low priority. The effort made to clear the arrears, and the lack of fuss about arrears afterwards might be taken as an indication that this problem had been permanently solved, were it not for the case of Basil Cochrane, which took over fourteen years to resolve.

The day-to-day accounting work was of four types: for suppliers of bulk items, where the individual transactions were large but few in number, for agents, storekeepers and sea provisions contractors where transactions were numerous, for pursers where the transactions were numerous and had to be cross-checked against those of the second group (and also against other pursers where ship-to-ship exchanges took place), and for other ships' officers who might have had some involvement with victuals and who, like the pursers, could not receive their pay until the Victualling Board certified they had no debt.[10]

The situation with officers' debts eventually changed to one where pay due was actually handed over to the Victualling Board to pay off the debt; concern over the legality of this practice led to the Admiralty obtaining counsel's opinion. This made it clear that although such a

8   BOR 9, pp. 22–3; see also J Knox-Laughton (ed.), Letters of Lord Barham, Vol. III, pp. 120–36.
9   TNA ADM 110/73, ff. 252–7, 15 January 1817.
10 See for instance NMM ADM C/722, 16 May 1809, Navy Board to Victualling Board.

practice could be used as a last resort, it could only be done if all the necessary accounting work had been done to prove the debt, not as a shortcut to doing that work.[11]

All this work on pursers' accounts would have been onerous enough if the documentation which arrived in the victualling office was in proper order and complete. All too frequently it was not, as evidenced in a letter of May 1813 to the Admiralty which set out the problems in detail: many pursers sent only part of their accounts, and did not send them direct to the victualling office but to their agents who were often slow in passing them on.[12] Although the *Regulations and Instructions* stated that accounts should be made up every twelve months, many pursers delayed sending them for years, and some had to be threatened with prosecution before they did so, finally producing papers 'in so confused and defective a state as to occasion great loss of time and labour in the [victualling] office'. When pursers had left the service, many never bothered to send their accounts at all, nor did the executors of many of those who had died. Pursers were not the only culprits: in 1803, the Victualling Board had complained to the Admiralty about captains and commanders who were failing to send in their accounts, as required by article 19 of the *Regulations and Instructions*, and had asked the Admiralty to put out a general reminder.[13]

In the 1813 letter, the Victualling Board proposed a new set of regulations for pursers. These would not only serve to emphasise the necessity of sending their annual accounts in at the proper time, but would also require them to be made up properly and balanced, with all supporting vouchers attached and also to send quarterly accounts, without which the office could not reconcile the quarterly accounts of agents, storekeepers and other correspondents. Muster books should also be sent promptly; monthly instead of two-monthly. Because the Victualling Board believed that part of the problem stemmed from the appointment as pursers of people who were completely unqualified to do the job properly, they were in future to undergo examination by a panel of three experienced pursers and produce a certificate of their suitability before being given a warrant.[14] Finally, in order to ensure that pursers and others complied with these new regulations, it would be necessary to include flag officers, captains and commanders. All this was approved and duly incorporated in the new *Additional Instructions to the Flag-Officers, Captains, Commanders, Commanding-Officers and Pursers of His Majesty's Navy*.[15]

11   NMM ADM C/723, 2 August 1809.
12   NMM DP/33A, 17 May 1813.
13   TNA ADM 110/49, ff. 373–82, 3 October 1803.
14   NMM ADM DP/33A, 17 May 1813.
15   These were issued on 4 November 1813 and were supplementary to the *R&I* 14th edition; for details and some examples of the *R&I*, see Brian Lavery (ed.), *Shipboard Life and Organisation 1731–1815* (London, 1998), pp. 1–57.

This whole situation serves as yet another demonstration of the relative unimportance of the Victualling Board (and perhaps also the other subordinate administrative boards) in the matter of enforcing compliance from ships' officers with the *Regulations and Instructions* under which those officers were supposed to operate. At the beginning of the French Revolutionary war, the current *Regulations and Instructions* was the thirteenth edition, issued in 1790. These regulations consisted of sections for each type of officer, from fleet commanders-in-chief down to the different types of warrant officer, with other sections relating to specific types of supplies. Thus although there is a section entitled 'Of the Provisions', there are also some 'articles' on provisions under the sections for the various officers. These latter articles are on the accounting requirements, together with sample forms. By the fourteenth edition, issued in 1806, the forms were printed and issued to ships' officers, instead of their being allowed to use any paper which they had available and in no fixed format.

In addition to the *Regulations and Instructions*, fleet and ships' commanders issued their own additional orders on various aspects of shipboard life and administration.[16] These seem frequently to have been ignored; for instance Nelson issued an order to the ships of his Mediterranean fleet in 1803 which stated that all provisions received on board should be listed, in detail, in the ships' logs, yet a study of over thirty sets of logs of that fleet showed that only a few complied fully with this order, a few more remarked that provisions had been received, without giving any detail, and most made no entries at all.[17]

If, as seems likely, such orders were ignored throughout the whole of the navy and with them the requirements of the *Regulations and Instructions*, it is small wonder that the victualling office found this aspect of its work so onerous. This could hardly have arisen as a new situation in 1813 when the Victualling Board listed the problems, although no earlier formal complaint has emerged. Perhaps it was the new spirit of reform which was emerging at that time which encouraged them to complain, or perhaps their failure to do so earlier was due to the fact that such complaints to one's superiors can be seen as an admission of failure to do one's job. Or, and more likely, it is evidence of an attitude which stretched up through the Board of Admiralty to the government and which saw concern over the administrative functions as being of little importance and beneath the notice of a gentleman: what had been scornfully described by one of the victualling commissioners as 'taking a clerk-like interest'.

---

16 See Lavery, *Shipboard Life*, pp. 59–201, 210–37.
17 British Library, Add. MSS 34970, f. 3 (Nelson's order book); Macdonald, 'Victualling', pp. 54–63.

In 1811, a new set of rules for the appointment and promotion of pursers added another layer of work for the victualling office staff, who had to certify that there were no debts; regular letters from the Navy Board asking about this began to arrive; there were often more than twelve of these queries each month which meant that any outstanding accounts for the listed pursers had to be moved up to the head of the queue.[18]

The correspondence between the Victualling Board and the Navy Board includes many letters about pursers' and officers' accounts, often prompted by the officer requesting exemption on the grounds of lost documents. Reasons for this ranged from the purser whose stores had been plundered by mutineers to the loss of a ship and all its books as a result of enemy action or shipwreck.[19] There is also much correspondence about log books and victualling books: requests to the Navy Board to borrow these, acknowledgements of receipt and covering letters on their return. Over several months in 1811, a series of letters were exchanged about the paucity of victualling books being sent by the Navy Board: the Victualling Board wanted sixty sets of victualling books each month but the Navy Board were only sending forty; these letters became sharper as time went by, mentioning that 300 sets of accounts were waiting for the victualling books, finally threatening to complain to the Admiralty.[20] The Navy Board replied that they had got three more clerks working on these, but it took another four months before they got things moving and the situation came up again three years later, the number of victualling books being sent having dropped from more than seventy each month to only thirty-three. The Victualling Board was concerned that this could only get worse once the new system was in place, but it seems that the Navy Board was suffering a staff shortage and the situation continued through into 1815.[21]

18 Sometimes many more: TNA ADM 110/70, ff. 176–7, 12 May 1815 lists forty-four pursers with no debt, fifty-four with accounts still open but against whom there was no objection, and twenty-seven with debts.

19 NMM ADM D/41, 11 November 1799 (Richard Holmes, late purser of *Impregnable*, provisions lost with the ship); ADM C/721, 7 February 1809; (purser Fitzgerald of *Beaulieu*, referring to the 1797 mutinies). This illustrates the long periods which could pass before accounts of this sort could be finalised. See also Macdonald, 'Documentary sources', pp. 239–62, which shows the numbers of letters received for this and other standard matters.

20 TNA ADM 110/63, f. 218, 20 February 1811; 110/64, f. 71, 4 July 1811, Victualling Board to Navy Board.

21 NMM ADM C/731, 6 July 1811, C/741, 10 June 1814, Navy Board to Victualling Board; TNA ADM 110/68, ff. 350–1, 2 March 1814, 110/70, ff. 284–5, 15 June 1815, Victualling Board to Navy Board.

Work for external organisations

Work for external organisations fell into three categories: that for Parliamentary inquiries, that for other government departments, and that for other naval boards. The work for Parliamentary inquiries consisted partly of producing reports of expenditure under various headings (for instance, of pensions paid from the Civil List, for the Committee on Public Accounts)[22] and partly of being interviewed and questioned by members of the relevant committees.[23] As well as the two major enquiries into the work of the victualling office itself, and the two general enquiries discussed in Chapter 9, there were others such as that on supplies sent to Portugal and Spain in 1808.[24] All these were ordered by precept from the enquiring committee and thus needed immediate attention. In addition to the time taken up by the actual interview, preparation of the reports would have taken considerable work by the two accounting department heads and their senior clerks.[25] This also applied to the reports requested by other government departments such as the Treasury's request for 'a specification of the Warrants, Delegations, Commissions or any other instrument by which appointments of honour, trust and emolument are conferred on the department of the Victualling Board [and the stamp duty paid on these]'.[26] This type of work, although also requiring immediate attention, was intermittent.

The work for other naval administration departments was mainly for the Navy Board and included regular (mostly annual) requests for information required for the annual estimates, such as the anticipated cost of victualling a certain number of men for the following year.[27] There were also frequent requests for the amount of cash which would be needed to meet Bills in the next week or month.[28] There is no indication that this regular work was diarised so that it could be prepared in anticipation of the expected request, however, the same might be said of the Navy Board, as these requests did not always come at the same time each year.[29]

---

22 NMM ADM C/715, 10 July 1807.
23 See, for example, the reported interviews in *Fees 8*, pp. 591–673.
24 BPP 1809 (102) *Papers relating to Supplies embarked for services in Portugal and Spain 1808 (victualling office)*.
25 Whether the internal papers were kept in a form which enabled the relevant information to be extracted is not known, as the surviving documentation on contracts and accounts is patchy.
26 NMM ADM C/719, 19 February 1808, Treasury to Victualling Board.
27 For instance, NMM C/679, 8 February 1793; C/731, 11 September 1811.
28 These are seen throughout the in-letters from the Navy Board in NMM C series.
29 For instance, in 1795 the request arrived in January, in 1799 and 1803 it was September, in 1800 November and 1804 December.

Other dealings with the Navy Board

There was also a regular exchange of letters between the Victualling Board and the Navy Board about items of stores required at the dock or victualling yards: for instance, the Navy Board supplied cordage and anchors for the Victualling Board's boats or sailcloth for the sawing stages and to cover waggon-loads of biscuit, the Victualling Board supplied the Navy Board with buckets, buoys and other items made by the coopers.[30] There were comparatively few of these requests before 1803 (a total of twenty for the period 1793–1802) and although not specifically stated, it seems that the Navy Board had been purchasing such items from outside; in March 1803, not wishing to set up their own cooperages, the Navy Board started 'buying' them from the Victualling Board.[31] Between that date and the end of the war in 1815, over 800 such requests were received by the Victualling Board.[32]

Another area of regular communication with the Navy Board concerned the supply and maintenance of the Victualling Board's boats and other vessels. This included some of the depot ships (others were hired and thus maintained by their owners), for instance the *Irresistible*, stationed at the Nore, required accommodation for her storekeeper and his clerk, hammocks for coopers and labourers, a bulkhead and bower cable, some deck caulking and other alterations, all of which were done in the dockyard at Sheerness.[33] The other vessels and boats suffered all the problems of wear and tear common to vessels in constant year-round use. These were reported by the agents victualler, and the Navy Board was asked to survey the vessels and either to make the necessary repairs or to have them broken up and provide new.[34] They also needed new boats for new situations, such as launches for Heligoland.[35]

All these tasks required little more from the Victualling Board than receiving and writing letters, although in some cases, such as the ongoing problems with launches for Heligoland, where the physical conditions of the site and the bad winter weather were particularly hard on boats, this took more than the receipt and writing of one letter in each direction.[36]

---

30 NMM ADM C series, passim.
31 NMM ADM C/699, 2 March 1803.
32 NMM ADM C/699 to C/748, passim, Navy Board to Victualling Board.
33 NMM C/700, 8, 15 & 26 July, 1 August, 21 September, 4 & 7 October and 16 November 1803, Navy Board to Victualling Board.
34 For instance, NMM ADM C/710, 26 April & 5 & 13 June 1805, Navy Board to Victualling Board re the Chatham yawl, and the *Resolution* smack at Deptford.
35 NMM ADM C/730, 15 April 1811, Navy Board to Victualling Board.
36 The first launch required oak planking for repairs, then had to be replaced when it was lost from its moorings overnight, then the order for this was countermanded and the agent at Heligoland instructed to find one locally. TNA ADM 110/62, f. 311,

There do not appear to have been any difficulties or delays over handling such matters, perhaps because they all came into the 'acute' category where a simple decision could be made and acted on as soon as the matter came to the Board's attention.

Property management

The Victualling Board had the responsibility for a great deal of real property, from the offices and victualling yards at home to the premises at the yards abroad. Many of the facilities abroad, especially at the places not considered to be permanent, were rented or leased, but the facility at Gibraltar was owned. These buildings had suffered badly in the Great Siege, they were inconveniently placed, and as St Vincent had remarked, the wharf was 'the vilest in the universe'. The solution was to sell the two sets of buildings and build a new facility immediately south of the town at Rosia Bay.[37] The process, from the decision in 1799 to the completion, took some twelve years and in the meantime the Victualling Board were reluctant to spend any money on the existing buildings. In early 1801 the agent victualler, James Cutforth, requested permission to make some essential repairs to his house, a part of which was collapsing. The Admiralty initially refused, on the basis that he would shortly be moving into the new premises, but after details of the problem were sent, they relented.[38] It was 1807 before plans for the new yard were approved and contracts issued for the building work; in the meantime Cutforth had requested and been granted a floating wine depot.[39]

Part of the arrangement at Gibraltar was that the Board of Ordnance took over the old victualling premises; a similar arrangement was utilised at Portsmouth in 1796 when the Victualling Board purchased a piece of land next to the brewhouse at Weevil from the Board of Ordnance. This was followed by an exchange of property when the Board of Ordnance objected to the Victualling Board's plans for new storehouses, as these would, they said, mask the battery and allow an advantage to 'hostile attackers'.[40]

Since many of the senior officers at the yards lived in houses on the premises, and some of the commissioners of the Victualling Board in houses at Somerset Place, there were various alterations to these properties

---

Navy Board to Victualling Board; 25 August 1810, 110/63, ff. 298–9, f. 369, 10 March & 14 April 1811, Victualling Board to Navy Board.

37   NMM ADM C/691, 4 & 10 January 1799.

38   NMM ADM C/695, 8 January 1801; C/696, 14 November 1801; D/43, 15 May 1801.

39   NMM ADM C/715, 14 July 1807; D/47, 12 June 1805; D/48, 5 September 1805. See also Macdonald, 'The victualling yard at Gibraltar', pp. 55–64.

40   NMM ADM C/686, 21 October 1796; C/693, 8, 17 & 21 April 1800.

to suit the families of these men, and, when the reorganisation at Deptford took place in early 1809, some of the houses were converted to storehouses and vice-versa (for instance, the two houses previously occupied by the clerks of the brewhouse and dry stores were converted into a single house for Henry Garrett, the new agent victualler).[41] And of course, these houses, along with all the other premises, required regular maintenance and occasional repairs.

Although no evidence relating to victualling staff's houses has emerged, it seems that there was a general problem over the maintenance and redecoration of buildings throughout the shore-based officers and civil employees of the navy, as in 1804 Samuel Bentham drew up a schedule of regulations for the general repair of all buildings at naval establishments.[42] These were, said the Admiralty order which accompanied the schedule, to be followed without deviation unless expressly directed. The schedule consists of fifty-one clauses, including the inspection of roofs after heavy snow, chimney cleaning, bricklayers' and masons' work, painting, paper hanging and internal fixtures.[43] The actual work was done by tradesmen from outside, usually arranged by the Navy Board's Civil Architect and Engineer or, when large works were required, by a builder contracted to do the work.[44] The same applied to the work on the various victualling yards, such as the paving and erection of stables at Deptford.[45]

There was ongoing work at all the yards and other places where ships went for water: pipe was laid at Brixham, reports and chemical analysis were commissioned for the two alternative wells at Chatham, and a well was sunk at Dungeness and fitted with a pump and hoses. A steam engine was ordered, but on Bentham's recommendation this was changed to a horse-operated pump, as being more easily managed and repaired.[46] Sometimes the Victualling Board needed to borrow heavy equipment from the Navy Board for this and other work, such as the floating steam dredger to remove mud from the camber at Weevil, or the pile driver to assist in sinking a well at Deptford.[47] All this involved a steady stream of correspondence, but as with the maintenance and replacement of boats, the role of the victualling office was mainly one of receiving requests, passing them on to the

41 NMM ADM C/721, 17 January 1809; DP/20A, 27 April 1809.
42 J Macdonald, 'Regulations for preservation and repair of buildings', *Newsletter of the Naval Dockyards Society*, December 2008, vol. 13, no. 2, pp. 18–19.
43 NMM ADM C/701, 21 February 1804.
44 For instance, NMM ADM C/706, 25 May 1805.
45 NMM ADM C/683, 13 October & 18 November 1794.
46 NMM ADM C/694, 8 October 1800; C/700, 28 December 1803; TNA ADM 110/48, ff. 183–4 & 243–5, 2 November 1802; 110/50, ff. 116–17, 5 January 1804.
47 NMM ADM C/704, 19 October 1804; C/705, 9 January 1805.

Admiralty for approval and passing that approval on to the people who arranged the actual work.

The only situation which seems to have caused the Victualling Board and its staff any personal inconvenience was the length of time it took to take possession of the extra space at Somerset Place which had been occupied by the Sick and Hurt Board. They had raised this matter with the Admiralty in December 1805 and again with the Board of Revision, complaining about the cramped conditions under which they had to work: staff numbers had increased from 64 clerks to 105, so that they were working in basements and garrets, and rooms which were designed for four or five clerks now contained eight, nine or even ten; they needed candles all the time, and there was nowhere for the commissioners to work on confidential matters; even the secretary lacked a private office.[48] From the Admiralty approving the scheme and instructing Bentham to propose a plan, to the Victualling Board finally taking possession of the space (after having to chase the Transport Board to have the Sick and Hurt Board's books and papers removed) took over two years, during which the clerks continued to suffer dark and cramped working conditions.[49]

Medical supplies

The Victualling Board provided some of the meat which was used to make portable soup, sending this to the soup house at Ratcliffe Cross which was run firstly by the Sick and Hurt Board and later the Transport Board. This was a winter task, and as far as the Somerset Place staff were concerned, involved no more than a letter stating that they were about to commence killing oxen and enquiring how much meat would be needed, then instructing the agent victualler at Deptford to send it. After the Transport Board took over the work of the Sick and Hurt Board in 1806, and the Victualling Board took on the task of distributing lemon juice on behalf of the Transport Board (anti-scorbutics were deemed to be medical supplies, and thus not the 'property' of the Victualling Board)[50] there was a steady flow of letters on this subject: requests for supplies, complaints about broken bottles or damaged cases, and offers received of orange or lime juice.[51] The Victualling

48   TNA ADM 110/53, ff. 454–60, 3 December 1805.
49   NMM ADM C/706, 7 December 1805; TNA ADM 110/56 ff. 309–11, 19 October 1807, Victualling Board to Navy Board; ibid. f. 335, 9 November 1807, Victualling Board to Transport Board.
50   Macdonald, 'Two years off Provence', pp. 448–50.
51   For a typical batch of these letters, see TNA ADM 110/55, ff. 57, 99–100, 172, 258–9, 417–18, 475, 508–10, 520–1, Victualling Board to Transport Board, between 6 October 1806 and 30 May 1807.

Board did not concern itself otherwise with the relationship between food and health, a comparatively modern concept which did not exist at that time.

Ad hoc tasks

Amongst the non-core tasks which can be described as ad hoc was that of dealing with suggested innovations and 'improvements'. Most of these were suggested by members of the public, either direct to the Admiralty or through some influential person, but some came from serving officers (and in one case, a resident naval commissioner) or from commercial firms. In all cases other than those which were repetitions of suggestions received and rejected earlier, the standard response was to conduct experiments. These were usually done at the Board's expense, but if expensive equipment was involved the inventor was expected to pay. In a few cases, the suggestions were so strange, and their effectiveness so unlikely, that one can only assume that the experiments were conducted in deference to the status of the inventor or his patron rather than any expectation that they would produce a useful result.

Probably the most frequent suggestions were those dealing with the ongoing problem of keeping biscuit in edible condition. These ranged from soaking the biscuit bags in nitre (rejected on the grounds of flammability) and putting live lobsters in casks of flour to 'extirpate' weevils (the first experiment failed as the lobsters died and the weevils crawled on their bodies; further experiments were declined as the yard workers complained of the offensive smell of the dead lobsters), to Captain J Yule's suggestion for preserving biscuit on long voyages by dividing the bread room into several sections, each of which was to be sealed by caulking until the contents were needed (the Victualling Board quite liked this idea, but there is no evidence that it was ever put into use).[52]

Other suggestions were Sir John Dalrymple's plan for brewing beer and making bread on board cruisers using 'yeast powder'; Sir John also experimented with making beer using 'wort cake', which included oil of hops. The results were deemed tolerable, although the beer was 'a little volatile in the making', but again there is no evidence that this ever became normal practice.[53] At about the same time, Lord Spencer's private secretary, J Harrison, sent details of Mr Thomas Sherlock's 'yeastless' bread. No detail

52 NMM ADM C/711, 24 July 1806; TNA ADM 110/54, ff. 268–9, 6 August 1806 (nitre); NMM ADM DP/33A, 24 June 1813; DP/33B, 8 July 1813 (lobsters); C/732, 10 December 1811; TNA ADM 110/64, ff. 452–3, 11 December 1811.
53 NMM ADM C/683, 12 May 1795; C/684, 11 & 28 September 1795; D/39, 9 May 1795.

of the method was given, but this sounds like what we now call sourdough bread, which relies on natural airborne yeasts getting into a wet mixture of dough.[54]

One suggestion which the Victualling Board declined to test at its expense was the 'perpetual oven' invented and patented by Vice Admiral Sir Isaac Coffin;[55] this oven was longer than the existing ovens and instead of being heated by lighting a fire of bavins inside it between each batch of baking, had two fire boxes (one each side running the whole length of the oven) and a conveyor belt which took the bread/biscuits through the length of the oven and out the far end. However, the Victualling Board remarked that 'our people at Deptford' were unable to see that it would need fewer people to operate and thus it would not save wages. Since the existing ovens were back-to-back and thus could not be modified, it would cost some £250–350 to build an experimental oven (the Victualling Board had tried, but failed, to find anyone in London who had used one). The Navy Board, on being consulted, said that it was normal for inventors to erect their inventions at their own expense to prove that they worked.[56] One can see that the Victualling Board would be reluctant to spend this sort of money when their general experience of suggested innovations was that few were effective, and this suggestion seems to have gone no further.

Another type of food which was the subject of numerous suggestions was meat. These ranged from the Bishop of Durham's supposedly more humane method of killing oxen by 'pithing': inserting a sword between the cervical vertebrae to sever the spinal cord instead of using the traditional pole-axe (two experiments were tried but it was rejected on the grounds of being agonising to the oxen),[57] through Dr Blane's suggestion that pimento powder and bruised juniper berries should be added to the rubbing salt when curing beef, Mr Eckhardt's method of preserving meat without salt, and what its inventor called 'par-boiled' beef. Mr Eckhardt's method seemed, reported the Victualling Board, to involve boiling the meat in acid and then covering it with melted fat. He had brought some samples of various types of meat in for the board to try; it was, they said, 'unsightly and disgusting in appearance', smelt unpleasant and tasted 'sour and unpalatable'.[58] The par-boiled meat was prepared by immersing pieces of beef in

54   NMM ADM C/684, 2 September 1795, J Harrison at Treasury to Victualling Board. Details of the sourdough method can be found in any book on home breadmaking.
55   Patent no. 3337 of 1810.
56   TNA ADM 110/62, ff. 146–7, 15 June 1810 (to Navy Board), ff. 258–61, 3 August 1810; 110/69, ff. 413–4, 9 January 1815.
57   NMM ADM C/705, 15 March 1805; D/47, 10 May 1805.
58   NMM ADM C/709, 24 January & 22 February 1806; TNA ADM 110/54 ff. 160–6, 30 March 1806.

boiling water for twenty minutes, hanging it up to dry and lightly salting it the following day; this method had, apparently, been tried with some success by the army during the 1799 expedition to Holland, and samples were duly sent to St Vincent's fleet blockading Brest, as an alternative to sending out live oxen. Some time later St Vincent wrote to request a supply for use 'in certain seasons' and this was duly sent, along with fresh vegetables, and barley to thicken the broth.[59] Despite this, the use of par-boiled meat does not seem to have become common.

Perhaps the most successful of all the ideas for meat was canning, known at the time as 'preserved meat'. Invented by the Frenchman Nicolas Appert, the process had then been patented in Britain by the firm of Donkin & Hall, who had sent samples to the president of the Royal Society (Sir Joseph Banks) and the foreign secretary (Lord Wellesley) before persuading the Victualling Board to try it at sea, which they did in 1813. The captains who conducted the trials were enthusiastic, but the process was costly and by this time it had become obvious that the war was coming to an end; this was going to leave the Victualling Board with a great deal of salt meat on their hands, so although canned meats and soups were used on voyages of exploration, they did not become a standard item of the naval seaman's diet until 1847.[60]

There were also several suggestions on dealing with the other ever-present problem of rats in the storehouses. Despite keeping cats in the stores (which caught two or three rats a night) and the work of the resident ratcatcher, Mr Inkpen, there was a constant influx of new rats from the craft on the river. Mr Inkpen's method involved traps, but a new method proposed by Mr Broad, suggested in 1813, used a combination of traps and bait, which seemed to be more successful, and was thus approved.[61]

Other innovations suggested to and tried by the Victualling Board during this period included spruce beer, the use of ale instead of the 'small' beer which was in common use (the idea here being that since ale was stronger, it could be diluted with water and thus less beer would have to be carried), several methods of purifying water, whitewashing cheese to preserve it, and shipboard melting of tallow from the live oxen slaughtered on board ship, thus reducing the space required to carry the raw tallow (rejected as too dangerous), and the use of various new types of soap for personal washing (reported to shrink in keeping and be wasteful in use).[62]

59 TNA ADM 110/54, ff. 295–6, 19 May 1806; 110/55, ff. 98–9, 5 November 1806.
60 Stuart Thorne, *The History of Food Preservation* (Kirkby Lonsdale, Cumbria, 1986), passim; Macdonald, *Feeding*, pp. 171–2; Christopher Lloyd & Jack L S Coulter, *Medicine and the Navy*, Vol. IV, p. 99.
61 NMM ADM DP/33A, 25 June 1813.
62 NMM ADM D/38, 3 April 1793 (spruce beer); C/707, 11, 13 & 23 September 1805; C/683, 19 June 1795; D/39, 23 June 1795 (purifying water); C/688, 1 September 1797

Iron water tanks

The use of iron water tanks was probably the most successful of all the innovations embraced by the Victualling Board during this period. The steady increase in numbers of ships meant the navy had a growing requirement for casks of all sizes; these were the equivalent of the modern shipping container, and were used for small items such as boatswains' stores as well as the wet and dry provisions.[63] Good quality staves, from which these casks were made by the Victualling Board's coopers, became more difficult to obtain and more expensive, so when in 1809 Messrs Trevithick and Dickinson suggested that the Victualling Board might be interested in their newly patented iron water tanks, available at considerably lower cost than the wooden equivalent, the Admiralty agreed with the Board that experiments would be advisable and iron tanks were fitted to five vessels. Favourable reports were received and a contract was made with the ironmaster Henry Maudsley. The precise number of tanks supplied under a series of contracts is not recorded, but by December 1814 the Victualling Board had concluded that in terms of durability over a five-year period, the amount of water held, and general efficiency and cost-effectiveness, iron tanks were better than wooden casks. In early 1815 the Admiralty decided that the tanks should be considered articles of ships' stores, and as such handled by the Navy Board.[64]

It seems a little strange that it had taken the Admiralty so long to decide that these tanks should be handled by the Navy Board, but presumably the thinking was that water and the containers for it had always been the province of the Victualling Board and that the material of which the containers were made was irrelevant. The Victualling Board, however, had handled the whole business with efficiency, as could be expected for a matter which, although it lasted for over three years, came into the acute category.

Feeding civilians and other countries' seamen

At various times during the period, the Victualling Board became involved in feeding people who were neither Royal Navy personnel nor British soldiers. With one exception, these were one-off tasks, and included some

(whitewashing cheese); TNA ADM 110/54, ff. 91–4, 21 February 1806 (ale); 110/69, ff. 224–6, 21 October 1814 (melting tallow); 110/62, ff. 387–8, 22 September 1810 (Baron von Doornik's patent soap).

63 'Wet' provisions included salt meat as well as water, wine and spirits, 'dry' included grain products, pease and cheeses.

64 For full details, see J Macdonald, 'The introduction of iron water tanks in the Royal Navy', *Mariner's Mirror*, vol. 95, no. 2 (May, 2009), pp. 215–19.

French emigrants seeking passage to Ostend, the royalist army in Quiberon Bay, the crews of some captured Dutch ships held off Sheerness, supernumeraries on Lord McCartney's embassy to China, and, in 1803–04 and again in 1813, when harvests failed in the north of Scotland, the 'poor inhabitants' of Shetland and the Orkneys.[65] All these situations required the Victualling Board to do little more than instruct the appropriate agent victualler to provide victuals, or obtain Admiralty approval to pass such items in pursers' accounts.

A more onerous task, which had to be dealt with over three separate periods, was feeding crews of the Russian navy when they were either interned or wintering in Britain. The first period commenced in 1795 when Admiral Duncan's command included two Russian squadrons which wintered at the Nore, the Downs and Yarmouth; this continued through the next five winters and the summer of 1800. Provisions were supplied for the crews, but the officers were supplied with table money in lieu, originally at £1.9.0 per officer per month, then at the rate of £1.4.5 per month multiplied by the number of rations 'usually allotted' to each rank of officer in the Russian navy.[66] Over the winter of 1799/1800, Russian troops were added to those to be victualled; many of these were sick and required a different ration (additional bread, less meat, butter and cheese). Then a further order directed that healthy Russian troops should have more bread and less butter.[67]

The second period involved the Russian squadron which had aided the French in Lisbon in 1808; omitted from the convention of Cintra, they had negotiated a separate convention which interned ten ships and some 5,685 crew at Spithead until such time as the two countries were at peace again'.[68] The third episode started in 1812, when the Russian Baltic fleet (from sixteen to eighteen sail of the line and from eight to ten frigates) over-wintered in British ports. This time they were supplied with wine, soft bread, fresh

---

65 NMM ADM DP/13, 11 July 1793 (French emigrants); C/685, 20 February 1796 (Quiberon Bay royalists); C/693, 10 September 1799 (Dutch); C/679, 12 February 1793 & C/683, 10 February 1795 (Lord McCartney's embassy); C/700, 13 December 1803 & C/738, 20 April 1813 (Shetland and Orkneys, Treasury secretary to Victualling Board).

66 NMM ADM C/684, 16 & 27 September 1795 (orders to victual); C/685, 1 January & 23 February 1796 (frigate *Riga* at Yarmouth, brig *Despatch*); C/684, 27 & 29 October 1795 (table money); C/686, 22 December 1796 (query about Russian officers); C/690, 5 October 1798 (rate of table money for officers. The precise numbers of rations for each rank of officer is not specified.)

67 NMM ADM C/692, 26 December 1799, C/693, 1 & 4 January 1800.

68 Christopher Hall, *Wellington's Navy: Sea Power and the Peninsular War 1807–14* (London, 2004), pp. 36–7.

beef and vegetables, and buckwheat in lieu of flour and the officers were supplied with free tongues in the same way as were British officers.[69]

All this involved not only much of the Board's time, but also that of the agents victualler at the various ports; it also required a separate accounting function as, in all such cases, the cost of such extramural victualling had to be recovered through diplomatic channels.[70] There is, however, no indication that any of these victualling situations ran other than smoothly.

The 'pursers' eighth'

One ad hoc task which required a major effort at the beginning and further less complex efforts at intervals over the following few years was the aftermath of the Spithead mutiny and the decision to issue provisions at the full rate instead of the traditional seven-eighths. No one knew how the tradition had started; in 1773 Henry Pelham at the victualling office had investigated the origin of this practice, but reported to Lord Sandwich that he 'never could find any orders … for allowing the pursers of His Majesty's ships the eighths'. The purpose was to give pursers an allowance for the inevitable wastage that comes from breaking bulk and doling out provisions on a per-man-per-day basis, but the practice seems to have had official sanction because after having notices printed which outlined the new rules and sending these to all pursers, the Victualling Board had to obtain and issue new sets of weights and measures and recover the old ones (which presumably were marked with the full measure while actually measuring seven-eighths of it).[71]

They then had to devise a new method of compensating pursers for wastage losses. This was done by adding a credit (equivalent to one-ninth of the total amount issued) when the purser's accounts were completed and passed. This was changed in 1804 to one-eighth, then in 1805 to one-tenth, and finally in 1806 this was discontinued and the credit prices for all provisions (except oatmeal) were increased in lieu. This meant, of course, that the clerks dealing with pursers' accounts had to make the necessary

69 NMM ADM C/736, 12 November 1812 (numbers of ships); DP/32B, 12 December 1812 (fresh meat and vegetables); C/737, 6 January & 3 February 1813 (buckwheat, wine and soft bread); TNA ADM 110/67, ff. 12–13, 7 April 1813 (tongues) The number of tongues was proportional to the rank of the officer: Macdonald, *Feeding*, p. 121.

70 For example NMM ADM G/792, 24 & 27 August 1798 ('the Russian squadron at the Nore'); TNA ADM 110/62 ff. 445–6, 10 October 1810 (Portuguese ships).

71 NMM ADM DP/105, 23 July 1773; C/687, 11 & 17 May 1797.

adjustments to these accounts at different rates for different periods, with all the inherent potential for error which such changes incur.[72]

Handling food on captured neutral vessels

At the beginning of the French Revolutionary war, the Victualling Board was involved in a prolonged, but ultimately abortive, attempt to purchase food intended for France and other newly enemy countries carried on neutral vessels which had been seized by British cruisers or detained in their port of loading. The first instruction was in February 1793, with an Admiralty Order to send 'two competent persons' to Ireland (where numerous ships had been detained) to purchase the beef and pork for naval use, and to sell the wheat and flour for the best possible price; the Board sent their secretary, John Watts, with a clerk from Deptford and a cooper. Two other neutral ships were taken into Alderney and Guernsey, and the Victualling Board asked the Admiralty to arrange for some warship officers from the Channel fleet to carry out the inspections. This instruction was followed by one from the Treasury to buy any provisions deemed 'not fit for the navy' and to send this to New South Wales; there was 421,560 lbs of meat in this category. This required the board to write to the agents of the ships' owners to enquire where the cargoes could be seen. On inspection, the cargoes proved 'wholly unfit for the service [for which it was intended]': (the beef lacked sufficient brine and the wheat needed constant turning to prevent it heating), which the Victualling Board duly reported to the Admiralty.[73]

Next, the Treasury informed the Victualling Board that they had appointed the firm of Brickwood and Inglis to deal with claims from the owners of these cargoes, and that the Board's agents were to follow this firm's instructions; the Treasury then announced that the firm of Messrs White and Son were to purchase the items which the Victualling Board did not want, and that they were to be granted an imprest to do so (in other words, the Victualling Board were to lend this firm the money).[74] Shortly after, the Victualling Board wrote to the Admiralty that, given the poor quality of all these cargoes, it might not be desirable to continue the operation; this suggestion seems to have been ignored.[75] A further complication was the necessity to deal with Customs officers; the Treasury took until

---

72   NMM ADM C/702, 25 April & 10 May 1804; C/708, 29 October 1805; C/711, 22 August 1806.

73   NMM ADM C/679, 15 February, 28 May (endorsement), 12 June 1793; D/38, 26 June 1793; C/680, 24 July 1793; D/38, 10 & 22 July 1793.

74   NMM ADM C/679, 18 February, 26 April, 4 & 11 May & 5 June 1793, Treasury to Victualling Board.

75   NMM ADM D/38, 22 July 1793.

September to decree that the cargoes were to be free of duty, but that would not have prevented the Customs officers from inspecting them for contraband. In November, the Treasury decided that Watts and the clerk could return to London (having been in Ireland since February), and in December that the Victualling Board should pay the difference between the owners' claims and the amounts raised by selling the cargoes. Three merchants (J Brickwood, J Inglis, and the corn factor Claude Scott) had been appointed to adjust the immediate claims; a couple of weeks later, the Treasury instructed the Victualling Board to appoint selling agents at the various outports where detained vessels were being held, having first conferred with the Ordnance Board over these appointments (some of the ships also carried 'naval stores', which presumably included guns and powder). This was delayed at the end of the month by a further instruction that all claims for cargoes deemed to have been sold to 'government' were to be referred to the Admiralty Court; (this caused yet more delays, and it was not until January 1796 that the Admiralty professed themselves satisfied with the Victualling Board's explanation for this).[76] In May of the following year, the corn factor Claude Scott was appointed sole agent for selling all neutral cargoes (as opposed to enemy cargoes on neutral vessels).

This exercise had taken some three years to resolve, during which time the Victualling Board had been put to considerable trouble, lost the services of its secretary for some nine months, and had to lend money to a commercial firm to relieve it of the low-quality foodstuffs it had rejected for naval use, and been obliged to fund the discrepancy between the net proceeds of the sales of these goods and the amounts claimed by the owners. As early as the end of December 1793, this stood at almost £10,000.[77] The Treasury summed it up quite neatly:

> … altho' it may be thought expeditious for the purpose of government that the cargoes should be prevented getting into the possession of the enemy … by reason of the high rates of the invoices, freights, demurrage, frequent damage to the ships and their cargoes, the inferior quality of the articles, the expenses of the captors and of the claimants, the proceedings of the Court of Admiralty and many other attendant expenses, the whole then charged to government, if they should not be condemned as prizes to the captors, and over which with all our endeavours, we have very little control, the expense to be borne by the public will very much exceed the real value of the goods in this country.[78]

---

76 NMM ADM C/680, 26 September, 18 November & 23 December 1793; C/681, 8, 15 & 28 May 1794 (Treasury to Victualling Board); C/685, 7 January 1796 (Admiralty to Victualling Board).

77 £14,698.11.7½ was raised by sale, but the owners claimed £24,324.5.1¾.

78 NMM ADM C/681, 8 May 1794, from Treasury.

It was a pity that the Victualling Board were not in a strong enough position to decline the job but presumably, to use a modern idiom, it must have seemed like a good idea at the time.

As with the core tasks, most of these ad hoc tasks, especially those of an 'acute' nature, were dealt with as promptly and efficiently as the situations allowed. However, one suspects that these tasks would have been prominent in the way the Board were judged; the end result was to paint a rosy tinge on what might otherwise have been judged less than satisfactory performance. The chronic failure to deal with massive arrears of accounts cannot, by any standards, be seen as adequate performance.

6

Head Office Staff

WHEN ATTEMPTING to judge the competence and efficiency of the Victualling Board operation, it is necessary to know something about the people who ran and staffed that organisation: their political and social affiliations, their position in the overall naval and government hierarchy, their career paths and salary structures and how they were recruited. These issues did not remain static throughout the period; the salary structure changed in 1800 as a result of the deliberations of the Fees commissioners; and the hierarchical structure of the department, staffing and department functions were subjected to major changes in 1809 as a result of the recommendations of the Board of Revision. Here the personnel at the victualling office at Somerset Place in London are considered; clerical staff, artisans and other personnel at the victualling yards are considered in the next chapter, as is the general issue of staff supervision, disciplinary techniques, and the inter-relationships between staff and commissioners. With the sole exception of Mrs Bull, the housekeeper at Somerset Place, all the head office staff were male.

Problems of locating information on staff

Most of the people who worked in the victualling office at Somerset Place are shadowy figures, of whom little is known except their names. There are a few exceptions to this, mostly commissioners, for some of whom a little personal information is known, and for one department head whose career can be traced. It is possible, through the intermittent staffing and salary reports, and the occasional mentions in correspondence with the Admiralty, to track some of the career paths within the Victualling Office, together with salaries and retirement benefits, but with only a few exceptions that is all that can be found about them; there are no extant documents of the sort which would today be designated personnel files, nor is there any indication that such files were kept. Staffing levels were not high and it seems likely that on occasions when information was required about individuals, their department head would be able to supply it from memory. Where that information is recorded, in letters and minutes recommending promotions or superannuation, it is rarely more than a statement of length of service and comments to the effect that the individual was hardworking and deserving; or, even more rarely, that he was not.[1]

Some salary information has survived, mainly in the form of payment books, but with the exception of department heads and commissioners, where there are alphabetical indexes, this is mostly in the form of quarterly listings of actual payments, which are in the order in which the individuals collected their payments rather than any alphabetical or department order.[2] Some reports were produced when required for official enquiries, or when increases were mooted, and thus not at regular intervals. Some of the available reports list staff by name, others only by position within department; it is thus only possible to track the career movement of individuals at wide intervals, or when recommendations for promotion list the current position of the individual being suggested.

There is an equal dearth of information about the recruitment process, apart from a recommendation in the tenth report of the Board of Revision that each commissioner should take it in turn to nominate a candidate for vacant posts, with the chairman having the right to two nominations when his turn came round.[3] This wording suggests that a less organised nomination system had operated before, but no direct evidence for this has emerged from the correspondence or minutes, nor is there any evidence that any other method, such as advertising for candidates, was used. Whilst the commissioners could appoint junior clerks without referring to the Admiralty, they had to seek Admiralty approval for senior clerks and officers, who were then appointed by warrant.[4] Other than the occasions when internal scandals prompted replacements of department heads and others, there are few records of new clerical staff joining from outside, or of clerical staff departing except on retirement or death.

Nor is there any record of the basic competencies required of clerks; here, however, the official documents show that an ability to write a clear hand was desirable; whether it was an absolute requirement is not known, but it is noticeable that almost without exception, the writing in the letter and minute books, original out-letters, contracts and ledgers is clear and easy to read; the same cannot be said of the notes written by the commissioners.

---

1   For instance, the clerk Francis Meheux was described as generally indolent and with an 'inclination to tipple whenever he had an opportunity to do so': TNA ADM 110/69, ff. 261–4, 5 November 1814.
2   These listings are at TNA ADM 7/869–871 but are not complete for the period.
3   *BOR 10*, p. 31.
4   *Fees 8*, p. 555.

Spelling ability was not always as good as it might be, with some words consistently mis-spelled (for instance the word gauger is frequently spelled guager); and although arithmetical ability should have been a prerequisite for staff in the accounting departments, the addition in the contract ledgers is frequently faulty. There were numerous technical schools in London and other large cities, offering tuition in 'Italian' book-keeping (what is now known as double-entry book-keeping) and other subjects designed to suit the pupils for a career in commerce; this sort of training would have been equally useful for government employees, but there is no mention of any of the Victualling Office clerks having attended such schools.[5] The Board of Revision did remark on the recruitment of new clerks but it did not specify any basic qualifications, merely recommending a month's trial to ensure that they were 'properly qualified'. They also stated that such new entrants should be 'fifteen years of age', which suggests that younger boys had previously been acceptable.[6]

Hierarchical structure

Although it has been stated that the Navy Board was at the *centre* of the naval system, it was the Board of Admiralty which was at the *top* of the naval hierarchy, taking its directions from Parliament, through a secretary of state and the cabinet.[7] It is certainly the place from which most of the instructions and orders for the Victualling Board emanated and it is clear from the nature and tone of the correspondence that the Admiralty was superior.[8] The head of the Admiralty was known as the First Lord and was a member of the Cabinet; all the seats on this board were political appointments, although many were held by naval officers who were also Members of Parliament. As well as having the overall responsibility for naval operations and strategy under the Secretary of State for War, the Admiralty directed the civil side of the navy, commissioned naval officers and their appointments to ships, and had some influence in the promotion of warrant officers.

Below the Admiralty were the four subordinate boards.

---

5   Nicholas Hans, *New Trends in Education in the Eighteenth Century* (London, 1951), passim.
6   *BOR* 10, p. 31.
7   Rodger, *Command*, p. 256.
8   The correspondence from the Admiralty to the Victualling Board is at NMM ADM C series.

The Navy Board

Its functions were more wide-ranging than any of the others: it had the responsibility for the fabric of all His Majesty's ships and vessels, including small boats; and it not only maintained such vessels but when new ones were needed built these in its own dockyards or arranged for them to be built in commercial yards under its supervision; its British dockyards alone employed over 15,000 workers.[9] It also kept the yards round Britain and abroad supplied with naval stores such as timber, masts and spars, sails, cordage and all the other items needed to keep ships in good repair; and supported the Civil Architect and Engineer whose responsibility for the fabric of the dockyards extended to other naval real estate. Due to its earlier inception, it was perhaps on a slightly higher level than the other three subordinate boards, but it did not stand in the reporting line between the Victualling Board and the Admiralty. To the casual reader some of the correspondence, notably instructions to victual individual ships, might appear to show that the Navy Board was superior to the Victualling Board but its function here was merely to pass on instructions from the Admiralty.

It also asked the Victualling Board, on a regular basis, for fiscal information on anticipated victualling costs and outstanding bills of exchange, told it how many men were to be fed in the coming year, and asked for an estimate of cost, but this was because one of its functions was the consolidation of such figures for the annual estimates and to pass on to the Treasury. It also had control of warrant officers, and dealt with wages payments for ships' crews at all levels. Although it organised all other supplies which were neither medical, edible nor considered 'victualling stores', the Navy Board did not handle any of the armament; this was the exclusive province of the Board of Ordnance, a separate organisation outside the naval administration, which also supplied the army. There were many regular interactions between the Navy and Victualling Boards including exchanges of information and paperwork on pursers' and commissioned officers' accounts, and the supply of items such as coopers' goods or cordage from the yards of one board to the other.

The Board for Sick and Wounded Seamen (the Sick and Hurt Board)

Its function was to care for the medical needs of seamen, by providing and supervising naval hospitals both afloat and ashore, and by running the system of naval surgeons and their equipment and medicines on warships. This board was notoriously incompetent in its administration, and in 1806 it was disbanded and its function taken over by the Transport Board as its 'medical department'; in 1817, when the Transport Board itself was disbanded, the medical department passed under the control of the

9   R Morriss, *Royal Dockyards*, passim.

Victualling Board. Prior to this date, the dealings between this board and the Victualling Board consisted almost entirely of the arrangements for delivering meat for portable soup to the soup house at Ratcliffe Cross, and receiving lemon juice into the victualling stores and issuing it on behalf of the Sick and Hurt Board/medical department of the Transport Board.

The Transport Board[10]

Both historically, and during this period, the Transport Board was set up for the duration of a specific war and disbanded during peace. Its main function was to obtain shipping for the other naval boards, the Ordnance Board and the army at reasonable rates; there was no Transport Board during the American war and this led to unnecessary competition between the various boards and the Treasury (who during much of that war were handling the food and other supply requirements of the army) which had caused a sharp increase in freight charges.[11] When the Victualling Board needed shipping to send provisions and victualling stores to its yards abroad, or needed a vessel to serve as a victualling depot at one of the main anchorages, it wrote to the Transport Board stating what tonnage was needed; the Transport Board then found, surveyed, and hired appropriate vessels.[12] Occasionally, when the required tonnage was insufficient to warrant hiring a whole ship, the Transport Board found a merchant vessel going in the right direction which was prepared to take the cargo on ordinary freight terms. The Transport Board also had responsibility for sick prisoners of war after 1795, and it may have been this function which led to its inheriting the functions of the Sick and Hurt Board in 1806.[13]

The Victualling Board

Its functions were to provide the Royal Navy, and during the French Revolutionary and Napoleonic wars, part of the army, with provisions and to account for these to government. Like the other three boards, the Victualling Board was run by a number of commissioners appointed by letters patent.[14] It had no responsibility for the health of seamen and did not consider this issue when dealing with foodstuffs.

---

10   Strictly speaking the Transport Board took its directions from the Treasury, but it has always been considered to be one of the subsidiaries of the Admiralty and took much of its direction from the latter; its correspondence and minutes are held at TNA under the 'ADM' prefix.

11   Syrett, *Shipping and the American War*, pp. 101–2.

12   Shipping to send provisions etc. between Deptford and the other British yards was arranged by the Victualling Board's own hoytaker.

13   Rodger, *Command*, p. 475.

14   These are in the Patent Rolls at TNA C66.

The Commissioners

These commissioners were chosen by the Admiralty and it is probable that, at least before 1809, the criteria for choice were more likely to be based on the pressure of political patronage than any consideration of the managerial competence of the individual or even their experience in naval matters. (There was a long-standing tradition of giving such board positions to people acting as private secretary to the first lord of the Admiralty to provide them with an enhanced income.)[15] However, since the victualling commissioners were excluded from sitting in Parliament by the 'Place' Act, such appointments could only have been in the nature of favours to people who did have a vote or could influence a vote.[16] Once appointed, regardless of the frequent changes in the government and the Board of Admiralty, they were secure in their position until such time as they died or chose to leave (usually because they had obtained a better position, or had became too ill to continue) or, as happened in 1808 and 1822, were found out in some misconduct or deemed to have failed to perform their duties satisfactorily.[17] To what extent the commissioners were politically useful to their patrons has not emerged; without a vote, they could not directly affect events in Parliament, but may have had friends or relatives who could.

The events of late 1808/early 1809,[18] when a combination of the Board of Revision's reports and the discovery of misdeeds by victualling office staff led to the replacement of three commissioners, demonstrate that such action could create political embarrassment in Parliament. A motion was proposed by Admiral Sir Charles Pole (chairman of the Commission of Naval Enquiry and an ally of St Vincent) on the necessity to appoint 'professional' and 'indefatigable' commissioners, and questions were asked about the reasons for the changes and the decision to replace two of the commissioners with 'military' men (i.e. ex-army). One member remarked that from conversations overheard 'both within and without this house' the purpose of the motion was to lay the blame for the arrears of accounts on the 'present Board of Admiralty'; the whig, Henry Martin, questioned the decision to retire John Marsh 'in pretense of his age and infirmities' and replace him as chairman by 'a person much the senior of him and the person so appointed had been longer in the victualling office than any other'. This can only have been Towry, who (as reported by Basil Cochrane) was originally appointed Chairman in place of Marsh, a decision which was then changed

---

15   Sainty, *Admiralty Officials*, p. 65 gives the salary for these private secretaries as £300 p.a., but this only commenced in 1800.

16   15 Geo II, c. 22.

17   See Chapter 8 for the 1808 and 1822 incidents.

18   See Chapter 8.

to make Searle chairman.[19] Martin went on to query the forced retirement of Budge and Moody, remarking that since there was a problem with arrears of accounts, surely Moody, 'who was allowed to be one of the best accountants in the country' was the best person to sort out the problem. (It does not seem to have occurred to him that Moody had, despite his long service, failed to do so.) The Admiralty secretary, Wellesley Pole, defended the changes: Marsh, he said, had been allowed to retire at his own request (this does not correspond with Marsh's version of events: 'to my great surprise [Lord Mulgrave will be making changes and has arranged for me to have a pension …]'),[20] Budge was incapacitated by gout and Moody had suffered a physical decline and was 'as incapable of discharging the duties of his office as if he was defunct'. William Windham asked why, 'if age were considered a ground for removal … Towry was retained?' (Towry was aged 76 at that time). Knight suggests that it was Towry (who had whig connections through the Grey family) who had 'blown the whistle' on the situation; this is unlikely, given that it was Towry's department which was at fault, but even so, one wonders why the debate did not cover the misdeeds of the victualling office clerks who were fired earlier that year.[21]

During the whole of the period of this study, this board consisted of seven commissioners who, until the recommendations of the Board of Revision were put into effect at the beginning of 1809, operated as a single body under a chairman; after this date they operated as two committees, only coming together as a full board twice a week. Three commissioners constituted a 'board' (quorum).[22]

During the 1793–1815 period a total of twenty-one individuals served as victualling commissioners, their periods of service shown in Table 2. The sources of information on these commissioners are varied and widely spread. Hardly surprisingly for men who were prepared to abandon an active naval career for a civilian role, those who had been commissioned naval officers do not seem to have distinguished themselves at sea.[23]

19   Cochrane, *An Enquiry* (1823 version), pp. 110–12.
20   NMM BGR/35, 14 October 1808, Marsh's autobiographical account.
21   The Parliamentary debate is reported in Cobbett's *Parliamentary Debates*, vol 13; and in *The Times*, 27 March 1809. The misdeeds of the victualling office staff are discussed in Chapter 8.
22   *SCF* 32, p. 3. See also R J B Knight, 'Politics and Trust in Victualling the Navy, 1783–1815', *Mariner's Mirror*, 94.2, p. 143.
23   An alphabetical listing of all these commissioners, together with such bibliographical information as has been found, is in Appendix C together with a full listing of sources.

Table 2: Victualling Board Commissioners – period of service

	S Marshall	A Chorley	G Cherry*	F Stephens	W Boscawen	G P Towry	F J Hartwell	J Hunt	R S Moody	Hon J Rodney	J Marsh*	J Harrison	C Cunningham	W Budge	J C Searle*	T Welsh	Hon E Stewart	N Brown	J Aubin	F E Edgecumbe	R W Hay
1815						till 1817									till 1822	till 1822		till 1830	till 1822	till 1832	till 1825
1814						×									×	×		×	×	×	×
1813						×									×	×		×	×	×	×
1812						×									×	×	×	×	×	×	×
1811				×		×									×	×	×	×	×	×	
1810				×	×	×									×	×	×	×	×		
1809			×	×	×	×			×						×	×	×	×			
1808			×	×	×	×			×		×				×	×	×	×			
1807			×	×	×	×			×	×	×				×	×					
1806			×	×	×	×			×	×	×	×		×	×	×					
1805			×	×	×	×			×	×	×	×	×	×							
1804			×	×	×	×			×	×	×	×	×								
1803			×	×	×	×			×	×	×	×	×								
1802			×	×	×	×			×	×	×	×									
1801			×	×	×	×			×	×	×	×									
1800			×	×	×	×			×	×	×										
1799			×	×	×	×	×	×	×	×	×										
1798			×	×	×	×	×	×	×	×	×										
1797			×	×	×	×	×	×	×	×											
1796			×	×	×	×	×		×	×											
1795			×	×	×	×	×		×												
1794	×	×	×	×	×	×	×														
1793	×	×	×	×	×	×															

Those marked * served as chairman.

Five were captains (Cunningham, Hartwell, Marshall, Rodney, Searle), one had been a lieutenant (Towry), one a midshipman (Edgecumbe) and four had been pursers (Aubin, Brown, Cherry, Stephens). Two had been army officers (Stewart, Welsh). Two had been Members of Parliament prior to joining the board (Rodney, Stewart). Only two commissioners are to be found in *The Dictionary of National Biography*, one with his own entry (Rodney) and one (Towry) mentioned in an entry for someone else (Lord Ellenborough). For some there is a little personal information in the appendices to the Eighth Report of the fees commissioners. Seven had worked for other naval boards or government departments (Aubin, Budge, Chorley, Edgecumbe, Hunt, Marsh, Stephens) and seven went to other boards or government departments when they left the Victualling Board (Cunningham, Hartwell, Hay, Hunt, Marshall, Rodney, Stewart); four had been admirals' secretaries (Aubin, Brown, Hunt, Stephens) and five had been or were simultaneously secretary to first lords of the Admiralty (Budge, Edgecumbe, Harrison, Hay, Hunt). But for the rest there is no widely available information other than their appointments, retirement or death in the correspondence between the Admiralty and the Victualling Board. These retirements and deaths are of interest; four commissioners (Boscawen, Brown, Chorley and Towry) died in office and six were stated to have 'retired' but were actually removed (Aubin, Budge, Marsh, Moody, Searle, Welsh) although several of these were in poor health. It is likely that all these elderly or ill commissioners would have functioned at considerably less than full capacity for some time before they retired/died, which suggests a willingness on the part of the other Board members and the Admiralty to tolerate this situation.

For only a few of the commissioners is there any strong indication of character: Searle in his Victualling Board correspondence on various matters; Towry in his reaction to the 1784 case of the Navy agent Robertson, his responses to the enquiries of the Board of Revision and in Basil Cochrane's published complaints about the handling of his accounts; Marsh in his journal; and the Hon. John Rodney in various sources including *The Dictionary of National Biography* and O'Byrne's *A Naval Biographical Dictionary*.

Searle seems to have been very status conscious. When there was a general change in naval uniforms in 1810, he wrote to the Admiralty wanting a ruling on the appropriate uniform to be worn by 'post captains now being commissioners of the Victualling Board'; the result of this was an Admiralty Order founded on an Order in Council stating that those who had been passed over for promotion should wear buttons showing the arms of the Victualling Board, but those who had not been passed over for promotion could continue to wear the same uniform as serving post captains. [24] Searle was also keen on improving his finances: for instance in 1807 he pointed out that the clerk of the survey at Deptford dockyard got £100 for house rent while he only received £65; he did have a point here as the rate had been set in 1704, but perhaps he would not have made a fuss had he not discovered that the dockyard official was getting more than he was; the result of that plea was an increase to £130. [25] He also, in May 1807, wrote to Thomas Grenville, who had just stepped down as First Lord of the Admiralty, suggesting that he might transfer to a Navy Board post (which would have paid more). [26] There also came a point when he decided he should be paid more for his additional duties in connection with army victualling, despite an additional amount already having been granted for these duties; now Searle wanted more, mainly, it seems, because he had discovered that the Deputy Comptroller of the Navy Board was paid considerably more than the Chairman of the Victualling Board. In 1811 he wrote a personal note to Charles Yorke, the current first lord of the Admiralty, then sent a memorial to the Admiralty to pass on to the Treasury to ask for this; it was refused, but he must have persevered because the next item in the files on this topic is a letter from the Prince Regent remarking on the 'very zealous, able and efficient manner in which he has discharged the important duties of his situation [with especial regard to the army in the Peninsula]' and awarding him an immediate lump sum of £1,000 plus an annual salary increment of £300 for the duration of the war. [27] Searle had had a varied career at sea, much of it under Lord Keith, who was probably influential in Searle's move to the Victualling Board in 1806. No explanation has been found for his abandoning his sea-going career; it may have been for some family reason, or for the considerable difference in salary: a post captain at that time earned less than half of the amount paid to Victualling Board commissioners. [28]

The main impression of Towry is of pomposity (this being evidenced by various comments made by him to the Board of Revision) and of a desire to have his own way. An early incident demonstrates this: in 1783, the navy agent William Robertson had been accused by his clerk Robert Douglas of passing counterfeit affidavits to obtain half pay for a surgeon who was not

---

24   NMM ADM C/727, 22 September 1810. Searle's query was worded in a way that suggests he was enquiring on behalf of other commissioners in the same position, but since he was the only one at the time, that seems to have been an attempt to disguise his personal interest.
25   NMM ADM D/49, 6 June 1807.
26   I am grateful to Roger Knight for this piece of information.
27   TNA ADM 109/102, 24 October 1793; 109/108, 9 September 1813; NMM YOR/ 16a/92–8 (Yorke papers); NMM ADM DP/31A, 29 April 1811.
28   £800 for a victualling commissioner, £364 for a post captain. Michael Lewis, *A Social History of the Navy 1793–1815* (London, 1960), p. 294.

entitled to it as he was employed at Haslar Hospital at the time; Robertson was tried at the Old Bailey but acquitted on this case.[29] An anonymous letter, which was probably written by Douglas, then accused Robertson of obtaining a balance bill from the Victualling Board for the purser Gambold, of the *Superb*, again using counterfeit papers. The Victualling Board secretary's chief clerk, Wilkins, was then accused of communicating the contents of this letter to Robertson before the original reached the victualling commissioners. When called before the Board to explain this, Wilkins suggested that he might have left the letter open on his desk when he went out of the office, where Robertson could have read it if he had come in. The Board did not accept this explanation and Towry, who had oversight of the secretary's department, stated that 'he could no longer confide in his clerk'.[30] Wilkins was suspended pending a better explanation. Maurice Burgoyne, the chairman at the time, ordered that 'suspicion [of Wilkins] should be made public' in every Victualling Board office as a deterrent to others who may have been tempted to copy him.[31] Over the following twelve weeks Wilkins was called before the Board several times, but as he was unable to provide a better explanation, a vote was taken at a board meeting when only five of the commissioners were present; the result was three against two for his dismissal. A further meeting, with all the commissioners present, voted again and this time the vote was four to three to retain Wilkins. This was deemed so unusual that the matter was referred to the Admiralty, which required each commissioner to explain why he had voted as he did. Burgoyne explained that there was a long-standing problem of official papers being communicated to people who should not have seen them, and that clerks had been admonished for this many times but the practice continued; thus Burgoyne wanted Wilkins dismissed not only to get rid of a person under suspicion but also to serve as an example to the other clerks.

The commissioners who wanted Wilkins reinstated felt that although he may have been indiscreet, no motive had been proved for his deliberately passing the content of the letter to Robertson as a favour; if he had wanted to do this, they said, it would have been better to hide or destroy the letter. Towry demanded to be permitted to dismiss Wilkins, asking the Admiralty to decide whether he or whether the Board as a whole was in charge of the staff of his office; the Admiralty decided it was the latter, and Wilkins was

---

29 NMM ADM DP/4, 23 July 1784.
30 Morriss states that Towry was the secretary himself; Morriss may have gained this impression from Towry's statement that he had been 'entrusted with the care of the branch of secretary beside the general business of the board' as meaning that he was the secretary. (*Naval Power*, pp. 111–15.) This is incorrect, the secretary at that time was John Watts.
31 NMM ADM DP/4, 14 April 1784. Morriss gives this as being in DP/3.

reinstated after an eleven-month suspension.[32] At this time the Atkinson affair was at its climax and there was a desire to restore confidence in the victualling office; one can understand that Towry agreed with Burgoyne that this would be served by dismissing Wilkins, but given Towry's very recent appointment to the Board, the incident does suggest not only a desire to assert his personal authority above the usual joint decision-making of the board, but also a confidence in the influence behind him.

This influence stemmed from the Grey family of Howick; Towry's grand-mother was Mary Grey, and a letter in the St Vincent papers referring to a Towry visit to Howick shows that he maintained contact with this family. (The 2nd Viscount Howick was First Lord of the Admiralty from February to September 1806.) He must also have benefited from the influence of his son-in-law Lord Ellenborough (Chief Justice on the King's Bench from 1802 and part of the 'ministry of all the talents').[33] Basil Cochrane certainly saw Towry as the chief cause of delay in passing his accounts and did not hesitate to say so in his various pamphlets. Cochrane alleged that Towry had, in order to retain his position as deputy chairman of the Victualling Board when the recommendations of the Board of Revision were put into effect, pulled strings to have the Order in Council outlining the new Board scrapped and replaced with another. The Board of Revision had recom-mended that the chairman of the Victualling Board should be a civilian and the deputy chairman a naval captain; Towry had never risen beyond lieutenant and Searle, who became the chairman, had been a captain. This certainly does appear strange, as the Admiralty's order on the Board of Revision's recommendations was that the whole thing should be put into effect, this after the Victualling Board had stated that they agreed with all the recommendations. Cochrane said that Towry should have retired due to his age rather than continuing as deputy chairman. Towry remained in that position until his death in 1817 aged 84; by 1813 his handwriting had become rather shaky.[34]

The Hon. John Rodney was the elder son of Admiral George Bridges Rodney and had been promoted by his father to post captain at the age of fifteen. There is some subsequent confusion over his naval career: O'Byrne says (without stating the reason) that he was court-martialled and dismissed the service in 1799, before being reinstated in the same year; however, his name does not appear on the list of court-martials at the National Archives. Another story says that he had a leg amputated in 1785 and was super-seded from his command of *Vengeance* as a result. In 1789 *The Naval Atlantis* wrote scathingly of his character 'Volatility of spirit and the aspiring ardour

32   Morriss gives this story in more detail, *Naval Power*, pp. 111–15.
33   www.oxforddnb.com/articles/1616142-article.html, downloaded 19 March 2007.
34   For instance, see his signature on NMM DP/33b, 25 October 1813.

of youth, which often leads to vanity, are very strong traits in Captain Rodney's character.'[35] In view of all this it is no great surprise that when he obtained what he presumably thought was a better appointment as Chief Secretary to the Government of Ceylon he just went off in August 1803 without bothering to inform the Victualling Board. It was not until October that the Board discovered why he had not attended the office and reported this to the Admiralty; it is strange that they had left it so long.[36]

John Marsh's family included a Navy Board commissioner who had also served on the Victualling Board (George), a banker whose firm also acted as navy agents (William, of Marsh and Creed) and a daughter-in-law whose father had been the agent victualler for the East Indies (Arthur Cuthbert); he had himself served as Consul at Malaga and on the Transport Board. His cousin Milbourne had married a Lucy Gosling, who may perhaps have been related to William Gosling, the Victualling Board secretary. His journal and copy letters do not give the impression of a particularly dynamic man and this may have been part of the reason he was forcibly retired in 1808.[37]

Commissioners' duties

Before the start of the French revolutionary war, the Board met regularly on four days each week, with an occasional fifth day, until the middle of December 1792 when they met regularly on five days each week.[38] After the war started they met every day except Sunday, including holidays (and including Christmas Day).

Like all other naval departments of the time, the Victualling Board operated on the principle of collective responsibility, with all correspondence being signed by a minimum quorum of commissioners. This makes it difficult, if not impossible, to gain a picture of the competence of the individual commissioners, as with only a few exceptions such as visitations to the victualling yards, and some comments from Towry, the commissioners responsible for particular actions cannot be identified.

Until 1784 the commissioners took it in turn to act as chairman; then the Admiralty directed that the commissioner in charge of the department of the Accountant for Cash should take the chair, the others taking precedence in this order of department: the accountant for stores, the hoytaker, the brewhouse, the cutting house, the bake house, the cooperage.[39] There were

35 'Nauticus Junior', *The Naval Atlantis; or a Display of the Characters of Post Captains who Served During the Late War*, Pt II (London, 1789), pp. 111–12.
36 TNA ADM 110/49, f. 372, 1 October 1803.
37 NMM BGR/35; www.jjhc.information/ (family history website).
38 As evidenced by the minutes: TNA ADM 111/125.
39 TNA ADM 12/55, section 102.5, 3 November 1784.

some shifts of these departmental responsibilities over time, for example in March 1794 Francis Stephens was assigned the task of looking after the brewhouse 'instead of the branch of the Inspectorate of the Cutting House and Master Butcher'.[40]

The system of allocating a specific department to each commissioner did not, unfortunately, give the degree of efficiency which was its intended purpose. Two of these departments were based in Somerset Place (those dealing with cash accounts and store accounts) and the others mainly at Deptford. A large part of the hoytaker's job disappeared in 1794 when the Transport Board was reinstated, the cutting house functioned for no more than six months each year, and brewing at Deptford was only on a minor scale. None of the commissioners responsible for the manufacturing and packing branches at the outports seem to have made regular individual reports on their departments; nor is there any evidence of these individual commissioners paying regular visits to Deptford; the minutes show that the commissioners spent almost all their time at Somerset Place and the Board of Revision report remarks on the amount of time spent by the officers from Deptford coming to London to consult 'their' commissioner.[41] Visits to Deptford would have been comparatively easy as the board possessed a barge with an enclosed passenger compartment; but on the few occasions when travelling arrangements for visits of commissioners to Deptford are reported in the minutes these are, as with visits to the other yards, in the context of agreeing their expenses for chaise hire. [42]

The only evidence, if indeed it is such, of direct control of each department reporting to, or taking instructions from, 'their' commissioner, is the comment in the Board of Revision 11th report to the effect that this reporting line was used by the heads of departments at Deptford as a reason for refusing to take instructions from, or report to, the superintendent of the yard.[43] It was not until 1809 when Deptford was put on the same footing as the other yards and the superintendant was replaced by an agent victualler that this situation changed.

As well as the changes at Deptford in 1809, the day-to-day activities of the Board were changed so that they operated as two committees (one for general business and the other for cash and store accounts), each of which met on two days each week, with the full board meeting on the other two days. At this point, the precedence changed to: the chairman, the deputy chairman, the first commissioner of the committee for cash and store accounts, the other commissioners according to their appointment date.

---

40   NMM ADM C/681, 15 March 1794.
41   *BOR 10*, p. 22.
42   TNA ADM 110/70, f. 71, 7 April 1815, request to Navy Board for new cushions and curtains for the barge.
43   *BOR 11*, p. 27.

Each committee dealt with all the departments, but the committee for general business, as well as dealing with all the correspondence and pursery accounts, dealt with the parts which related to 'the provision, care, conversion and distribution of stores, [both at home and abroad] and to the economy of manual labour', while the committee for cash and store accounts dealt with 'the receipt and disbursements of money and to the receipt, issue and remains of stores', which included dealing with all accounts except those of pursery, and 'the speedy recovery of all outstanding balances and money'.[44]

The chairman's duties were also stated for the first time: as well as the obvious tasks of presiding at board meetings (at which he had a second vote) and superintending the work of the committees, he was authorised to grant leave of absence to the other commissioners but had to obtain this for himself from the Admiralty.[45] He was to serve as the interface between the Victualling Board and the Admiralty, Treasury, and 'the great offices of state' and, more interestingly, to handle secret services. The latter were, not surprisingly, undefined, but they would originate with the First Lord of the Admiralty and were not to be reported to the Victualling Board until after the event.

The new arrangements also moved the tasks of signing minor letters and minutes from a quorum of commissioners to the secretary, tasks which the Board of Revision described as '[diverting] a considerable portion of their time … from the business of greater importance'. This was clear recognition of the necessity for the commissioners to concentrate on important matters instead of micro-managing every minor task as had been their practice. That they did so is shown not only from this report but also from the minutes and the endorsements on the in-letters, all of which are marked as having been read at the Board meetings; many include instructions on the action to be taken which should have been unnecessary: for instance the instructions to victual named ships at named yards are endorsed 'write the agent'.

Clerical departments at Somerset Place

There were three departments at the Victualling Office in Somerset Place: those of the secretary, who supported the Board and dealt with all correspondence, and those of the accountant for cash and the accountant for stores, the latter two divided into smaller sections dealing with specific aspects of the work. The clerks in these departments consisted of the

---

44   *BOR 10*, pp. 26, 35–44.
45   Before this date, there are several letters from the Admiralty authorising such leave of absence for various commissioners, for instance NMM ADM C/696, 20 October 1801, Commissioner Harrison was granted six weeks leave of absence.

established (i.e. permanent) staff and other clerks who were employed when additional help was needed; the latter are listed as 'extra' or 'temporary supernumerary' clerks. The extra clerks could be, and often were, promoted into permanent positions, for instance in 1811 when an additional thirteen clerks were agreed for the establishment, the order required that they be taken from the existing extra clerks, not recruited from outside.[46] The established and extra clerks received an annual salary paid quarterly, the temporary supernumerary clerks were paid weekly.[47]

Inevitably the pressure of work in wartime meant more staff were required; in 1788 there was a total of sixty-three clerical staff at Somerset Place, by July 1815 this had risen to 151.[48]

Career progression

There was no guarantee of any sort of career progression at any level, although before 1809 the commissioners did expect to be moved up the precedence list of departments. This did not necessarily mean that the deputy chairman could expect to inherit the chair in due course; Towry did not do so, and Searle, who took the chair in 1809 was not deputy prior to that time. Indeed, Searle was made chairman so quickly after his initial appointment to the Board, and without serving a period as deputy chairman, that one might surmise that he was recruited specifically to fill that role.

As far as the junior clerks were concerned, as they remarked in their 1811 petition, progression through the ranks was extremely slow. Far from being, to use a modern metaphor, a simple climb up a ladder, the progression could be better described as a slow climb up a mountain comprised of cliffs and plateaus. In the early stages the plateaus were comparatively narrow and the cliffs were low, and the view from the top of one cliff was little different than from the plateau below. As the climb continued, the plateaus grew wider and the cliffs higher, and the chance of any real likelihood of reaching even the position of chief clerk receded; there was only one during this period who rose all the way to a seat on the board (this was Moody, who joined the victualling office in 1759 and became a commissioner thirty-five years later in 1794).

For instance, in the secretary's office at the end of 1815, the time gap in length of service between the eighth and first extra clerks was two years

---

46 NMM ADM C/731, 11 September 1811.
47 NMM ADM D/49, 4 February 1807.
48 On 6 December 1815 the number of staff required at Somerset Place for a peacetime establishment was set at 115 (this number excludes commissioners, the warders, messengers and housekeeper): TNA ADM 110/71 ff. 263–5. The 1788 figures are taken from *Fees 8*, pp. 584–5. See Appendix D for details of the positions.

and two months (four years six months and six years eight months service respectively) and the gap between the first extra clerk and the eleventh
established clerk one year four months (six years eight months and eight
years respectively) between the eleventh and fourth clerks three years nine
months (eight years exactly and eleven years nine months respectively) but
between the fourth and third clerks it was eight years eight months. The
second clerk had twenty-eight years six months service and the chief clerk
had thirty-six years two months service. The chief clerk had been in that
position for twenty-one years and eight months, and the secretary himself had a total of thirty-five years service and had also been in position
for twenty-one years and eight months. Both these, and the second clerk,
remained in those positions for a further six years.

Unfortunately we lack data on staff turnover; the fact that names disappear from such lists as are available without being reported in the
correspondence as retiring, dying or being sacked for misconduct, indicates
that many did leave for other reasons and suggests that the popular impression of people staying in such jobs for life may be mistaken.

Sparse as the information on the commissioners is, there is even less on
the department heads. Apart from the details in the recommendations for
superannuation, which are usually confined to their age, length of service, deteriorating health and the Board's judgement on the fact that they
had been hard-working and deserving, information on the career paths of
these clerical staff is only that which can be garnered from the intermittent
listings of staff which mention names as well as positions, and occasional
recommendations in the correspondence for someone (who was, of course,
hard-working and deserving) to be promoted into a vacant position, or who
was being sent off on some special duty, as was Richard Ford on several
occasions.[49]

Recruitment premiums and salaries

Philip Harling deals with the issue of fees and perquisites, and of recruitment premiums, patronage and sinecures, taking one of the contemporary
descriptions of 'old corruption' as part of his title in *The Waning of 'Old
Corruption'*. According to the jacket description of this book, Harling

> argues that the mostly Pittite governing elite helped to allay the suspi-
> cions of parasitism at the root of the familiar critique of 'old corruption'
> by responding to intense pressure to sanitize government; [this was

---

49   Information about Ford's career occurs throughout the correspondence. See par-
     ticularly his post-'retirement' letter of 28 January 1822 which outlines his career
     (TNA ADM 1/4601).

done] by eliminating … the grant of lucrative sinecures and unmerited pensions, and by ostentatiously dedicating themselves to public business rather than the pursuit of wasteful privileges for themselves and their hangers-on.

The controversial issue of sinecures and patronage was seen by radical politicians as corruption; the system had arisen from the concept that government offices were freehold property and thus could be bought and sold, such offices having originally been at the gift of the monarch, or in some cases (as far back as James I) having been sold by the monarch. This latter practice was less prevalent in Britain than elsewhere on the continent but there were still numerous sinecure offices.[50]

The British navy, being run by a hierarchy of boards, was less prone to the purchase of positions than some other government departments, but at the beginning of this period it still operated on the basis of paying its civilian personnel small salaries which they boosted by collecting fees, gratuities and perquisites from various sources. The nature and amounts of these augmentations, and the officers and clerks who received them at the Victualling Office in London and at the outports, are detailed in the eighth report of the Fees commissioners.[51] These are numerous and complex, but to give some examples:

- The accountant for cash and his chief clerk each received 2/6 per bill for despatching bills of freight and demurrage, and from 2/6 to £2.2.0 (depending on the amount involved) for bills to tradesmen and artificers.
- His first and second extra clerks received respectively 2/6 per search for checking that masters of victuallers had accounted properly for returned casks, and 2/6 to 5/- for entering each bill of exchange.
- The clerk of the cheque's first clerk received 1/- per man for making out monthly pay notes for day coopers (which allowed them to borrow on their unpaid salaries).

In 1798:

- The accountant for cash reported an average income over the past three years of £3,169.13.0, of which only £120 was salary.
- His chief clerk reported an average income over the past three years of £1,722.2.2 of which only £60 was salary.
- His second and third clerks reported an average income over the past three years of £688.10.0 and £574.0.6 respectively of which only £80 in each case was salary.[52]

---

50   Brewer, *Sinews*, pp. 16–17.
51   *Fees 8*, pp. 695–706.
52   Ibid., pp. 20–1.

With such substantial rewards available at the higher levels, in several cases totalling more than the salaries received by the victualling commissioners (who did not receive any share in the fees) it is not surprising that the officers and clerks would have been prepared to pay premiums in order to obtain their jobs.[53] In some cases these would have been lump sums, in others they took the form of paying an agreed annual amount. The victualling commissioners told the Fees commissioners that although it had been the practice to receive premiums on the appointment of clerks in the Victualling Office, it was no longer done, although the custom did still prevail at the outports.[54]

No premiums as such were paid at the Victualling Office during the period studied, although they had been earlier; they were specifically forbidden after 1800.[55] However, in 1800 when the fees were stopped and larger salaries were awarded (but not large enough to compensate for the loss of fees), it transpired that in 1794, the then secretary, John Watts, had benefited from an arrangement with his immediate subordinates which effectively enhanced his pension. The chief, second, third and fourth clerks in the secretary's office had agreed between themselves to pay Watts an annual annuity totalling £200 to top up the officially offered pension of £150 so that he could retire and they could each move up one position. This was made up of £115 from the new secretary, £55 from the new chief clerk, £20 from the new second clerk, and £10 from the new third clerk.[56]

This had obviously been acceptable to them when Watts' retirement allowed each of these clerks to move up a step, thus bringing a large increase in fee income, but less so when they lost the fees which they would have enjoyed.[57] Having to continue this annual payment on their new salaries would, they said, cause them 'peculiar hardship' and they requested that the Crown should take over this payment: it would not, they pointed out pragmatically, continue for too long as Watts was 'upwards of seventy years old [and thus could not] in the ordinary course of nature, continue [to be] a charge to the public of long duration'.[58] After some deliberation, the Admiralty passed this request on to the Privy Council and an Order in Council was made in February 1801 to increase the pension paid to

---

53   Nor, as will be seen in Chapter 8, that after their overall income was reduced in 1800 to a 'salary only' basis, some found other ways to augment their income.
54   Ibid., p. 575.
55   *SCF* 32, pp. 101–2.
56   John Watts retired in 1794. TNA ADM 111/130, 18 January 1794; 110/46, ff. 122–4, 18 April 1800.
57   Their total average income for the three years to 1797 had been £3,169.11.3, £1,699.7.2, £899.3.4 and £498.14.8 respectively (*SCF* 32, pp. 26–7); their new salaries from 1800 were £880, £600, £350 and £200 respectively.
58   TNA ADM 110/46, ff 122–4, 18 April 1800.

Watts to £350 pa, on condition that he relinquished all claim to the four clerks who had been topping up his pension; however, this came with a strongly worded directive that such a solution would not be countenanced in future.[59]

The Fees commissioners recommended that the system of fees as part of salaries should be replaced by a salary-only system. They also recommended that clerks should no longer be allowed to act as agents for contractors and naval officers. Although not stated in these terms by any of the historians noted above, or by the Fees commissioners, encouraging what should have been exclusively government servants to derive a major part of their income from that government's suppliers and what we might call franchisees (i.e. the ships' pursers and other officers), inevitably created a conflict of interest, so it is hardly surprising that some clerks were persuaded to push the interest of their 'clients' before that of others. It is, however, surprising that no-one foresaw that the large (in some cases, very large) differentials between the new salaries and the old fee based incomes, imposed without compensation, would inevitably lead to trouble.

However, what the members of the enquiry saw as desirable and what the politicians of the day saw as feasible and likely to be popular were two different things. Although the Fees commissioners had finished their work and reported in 1788, it was not until 1800 that their salary recommendations for the Victualling Board and its staff were put into effect (and not until 1809 that the sale of offices was forbidden by statute).[60] John Breihan believes that the delay was caused by Pitt's procrastination and political manoeuvrings.[61] The norm was for such enquiries to be conducted, as was the predecessor to this enquiry on public accounts,[62] by a board of seven or eight members; the enquiry into fees had only three members, and these less than impressive choices; it was also the norm for the results of such enquiries to be presented to Parliament, but this one was to go to the Privy Council, with any reforms established by Order in Council.[63] The reports relating to the naval offices were delivered in 1788 but before they could pass the Privy Council the King's illness and the regency crisis intervened

59 NMM ADM C/695, 29 April 1801, referring to an Order in Council of 20 February 1801.
60 49 Geo III, c126, ss. 3 & 4.
61 John R Breihan, 'William Pitt and the Commission on Fees 1785–1801', *The Historical Journal*, 27 (1984), pp. 59–81.
62 20 Geo III, c54 'For appointing and enabling commissioners to examine, take and state the public accounts of the Kingdom ...'
63 The commissioners were Sir John Dick, 'aged former diplomat', and nearly blind; William Molleson, 'a shady character, eventually dismissed in 1794 for official improprieties', and Francis Baring, 'becoming deaf'. (Breihan, 'William Pitt', p. 63).

and they were effectively shelved, to the disgust of the comptroller of the navy, Charles Middleton, who had been a prime mover in their instigation. They did not emerge again until 1793, and then with excuses about the cost of having them printed. There was more procrastination, this time taking the form of consultation with the Admiralty; it was 1796 before the recommendations to split the Navy Board into committees was adopted, but 1799 and 1800 before the new pay systems for the Navy and Victualling Boards were put into force.[64]

Salaries under the new system

In 1799 the total amount paid out in salaries was £13,926; in 1800, the year when the new method of payment started, the total amount was £28,745. The figure then rose steadily until 1812 when it totalled £52,290.[65] Some of these increased amounts were due to increasing numbers of staff; but there were some general pay rises due to inflation. Agitation for inflation pay rises started in July 1804, with requests coming first from Somerset Place staff and then from the clerks at Portsmouth.[66] There was also a protest at the rule which had been added in 1800 without the clerks realising, that salaries would automatically reduce by one-sixth three years after the end of the war.[67] The Board supported these requests, pointing out to the Admiralty that they were losing clerks to better paid positions elsewhere. The Admiralty responded by asking the Board's opinion on the appropriate amounts, but despite the Board's detailed response, no action was taken; the following May brought a further petition from the London clerks, with another the next year.[68] This time there was an additional request, that clerks should receive automatic regular increments based on length of service. The justification for this request was that as the salary structure stood, with the junior clerks all receiving the same amount, regardless of their position on the 'ladder', there was no incentive for them to improve their knowledge of the tasks which would suit them for the higher positions.[69] Thus, for instance, in the secretary's office, the chief, second, third, fourth, fifth and sixth clerks received £600, £350, £200, £150, £130 and £100 respectively, but

64   By an Order in Council dated 29 January 1800.
65   TNA ADM 110/46, f. 128, 21 April 1800; 110/47, f. 342, 9 March 1802; 110/65, ff. 30–31, 31 January 1812. These figures were reported annually until 1812 in the format of 'increases/diminutions'.
66   TNA ADM 110/51, ff. 88–96, 6 July 1804; NMM ADM DP/24, 12 July 1804.
67   TNA ADM 110/51, ff. 88–96, 6 July 1804.
68   TNA ADM 110/51, ff. 88–96, 6 July 1804; NMM ADM C/704, 18 October 1804; DP/24, 19 October 1804; DP/25 27 May 1805.
69   TNA ADM 110/54, ff. 352–4, 20 June 1806.

the five other clerks (seventh to eleventh) all received the same amount of £80. The request for this pay system was ignored at this time, but a round of rises was effected in 1807.[70]

A further sequence of requests, again based on length of service increments, started in April 1809.[71] Although supported by the Victualling Board, and already in place in the Admiralty and War offices, this received little enthusiasm from the Admiralty and it was not until September 1811 that an Order in Council was granted which gave increments to junior and extra clerks in London every two years, with the annual salaries of the junior clerks rising to a maximum £200 after twelve years, and those of extra clerks rising to a maximum £110 after six years; however, regardless of length of service, no clerk was to have a higher salary than the clerk above him. This Order also increased the salary of the secretary to the Committee of Accounts from £700 to £750, and allowed an addition of thirteen clerks to the establishment.[72] There were no further rises until 1816, when there was a general rearrangement of the pay structure, with all clerical staff (i.e. department heads and clerks) being arranged into three classes as well as continuing to receive length of service increments.[73]

When passing on the request from the junior clerks in 1811, the Victualling Board remarked that the circumstances in the request (on the inadequacy of the present salaries and the 'distant prospect of promotion') were true and that the facts stood for themselves. When it came to the matter of pay rises, the Board did seem to fight for its clerks, but this may have been for a pragmatic desire to retain staff rather than for humanitarian considerations. As they had told the Admiralty before, since promotion prospects were remote, many of the junior clerks were leaving as soon as they had become 'sufficiently qualified' (i.e. experienced) to be really useful. This unfortunately also qualified them for better paid work in other government departments, the Bank of England or merchant counting houses; they could only be replaced by young and inexperienced clerks.[74]

For the department and section heads and the officers at the yards, pay rises were often given, on a basis of merit or for parity with equivalent positions, when they were individually requested. For instance Michael Elwin, the storekeeper at Dover, asked for parity with other storekeepers at the

---

70   The new salaries granted in 1807 are taken from TNA ADM 110/71, ff. 34–42, 1 October 1815, being those paid at that time (there were no further rises between those two dates). See Appendix E. (All salaries were paid free of tax: TNA ADM 110/59, f. 504, 8 May 1809.)

71   NMM ADM DP/31B, 15 August 1811, referring to previous requests of 26 April 1809, 9 November 1810, 8 March, 20 April & 15 May 1811.

72   NMM ADM C/731, 11 September 1811.

73   NMM ADM DP/36A, 30 April 1816.

74   TNA ADM 110/63, ff. 278–86, 8 March 1811.

outports and was awarded an additional £20, three of the Somerset Place chief clerks requested and were awarded an additional £20, and the super-intendant at Deptford had his pay increased to £400.[75] The Admiralty seems to have been able to authorise these individual merit or parity rises on their own, but any alterations to the overall salary levels had to be referred to the Privy Council.

The commissioners, who had not received any part of the fees, received a flat sum of £400 each until June 1793 when the Board was given the addi-tional task of handling army victuals; for this the chairman was given an additional £500 per annum and all the other commissioners an additional £250 (the clerical staff involved in this work also received additional sums ranging from £100 for the secretary down to £10 for the junior clerks).[76] They also had either the rent-free use of a house or a rent allowance of £65, coals and candles to the value of £80, and free stationery and postage for their personal letters. This gave the commissioners a gross income of £795 and the chairman £1,045. They did not receive a rise until 1800 (when their salaries were increased to £1,200 for the chairman, £1,000 for the deputy chairman, and £800 for each of the other five commissioners),[77] despite a plea to Lord Spencer in 1797; interestingly, that request includes the information that 'from the time the Victualling Board was established [the commission-ers' salaries were] in the proportion of four-fifths of the salaries and house rents of the commissioners of the Navy ...' The victualling commissioners were basing this request on the fact that the Navy Board commissioners had received a pay rise and thus the differential had been increased.[78] It is also of interest that the chief clerks at the Treasury were paid £800 per annum from 1780 (at that time, the victualling commissioners were paid £400), another example of the government's opinion of the latter's place in the scheme of things.[79] Due to the erratic survival of documentation on pay, it has not been possible to compile comprehensive information on pay scales in other naval departments; however, it is clear that there was no standard pay system across government departments at that time.

75 TNA ADM 12/63, 29 November 1793 & 7 April 1794; ADM 12/75, section 102.5, 10 October 1797.

76 TNA ADM 109/102, 24 October 1793; PRO 30/8/246 (copy Treasury minute 16/8/93, ff. 57, 125–6).

77 TNA ADM 181/13–16, 'ordinary estimates'. Sainty, in his internet listing, states incorrectly that these increases took place in 1803: www.history.ac.uk/office/comms_victual.html

78 Petition to Spencer signed by all seven commissioners, TNA ADM 110/43, ff. 304–5, 26 October 1797.

79 Henry Roseveare, *The Treasury, 1660–1870, The Foundations of Control* (London, 1973), pp. 122–3.

Retirement benefits

As evidenced by the case of the Victualling Board secretary, John Watts, as reported above, prior to 1800 there was no automatic right to pensions for government employees and those wishing to retire had to fund this from payments (either regular or lump sums) from those who succeeded them. Such official pensions as were paid to Victualling Board employees came from petitioning the Admiralty.

Under the recommendations of the Fees commissioners, pensions were made available to those who were deemed worthy (hence the statements in requests that they were hardworking and deserving) and whose health rendered them incapable of further work. The latter required the applicant to be 'surveyed' by a doctor and sometimes also by attendance at the Admiralty board.[80] Such pensions as were paid were funded by the sale of offal and old victualling stores.[81]

These meagre arrangements had the inevitable effect of discouraging elderly personnel from retiring and must have contributed to the general inefficiency in the offices; the extremely shaky writing of the elderly John Watts gives testimony to this. The demoralising effect of this on younger clerks would also have contributed to the turnover of staff to other situations; it was a general problem in all government offices and eventually led to the Superannuation Act of 1810.[82] The terms in this Act were taken from the formula used by the Treasury: two-thirds of the final salary after twenty years' service, or fifteen years if over 60, and half of the final salary for those under 60 with ten to twenty years service.[83] These were rather more generous than the terms proposed by the Board of Revision, as shown in Table 3.[84]

Table 3: Pension rates

Length of service	Retiring from old age/infirmity	Retiring from incapacity
Between 10 and 15 years	One-quarter salary	none
Between 15 and 20 years	One-half salary	One-quarter salary
Between 25 and 35 years	Two-thirds salary	One-third salary
Over 35 years	Three-quarters salary	One-half salary

80 For instance, John Rickards, clerk of the issues: NMM ADM C/722, 24 June 1809.
81 TNA ADM 111/130 18 January 1794.
82 50 Geo III cc. 56, 117.
83 Roseveare, *Treasury*, p. 131.
84 *BOR 10*, p. 32.

Since all the extant recommendations state the deserving character of the retiree, the implication is that the undeserving would not get a pension; this is borne out by the arguments in 1822 on whether dismissed clerks, officers (and one commissioner) should have pensions.[85] Some of these were eventually given reduced pensions, but the widow of the clerk Glasspoole (who had committed suicide, inferably because of the shame attached to his involvement in the forbidden activities) was refused a pension on the grounds that her husband was about to be dismissed for misconduct.[86]

Clerical employment in other government departments

Whilst there is some information on salaries in other government departments in the Sainty and Collinge series of books on government officials, neither these nor other literature offers much information on working conditions or job content;[87] thus although it would be desirable to make comparisons between them and Victualling Board officers and clerks it is not possible to do so in a meaningful way. Morriss makes some useful comments on the Navy Board and H M Boot and H V Bowen also comment usefully on some aspects of the administration of the East India Company.[88] Life at the East India Company office in London was, for all but those at the highest levels, lacking any form of intellectual interest and for most of the junior clerks, consisted of no more than boring repetitive tasks. The salaries were generous and there were pensions, but since competition for jobs was high and most clerks entered the office aged fifteen or sixteen to serve an unpaid 'apprenticeship' of up to three years, this was not an opportunity for victualling office clerks to better themselves.[89]

Much the same situation of stultifying boredom applied to the Colonial Office, with most of the clerks spending their whole working life copying documents. D M Young reports that in 1854 it was suggested that civil servants were of two sorts: 'mechanical' and 'intellectual'; and remarks that twenty years before then 'the idea that clerks should be expected to perform

85 See page 185 below.
86 TNA ADM 12/210, section 102.5, 19 September 1822.
87 J M Collinge, *Navy Board Officials 1660–1832* (London, 1978), p. 14; Sainty, *Admiralty Officials* (London, 1975), pp. 10–13; *Officials of the Board of Trade* (London, 1974), pp. 44–5; *Home Office Officials* (London, 1975), pp. 3–4; *Colonial Office Officials* (London, 1976), pp. 1–2.
88 H M Boot, 'Real incomes of the British middle class, 1760–1850: The experience of clerks at the East India Company, *Economic History Review*, LII, 4 (1999), pp. 638–68; Bowen, *Business of Empire*.
89 Bowen, *Business of Empire*, pp. 141–6.

intellectual duties was not even accepted by the clerks'.[90] These descriptions were probably just as applicable to the victualling office clerks in the French Revolutionary and Napoleonic wars; given the victualling commissioners' practice of micro-managing, one can accept that it could only have been the senior clerks who might aspire to the 'intellectual' status.

Even Sidney Pollard, in his seminal *The Genesis of Modern Management*, has little to say on staff prospects, but he does make one comment which might apply to the Victualling Board, suggesting that salaries were set according to the social class of the job holder rather than the content and responsibilities of the job, a practice which pertained until the 1790s and was only gradually changed. This could account for the large differentials between the salaries of the victualling commissioners and most of their clerical subordinates.

Henry Roseveare devotes a little space to administration in his book on the Treasury. In 1782, Lord Shelburne, aided by the Treasury secretary George Rose, substituted fixed salaries for a fee-based income, five years before the Fees commission sat. He also established the principle that promotions should be based on competence and diligence rather than seniority, and required punctual and personal appearance (emphasising this by dismissing a clerk who had not been seen for two years).[91] The attempt to reform promotions was not entirely successful as 'few promotions flouted the claims of seniority'. And the senile were allowed to remain in their posts, the best known of these being Thomas Pratt, whose post had been secured for him when he was seventeen by his father Sir John Pratt (who was caretaker Chancellor of the Exchequer for a mere eight weeks). 'Old Pratt' remained in his job until he died in 1805 aged ninety-seven, being thought 'too venerable to sack, although there is little evidence that he had done a stroke of work since the 1760s'.[92]

Roseveare goes on to make a telling comment on the quality of Treasury staff: 'To believe that the Treasury lords wanted to be served by a troop of nimble-witted young clerks, with thrusting personalities and first-class minds, underrates their ministerial sense of self-importance'.[93] This reinforces the impression gained of contemporary management attitudes and the question of whether the victualling commissioners also had such a sense of self-importance, a possibility which comes to mind when considering their tendency to micro-manage instead of delegate, and the grovelling level of language used in petitions and memorials submitted by their staff.

---

90 D Murray Young, *The Colonial Office in the early Nineteenth Century* (London, 1961), p. 5.
91 Roseveare, *Treasury*, pp. 122–3.
92 Ibid., pp. 103, 123.
93 Ibid., p. 123.

Non-clerical staff

There were also a few non-clerical staff at Somerset Place; these included Mrs Bull the housekeeper, several messengers (who would have carried post to the other naval offices in town, to Deptford and occasionally to the outports) and to the coffee houses and exchanges where the contractors congregated, one warder (ie a porter), what the Fees commissioners described as 'attendants on three several offices' (no definition of their duties is offered, but one can surmise that they would have performed such duties as making up the fires) and a bargemaster.[94] The bargemaster (who also operated a wherry to carry small quantities of provisions to warships in the Thames) was retired in 1802 and does not appear to have been replaced. Other bargemen were hired by the day as needed, and provided annually with a livery of 'scarlet clothes, velvet caps and burnished badges'.[95]

---

94   *Fees 8*, pp. 585–6.
95   NMM ADM 111/184, 11 July 1807 (minute on livery); 110/48, ff. 172–5, 1 November 1802 (employment details).

7

Yard Staff

STAFF AT THE Victualling Board's yards were of two types: clerical and manual, each type being supervised locally by persons known as officers. The officers responsible for the main accounting and clerical functions in each yard were known as 'superior' officers, those responsible for the manual workers were known as 'inferior' officers. The number of these inferior officers varied, according to the manufacturing activities carried out at the yard. At the outports, both sets of officers reported to the agent victualler who in turn reported directly to the board of commissioners; at Deptford the chief officer was known as the superintendant until 1809. In the yards abroad, although responsible to the board of commissioners, agents victualler were also required to take instructions from the local commander-in-chief and, after 1809, the local resident naval commissioner.

As with the staff at Somerset Place, the supervisory and clerical levels at the yards saw changes to the salary structure in 1800, and to hierarchical structures and retirement arrangements in 1809. The manual workers in the yards at home also saw changes during the twenty-three year period to working practices, wage payments and retirement arrangements.

The clerical staff at the victualling yards both at home and abroad are, to a large extent, like those at Somerset Place, shadowy figures. Many of the agents victualler and clerks in the yards abroad had worked in head office or the yards at home, and returned to these locations when the wars ended; a few of the tradesmen in the home yards also went to the yards abroad and returned to the home yards in due course. Very little is known about the manual workers, mainly their names and trades, but for some yards there are 'description' books, which contain physical descriptions of the workers with age, height, hair and eye colour and other distinguishing marks; these were probably to prevent unauthorised persons attempting to claim a worker's wages. With very few rare exceptions, such as Grace

George, who split twigs for the coopers at Deptford, all the workers in the victualling yards were male.[1]

Supervisory staff in the yards at home

The main British yard was at Deptford, with others at the outports of Portsmouth, Plymouth, Chatham, Dover and, later, Cork. With the exception of Dover and Cork, these yards were immediately adjacent to naval dockyards. In each of these locations, the principal officers (the agent victualler, the clerk of the cheque and the storekeeper) had departments of several inferior clerks, while the master tradesman officers (the master brewer, master baker, master cooper, master butcher and master miller) had one clerk each. The other inferior officers (the principal boatswain, the principal stevedore, the porter and the inspector of works) did not have clerks. At the army store at St Catherine's, the only officer was the storekeeper. There were also several depot ships run by storekeepers, and some situations where a clerk was seconded to supervise issues at fleet anchorages, such as Brixham and Yarmouth.

Deptford was a special case. The activities in this yard, and the way in which they were managed, were a relic from arrangements earlier in the eighteenth century when the yard was located at Tower Hill in the same premises as the victualling office itself. Then, although the yard activities were nominally run under the auspices of a superintendant, the head of each specific department reported to the commissioner designated as being responsible for that department. This chain of command continued when most of the yard activities were moved to the new yard at Deptford in the 1740s, which was not unreasonable whilst the yard and the office were separated by little more than the width of the Thames, but less so when the office moved up-river to Somerset Place in 1787.

As the Board of Revision noted in their Eleventh report, this reporting line was used by the department heads at Deptford as an excuse for refusing to take instructions from, or report to, the superintendent of the yard.[2] These officers' job descriptions did not, interestingly, contain the clause 'and to attend the agent in the other duties of the yard' which is seen in the job description of the officers at the outport yards.[3] It was not until 1809 when, as a result of this report, Deptford was put on the same footing as the other yards and the superintendant was replaced by an agent victualler that this situation changed; the report also recommended that the agents

---

1 TNA ADM 110/69, ff. 507–8, 25 February 1815.
2 *BOR 10*, p. 22; *BOR 11*, p. 27.
3 *SCF 32*, pp. 34–40.

victualler at all the yards should ideally be naval captains; this was put into effect at Deptford in December 1808 with the appointment of Captain Henry Garrett.[4]

The Board of Revision also concluded that the number and ranks of the officials at Deptford was excessive. Of the eight principal officers, five (the hoytaker, master cooper and the clerks of the brewhouse, dry stores and cutting house) were either unnecessary or could be reduced to the lesser inferior officer rank. The master cooper, whose job included an element of storekeeping, could be reduced to inferior status, the clerks of the brew-house and dry stores, whose functions were basically those of storekeepers, could be dispensed with and replaced by a single, dedicated storekeeper who would also take on the storekeeping aspects of the work of the clerk of the cutting house; the latter should be replaced by a master butcher. This allowed the thirty clerks who were attached to these functions to be reduced to nineteen: two for the agent victualler, eight each for the storekeeper and the clerk of the cheque, and one for the master cooper.

The hoytaker's current duties did not match the seniority (and salary) of his position. They had originally involved the care of some stores, which had been transferred to the clerk of the brewhouse in 1788, and the hiring and inspection of victualling transports, which had been taken over by the Transport Board in 1794. At about the same time, another of his duties, that of hiring small craft for conveying provisions to Chatham and ships in the Thames, had been passed to a contractor. All that was left of this part of the job was the occasional need to hire vessels to take provisions to the outports. He also attended the issuing of stores and the loading and unloading of vessels at the wharf, all of which activities were already supervised by other officers. He also 'took account of the remains on board ships, transports and victuallers', which could, and should, said the Board of Revision, be done by their pursers, and he employed three clerks to keep several sets of books and accounts, none of which 'has any connection with the nature of his present employment, nor were they of the slightest use whatever'. The Board of Revision's recommendation was that this position should be discontinued and the hoytaker (who had a salary of £400 and a house) be replaced by a boatswain of the wharf (at a salary of £200, without a house).[5]

The post of hoytaker was duly discontinued and the 'business of the wharf' (i.e. superintending the men engaged in loading and unloading vessels) was to be performed by a 'Boatswain of the Wharf'. This change did raise the problem of what to do with the current hoytaker, Lieutenant William Alder. Because he had been a commissioned officer but had given

4   BOR 11, pp. 34, 43.
5   BOR 11, pp. 28–9.

this up on taking up the position of hoytaker, the Board of Revision felt he was 'worthy of consideration' as he had thereby lost the chance of promotion. They suggested it would be better and less expensive to leave him in place than to compensate him financially and still have to pay a (albeit reduced) salary to his replacement.[6]

The Victualling Board had only one objection to this: the danger of a future successor to Alder expecting the same terms and conditions. They also pointed out that Lieutenant Alder felt 'a natural repugnance to bear the humiliating title of Boatswain, and to act under the orders of the storekeeper [instead of the agent]' and they suggested that he should be designated 'Superintendant of the Wharf'. They also remarked that to change people, at a time when the whole system was changing, would subject the department to serious inconvenience.[7] (To the modern management mind, that would be the best time to introduce a 'new broom'.) In the event, Alder did not stay much longer, being superannuated in September 1810 and replaced by a ship's master, William Wilkinson.[8]

The same points were raised over the abolition of the position of clerk of the cutting house, the transfer of his storekeeping duties to the storekeeper, and the recommended appointment of a competent master butcher to oversee the work of the slaughter and cutting houses. This change would leave the current clerk of the cutting house (Robert Bowring) without a job, and in view of his knowledge of the work the Board suggested that he would be the obvious person to appoint as master butcher with the temporary title of 'inspector of the cutting house'. This would also save the cost of superannuating him, which given his length of service would cost three-fourths of his present salary.[9] The Admiralty had directed chairman Searle to find a proper butcher, but this had proved impossible; William Mellish, the meat supplier, remarked that butchers no longer seemed to understand the business of preparing and packing salt meat. Bowring was the only person available (there was some urgency as the killing season was fast approaching) and he managed to negotiate not only a continuance of his old salary of £250 p.a. (the salary for a master butcher was £200) but also the use of a vacant house in the yard. Bowring had over thirty years' service at this time and thus was not far from retirement; in view of the difficulty in finding anyone with the necessary knowledge, one might think that the Victualling

---

6   *BOR 11*, pp. 29–30. The comment was whether it would be right to 'dispossess' him of his office, an interesting choice of word which indicates that the concept of an office as personal property was still a strong part of bureaucratic culture.

7   NMM ADM DP/29A, 15 May 1809.

8   TNA ADM 110/62, ff. 370–1, 14 September 1810.

9   NMM ADM DP/29A, 15 May 1809.

Board's suggestion that he should be given an assistant would have been welcomed by the Admiralty, but this suggestion was rejected.[10]

Duties of the officers

The duties of the agents victualler and other officers were defined in their letter of instruction and, after the recommendations of the Board of Revision were put into effect, by the printed *Regulations for the Guidance of the Officers of the Several Victualling Establishments At Home*.[11] Copies of the earlier letters of instructions to officers at the yards written between 1715 and 1805 were recorded in a separate letter book and also in the thirty-second report of the Select Committee on Finance.[12] These early instructions show some minor variations as time goes by but fewer than might be expected over such a long period; they consisted of twenty-five clauses with eleven sample forms. The 1808 version consisted of 289 clauses for the agent victualler with 124 forms, and between 14 and 36 clauses for each of the other yard officers, making a total of 154. However, the instructions for these officers which did not relate directly to their trade, such as those warning the officer to guard against pilferage, were identical for each officer. Such forms as they required are amongst those listed for the agent victualler.

In broad terms these duties may be described as overseeing the physical receipt, storage and issuing of provisions and victualling stores, manufacturing certain items from raw materials, and accounting for all these movements. The agent victualler's responsibilities included organising and overseeing all these activities, arranging contracts for local purchases, holding sums of cash to issue to pursers for necessary and short allowance money, arranging for and holding sales of unserviceable stores and offal, and dealing with the payment of clerks' salaries and yard workers' wages. Although not mentioned specifically in the instructions, those of his duties which involved delivering provisions to warships must have required regular consultation with the local port admiral or his equivalent.

10 TNA ADM 110/60, ff. 375–7; 417–19, 25 September and 7 October 1809; NMM ADM C/724, 9 & 10 October 1809.

11 TNA ADM 7/216, *Instructions and Regulations for the Guidance of the Officers of the Several Victualling Establishments at Home* (1808) for full title see Bibliography); a similar book was produced for the victualling yards abroad. (TNA ADM 7/217) (Hereafter these are referred to as '*Regulations … Home*' or *Regulations … Abroad*').

12 TNA ADM 49/59 'Instructions to victualling agents 1715'. These letters are copied in full on the first occasion each type was sent, with notes stating that such letters have been sent for those up to 1805; *SCF* 32, pp. 68–88 (these being for officers abroad).

Until 1809 there was no formal convention on who should take charge when the agent victualler was absent. In practice it had been his first clerk, but this was felt to be unsatisfactory and 'inconsistent with the regular subordination' normal in His Majesty's service (a interesting comment demonstrating another aspect of the mores of the period). The Board of Revision recommended that the clerk of the cheque should be deemed the second officer, with the storekeeper the third.[13]

The clerk of the cheque was, as the modern spelling of his title indicates, a high-level checker of yard activities. He, or his clerks, attended the receipt of stores and kept account of their issue, attended the daily mustering of yard workers, maintained records of the men's time, calculated their wages and physically paid them once a quarter. He also assisted the agent victualler in making local contracts for bulk supplies.

The storekeeper, as well as having responsibility for all the stores, assisted the agent victualler and clerk of the cheque in the tendering and contracting process.

Other clerical staff at the yards at home

The terms and conditions of work for the clerical staff at the yards were much the same as those at Somerset Place, and there is no more known about them as individuals. The only real difference was that some (and perhaps all) had contact with the actualities rather than the concepts of receiving and issuing commodities. The correspondence mentions clerks going out into the yard and storehouses to physically check receipts and issues, and it is probable that most did so at various times. Most would have had contact with warship personnel, from commissioned officers visiting the offices to warrant officers and seamen collecting from the yards; some accompanied deliveries to warships at anchor.

The new *Regulations … Home* had four articles on yard clerks.[14] These laid down the office hours as 9 a.m. 'until the people' (i.e. artificers and other manual workers) 'leave off work' and required that there should always be at least one clerk present in the office. They had to produce a certificate of their 'integrity, diligence and good conduct' before collecting their salaries. The agent was required to report his observations on the performance of his staff, not only to allow the victualling commissioners to deal with those who misbehaved but also 'in order that the able, diligent and active may be attended to'. He was also, at least once a year, to assemble the clerks, officers, masters of trades and yard foremen, to read the *Regulations* and to listen

---

13   *BOR 11*, p. 27.
14   *BOR 11*, p. 57, articles 29–32.

to 'such public remarks as he may judge proper, on any instance of neglect or inattention that he may have observed in any person, cautioning him against a repetition thereof …' This is another example of the rather draconian attitudes of the period; but whilst the threat of such public humiliation may well have kept some of the younger clerks up to the mark, the actuality would surely have caused such resentment that no wise agent victualler would have actually done this.

Career progression

The general pattern seems to have been of yard staff staying, if not in the yard where they started, in another yard. Since there were fewer staff in the yards than at Somerset Place, the possibilities of promotion were higher and this can be seen in the case of William Crees, agent victualler at Plymouth, who had entered as second clerk to the clerk of the cheque, risen to first clerk, then spent seven years as storekeeper before rising to be clerk of the cheque himself and finally to agent victualler.[15] This potential career pinacle as agent victualler was, of course, reduced to clerk of the cheque after 1808, with the requirement that agents victualler should be naval captains. Other agents victualler, particularly those abroad, entered that job via head office and the job of peripatetic agent victualler, such as Richard Ford (agent victualler Lisbon and later afloat in the Mediterranean), John Geoghegan (Ford's clerk and then agent victualler at Rio de Janeiro) and Manley Hulke (agent victualler Mediterranean).

Most of these men were well into middle age before becoming agent victualler; for instance Collier, the superintendant at Deptford, was 61 when he took that position.[16] This advanced age, although undoubtedly giving the authority which would have helped these agents victualler in dealing with commissioned officers, must have affected their energy levels and thinking and other work patterns, and may have been part of the reason for the stagnation of clerical and other work practices which the Board of Revision criticised so strongly.[17]

Some agents victualler, on the more remote stations, were appointed by the commander-in-chief, having been senior pursers or even admirals' secretaries, and these men tended to be younger. The Fees commissioners did not approve of this practice, stating that it should be discontinued; quite

---

15   Other agents victualler who had started in the office at one of the yards were Benjamin Collier (Deptford), Digory Tonkin (Plymouth), William Reeks (Portsmouth), John Dunsterville (Cork), William Crees (Plymouth), Joseph Matthews (Chatham) and George Desborough (Leeward Islands): *Fees 8*, pp. 642–71.

16   *Fees 8*, p. 582, Collier was appointed in 1787.

17   See Chapter 9.

who those commissioners thought would be suitable (and immediately available) so far from home was not stated, but the Victualling Board, in their response to this, pointed out that such people were actually ideal for the job.[18]

Until 1800, entry into clerical jobs at some yards was by payment of a premium.[19] The premiums required at Plymouth tended to be higher than those at Portsmouth and Chatham (none were paid at Dover), which would support the 'remote towns' theory. There was no consistency in the amounts paid and they do not appear to be related to the salary paid for each job; they may have been calculated on the fees available at the time of appointment, the availability of other clerical work in towns remote from London, or the amount the candidate (or his parents) was prepared to pay. In some cases, the premium was paid in a single lump, in others it was paid in installments over several years, and in some cases no premiums were paid. It is clear that the victualling commissioners did not approve of the practice; on more than one occasion premiums demanded were waived after appeal to the Board.[20]

There is no indication of regular movements of clerks from posts in the dockyards to victualling yards, or vice versa; given the general practice of promoting within departments, this seems to have been unlikely as a promotion strategy.

Salaries

The salaries of the superior officers were linked to the importance of the yard, as is shown in Table 4. Insofar as clerical salaries at the yards and at Somerset Place can be compared, those for the clerks at the yards were considerably less, both before and after 1800. They also differed from yard to yard, as can be seen in Tables 5 and 6.

Table 4: Annual salaries proposed for the officers of the yards

	Deptford	Portsmouth	Plymouth	Chatham	Dover
Agent victualler	600	600	600	450	400
Clerk of the Cheque	500	400	400	300	220

18 *SCF* 32, p. 216.
19 *Fees 8*, p. 575. Charging premiums for jobs was common practice at the Navy Office.
20 For full details of premiums paid, see *Fees 8*, pp. 658–74.

Table 5: Average total annual income of clerks at the yards before 1800[21]

	Portsmouth	Plymouth	Chatham	Dover
1st clerk to agent victualler	745	70	154	78
2nd clerk to agent victualler	300	155	166	30

Table 6: Annual salaries of clerks at the yards from 1800[22]

	Portsmouth	Plymouth	Chatham	Dover
1st clerk to agent victualler	300	200	175	80
2nd clerk to agent victualler	150	120	100	70

Supervisory and clerical staff in the yards abroad

None of the Parliamentary reports have much to say about the running of the yards abroad, mainly because they were unable to examine any of the agents victualler. The ninth report of the Fees commissioners was a joint report on victualling and naval yards; it did devote a little space to 'abuses' amongst pursers and contractors at Jamaica, and to what they felt were excessive prices charged by the two agents victualler for India and the Cape of Good Hope between 1780 and 1785, but the bulk of this report is on the naval yards abroad.[23] At the time this report was produced, there was only one victualling yard abroad, at Gibraltar.

The thirty-second report of the Select Committee on Finance was equally sparse on the topic, stating that there were three regular agents victualler abroad (at Gibraltar, the Leeward Islands and Lisbon) and one at the Cape of Good Hope who was considered temporary.[24]

The twelfth report of the Board of Revision on yards abroad is also sparse, consisting of only twenty-five pages, twenty-three of which were a draft of new instructions.[25] It remarked on the inadequacy of the existing

---

21 Figures taken from *SCF* 32, pp. 18–51, showing a three-year average of salary plus fee income. The low figure shown for the 1st clerk to the agent victualler at Plymouth is as shown in *SCF* 32, pp. 44–5.

22 Figures taken from yard pay books: TNA ADM 113/236 (Portsmouth), 113/203 (Plymouth), 113/22 (Chatham), 113/96 (Dover).

23 *Fees 9*, p. 725.

24 *SCF* 32, pp. 730–4.

25 *BOR* 12, pp. 5–25; also at TNA ADM 7/217.

instructions and made a strong recommendation that agents victualler abroad should work under the supervision of the resident naval commissioner; considered the current salaries for the staff at Gibraltar, Malta and the Cape of Good Hope, and suggested that 'to compensate for the danger and inconvenience of [their] working in a foreign climate' the officers and chief clerks should be entitled to return to a suitable permanent position at home after five years.[26] This, although fair to the person returning from abroad, was not necessarily so for those at home. In 1815, when the yard at Rio was closed, the agent victualler, John Geoghegan, who had been away for twelve years, came home and was slotted into the position of second clerk to the secretary. During his absence, William Wickey had risen to fill that post, and was most aggrieved to be demoted back to third clerk (as were, no doubt, all those below him who were also moved down one place). Despite his protests, this decision held and he was told in no uncertain terms that he should consider himself lucky to have had the advantage of his temporary positions and salaries.[27]

As the twelfth report remarked, 'Abroad, the agent victualler combines in his own person the duties of storekeeper, clerk of the cheque and agent'.[28] With the exception of Gibraltar, where for a brief period one of the clerks was designated 'storekeeper', none of the pay lists show any other supervisory staff. The agent victualler there was assisted by no more than four established clerks, although during busy periods extra clerks were taken on.[29] Most of the senior clerks appear to have been British, from their names and the fact that as well as a salary they received table money, which would not have been necessary for locals.

The only other mentions of clerks in the twelfth report are that one should be sent to attend issues of stores, either to individual ships, or of bulk stores for distant squadrons; that the agent victualler should ensure that they did their work diligently, and that neither they, nor the agent victualler himself, were to act as an agent for anyone or to be concerned in any business.

The thirty-second report of the Select Committee on Finance includes a 'draft' of the instructions given to agents abroad which corresponds to the handwritten copy letters dating from 1715.[30] In comparison with the new instructions, the old version is extremely sparse; running to a mere twenty-five clauses in ten pages, with eleven accompanying sample forms, its content is rather unbalanced. It takes up a page and a half on the subject of

---

26 *BOR 12*, p.4.
27 TNA ADM 110/71, ff. 147–55, 2 November 1815; 110/72, ff. 348–9, 13 August 1816.
28 *BOR 12*, p. 3.
29 At Malta, in 1810, there were three clerks and five extra clerks. TNA ADM 113/176.
30 TNA ADM 49/59. Although the wording is slightly different in some of these handwritten letters, the content is effectively the same.

issuing provisions, including the basic ration table. The Board of Revision version covers the whole topic of issues in one short paragraph with one sample demand form.[31]

Equally, the earlier version devotes two whole pages to detailed instructions on how to check pursers' accounts against their ships' muster books before paying over short allowance money; an auditing task which has disappeared from the later version to be replaced, as before, by a single short paragraph requiring the agent to do no more than view a certificate signed by three of the ship's officers and referring to two forms, one of which is the purser's demand and the other a receipt.[32]

However, these tasks were much the same as those required at home. Where the instructions for agents abroad differed was in the additional tasks of overseeing the artisans and labourers in the yard and calculating and paying their wages (tasks carried out by the clerk of the cheque in home yards), dealing with the maintenance and repairs of the yard buildings and/or hiring suitable premises where appropriate (tasks done by the surveyor of buildings at home), hiring vessels to carry provisions to remote squadron rendezvous (done by the Transport Board at home), and obtaining, handling and accounting for tranches of specie for squadron use.[33] This latter task could involve substantial sums; the agent victualler at Gibraltar, James Cutforth, dealt with regular tranches of Spanish $10,000 (about £2,250 sterling),[34] passing these on to the agent victualler afloat attached to the Mediterranean fleet, who used part of it to pay short allowance money to crews, issued part to pursers for necessary money, and used the rest to purchase fresh food and wine in areas remote from Gibraltar.[35]

The main reason for all the additional clauses in the new instructions was more stringent accounting requirements. Only six of the twenty-five clauses in the old version covered accounting procedures and formats; in the new version it was 52 of 100, many of these relating to daily receipt and issue books, expenditure books (e.g. for items lost by leakage or destroyed by vermin), sale of decayed provisions, etc. This desire for greater control can also be seen in the differences between the thirteenth and fourteen versions of the *Regulations and Instructions Relating to His Majesty's Service at Sea*, which had increased from 232 pages with a few printed forms to 440 with 29 forms.

31 BOR 12, p. 12, clause 36; Appendix 12.
32 SCF 32, pp. 75–77, clause 20; BOR 12, p. 21, Clause 88 & Appendices 45 & 46.
33 Ibid., p. 6, clause 7 (labourers); p. 7, clauses 13, 14 (buildings).
34 As shown in Richard Ford's accounts as agent victualler afloat in 1804: TNA ADM 112/46.
35 Nicolas, *Dispatches*, Vol. V, p. 445 (instruction from Nelson to Cutforth on specie); short allowance money: *R&I*, 13th edition, pp. 69–71; Macdonald, *Feeding*, pp. 66–7.

Insofar as agents abroad were responsible to anyone other than the Board under the old rules it was the commander-in-chief of the station, although the instructions only mention this in relation to purchasing provisions.[36] The new instructions placed the agent victualler under the direct supervision of the resident naval commissioner (where there was one), with the commander-in-chief retaining the right to suspend or dismiss staff and give directions to the agent, even where these orders might contravene the other instructions, providing this was done in writing.[37] This caused much friction between agents victualler and naval commissioners, notably at the Cape of Good Hope.

This facility seems to have been constantly troublesome; it had several changes of agent, two of whom failed to submit accounts and refused to answer questions about their activities,[38] as did the naval storekeeper, and another of whom got into a bad-tempered argument with the resident naval commissioner. This was Henry Pallister, who had been a clerk in the victualling office, and should have returned to that position, but due to 'the language used in his letter' to the commissioner, William Shield, the Victualling Board told the Admiralty that they would not allow this unless Pallister had a good explanation to give them when he returned to London. He was not able to do so, as he died on his way home, having been unwell for some time.[39]

However, this was not the only complaint Shield made to the Admiralty about personnel at the Cape. Of Andrew Millar, the agent of the Naval Hospital, he said

> having found great reason to complain of the loose and improper expenditure of money … and to remonstrate frequently with him on his extreme negligence in the performance of his duty, and improper conduct to the surgeon of the establishment, he told me in the most menacing way possible that it would be Death for Death … he told me that he was a gentleman and should make it a private business between him and me.

This presumably meant Millar intended to challenge Shield to a duel. Two weeks later, Shield complained again of Millar's 'ungentlemanlike and improper behaviour' and that he had been 'outrageously indecent'. Two

---

36 *SCF* 32, pp. 72–73, clause 12.

37 *BOR* 12, p. 5, clauses 2 & 3.

38 These were Maude and Robertson, TNA ADM 110/65, ff. 198–202, 22 December 1806; 110/58, ff. 527–8, 15 December 1812.

39 TNA ADM 110/62, ff. 353–4, 5 September 1810; TNA ADM 110/61, ff. 124–147, 11 December 1809; NMM ADM C/733, 24 April 1812, from Navy Board to Victualling Board. Unfortunately the letter from Pallister to Shield has not been found; in view of what follows it would have been interesting to see exactly what was deemed so offensive.

months after that, Shield was having trouble with Captain Robert Corbet, who offered to horsewhip him. Shield reported that Corbet had used his name 'with little decency, and [also] some expressions of great indecency he used in the naval yard, perfectly uncalled for'. This row seems to have blown up over Shield's intervention in the replacement of some rigging; Corbet's letter suggests that other officers had had similar problems with Shield.[40] This particular incident continued, with Shield refusing to supply various essential items for refitting Corbet's capture *La Caroline* (renamed *Bourbonnaise*).[41] Shield stated that to supply her from his stores would deplete them to an unacceptable level, to the fury of the commander-in-chief, Vice-Admiral Bertie; Corbet had to take the ship to England for refitting.[42]

The following year yet another person had found disfavour with Shield: Thomas King, who had been the naval storekeeper until he was seconded to be acting agent victualler at Mauritius. Shield's letter has not been found, but the Victualling Board, when returning it to the Admiralty secretary, remarked that it contained matter 'which had induced [Shield] to consider Mr Thomas King as an unfit person to hold a position of great responsibility'. But, continued the Victualling Board, in a letter of 29 August 1812, Shield had sent King's cash accounts without making any objection 'to any part thereof, or offering any comment on Mr King's character, or conduct'. They had found those accounts correct and had duly passed them.[43]

Shield's earlier career in the navy was not without relevant incident. As a lieutenant he had been privately prosecuted by a midshipman who accused him of assault and violence (the jury found for Shield), and as a captain part of his crew mutinied claiming ill-treatment. At the subsequent court martial Shield was acquitted, but sent home for the good of the service.[44] These early incidents do suggest that Shield was particularly irascible (a personality trait for which Corbet was also notorious), and it may be that his interpretation of comments made in haste by people he had managed to upset was stronger than they had intended. The alternative is to accept that he had arrived at the Cape and found a situation rife with corrupt

40 TNA ADM 1/3441 (Letters from Naval Commissioners Abroad to Admiralty), 18 September, 9 October & 4 December 1809; 1/3442, 25 June 1812. I am grateful to John Day for bringing my attention to these letters.

41 This may seem to be the wrong way round, but she was named *Bourbonnaise* partly because of the location of her capture, and partly because there was already a *Caroline* in the navy. I am grateful to Rif Winfield for this clarification.

42 John Day, 'The Role of the Resident Commissioner at the Cape of Good Hope 1809–1813' (MA Dissertation, University of Exeter, 2007), p. 60 and passim; Stephen Taylor, *Storm and Conquest: The Battle for the Indian Ocean, 1809* (London, 2007), pp. 246–7.

43 NMM ADM DP/33A, 4 May 1813.

44 Day, 'The Role', p. 47.

personnel whose response to his heavy-handed attempts to instil what he considered proper discipline was aggression, but for four separate people to react in the aggressive way Shield described is rather unlikely.

John Day suggests that although Shield was heavy-handed, the commander-in-chief at the Cape, Vice-Admiral Bertie, had been influencing the situation at both the victualling and naval yards to his own advantage. Day believes that it was Shield's reports on this situation which led to Bertie's abrupt recall and replacement.[45] That may have been the case, but it seems more likely that it was Shield himself who was the cause of all the other trouble.

Closer to home, in 1810 there was a long-running episode at Malta of ill-feeling between the agent victualler, Patrick Wilkie, and Commissioner Percy Fraser over the purchase of some bread. Wilkie accepted an instruction from the commanding admiral to buy bread; Fraser objected to this and the argument dragged on for several months. Wilkie prevailed here, as he was able to point to the second clause in the agents' instructions which stated that the senior admiral had precedence over the resident commissioner.[46] Trouble flared again in 1811 when there was a wheat shortage and Wilkie objected to Fraser's having instructed the agent at Gibraltar to buy some from American ships calling there. It transpires that Wilkie had had 'two fits of apoplexy' and was 'considerably advanced in years'; which may not have improved his temper; he retired later that year.[47] However, when an agent victualler had, as in this case, been doing his job for many years without complaints (and of whose performance the Victualling Board remarked that they had always been satisfied and that he had 'executed his duty to the best of his ability') it is hardly surprising that what appears to have been heavy-handed interference from an outsider would have caused resentment.[48]

Whilst the principle of placing an agent victualler in a remote location under the control of a senior Navy Board official can be seen as desirable in the context of the perceived threat of embezzlement, it had the unfortunate effect of putting the agent victualler under the potentially conflicting orders of three masters: the Navy Board commissioner, the commander-in-chief and the Victualling Board. This situation in itself put the Victualling Board to some trouble in dealing with the disputes. Together with the reluctance to pay a salary commensurate to the risk of working in unhealthy locations, this conviction that personnel would seek opportunities to defraud their employer illustrates the attitudes which were endemic in all naval administrators, not just the Victualling Board. In the case of Victualling Board

45 Ibid., p. 70.
46 TNA ADM 110/62, ff. 272–4, 9 August 1810.
47 TNA ADM 110/62, ff. 417–21, 6 October 1810; 110/63, ff. 152–8, 18 January 1811; 110/64. ff. 344–53, 1 November 1811.
48 TNA ADM 110/71, ff. 430–1, 14 December 1816.

establishments abroad during the French Revolutionary and Napoleonic wars, that conviction proved incorrect, as no such cases occurred.

Manual workers in the yards at home

The types of manual worker in any given yard were dependent on the activities carried out at that yard. All the yards received bulk supplies, put them into store and took them out again to issue them to individual warships and troop transports, or send them in bulk to other locations. This required numerous labourers throughout the yard, and stevedores or boatswains on the wharves. All the yards had messengers and what might now be designated security staff: porters at the gates, warders and watchmen inside the yards. All except Dover had some seamen to operate the delivery vessels (hoys, yawls, and at Plymouth, two sloops).[49] All the yards had coopers and their attendant sawyers. These, with the labourers, constituted by far the greater part of the workforce.

All the yards except Cork had bakers; most had brewers and millers, although at some yards these latter two activities were discontinued during the course of the period. Some yards had designated bread/biscuit bag menders and washers; it is unlikely that bags were not repaired or washed at the other yards but this may have been done by one of the other workers or on a local contract and thus not listed in the pay books.

Portsmouth employed a 'foreman of the flesh store'; Plymouth employed a 'weigher of fresh meat' and occasionally a couple of men in 'the seasoning house', but this would only have been to preserve excess quantities of fresh meat. Only Deptford regularly processed meat on a large scale; for this they employed randers, messers and salters.[50] These workers were only employed in the killing season from October to early April.

Plymouth had a designated cheesemonger, who would have unpacked the cheeses, put them in racks, scraped and brushed them to prevent decay, and repacked them in casks for issue.[51] Someone must have done this at the other yards without the specific designation.

Some yards intermittently employed building workers (carpenters, bricklayers, masons) and Deptford and Dover employed carters for moving provisions.

The depot ships had, as well as a dedicated clerk/storekeeper, a stevedore, labourers and coopers. There is no indication in the Victualling Board

---

49 These men had to be provided with protections against impressment, as did the watermen on contractors' lighters. See, for instance, NMM ADM C/682, 15 October 1794; C/687, 10 January 1797.

50 See the Glossary for definitions of these jobs.

51 *BOR 11*, pp. 64–5.

records of whether they had a permanent staff of seamen, or if not, who sailed them when they had to be moved. For the ships which were at more or less permanent anchor, they may have 'borrowed' officers and seamen from the local port admiral for this purpose, or the private owners from whom some of them were hired may have kept some crew on them. Equally, there is no indication of how they were restocked; one might surmise that they were sailed back to the nearest victualling yard for this purpose.

The army victualling store at Saint Catherine's employed only coopers and labourers, and only on an intermittent daily basis. This is not surprising as they only received and issued bulk supplies, and thus would only have required those workers for those events. The permanent staff consisted of four clerks, an 'Inspector of army provisions and victualling stores' and the storekeeper.[52]

All the above information is to be found in the pay registers;[53] the gaps in the coverage for some yards and the varied way in which the registers were kept, and the fact that some of the workers were employed by the day (and later by the piece), makes it impossible to give accurate numbers of workers. Other difficulties attached to this are that some individuals appear, by the repetition of their names, to have worked regularly by day as labourers and for one week at a time on a rotating basis as night watchmen. Thus what appears at first glance to be a large number of night watchmen is in fact a third or a quarter of the number listed, with these men already listed elsewhere. Another difficulty is that because the main wage payments were made on a quarterly basis, what might be counted as a high number of men would be shown to be less if counted on a 'number of jobs' basis allowing for leavers and joiners. This would be excessively time-consuming to do on a 'whole yard' basis, but can be demonstrated by examining the meat processors at Deptford. In the Christmas quarter of 1793, twenty-six names are listed (three inspectors, four messers, nineteen salters). However, one inspector and one salter left during the quarter and were replaced by other individuals, making a real total of twenty-four jobs, a number which remained static throughout the rest of the period. There are a few other apparent exceptions to this which turn out to be several men who worked only part-time.[54]

The meat processors were not the only workers employed on a seasonal basis; the coopers and labourers attached to the cutting house were only required when meat was being processed, and there was also a reduced need for coopers and other workers in the brewing departments at all the

52 *SCF* 32, pp. 50–1. Until 1806, when he retired due to ill-health, this was George Rose; given that the Treasury Secretary at that time was also a George Rose, there may have been a family connection: TNA ADM 109/106, 25 June 1806.

53 These are at TNA in the series ADM 113.

54 TNA ADM 113/159 to 163.

yards in the hot summer months when brewing ceased.[55] This seasonality of work was not exclusive to the victualling yards. As L D Schwarz points out in his *London in the Age of Industrialisation*, 'The concept of a single occupation, carried on throughout the year, was by no means universal … multiple occupations were commonplace and necessary' and that 'London consisted of a mass of people technically untrained but willing to learn any job that required a relatively short period of training.' He suggests that some 14 to 20 per cent of the population of East London could be categorised as general labourers.[56]

Given all this, one can offer no more accurate a number of victualling yard workers in the British Isles than approximately 3,000. This can be compared with the figures given for dockyard workers of between 13,000 and 16,000, although given the situation decribed above, which must also have pertained in the dockyards, those figures should not be taken as accurate or static numbers of full-time jobs.[57]

The Board of Revision had very little to say about the existing situation of the workers in the yards apart from comments on their wages and pension provision. They did, however, state that the numbers of labourers at Deptford seemed to be excessive, due to the practice of 'entering' them for specified departments. This made the labourers reluctant to do any work for other departments, which meant they wasted much time when there was no work in 'their' department. The same applied to the day coopers who worked for specified departments. In both cases the Board of Revision recommended that these workers should be entered into a common pool and sent to wherever they were required as and when the need arose. This, they said, should give a great reduction in total numbers employed.[58] It is difficult to tell if this happened, as most of the labourers continue to appear in the pay lists under separate departments.

There had already been a major reduction of workers in 1802. It is well known that St Vincent conducted a purge of old and infirm workers in the dockyards following a series of visitations to the yards; he also visited the victualling yards and effected a similar clear-out, though not on quite such a large scale. In the dockyards, over a quarter of the workforce (2,954 out of 10,756 men) were forced out, in the victualling yards it was about a tenth

55 For instance, as ordered on 6 July 1804, NMM ADM C/703.
56 L D Schwarz, *London in the Age of Industrialisation: Entrepreneurs, Labour Force and Living Conditions, 1700–1850* (Cambridge, 1992), pp. 48–50.
57 Morriss gives a total of 15,598 for March 1814 in *Royal Dockyards*, pp. 108–9; Haas gives 13,000 in 1814 in *A Management Odyssey: The Royal Dockyards, 1714–1914* (London, 1994), p. 3.
58 *BOR 11*, p. 38.

(338 men, of whom 212 were labourers and 37 coopers). About one-third of these men (101) were given pensions.[59]

At the same time, a rather tetchy letter from the Admiralty secretary asked the Victualling Board 'to explain to their Lordships' why six or seven men had been on the pay books for wages for more than six years when they were 'incapable from age and sickness from doing their duty or even attending the muster'. The reply was that with one exception, these men were between seventy-three and eighty-four years old and had worked in the yard for between twenty-five and forty-seven years; since they were all 'of good conduct' they had been left on the books. And anyway, due to their age and health, they were not likely to 'long remain a charge to the government'. It had, added the Victualling Board, long been the custom to indulge such old and faithful servants as an inducement to others to perform their duties 'industriously and faithfully'. The exception was Henry Dixen, aged forty and with eighteen years' service, who was stated to have caught a violent cold whilst at work which had turned into 'a deplorable paralytic affliction which has totally deprived him of the use of his limbs'.[60] He was the son of the ex-clerk of the cheque at the Port of London who had died in indigent circumstances, and like the others, if he had been granted a pension (referred to as 'the utter insufficiency of the Pension of £10') would not have been able to live on it, and if he had applied to the parish for relief, the parish would have seized that pension. This is much the same story told by the Navy Board about their elderly workers.[61]

Wages for manual workers

At the start of the period, wages for all manual workers were calculated on a 'per day' basis, and were paid once a quarter. This inevitably led to their having to borrow at high rates (10 or 15 per cent) to meet their household expenses.[62] In 1805, dockyard workers were granted weekly paid 'subsistence' money of two-thirds of their wages, with the balance paid quarterly; this scheme was then extended to the victualling yard workers in 1809.[63] Unlike the main wage payments, which went direct to the individual worker (who signed for it or made his mark), the men formed themselves into

---

59   NMM ADM C/698, 15 October & 1 November 1802. The minutes of these visitations to the yards are at TNA ADM 7/593 & 663–4.
60   Modern medicine would probably suggest a different cause of this paralysis.
61   TNA ADM 110/48, ff. 138–40, 21 October 1802; R A Morriss, 'Labour relations in the royal dockyards, 1801–1805', *The Mariner's Mirror*, vol. 62, no. 4, 1976, p. 342.
62   Morriss, 'Royal Dockyards', p. 102.
63   *BOR 11*, p. 41.

small 'parties' and designated a representative to collect their subsistence money.[64]

Meanwhile, the labourers had a major grievance which had to be dealt with: the Board of Revision had recommended a change to the payment system. Under the old system the men were paid the same daily rate throughout the year and had to attend for the same number of hours (which meant several hours in winter when it was too dark to work); under the new system they would work a shorter day in the winter, for which they would receive less pay. The difference was considerable: 20 per cent for coopers and first class sawyers, between 19 and 14 per cent for the other sawyers and the labourers.[65] When these reduced payments commenced in November 1809 the labourers at Deptford presented a petition, stating their living costs (which were higher in winter due to the need for warmer clothes and fuel costs) and the hardship caused by the new rates. The Victualling Board supported their case with the Admiralty, remarking that the new wage was 'inadequate to provide the poor men with the most ordinary means of support, particularly during the inclement season'.[66]

At this point Searle intervened: the idea of piecework for victualling yard workers had been mooted at various times but the yard officials were not convinced that it would be effective, despite its long-term use in the dockyards.[67] Searle demonstrated its advantage by supervising a gang unloading a barge on piecework; what would have otherwise taken a whole day took only two hours under the incentive of piece payment. Since this demonstrated that the labourers would be more productive under this system, and having conducted an investigation into pay rates for labourers across the whole of the naval yards, the Admiralty accepted that paying low wages led to the better workers going elsewhere; they conceded the point and the winter pay rates were suspended. The system was then extended to the coopers.[68]

The Victualling Board was not always so sympathetic to such requests. In late 1800, many of the bakers at Deptford, Rotherhithe and Dover requested a pay rise. This was refused and some of the men at Deptford and Rotherhithe went on strike; because this had involved a 'combination' they were committed to gaol under the Combination Act.[69] Then two foremen bakers and a cutting-house labourer paid for them to be bailed and were suspended for this. They wrote what can best be described as a grovelling

64   *BOR 11*, pp. 95–97, clauses 268 – 273. The pay lists for Dover show these 'party' payments: TNA ADM 113/99. The groups were to be of no more than twenty men.
65   *BOR 11*, p. 45.
66   NMM DP/29B, 9 & 15 November 1809.
67   Morriss, 'Royal Dockyards', p. 108.
68   Morris, *Naval Power*, pp. 231–2; NMM ADM DP/29, 15 November 1809.
69   39 Geo. III, c. 81.

letter, saying they had done it under the advice of the Justice of the Peace, hoping it would induce the men to return to work. This explanation was accepted and those three men were reinstated. Several of the striking bakers admitted that their actions had been improper and said that their demand for more pay was 'very improper'; they were also reinstated but the others were not.

Commissioner Towry went off to the north-east of England and Scotland in search of bakers who would come south to work. Meanwhile, the bakers at Dover failed to turn up for work, sending a letter to the agent victualler saying that they wanted an answer to their petition for more wages. He passed this to the Board, who replied that he should tell them they would have no more money and could either work or be prosecuted, in which case they would also never work for the Victualling Board again. Towry, meanwhile, had recruited 100 bakers in the north and sent them down to Deptford and Dover.[70] There was a further incident of bakers requesting more wages and receiving short shrift in 1814; they stated that the 'town' bakers got more money and were told that they could leave if they wished.[71]

Pensions for manual workers

Although there had always been some provision for workers to be super-annuated (i.e. retired on a pension), this was not automatically payable to all. This was probably a contributory reason for the high number of elderly men in the yards; as Morriss remarks 'the yard officials were reluctant to discharge these elderly men to penury'.[72]

The Board of Revision recommended this be changed to superannuation for all after thirty years' service, at the rate of £20 p.a. for coopers and saw-yers, £15 for warders and £10 for labourers; but if 'from length of service, or from injuries they may have sustained in faithful and diligent discharge of their duty, [they] shall merit particular indulgence, at the discretion of the Lords Commissioners of the Admiralty' these rates could be increased to £24, £20 and £15 respectively. This did not extend to widows, unless their husbands had been killed by an accident at work, in which case they were to receive half the amount 'during their widowhood'.[73]

From this date, numerous yard workers requested and were granted pensions, including several who had been injured at work. For the first few years of the scheme those seeking pensions from infirmity or injury had to be examined by a surgeon and/or appear before the Admiralty board,

70 TNA ADM 111/160, 7, 10, 11 & 13 August, 4 September 1801.
71 NMM ADM C/741, 1 January 1814.
72 Morriss, 'Royal Dockyards', p. 99.
73 *BOR 11*, p. 44.

but this requirement was soon dropped. As with the office clerks, requests for superannuation for yard workers were passed to the Admiralty by the Victualling Board with a letter which confirmed the loyalty, hard work and deserving nature of the worker, with the unstated implication that the undeserving would receive nothing.[74] But whilst one can understand that the Admiralty were following a government line which discouraged the additional burden to the public purse of such regular financial commitments, the amounts paid do seem somewhat niggardly at a time when it was known that the cost of feeding a seaman was a minimum 38s per lunar month, a fact reflected in the Victualling Board's own comment that a pension of £10 was utterly insufficient.[75]

Manual workers in the yards abroad

With the exception of a few British artisans sent out to foreign yards, most of the workers listed in such pay records as have survived appear from their names to have been locals.[76] By far the greatest number of these workers were labourers, but there were also some boatmen for deliveries from yard to warships, and some coopers performing the essential task of keeping the warships supplied with sound water casks. At a couple of the yards, where the agent victualler had discovered the economic benefit of making biscuit, there were some bakers. At Malta, while the ovens were being constructed, there were numerous building workers. At the Cape of Good Hope, some of the workers were slaves, whose owners collected their wages.[77]

The pre-1808 instructions say nothing about these workers; the 1808 *Regulations ... Abroad* only required the agent victualler to ensure that all workers were competent before engaging them, that they were to be listed in a 'complete' book and mustered regularly, that there were to be watchmen and gate porters (who were to search the workmen when they left the yard to prevent theft) and that there was to be a strictly enforced 'no smoking' rule. On the other hand, anyone injured at work was to be sent to the naval hospital.[78]

---

74   Correspondence between Victualling Board and Admiralty, NMM ADM C series, TNA ADM 110 series, passim.
75   See the estimate in Appendix B; TNA ADM 110/48, ff. 138–40, 21 October 1802.
76   Several coopers and bakers went out to the Mediterranean to work in the yards at Malta, Minorca and Sicily; others as far as Rio. TNA ADM 110/57, ff. 16, 338–40, 7 February & 9 May 1808; 110/61, ff. 165–7, 18 December 1809; 110/64, ff. 256–7, 267–8, 2 & 8 October 1811.
77   Pay lists for Malta are at TNA ADM 113/176; for the Cape of Good Hope, 113/2–3.
78   *Regulations ... Abroad*, articles 7 – 12.

There is no mention of the terms on which the wages were to be set; they were, presumably, close to the local norm for the various trades, and paid in the local currency. At the Cape of Good Hope, after Shield arrived, he signed the pay lists as having been paid in his presence, adding 'and it is my opinion they were paid at the lowest rate at which such persons could be procured'.[79] Nor is there any indication that any of these local workers were considered for superannuation in this period; the only yard which had been in operation for long enough in this context was Gibraltar.

Staff problems and discipline

Other than the actually criminal or morally unacceptable situations which are described in Chapter 8, or the mass rebellions described earlier in this chapter, there is remarkably little in the correspondence or minutes on difficulties with staff or yard workers. There are several possible reasons for this, which are worth examining.

The first possibility is that there really were very few problems, which seems unlikely given the numbers of people involved and the length of the period. The second is that they were dealt with 'in-house' and thus not mentioned in the minutes or otherwise brought to the attention of the Board. Whilst the agents victualler seem to have had the power to sack troublesome yard workers without consulting the Board, this did occasionally lead to spiteful accusations of wrong-doing by the yard officers, such as those made by the dismissed labourer Edward Mallard against the foreman cooper at Plymouth, who was, claimed Mallard, stealing staves with the assistance of yard labourers during work time. He was actually exercising his right to 'chips' by sending broken staves to his home by some of the labourers who did this in their dinner hour.[80]

With clerks, the threat of dismissal made by a department head or the board may have been sufficient but the actuality had to involve the Admiralty. One incident at Somerset Place illustrates this: in 1801, Holt, the accountant for stores, reported to the board the bad conduct of John Coulthred, the junior established clerk in his office: it was, said Holt,

> very improper, in making use of the most low, ungentlemanlike and indecent language, and he having continued to use the same, notwithstanding the repeated admonitions of the commissioner of the branch, and of [myself], and being convinced that he is in a very serious degree injuring the morals of the young men in his department, [I am] under the necessity of representing him as an improper person to remain in the

79 TNA ADM 113/3.
80 TNA ADM 110/51, ff. 440–3, 7 November 1804.

office. [Also the behaviour of Mr Halloran, a temporary supernumerary clerk] is equally improper, in shewing himself perfectly regardless to all admonition, and using language very disrespectful of [me] and [his] superiors ..., and so subversive of the order necessary to be preserved, that if he is continued, [I do] not think [I] shall be capable of conducting the business of the office ...

The Admiralty agreed and both Coulthred and Halloran were dismissed.[81]

This was, of course, an example of open aggression and disobedience; general incompetence would have been more difficult to manage, as there were no formally written office procedures or job specifications which could be used to measure performance, although such formal instructions were not unknown at the time.[82] It seems that there were no such instructions for the victualling office; there is no mention of such a thing in the correspondence or minutes, and when Sir George Clerk and Sir George Cockburn conducted an enquiry into victualling office staffing in 1821, they had to ask all the clerks to describe their own jobs.[83]

One difficulty for department heads would have been the fact that reporting difficulties with one's inferiors tends to be seen as a lack of ability to maintain discipline; the department heads may have elected to tolerate inefficiency for this reason, as may the commissioners. It is also possible that the department heads were either so busy themselves, or so physically isolated from their inferiors, that they were not aware of what was going on.

There is also evidence in the contract ledgers that the work done in the office was not checked: several of these ledgers contain pencil portraits (perhaps of other people in the office) and a caustic pencilled comment on a page where the detail had been crossed through: 'Mr Elliott says this is nothing, alias all my eye!' Such graffiti indicates not only a bored individual with nothing better to do, but is clear evidence that the clerk felt able to do this because he knew his comment would not be found.[84]

The final possibility is that the department heads did know what was going on but were unable to correct it because the employee had high-level patronage. In his introductory essay to Henry Taylor's *The Statesman*, Leo Silberman remarks on 'The backward nephews of influential men were

---

81 TNA ADM 111/160, 30 July 1801.
82 This is illustrated by Jacob M Price, 'Directions for the conduct of a merchant's counting house, 1766', *Business History*, vol. 28, 1986, pp. 134–50.
83 These job descriptions are in NMM ADM DP/201. When a new board secretary was appointed in 1822, he was given a set of instructions for the office staff: Admiralty Library, MSS 93.
84 For instance TNA ADM 112/184 f. 392 for a portrait; 112/189, no folio, last page of biscuit section for 'Mr Elliott' comment.

quartered for life upon the public, ... "vested interest" made these "sickly youths" good for nothing, "the unambitious and the indolent or incapable, well-nigh irremovable".'[85]

Such patronage may have been the reason for the astonishing level of tolerance shown by the Admiralty board for the behaviour of Lieutenant Fell Benamor at Portsmouth. Benamor was employed in April 1808, under the port admiral, to superintend the loading and unloading of the craft used to carry beer and water from the brewery at Weevil to the ships at Spithead and in Portsmouth harbour.

The first thing he wanted was a four-oared jolly boat (a not unreasonable request) which the Navy Board was told to supply. However, before many weeks had passed, he had started to annoy people by his 'frequent unnecessary and improper interference ... with the general duties of [the] agent and other officers' (one example of this was that in order to send water out to warships, he had commandeered a hoy which was intended to carry fresh meat, thus delaying that delivery by a day). The Victualling Board remarked to the Admiralty that they felt that since all that was needed was to see that the masters and crews of hoys were 'properly attentive', the task warranted no more than a master of the navy or a boatswain of the wharf. The Admiralty decided that as they did not want to remove him, Benamor should be put under Victualling Board orders and told the board to send him a letter containing precise details of his job.

By the end of the month, Benamor had asked for apartments in the brewery complex (none were available but he continued to request this), then a few days later he thought he should have a clerk and when asked why, he replied was it was obvious given his duties. The Admiralty agreed that these requests were unreasonable and wrote direct to Benamor telling him this and when he persisted, now suggesting he should take over some of the accounting work, asked caustically if he would prefer to go back to sea. He then proceeded to annoy various of the officers both at Weevil and in the yard at Portsmouth by demanding information on the duties of their clerks, and wanting to know the numbers of yard workers they commanded. Next, he took it upon himself to conduct an investigation and made accusations of irregularities in the brewery (which he conveyed to the yard officers in what the agent described as 'violent language'). Amongst other things, he said the behaviour in the tap made it resemble a 'beargarden', that the delivery crews were drinking the beer out of the casks, that staves were being left around on the wharf for weeks on end instead of being put away,

---

85   Leo Silberman in his introductory Essay to Henry Taylor, *The Statesman* (London, originally 1836, this edition 1955), p. xix, citing Parliamentary Papers 1854, XXVII, p. 405.

and that the accounting for cooperage stores was so lax that it would be easy to disguise embezzlement.

On investigation it turned out that some of his accusations were correct. However, this did nothing to reduce the irritation he was causing: in one letter about him to the Admiralty, the Victualling Board remarked that although some of his accusations were justified, others were frivolous or 'wholly unfounded', and that they had felt it necessary to instruct Benamor to conduct himself in future with 'becoming temper and moderation' since he had managed to provoke the normally calm agent victualler into unusual 'asperity'. Things then became quiet for some months, but the following April, it started up again, with a letter from the Victualling Board asking the Admiralty to request the commander-in-chief at Portsmouth, Sir Roger Curtis, to intervene in a dispute between Benamor and the master cooper. Sir Roger was duly asked to investigate, with the result that the Victualling Board was instructed to tell both parties that if they did not stop squabbling, they would both be dismissed. The Admiralty's patience did finally run out, although there is no indication of what caused this; the final letter on the subject is one which merely instructs the Victualling Board to appoint Mr W A Langton in Lieutenant Benamor's place.[86]

Given that this was a period when there were numerous lieutenants and warrant officers 'on the beach' who could have replaced Benamor, this 16-month-long saga is another illustration of the Victualling Board's place in the naval administration hierarchy: rather than remove a person who was causing major disruption in an important facility, the lords of the Admiralty expected the Victualling Board and its officers to tolerate this behaviour. This cannot be because the Admiralty expected the Victualling Board to dismiss Benamor, as it denied them the power to do so.

There is some other evidence that department heads and the Board were either unaware of staff activity (or inactivity) or chose to ignore this for various reasons. However, even when they were aware and wished to intervene, the courses of action open to them were controlled by the Admiralty.

---

86 TNA ADM 110/57, f. 340, 9 May; ff. 424–7, 7 June; ff. 495–6, 25 June; ff. 514–516, 29 June; 110/58, ff. 8–9, 2 July; ff. 23–31, 8 July; ff. 58–80, 20 July; ff. 111–14, 30 July; NMM ADM C/718 30 June; C/719, 6 July; 27 July; (all 1808); TNA ADM 110/59, f. 498, 28 April; NMM ADM C/722, 16 May; C/723, 28 August (all 1809).

8

Theft, Fraud, and other Misdemeanours

ALL ORGANISATIONS are, and always have been, vulnerable to people who seek to enrich themselves through means both unlawful and immoral; the Victualling Board, in common with other areas of naval administration in Georgian times, was no exception. What is important in the context of this study is how the Victualling Board managed this situation: what policies they had in place for prevention and early detection, whether these policies were actively pursued, what action they took on detection or complaint, and whether these policies were effective in reducing the incidence of misdemeanours over time.

In addition to the various cases where the Board's investigations produced evidence of wrongdoing (although this was often not sufficient to pursue legal action), there were also some cases where allegations appear to have been prompted by spite and where no evidence was found on investigation. Such allegations might be made by anonymous or pseudonymous letters, or, where officials were involved, by pamphlet, but as Morriss points out, despite the effort and time they absorbed, all had to be investigated as where officials were accused, such allegations undermined the credibility of both office holders and public finance.[1]

Theft

Knight tells of a culture of petty theft in the dockyards, encouraged by professional receivers and perhaps fuelled by low wages, long payment intervals

---

1 Roger Morriss, '"Corruption" in the management of the Royal Navy: The internal evidence of fraud, 1770–1820', p. 3. (I am grateful to Dr Morriss for letting me see this unpublished paper.)

and inflation.[2] His paper deals with the American War of Independence, but the situation cannot have changed much between then and the French Revolutionary and Napoleonic wars. Clearly there were parallels: the same financial situation for the workers, the same working practices which allowed workers' wives to bring meals into the yards in baskets which could then be used to remove plunder, the same opportunities for large groups of workers to 'surge' out of the gates at quitting time (and thus frustrating attempts to stop them for searches), the same impossibility for yard management constantly to observe the workers as they went about their tasks.

There were, however, differences between the victualling and dock yards, these being mainly that there were fewer small items of His Majesty's property available to be slipped into pockets (nails and fine cordage were particularly vulnerable in the dockyards) although a handful of corn or flour, a piece of meat or a couple of biscuits could be wrapped in a handkerchief and pocketed.[3] Most of the provisions were in large packages: casks of various sizes, or large single items such as whole cheeses, any of which would require some planning and transport to remove (although no doubt an enterprising and hungry worker could devise a way to remove a core from a cheese and disguise the hole). In several of the reported cases, items were stolen from the lighters or hoys employed by the yard: rope, empty casks or their iron hoops, casks full of foodstuffs, even the contents of casks were removed while in transit.[4]

In cases where the items could be positively identified as belonging to the Victualling Board (and this was easy enough with casks, or their component parts, which were all marked with the broad arrow) there were prosecutions, with yard officers attending the courts as witnesses to the ownership of the property. Punishment in such cases often included an element of warning to others who might be tempted: two of the thieves who stole rum and biscuit from one of the yard lighters at Chatham were given sentences which included two whippings outside the yard gates.[5] But it was not always possible to make the necessary positive identification, especially of loose foodstuffs: when in 1813 the Navy Board's embezzlement officer

2   R J B Knight, 'Pilfering and theft from the dockyards at the time of the American War of Independence', *Mariner's Mirror*, vol. 61, no. 3, pp. 215–25.

3   For example, see TNA ADM 111/188, 26 August 1808 (minute, baker caught with a handkerchief of grain); 111/188, 29 August 1808 (minute, cooper caught with nails); TNA ADM 110/66, 19 February 1813 (labourer caught with meat).

4   NMM ADM C/682, 21 August 1794 (theft of iron hoops); C/691 15 March 1799 (rope stolen from a lighter); C/727, 13 August 1810 (theft of hoops and staves); TNA ADM 110/58, 9 October 1808 (50 lbs of sugar stolen from a cask on the *Wanstead* hired transport); TNA ADM 110/69, 4 August 1814 (a barrel of flour stolen from *Rebecca* barge at Deptford).

5   TNA ADM 111/244, 31 August 1810.

caught James Everett of Northfleet in possession of some three hundred-weights of biscuit, two hundredweights of flour and some loose suet, the Victualling Board wrote that since they could not positively identify these items as being theirs, there was nothing to be done.[6]

Although there is a mention of 'depredations' in the minutes of the yard visitations made by St Vincent in 1802 there are very few such petty theft cases mentioned in the correspondence during the French Revolutionary and Napoleonic Wars. This is more likely to have been because most thefts were not detected than an indication of their actual rarity.[7] Such cases as are recorded all appear to have been detected by outsiders such as Customs officers or the Navy Board's 'embezzlement officer'. Since all these involved the thieves being caught 'in possession', it is not possible to tell whether these were single instances or merely the last of a series; the latter is more than possible, as it would be simple for petty thieves to repeat 'easy' crimes, especially where security was lax.

Today, even with modern security devices and cameras, such pilferage is endemic in warehouses and industrial worksites; all they had then was watchmen hampered by poor lighting at night. Storehouses would have been locked outside working hours, and some of the yard facilities were within walls with gate porters, but other victualling 'yards' (especially Portsmouth) were fragmented, consisting of different buildings situated around the town. Short of employing many more watchmen, and keeping all items under lock and key during the working day as well as at night, there was probably little more they could have done to prevent opportunistic picking up of unconsidered trifles. However, the pay books of the various yards show what appear to be the same men working as labourers during the day and watchmen on one or two nights each week, which would tend to invite collusion.

Such petty theft, provided it is kept within reasonable bounds, does little harm; constant repetitive thefts which built up to substantial quantities of goods can, if extended over a prolonged period, become expensive. However, lax storekeeping practices and inadequate stock-checks make it easy for thieves to ply their trade, especially when the goods involved are in substantial quantities and stored loose rather than bagged or casked, and when that store is constantly being drawn from. Although no such continuing thefts were reported, it becomes clear, when reading the report of the victualling commissioners' outport visitations in 1803, that such thefts, or regular embezzlement of stock by storekeepers, would not have been noticed.[8]

---

6   TNA ADM 110/66, ff. 473–4, 5 March 1813, Victualling Board to Navy Board.
7   TNA ADM 7/663, ff. 191–204, 30 September 1802.
8   NMM ADM D/45, 17 November 1803.

Fraud

With the exception of a few cases, such as the person who pretended to be a purser in order to obtain provisions,[9] or the person who forged bills of exchange in America,[10] most of those who committed fraud were pursers or junior officers in command of small warships who acted as their own purser. Almost all these offences consisted of variations on the themes of overcharging for items bought by pursers on the ad hoc basis (fresh beef, beer, etc.). An item which had cost the purser, say, 6d would be claimed at 7d or 8d, and/or the number supplied would be inflated. Since all such purchases entered in the purser's accounts had to be supported by vouchers from the supplier which had been countersigned by ships' officers (usually the captain), this required either alteration of the vouchers after signature, or the collusion of the officer and/or the supplier. For example Samuel Northcote, the purser of *Princess*, claimed for more than three times the amount of water actually collected at Liverpool.[11] This case came to light when Lieutenant George Peck happened to be with Captain Colquitt when the purser brought a bill for £34 drawn on the Victualling Board for signature; Peck thought the price was high and mentioned it later to the boatkeeper who said that the price had actually been £21.13.8. Peck then told the captain, who remarked that Northcote was 'a great scoundrel'; on being called to account for himself, the purser confessed and begged for forgiveness. Peck said he thought all the bills for water were too high and the captain replied that he knew they were but had not thought it was to such a great extent. Incensed by all this, Peck called for the captain to be court-martialled for signing false vouchers, knowing them to be false. Northcote's defence was that this was common practice at Liverpool, a statement which was confirmed by two other captains.[12]

The 1802 case of Lieutenant William Hicks and the gunvessel *Jackal* started out as a comparatively simple case of overcharging on beef and beer collected at Margate by one ship. Quite what prompted the investigation is not obvious, although it may have been a tip-off to the Admiralty, as between October 1802 and March 1803 there was a sequence of letters from the Admiralty secretary, William Marsden, querying Hicks' accounts, asking whether *Jackal* had actually received the provisions signed for, and finally asking whether there was a fraud between Hicks and the supplier. If this

---

9   NMM ADM D/43, 26 June 1801.
10 TNA ADM 110/47, ff 454–5, 20 May 1802.
11 Between August 1803 and June 1806 Northcote had collected just under 623 tons of water, but claimed for 1,980 tons: TNA ADM 110/55, ff. 329–333, 7 March 1807.
12 NMM C/713, 17 February 1807; TNA ADM 110/55, ff. 329–333, 7 March 1807; NMM ADM C/713, 30 March 1807.

was the case, said Marsden, they were to be prosecuted.[13] The Victualling Board sent one of their senior clerks, Brady, to investigate, and he reported 'gross frauds' in overcharging for beef and beer. He had questioned the butcher and brewer involved, but although they had verified the offence, the Admiralty solicitor felt that they would not be acceptable to a court as witnesses because they were too close to the offences themselves; a court martial was suggested as an alternative. The Admiralty ordered Hicks to be struck off the list of officers. Then a further letter listed six other ships which may have been implicated and directed that their accounts should be examined. Brady went back to Margate and reported that they all were implicated; after some deliberation, the excess amounts were charged to the respective commanders' imprest accounts.[14] As well as recovering the money through the officers' pay, the Victualling Board prevented a recurrence by making a local contract for supplies, thus giving them control over the prices of all the items required.[15]

As with the theft cases, there do not appear to have been a great number of purser frauds during this period. Nor were there any new major frauds perpetrated by contractors or agents victualler, although a couple of cases which had begun in the 1780s were still rumbling on, both from the West Indies. William Ward was the contractor for Jamaica; he and his associates Blackburn and Shirley were accused of frauds committed in 1778, 1779 and 1780 in Jamaica, Barbados, St Kitts and Grenada. The allegations, which came from the purser of the *Alert* sloop, Arthur Goate, concerned substitution of the cheaper sugar, or an amount of cash at the value of sugar for the more expensive butter or oil, and Goate stated that Ward and his partners had profited from this to the tune of some £300,000. Like many such cases, these allegations came long after the events complained of, seemingly as a result of Goate's failure to get his accounts passed. During the course of the correspondence between Goate and the Victualling Board, during which he stated that he had been 'well informed' that Commissioner Towry would allow no interference in his department from the other commissioners, matters had become so acrimonious that the Victualling Board remarked to the Admiralty that Goate's letters were 'in terms the most insulting and abusive' and that only Goate's insignificance had prevented their suing him for libel.[16]

13 NMM ADM C/698, 18 October, 15 November & 28 December 1802; C/699, 3 March 1803; C/700 24 September 1803; TNA ADM 110/49 ff. 354–6, 22 September 1802.
14 TNA ADM 110/50, ff. 34–6, 20 November 1803; NMM ADM C/704, 4 December 1804.
15 TNA ADM 110/50, ff. 126–8, 6 January 1804.
16 NMM ADM DP/2, 9 January & 19 February 1782; DP/9, 10 July 1787; DP/9, 22 July 1788, 18 & 28 July 1789.

Ward responded to the allegations by pointing out that substitutions were allowed by the contracts and after the case had been considered by three outside arbitrators (who found for Ward) the Victualling Board eventually had to abandon the action, although they did manage to collect contract penalties of £10,000 and the costs of the legal action.[17]

The amounts in the Ward case were substantial but those alleged in the case of the other fraud in the West Indies were much greater. This case involved allegations made by two merchants, William Wilkinson and Joseph Blake Higgins, against a set of people who included the merchant William Whitehead, the naval storekeeper at Antigua Anthony Munton, the agent victualler John Marr, and the deputy agent victualler at Antigua Thomas Druce. Whitehead, who had been a prize agent in the American war, was also alleged to have failed to pay out prize money. The amounts, stated to be annually £1,000,000 at Jamaica, £300,000 at Antigua, £300,000 at St Lucia and £250,000 at Barbados, were split between the Navy Board, the Sick and Hurt Board, the Victualling Board and the Ordnance Board.

It was the usual story of overcharging and overstating supplies and delivery costs but on a grand scale. The situation was somewhat muddied by Wilkinson's own situation: he was being sued by creditors and during the time covered by the investigation spent two periods of eighteen months in debtors' gaols in Antigua and Virginia. He claimed that these actions had been brought against him in an attempt to silence him and his letters became more and more incoherent as he railed against the malefactors. Like many of the informants in such cases, Wilkinson and Higgins wanted to be paid for their trouble; they had been in partnership with Whitehead, then bought him out but retained his books; they claimed these would give all the necessary proof, and suggested that they would carry out the investigation for 15 per cent on the first £100,000 recovered and 7½ per cent on other recoveries. It transpired that their motives were not entirely innocent: because they were heavily in debt they had first attempted to sell their silence to Whitehead and Munton and only turned to the naval administration when this attempt failed.

The documentation on this case is somewhat fragmented, but it seems that very little success was achieved, considering the magnitude of the allegations. Whitehead was found responsible for defrauding the public of £1,213 by the Assembly in Antigua and Munton was fined and imprisoned for his involvement. Although the sum mentioned as relating to the Victualling Board was originally stated to be between £50,000 and £60,000, it is not clear what the exact amount was, nor whether they succeeded in

17   NMM ADM C/690, 17 September & 24 November 1799.

recovering any of it. It does seem that the allegations were true in principle if not necessarily in amount.[18]

In both these cases the normal difficulties of getting to the truth of large numbers of transactions, involving numerous ships and a prolonged time period during which there were several changes of personnel on the station, were exacerbated by the communications difficulties associated with the distance involved and the fact that the navy (or at any rate, Nelson, as senior officer on the station) had not endeared itself to the local merchants by its insistence on adherence to the Navigation Acts. This combination of factors, with the multiple jurisdictions in the West Indian islands, the distances between the different islands as well as that between the West Indies and Britain, the unhealthy environment which eliminated many potential witnesses, and the number of government departments involved, meant that without some form of radical reorganisation of the whole system of oversight there was little that could be done to prevent a recurrence. The Victualling Board made no attempt to change the system of oversight at that time but it had realised that the whole voucher system was rather loose, and altered the documentation, requiring the ships' masters and captains to verify that the amounts shown were genuine.

The Board retained an agent victualler at Antigua until 1804 when it found itself unable to find a suitable replacement for George Desborough who had died; it finally put the task at Antigua out to a contractor, and continued to use a contractor at Jamaica, but set up separate contracts for all the other islands, although in practice most of these, with the exception of Jamaica, were held by one individual. Maybe they were lucky in their choices of contractors, for there were no further reported instances of grand fraud against the Victualling Board between 1793 and 1815. On the other hand, given the general personal debt situation in which Wilkinson and Higgins had managed to get themselves embroiled, and the almost unbelievably large sums of money which they claimed as having been defrauded, one does question whether the amounts involved were mainly figments of the overheated imagination of a near-bankrupt and over-stressed individual; perhaps the Victualling Board had also reached this conclusion.

Embezzlement

With three exceptions, the embezzlement cases were those where pursers, storekeepers or other employees were found to have sold provisions from

---

18   Morriss, *Naval Power*, pp. 115–18, believes the case fizzled out for lack of proper evidence and gives only one reference; John Sugden, *Nelson: A Dream of Glory* (London, 2004), pp. 352–5, 377–8, 393–5, gives much detail and copious references; see also TNA ADM 114/26; NMM CAD/D/15, Appendices 4 & 5.

their stock, or made private use of His Majesty's property and employees. As far as cases of illicit disposal of stocks on board ship were concerned, more of these cases involved masters of transports than pursers of warships, and all but one involved single ships.[19] The exception to this was the case where the pursers of a group of blockships employed under Trinity House were accused of false musters and sale of provisions.[20] Unfortunately reports of the resolution of this case have proved elusive.

There was one more substantial case, that of Lambert Middleton, the storekeeper of the depot ship *Harmony* which was stationed at The Downs. He, with his clerk Arthur Bryan, the ship's master Thomas Clark and the mate Henry Rimington, had been sending boatloads of biscuit and spirits ashore, presumably for sale. Middleton had also, a few months earlier, been reprimanded for sending coal ashore 'for his own use'. The ensuing prosecutions took place at Maidstone Assizes and the Old Bailey; unfortunately the results of these two trials are not reported in the Victualling Board documents and cannot be found in the surviving records of either court or the Home Office lists.[21]

The cases which involved private use of His Majesty's resources featured either storekeepers or millers. The most interesting of these cases, for its audacity if nothing else, was that of Thomas Watts, the master miller at Rotherhithe, who was running what can only be described as a mini-farm on the mill premises. He had converted one of the tanks to a duckpond, built a large hogsty which housed between twenty and thirty hogs 'which could not all be for the domestic use of his family', and also constructed an enclosure for a large number of turkeys and other poultry. All this livestock was being fed corn or pollard from the mill, and several of the labourers employed 'by the Crown' were working full-time caring for the livestock. Acting on information received, a Board inspection verified these offences; Watts was suspended immediately and subsequently dismissed.[22] Although the Victualling Board acted swiftly when they were informed of this case, what sounds like a long-established practice, and one which would have been immediately visible to anyone walking round the premises, should have been detected earlier.

The first two exceptions both involved cash: Payne, the purser of *Hindostan* who 'ran' with the short allowance money he had collected from the agent victualler at Plymouth, and which he should have paid over to

---

19 For example: NMM ADM C/690, 28 September 1798 (the purser of *Fame* selling brandy); TNA ADM 110/60, ff. 104–5, 17 June 1809 (master of transport *Bellona*); 110/64, ff. 432–5, 3 December 1811 (master of transport *Christiana*).

20 NMM ADM C/709, 29 January 1806.

21 TNA ADM 110/65, ff. 48–9, 186–7, 200–1, & 442, 7 February, 30 March, 6 April & 21 July 1812; 110/67, ff. 274–5 & 387, 29 & 30 June & 10 August 1813.

22 NMM ADM D/40, 15 September 1796; C/686, 27 September 1796.

the crew, and William Bishop, a victualling yard worker at Portsmouth who absconded with the weekly subsistence money he had collected for his party of labourers. In Payne's case, the Admiralty's initial reaction was to stop Payne's pay and the payment of any balance due on his pursery accounts, using this to pay the crew as far as it would go, giving preference to the seamen over officers. The Victualling Board protested against this on the grounds that it was not right that the crew should be disadvantaged by Payne's fraud. Payne was apprehended and sent for trial at Plymouth, where he was found guilty and given a six-month gaol sentence. He was also court-martialled and sentenced to lose all pay and allowances due to him.[23] Bishop's case came to light when the party of labourers sent a petition to the Admiralty; after a brief exchange of letters the Admiralty instructed that the labourers should be reimbursed for the missing money.[24] These were both cases which probably could not have been predicted (and they were the only two reported during the whole of this period) and thus there was little which could have been done to prevent them. When they were notified, the Victualling Board moved with commendable speed and sympathy to ensure that the potential victims did not suffer.

The third exception, that of Joseph Matthews, the agent victualler at Chatham, started with other misdemeanours, and it was not until after his dismissal that the embezzlement came to light. He had already been strongly reprimanded in 1797 for 'great neglect and inattention … to the duties of his office' after complaints from naval officers,[25] then in December 1799, the Victualling Board reported to the Admiralty that the preceding April, the Commissioners of Customs and Excise had received intelligence that Matthews and his second clerk, J Stephens, had smuggled spirits and wine ashore to Matthews' house; having obtained a warrant, Customs officers had searched the house and seized 34 gallons of rum and more than 260 gallons of wine. Matthews was prosecuted before the local Justices of the Peace and as well as having the rum and wine confiscated, had been fined 500 guineas, which he paid immediately. Now it transpired that further smuggling offences had been committed at various times by Matthews and by other officers of the yard, as a result of which Commissioner Towry had been sent to investigate and report. He had found that in addition to the accusations of the Customs officers, Stephens had been in the habit of hiding rum in the victualling stores before taking it home, so the Board dismissed him 'as a punishment and an example'. Towry had also found that pursers having their stock surveyed at the Nore had been giving rum to the clerks

23 NMM ADM C/695, 15, 18 & 30 April 1801; TNA ADM 110/46, f. 621, 21 April 1801; ADM 1/7353, 7 May 1801.
24 NMM ADM C/735, 9 & 12 September 1812; TNA ADM 110/66, ff. 19–21, 10 September 1812.
25 TNA ADM 111/143, 4 April 1797.

and their boat crews, and he had forbidden this. At this time, Matthews escaped with no more than a warning about his future conduct.[26]

After this incident, all was quiet until 1802, when questions began to be asked about the well used to provide water at Chatham. It transpired that the original lease for this well, which was on land opposite the yard, had been made in 1778 (when the other well which served both the victual-ling and dock yards had proved inadequate); this well was on land which at that time belonged to the father of the current agent victualler, and the lease, at £42 p.a., was for twenty-one years. In 1799 this lease had been renewed for £100 p.a. for twenty-nine years, after some negotiation with Joseph Matthews, who had inherited the land when his father died; the original asking price had been £300 p.a. Prompted by the Admiralty, two commissioners, Towry and Moody, went to Chatham and made enquiries from various locals, including a brewer who drew water from a well near that of Matthews. They found that there was plenty of good water available (including river water near Rochester Bridge which was usable for a few hours each tide) and that local opinion was that the price they had been obliged to pay was excessive. It also transpired that there was a perfectly good well in the laundry yard, although this had been closed up for some time; the Inspector of Repairs from Deptford said this well could be deep-ened and made usable with a pump for a cost of £260, and that it would then supply all the water needed.[27]

Matthews was then asked why he had not disclosed this alternative source or the cost of other sources of water, and as his answers were not satisfactory, the Admiralty, feeling that he had failed in his duty to the Board, ordered that he be dismissed.[28] Three weeks later, it was reported to the Board that Matthews had for 'a considerable time before his dismission [been] in the constant practice of rendering fallacious accounts of the monies remaining from time to time in his hands'. This added up to a substantial sum, so a warrant was put out to seize both his person and his property. An auction-eer from Rochester was employed to value the contents of Matthews' house and the new agent victualler, Henry Stokes, was instructed to view these contents and identify any items that belonged to the Crown. Meanwhile, Joseph Matthews' brother John was accused of breaking the new lock which Stokes had put on the office door, stealing various papers and passing them to his brother; he was to be tried at the next Kent Quarter Sessions.[29]

---

26 NMM ADM D/41; 27 December 1799, C693, I January 1800.
27 TNA ADM 110/48, ff. 161–72, 30 October 1802.
28 NMM ADM C/698, 4 November 1802.
29 TNA ADM 111/165, 26, 29 and 30 November 1802. There was a John Matthews working in the Chatham office as a clerk, it is not unreasonable to suggest that this was the brother, who thus had access to the premises.

One must ask why the Board did not wonder, in 1799, how it was that the agent victualler, whose income from his victualling duties was little more than £250 per annum, had been able to 'immediately' pay a fine of 500 guineas;[30] why the reason given for dismissing Stephens was 'as a punishment and an example' rather than because he had been demonstrated to be dishonest and thus not a suitable person to be employed in a position of trust; and why, given that it had been necessary to reprimand him for neglect of duty and that he had also been found guilty of the smuggling offense, Matthews was not also dismissed at that time. Equally, one wonders why it did not occur to anyone that a person who had just been dismissed from a lucrative job and who had been shown to have been embezzling substantial sums of money for several years would not hesitate to arrange for incriminating documentation to be stolen from his old office, and that this could have been avoided by arranging for those documents to be held in a more secure place.

One final case, which is reported in the Eighth report of the Commissioners of Naval Inquiry,[31] involved embezzlement of casks from the Southdown brewery at Plymouth. In December 1801, the agent victualler, Thomas Miller, was informed that some casks belonging to the victualling office were hidden at the Tamar Brewery in Maurice Town near Plymouth Dock, the largest of the local private breweries. Miller obtained a search warrant, and with Joseph Pridham (an attorney), Samuel Triscott (a foreman cooper from Southdown) and a constable, conducted a search of the Tamar Brewery's premises, escorted by the managing partner John White. In a locked cellar they found three empty butts marked with the broad arrow and coopers' marks showing they had been made at Southdown, and eleven other butts with the broad arrow freshly chipped out. Elsewhere in the brewery they found a further fifty-five butts with the marks chipped out.

The clearly marked butts were marked again by Miller and Triscott for identification and returned to the victualling office; the others were left until a decision could be made on how to proceed. On the following day they returned and found that all the suspect casks had been shaken. White, when summoned before the magistrates, stated that these casks were part of a batch of 100 purchased in London. The court case did not reach a satisfactory conclusion.

When the Commissioners of Naval Inquiry visited Plymouth in 1804 they felt the investigations had not been properly carried out, and proceded with their own investigation. After the time which had elapsed between

30   Matthews' income as agent victualler at that time was £252.17.6: SCF 32, Appendix A, pp. 48–9.
31   *Eighth Report of the Commissioners of Naval Inquiry: His Majesty's Victualling Department at Plymouth – Embezzlement of the King's Casks*, pp. 648–53.

this and the original incident it was difficult to establish the true story, but one informant, Gilbert Heard, who had worked at the Tamar Brewery, said that it was well known that Victualling Board casks were brought to the brewery, that between Miller's first and second visits a group of coopers had worked all night under White's supervision to shake the casks and erase markings, and that he (Heard) had been given £10 for 'expenses' and told to absent himself so that he could not be questioned.

Other than report their conclusion that the original investigation had not been carried out sufficiently thoroughly, there was little that could be done by the commissioners except recommend tighter procedures for handling casks returned from warships, this being thought to be the origin of the diverted casks. The victualling yard personnel responsible for these diversions were not identified. There was, however, a query as to why Miller had chosen Pridham to act in the matter instead of Mr Eastlake, the attorney previously used in such cases at Plymouth. It seemed that Miller had chosen Pridham 'as a matter of private regard'. The inference here is that Pridham was inexperienced in such matters and thus a poor choice. This may have been a naïve decision by Miller, but it was not contrary to his instructions, which did not contain anything on how to proceed in cases of theft or other misdemeanours.[32] Nor did the new instructions of 1808 include anything on how to deal with such matters. Although it was clearly expected that commissioners and officials at the yards should deal with such situations when they arose, it seemed that it had never occurred to anyone that they needed guidance on how to do so.

Misfeasance

There were few cases under this heading, but one of these was extremely serious. Like many others, this case started with an anonymous letter. Signed 'A Contractor' and passed on to the Victualling Board by the Admiralty secretary, the letter stated that the accountant for cash, Denham Barons, discounted bills drawn on the cash department,[33] that he and other clerks not only expected presents from contractors but actually made out lists, with their addresses, of the items they wished to receive, and that if contractors did not comply with these demands their business was neglected and preference given to contractors who did comply.[34] A second letter from 'A

---

32 TNA ADM 49/59.
33 Discounting bills was the process whereby the holder of a bill could obtain cash for its face value, less a discount. This discount reduced in size as the due date of the bill got closer.
34 The named clerks were John Arthur Smith (Barons's first clerk), William Elliott senior (his second clerk), and other clerks of the same department, namely

Contractor' stated that another contractor had experienced difficulty until he sent 'three dozen of sherry each', the writer said that he had not received proper attention until he had sent some 150 bottles of wine: 'but before that I could not get a civil answer from Mr Todd or Mr Richardson and every impediment is thrown in my way by Millman being [continually] absent from the office'.[35]

The background to this was the changeover of salary systems.[36] This had been formalised by an Order in Council dated 29 January 1800, and all the clerks were required to take an oath, as given in the Order. The claimed offences were therefore not just dubious behaviour, but behaviour which was specifically forbidden.

The Board responded to the anonymous letters by conducting an investigation with the assistance of Mr Read, the chief magistrate of Bow Street. They interviewed all the clerks and nineteen contractors, of whom thirteen were major suppliers of bulk products such as Irish meat, flour and biscuit; two others were less important bulk suppliers and the remaining four were the largest of the sea provisions contractors. Five of the contractors said they had discounted bills through clerks, three of them naming Barons; one said he had received hints about presents 'in a round-about way' but had ignored this, six denied having given presents at all, the other nine said they had given presents but had not been asked for them. Of those who had given presents, six described them as 'trifling' or 'small', these involving a case of wine or, in one case, a small keg of biscuit. One had given two hampers of a dozen bottles of wine, another presents of wine and lottery tickets at Christmas, another had given 'a couple of dozen of Madeira' to several of the clerks, one gave an annual haunch of venison to Barons, and William Mellish, the fresh meat supplier, had made annual presents to several of the clerks of 'from two to eight dozen of Madeira, port or wine'. Mellish had also, in the past, discounted bills with Barons and paid a brokerage fee, but had concluded this was not proper and asked for the brokerage fee to be returned, which Barons did. The contractor Glenny said he had not given presents on a regular basis but when his agency with another of the sea provisions contractors, Alexander Donaldson, had ceased, he had sent hampers of wine to 'five or six' of the clerks 'out of gratitude for past favours'. He had also occasionally procured loans of £2,000 to £3,000 for 'one or two' of the clerks (not named), on which they stood the risk.

Ralph Watson, Manley Hulke, Charles Moss, Richard Hawes Harman, Thomas Richardson, William Todd and George Millman.

35   NMM ADM C/717, 30 March 1808, C/718, 9 April 1808.
36   The difference between the two salary systems, especially for the heads of departments, could be significant: the average annual income of the accountant for cash preceding Barons was stated to be £3,169 in 1798, the new salary was £700. SCF 32, Appendix A, pp. 20–1; TNA ADM 110/72, ff. 164–75, 17 May 1816.

Of the ten clerks whose evidence is detailed, two 'extra' clerks, Henry Park and William Elliott junior, stated they had neither accepted presents nor discounted bills. The others, with the exception of John Guyer (Barons' sixth clerk) in his first statement, all said they had accepted presents of wine and/or lottery tickets. William Elliott senior said that he had given his home address to contractors when asked for it. Of those who confessed to having discounted bills, four said they had done so (one using money from friends who saw it as a good investment) but not charged a brokerage fee; four others used the careful wording 'never discounted bills for any person on which [they] charged or received brokerage', which seems to imply that they had discounted bills, but without a brokerage fee, rather than that they had not discounted bills at all. The tenth statement, that of the accountant for cash, Denham Barons, was rather more detailed. He said that friends had occasionally left sums of money with him for purchasing victualling bills on their behalf and that all he had received was a commission for his trouble which was less than the brokerage fee charged by professional bankers. He then added that he had never thought he might be doing wrong or that there was 'any possible impropriety, but on the contrary some public advantage might rather result from the transaction by giving additional facility to the circulation of this description of Government bills', and went on to say that he thought he was helping the contractors to get ready cash, as they could not do so on these bills until twenty-five or thirty days of the ninety had elapsed. He then added that he had never thought this incompatible with his official duties until a friend suggested that it might be wrongly construed, so he immediately stopped, and had 'made myself responsible to Mr Mellish for repaying to him the whole of the brokerage I had received from him' (a slightly different story to that given by Mellish). Barons added that the charge of taking presents was 'totally false' but went on to say that he had received some 'objects of friendly notice' such as occasionally a haunch of venison (again a different story to that of the donor) or a dozen or two of wine.[37]

John Guyer, who was the first of the clerks to be questioned, said in his first statement that he knew of no instance of presents being made or of any bills discounted; twelve days later he was questioned again and this time told a different story. In 1804 he had been working out of office hours in the counting house of Alexander Donaldson, the sea provisions contractor for Jamaica; Donaldson told him that Elliott had asked for presents for himself and the other clerks and that he had asked his partner Glenny to deal with it, telling him 'Spend no more than two hundred pounds or guineas in wine'. Glenny bought a pipe of Madeira and bottled it, sending either six or four dozens each to Elliott, Watson, Hulke, Moss and others, but none to

37   TNA ADM 110/57, ff. 230–57, 19 April 1808.

Barons who had a loan instead. Guyer also bought four half lottery tickets at a cost of 36 guineas, which went to Harman, Watson and another clerk named Mobbs who had subsequently left the office. Guyer said he had no knowledge of other presents nor of who wrote the anonymous letters.[38]

The Admiralty, on receiving this report, ordered ten of the main offenders to be dismissed immediately, and four days later, added Guyer to the list. The Victualling Board acknowledged these orders, but pointed out that this would take a little time as the department would need to be reorganised to be able to carry on business, and the Admiralty agreed to suspend the order consistent with getting work done.[39] Before the dismissals could take place, William Elliott sent a personal memorial and seven of the other clerks sent a joint memorial to the Admiralty, pleading for their jobs and enclosing a copy of the oath which they had taken. This was not in the form in which it had been laid down in the Order in Council. They also enclosed a letter from the officers of both the cash and stores departments, stating that they thought they were allowed to act as they had done. The Admiralty in reply wished to know why the Victualling Board had altered the form of the oath without permission.[40]

The Victualling Board replied that when the oath was originally required they had minuted the requirement on 14 March requiring all staff to take the oath. By 'the following July'[41] all the officers and clerks at Plymouth and Dover had taken it but those in London did not wish to do so in that form, objecting on the basis that they might 'on trifling occasions inadvertently deviate' and wanted to lodge a bond which could be exercised instead of being dismissed. In May 1802, this suggestion had been passed to the Admiralty secretary of the time, Evan Nepean, who replied that their lordships insisted that the oath should stand. Acting on the assumption that the wording given in the Order in Council was not intended to be rigid, the Victualling Board changed the wording to what was thought to be more appropriate (but still meeting 'any conscientious scruple … without diminishing its efficiency'). This version was thought by the clerks to permit them to accept 'presents of game or other similar marks of attention which a gentleman may honourably receive from another'.

On 2 June 1802 the Victualling Board minuted the decision that anyone who had not taken the original oath should now take the new one, which

---

38 Ibid.
39 NMM ADM C/718, 22, 25 & 26 April 1808; TNA ADM 110/57, ff. 268–9, 23 April 1808. The ten to be dismissed were Denham Barons, John Arthur Smith, William Elliot senior, Ralph Watson, Manley Hulke, Charles Moss, R H Harman, Thomas Richardson, William Todd and George Millman.
40 NMM ADM C/718, 28 April 1808.
41 Whether this means 1800 or 1801 is not stated, but in view of what follows, it probably meant 1801.

they all did. The victualling commissioners said that they had not consulted the Admiralty lords on the changed wording as they saw no need to trouble them again and felt their changes made no real change to the intention of the order. They did remember a conversation with some officers about the propriety of accepting 'such trifling presents as a brace of pheasants or a turkey at Christmas' but did not think this could reasonably be interpreted as including wine or spirits. They added, almost as an afterthought, that about a year and a half previously, despite having thought they had taken every means in their power to prevent abuses, they had found it necessary to reprimand Guyer for 'great misconduct' (not specified), and as a result had put a notice in the public entrance hall of the offices stating that 'all victualling and other bills made out in this office are to be passed in regular course without favour or partiality to any person' and that anyone who felt they had a complaint on this should address it to the Board.[42]

In a further letter to the Admiralty, the Victualling Board enclosed another letter from eight of the clerks (Smith, Elliott, Richardson, Harman, Todd, Watson, Hulke and Millman) begging the dismissal order to be reconsidered, apologising and promising not to offend again; the Victualling Board remarked to the Admiralty that they would be loth to lose the experience these clerks had.[43] The Admiralty replied that they would accept this for seven of those named, but that the four others (Barons, Smith, Elliott and Guyer) should be dismissed (the original ten plus Guyer). The rest were to be retained, but were not to benefit from promotion in the process of replacing those who had gone.[44] The replacements came from other departments in the victualling office.[45] Two weeks later, on 12 May 1808, a board minute records 'Ordered that the practice of discounting or negotiating Bills in this office, be for the future discontinued'.[46] After some discussion, a final wording for the oath was agreed and all officers and clerks were obliged to take it.[47]

Four thoughts come to mind in connection with all this: why it took so long for the oath situation to be resolved; why the commissioners had allowed themselves to be persuaded that some of the staff should be allowed to take a different form of oath; why this situation of blatant disobedience to the spirit, if not the actual form, of the oath had been allowed to continue so long without detection by the commissioners; and why Guyer had been merely reprimanded when he had been detected in contravention (whether

---

42 TNA ADM 110/57, ff. 301–4, 30 April 1808.
43 Ibid., ff. 305–9, 30 April 1808.
44 NMM ADM C/718, 4 May 1808.
45 TNA ADM 110/57, ff. 330–4, 6 May 1808.
46 TNA ADM 111/187, minute, 12 May 1808.
47 For the first two versions of the oath: NMM ADM C/718, 28 April 1808, enclosures 1 & 2; TNA ADM 110/57, ff. 336–8, 346–8, 6 & 11 May 1808.

the commissioners were aware of his 'moonlighting' is not stated). The Admiralty clearly thought this way when they expressed their surprise that 'the system of corruption' had gone on for so long in direct violation of the office regulations without the victualling commissioners having discovered it: 'Their Lordships cannot but feel that there must have been great want of vigilance on your parts, or such disgraceful practices could not have prevailed unnoticed'.[48]

There is, however, a possibility that some of the commissioners may have been not only aware of the practices but actually involved themselves. By the end of May, replacements for the dismissed staff had been approved and all should have proceeded smoothly, but on the eighteenth, another anonymous letter arrived, this time signed 'A Friend to the Cause'. This one suggested that the method of investigation had been faulty: 'had not the investigation been conducted in a particular way when Mr Read presided, I am fully convinced has [sic] many more [than the four dismissed] would have been found guilty of the same offence … it is well known for greater men than the Accountant for Cash [to have] participated in the same illicit practices.'[49] This echoes a comment made by William Elliott in his individual memorial of 25 April: 'without mentioning any names in particular, he [Elliott] conceives there is hardly a person of any rank or consequence in the department who has not done so either for himself or for friends.'[50]

Whether or not these allegations were true, the investigation seems to have stopped at that point, or at any rate, no more appears in the correspondence. What did happen, at the very end of 1808 and the beginning of 1809 was that three commissioners departed: John Marsh the chairman, William Budge and Robert Sadleir Moody, to be replaced by Nicholas Brown, John Aubin and Edward Stewart. Although the main reason given for these changes was the reports of the Board of Revision, this scandal must have been influential in the Admiralty's decision. Marsh was only 62, and his enforced retirement certainly came as a great surprise to him, and it was later referred to as his having been 'turned out' to make way for Searle;[51] equally, it is clear that Budge's departure was not voluntary either: he referred to this in a later letter as 'my removal from the Victualling Board'.[52]

To the eye that reads no further in the correspondence than the end of the war in 1815, it appears that everybody concerned had taken the lessons of the dismissals to heart, or that the Board had found a way of keeping an

48   NMM ADM C/718, 22 April 1808 .
49   NMM DP/28, 18 May 1808.
50   NMM DP/28, 25 April 1808.
51   NMM BGR 35 (Marsh's journal); *The Times*, 19 March 1822. Searle was, of course, already on the board.
52   NMM ADM C/723, 25 July 1809.

eye on the extra-mural activities of their staff. This, however, was not so: in 1821, another series of anonymous letters arrived at the Admiralty. There had been several of these, but only one survives; it is given here as written to show its rather chaotic nature in spelling, punctuation and thought processes, a common feature of such letters.[53]

To Sir George Cokborn B[t] KB and Sir George Clark B[t]

I have just heard that a complete history of the Black Deeds of the Victualling Board, has been or is about to be forwarded to the famous Mr Hume. I have endeavoured to learn the substance thereof – that I might myself inform you and can only gather in addition to what I have already informed you, that, one of them charges Capt Serle, and others of having participated in a Contract for Biscuit with a person named Solly – also that a pretty 'Flower' of the city had a contract for Butter and on the price of that Article advancing he asked of the Board <u>and obtained permission</u> to pay the fine on his Contract, that, it might be vacated, that this was done by an infamous negotiation with the person who always held such disgraceful influence in these cases, and who thus betrayed the Govt. who employed them but most of these persons are now happily removed – the result was a new Contract.

When Lo! all the Butter was found to be bought up by <u>one Person</u> and <u>this Person</u> was the <u>late contractor</u>, a new Contract was taken with this Man at an advance of 25 p[r] cwt on the former price . – I am told that on the Exchange, it is roundly stated, that the <u>whole of the Board</u> except the two present Jun[r] members have been concerned in these Transactions, that the Public Confidence in them, is for ever gone, the Collusions with the House of Scot Idle & Co, from what is stated, appear black indeed. It is inconceivable, how a set of Men holding Public Situations could so far commit themselves, and betray for base lucre, the Interests of their Country, an Awful Responsibility hangs over them. let the present Admiral Commanding at Chatham, speak, his opinions of one of the Gent[n] now in the office, when in the Mediterranean Contracts for Shoes – it was recently stated, was made, and all was found to have been bought up a few days before, by the only person who could know the Contract was contemplated. Shoes for the fleet then purchased at Leghorn a few days before the Contract, at under 4/- per pair, was supplied, I am told to the Govt. at 7/-. If these Acts were perpetrated in the Mediterranean what else could be expected to prevail afterwards at home. – I tell you my Lords, of these Deeds that they may not be detected by any other parties, an Exchequer process is talked of, as about to be petitioned for,

---

53   This letter is with a bundle of papers relating to an investigation carried out in 1821 by Sir George Cockburn and Sir George Clerk (Admiralty lords) with a view to reduce staff numbers in the victualling office and reorganise the pay scales: NMM ADM DP/201A.

by the Merchants against this man, and others, who have made Splendid Fortunes, in a very short space of time. this Ex Sec^y be assured, my Lords, is as corrupt as old 'Nick', and if you suffer him to remain I am told that no confidence will be felt in the City in the new Board's integrity. it is considered hard and complained of as a favour to Mr Briggs, that, he should escape your censure when others are discharged for the same offence they say he <u>knew well</u> of the Board's minute, against discounting Bills, but he found the sweets of 5 per cent, above the 3 per cent on Exchequer bills, too tempting to resist. they add his having had only one bill is all a farce. – the clerk Wickey also did not tell them half he knew, if these persons remain, and a man named Perigal, who was discharged at first, with great reluctance to save Mr John Gosling, but is since to be retained through the influence of Brown, Gosling, Serle & Co you will not have completely cleaned out the Augean stable. this last man has been, I am told, 37 years, next in office, to John Gosling, he was the jackal of these brothers, and if he remains, no good will result to the public therefrom – he is Brother to the Storekeeper at Deptford, who receives all provisions Contracted for, and is closely closeted on contract days. my brother tells me a man named Riely, is to be kept but I hope you will send him away to imploy all his time to his business as an undertaker. a Subordinate officer of Deptford went I am told some time ago to order a Service of Plate at Green & Co of Ludgate Hill, they demurred at first to supply it on learning the Situation held by the person for whom it was intended. Surely, my Lords, men of your superior Talents, will not believe these things would be done fairly. How did Messrs Gosling, Holt, Brown, Ford, and others make the fortunes they possess? Certainly not from their official salaries.

With much respect, I am my Lords, yours obediently. Veritas.

This letter is undated, but from its content it appears that it arrived towards the end of the investigation which had been sparked off by the earlier letters. The various topics covered in it require some explanation and comment. The 'famous Mr Hume' is, presumably, the radical politician Joseph Hume, who was notorious for exposing corruption. If this is the Hume intended in the letter it seems unlikely that any 'history' did go to him, as there is no evidence that he had brought it up in Parliament as was his wont in such matters.

The biscuit contract accusation appears to be pure fabrication. There was a contractor named Isaac Solly but his family's involvement with the Victualling Board, which extended from the Seven Years' War until at least 1826, was only ever for staves from the Baltic countries (and the incident with the cattle in Dantzic mentioned earlier); he also supplied timber for the Navy Board.[54]

The 'pretty Flower of the City' was the bulk food supplier, Charles Flower. This designation is not an invention of Veritas: there is a Rowlandson cartoon of Flower showing him as a sunflower growing in a barrel of rancid butter standing on two stinking cheeses, which suggests that his general reputation was dubious.[55] However, the correspondence relating to this particular incident starts with a letter from Flower on potential difficulties with his contracts for butter and cheese. The problem was partly that Bonaparte had banned exports of butter and cheese from Holland and partly that because a dry summer had reduced the growth of grass there was less milk and thus less butter and cheese available; these situations had caused shortages and raised prices in Britain. Flower had purchased all he could obtain, but at inflated cost and thus he wanted a higher price for it. Even so, he did not have sufficient to fulfil his contracts, and rather than sully his reputation at a time when he was about to take on 'a very responsible situation' (probably the Lord Mayorship) he offered to pay the penalty on the contracts.[56]

This seemed to be acceptable, but some eighteen months later, the ex-commissioner William Budge, apologising for the delay caused by his ill-health, wrote to the First Lord of the Admiralty Lord Mulgrave to say that 'notwithstanding my removal from the Victualling Board, I still feel myself bound in honour to bring this case under your lordship's view'.[57] His letter is a little rambling, but basically suggests that Flower had been in possession of enough butter and cheese to fulfil the whole of his contracts and even with the penalties, had still made a profit. Budge then rambled on about a £500 penalty on a stave contract with Flower, but this, as the Victualling Board pointed out in its response, was nothing to do with Charles Flower, being the unrelated firm of Matthew Flower & Co. They also corrected Budge's statement on quantities: Flower had delivered about 62 tons of butter and 71 of cheese, and was offering sufficient to bring the total amounts to 200 and 300 tons respectively, about three months' supply. A price was negotiated on this, Flower paid the penalty and new contracts were tendered for and awarded, Flower sharing in these as before. The Admiralty accepted this and no more was heard. Budge's confused recollections and prolonged ill-health do, perhaps, throw some light on the reason for his 'removal'.[58]

The 'collusions with the house of Scot Idle & Co' refers, as evidenced by a letter in *The Times* from John Robertson Bell, to the prolonged and less

---

54 For the Seven Years' War, Buchet, *Marine* (who refers to him as Sally), p. 47; for the later period from 1776 to 1826, contract ledgers TNA ADM 112/162–212.
55 Painted 1809, Guildhall City Library Print Room, 20155.
56 NMM ADM C/716, 17 October 1807.
57 NMM ADM C/723, 25 July 1809.
58 TNA ADM 110/60, ff. 240–8, 7 August 1809; NMM ADM C/723, 9 August 1809.

than successful attempts to obtain a supply of staves from Canada when Bonaparte's Continental System had cut off the supply from the Baltic.[59] Bell states, in this letter, that he had worked for some time for the Victualling Board and that his father had been involved in the purchasing of staves.[60] Bell junior had given up his position in order to set up on his own as a 'merchant and agent', and had been employed by Christopher Idle to negotiate the contract for Canada staves. Then, 'I found I was likely to be made a mere tool of by Mr Idle'; a comment which suggests that Bell thought he was to be a partner in the contract and was aggrieved to find he was only to be an agent. Both Bell's letter and *The Times* editorial comments implied that Idle and the victualling commissioners had colluded to push the deal through. In fact, the correspondence shows that the Victualling Board actually resisted the use of Canada staves, having tried them in the past and found them unsatisfactory, but had been overruled by the Admiralty under the prompting of the Board of Trade, and that far from allowing the Victualling Board to make an uncontested contract with Idle, the Admiralty had insisted on public tendering. As it happened, Idle's was the best of the tenders and they agreed a contract with him, but six weeks later Idle withdrew his offer and the contract eventually went elsewhere. Throughout this period the price of Canada staves fluctuated wildly, from a high of £185 per mille to a low of £133, which explains the reluctance of the suppliers to commit themselves for three years.[61] As with the letter from Veritas, the allegations in *The Times* can be refuted by the facts, which suggest that the motive was spite rather than a genuine desire to unmask corruption. Which is not to say that the victualling commissioners never engaged in lucrative collusion with contractors (something which would be almost impossible to prove) but that it appears unlikely in this case.

The only detailed accusations about members of the Victualling Board being in collusion with contractors were the Idle/Bell items in *The Times*, although that newspaper made some heavy hints of other incidents; none of the other newspapers reporting the situation, with one exception, suggested any other misdeeds than taking up victualling bills. The exception was *The Morning Post*, which reported that there had been 'some dismissals'

59   *The Times*, editorial 26 January 1822; Bell's letter 28 January 1822. However, the firm of Scott Idle were wine merchants, and do not appear to have had any connection with Christopher Idle.

60   This is, presumably, the Adam Bell who was Master Cooper from 3 January 1788. His duties did not involve purchasing staves or anything else. SCF 32, p. 40.

61   NMM ADM C/714, 15 May & 1 June 1807; C/716, 23 Oct & 5 December 1807; C/717, 15 & 21 January 1808; C/722, 17, 21 & 28 April 1809; C/726, 23 May 1810; TNA ADM 110/55, ff. 514–16, 7 May 1807; 110/56, ff. 444–5, & 500–1, 2 & 20 January 1808; 110/57, f. 73, 25 February 1808; 110/59, ff. 196–7, 17 February 1809; & ff. 458–64, 27 April 1809; 110/62, ff. 98–106, 29 May 1810; 110/69, ff. 200–5, 17 October 1814.

when the Cockburn/Clerk enquiry had uncovered collusion between some clerks and pursers. This involved overstating the balance of remaining stocks of provisions, for which the pursers were paid. There is only one reference to this in the correspondence/minutes: a letter from the Admiralty which instructs that 'the clerk Mason' was to be dismissed for lying under oath.[62] The chief clerk of that department, A Stokoe, was one of those later compulsorily retired.

The shoe story refers to an incident in 1800/01 when Lord Keith was commander-in-chief in the Mediterranean and Nicholas Brown (who became a victualling commissioner in 1808 and at whom the reference to 'old Nick' is aimed),[63] and Brown's assistant James Meek, were pursers with the fleet and also served as purchasing agents; both also later served in turn as Keith's secretary.[64] The allegations about the shoe price (which was actually 4s 4d, not Veritas's stated price of 7s) was part of a series of accusations against Keith and his entourage made by a small coterie of his subordinate captains, orchestrated by Alexander Cochrane. One of these captains, and the one who raised the shoe issue, was Benjamin Hallowell, who was the 'admiral commanding at Chatham' mentioned by Veritas. Despite Keith's investigation into the transaction and his declaration that he had examined and was satisfied with the vouchers, Hallowell continued his assertions with a complaint to the Admiralty. They passed it to the Navy Board (who had the responsibility for seamen's clothing), who in turn investigated and stated that they were satisfied with the transaction.[65]

The only Briggs to be found in the pay books was the master butcher at Deptford between 1782 and 1787 but he had long departed by 1821, when there was no one of that name listed.[66] In 1821, Wickey, the Gosling brothers and Henry Perigal were all employed in the Victualling Board's secretary's office: William Gosling had been the secretary since 1794, his brother John was the chief clerk, Henry Perigal was the second clerk and William Wickey the fifth clerk. There was an Edward Perigal working as a third class clerk in the stores department but his duties were confined to pursers' accounts and

---

62 *The Morning Post*, 24 & 25 January 1822; TNA ADM 109/25, 5 January 1822. This would have been Samuel Mason, third class clerk in the department for stating and balancing pursers' accounts.

63 'Old Nick' is one of the many euphemisms for Satan.

64 Meek joined the Victualling Board in 1830 and remained as Comptroller of Victualling and Transport Services from 1832: MacDougall, 'Somerset Place to Whitehall: Reforming the civilian departments of the navy' (Unpublised Ph.D. Thesis, Kent, 1995), p. 71.

65 W G Perrin (ed.), *The Letters and Papers of Admiral Viscount Keith, vol. II*, pp. 234–5, 292–3.

66 *Fees 8*, p. 636; *BOR 11*, pp. 38–9.

occasionally making entries in the book of tenders.[67] Unless their mother had remarried (which is, of course possible) neither of the Perigal brothers could have been 'the brother of the storekeeper at Deptford', who was Anthony Bowring.[68] The only 'Riely' to be found in the staff lists was a Reilly listed as 'clerk of the repository' in the stores department; this job involved little more than filing pursers' and transport accounts.[69]

The story of the order for a service of plate cannot be authenticated,[70] nor can the size of the 'fortunes' of the named persons; such fortunes, had they existed, could have been acquired from perfectly legitimate sources such as marriage or inheritance. One final point of interest is that Searle's will names 'my good friend William Henry Wickey of the victualling office at Somerset House' as executor and trustee of a substantial portion of his estate. Wickey had been appointed Searle's private clerk in December 1808 with a salary increase of £50 p.a. for his additional duties.[71]

So, this letter contains a mixture of very old inaccurate stories, incorrect assumptions connecting similar-sounding names, wild undetailed accusations and dubious innuendo. It smacks of partially overheard (and possibly drunken) conversations in a public house, between disaffected lower-level clerks or messengers, put together by a troublemaking conclusion-jumper. Yet it, or the earlier letters, had been sufficient to spark off an Admiralty investigation. Early in 1821, Cockburn and Clerk (both Admiralty Lords) had been conducting an investigation into staffing levels and salaries with the Victualling Office and Navy Office, and they were then instructed to carry out a full investigation into the anonymous allegations.[72]

The report of their findings does not appear to have survived, so we cannot know the full details of what they discovered, but it involved 'abuses conducted in the stores department' relating to 'fraudulent alterations and surreptitious interpolations' in the office pursery accounts ledgers amounting to 'several hundred pounds';[73] and, to judge by the indignant tone of the letter from the Admiralty secretary, what was considered the more heinous 'great irregularities' in the Secretary's department. These included discounting bills for an unnamed 'agent employed under the Board in the purchase of provisions', which had been going on 'from a distant, up to a very late,

---

67   NMM ADM DP/201A.

68   *SCF 32*, p. 36.

69   NMM ADM DP/201A.

70   The inclusion of this little story is strange, unless the purpose was to indicate another person living beyond his salary, 'plate' meaning silver-plated tableware.

71   TNA PROB 11/1694; TNA ADM 111/189, minute, 16 December 1808.

72   TNA ADM 109/21, 21 February 1821; NMM ADM DP/201B, 21 April 1821; TNA ADM 111/256, minute, 1 January 1822.

73   TNA ADM 111/255, minute, 24 December 1821. These offences had taken place in 1817–19, but had not been detected by the responsible clerks' supervisors.

period' despite this practice having been prohibited in May 1808.[74] What was particularly bad about the behaviour of the secretary and his immediate subordinates is that they were in their positions during the previous scandal and would have written and copied the minutes and letters dealing with it; there was no possibility of their not understanding the nature of what they were doing.

There was a round of dismissals and enforced retirements; the clerk Glasspoole committed suicide.[75] Some clerks in the department dealing with pursers' accounts, and the board secretary William Gosling and his brother John were summarily dismissed without compensation and several other clerks in the secretary's department were implicated, but perhaps without absolute proof; they, together with numerous other clerks in the stores and cash departments were retired on pensions, as were the heads of those departments, Henry Holt and Richard Ford. Holt was specifically stated not to be implicated in the misdeeds, but it was felt that he should have been aware of what his staff were doing. His 'advanced period of life' (age 69 and with 55 years' service) was thought to have rendered him less active and efficient than he should have been. Ford's retirement has more interesting implications: the correspondence says no more than that he should be 'selected for retirement'. He was at that time only 47 and there was no suggestion of ill-health (he lived to 65); he had served 31 years. Given all this, the obvious inference is that he was suspected of involvement in the misdoings but that this could not be proven; he did, however, give himself away in his letter to Croker following his enforced retirement, in which he said

> [when the minute was] issued directing the discontinuance of the practice of discounting victualling bills on 12 May 1808, I was at Palermo as agent victualler and did not return to England to take possession of my appointment at this office until February 1809 and consequently could know nothing of the existence of such a document which I beg most unequivocally to state you Sir, that I was ignorant of, as the child unborn.[76]

This statement is not believable: although Ford might not have been aware of that document at the point when he returned, it is unlikely that he would not have been made aware, very rapidly, of the reason for his having been promoted, and should also have made the required oath himself. It is

74 TNA ADM 111/256, 19 January 1822; ADM 109/25, 21 January 1822; 111/187, 16 May 1808. The identity of this person is not disclosed but since the use of agents, with the exception of William Mellish, had been almost abandoned since the BOR's 11th report, this may have been Mellish, who was certainly involved in this practice before 1808.

75 TNA ADM 12/210, section 102.5, 19 September 1822.

76 TNA ADM 1/4601, 28 and 30 January 1822.

interesting that he referred to '[taking] possession' of his new job: a clear indication that jobs were still considered to be personal property. It is also of interest that at a time when the office must have been in turmoil and the commissioners' priorities should have included settling it down, they were prepared to appoint as a replacement department head a man who was going to take, at best, many weeks to receive his instruction and return from the Mediterranean to take up the post; in fact it took almost ten months.[77] This is not to say that Ford was not a good candidate for the job, but there must have been many other suitable candidates in other naval departments who could have been slotted into the position immediately. Various events in Ford's earlier career suggest that he was a favourite of Towry, who may have used his influence to obtain this position for him; by 1822, Towry was dead and Ford would thus have lost his patron and protector.

The final retirements were three of the commissioners: the chairman Searle, John Aubin and Thomas Welsh. Searle's retirement was handled in a way that led to questions in Parliament: the tradition was that commissioned officers who had left active service to take up a civil appointment should not be allowed to return to active service, but Searle, when he left the Victualling Board, was returned to the list of active officers and given the promotion to rear admiral which he would have received had he remained on the list.[78] Despite public statements that there was no suspicion against him, his abrupt departure seems to have been part of an attempt to keep matters from developing into a major public scandal. Whether Searle was thought to have been implicated in the 'improper conduct' or merely, like Holt, failed to have spotted what had been occurring under his nose since 1808, can only be a matter of speculation, but the whole incident provided fodder for the newspapers for several days.[79] *The Times* stated that Searle and Aubin had been dismissed; it did not mention Welsh, who went at the same time.[80] There is, however, another possible explanation for Searle's departure, which is that his mental faculties or general health were failing. This can only be conjecture, but there are two pieces of evidence which support this: firstly that the vigorous and pushy man of a decade before was, when interviewed by the Select Committee for Finance on 28 May 1817, unable to remember the precise dates of two major events which had occurred less than three months previously (Towry's death on 8 March, of which he said 'about five weeks or two months ago' and the medical department from the Transport Board being passed to the Victualling Board on 20 March, of

---

77 The decision was made in early May 1808: NMM ADM DP/28, 9 May 1808.
78 *The Times*, 19 March 1822. This allowed him to receive his half-pay; he had not served long enough on the Victualling Board to receive a pension.
79 *The Times*, 23 to 29 January; *Morning Chronicle*, 23, 25, 26 & 29 January; *The Morning Post*, 24 & 25 January; *The Glasgow Herald*, 28 January; all 1822.
80 *The Times*, 29 January 1822.

which he said 'I cannot specify the exact date but I believe about six weeks or two months ago'); secondly that he died only two and a half years after his 'retirement', at which point he was aged only 67.[81]

Searle probably knew well in advance that his services were about to be dispensed with, as he did not attend any of the board meetings after 22 January, the day on which the Admiralty secretary's letter informing the board of Cockburn and Clerk's findings would have arrived (by 4 February he had submitted a memorial to the Privy Council 'praying to be appointed one of the flag officers'; after referring this to the Admiralty, it was approved on 8 February).[82] The wording of the minute of 21 February indicates the desire to keep such matters quiet: it states only that a new patent had been received, lists the commissioners on that patent, then orders that Searle, Welsh and Aubin, 'whose names are not in the new patent' should be paid up to that day. At no point in that minute, or those preceding, does it state that these commissioners will be leaving.[83]

In all, as a result of this investigation and the preceding investigation into staffing levels, three commissioners, all three department heads (the secretary and the two accountants), five first class clerks, two second class clerks, sixteen third class clerks and ten extra clerks left the office. The reasons given are interesting: four were summarily dismissed for misconduct (and one other would have been had he not committed suicide), five were just stated as 'by Admiralty Order', which implies not-quite-provable misconduct, eight had serious health problems, three were for 'reduction of his class' (these having thirty-three, thirty-four and forty years' service) and eight were declared unable to do their job (i.e. incompetent). Only two of these had worked long enough to receive any pension (twenty-seven and twenty years), the others had between thirteen and eighteen years' service. All in all, 39 out of a total staff of 108 were found to be either dishonest, incapable of doing their job, or performing unnecessary tasks. Whether or not improper conduct was involved, and despite the events of 1808, the board of commissioners was clearly still not aware of what went on in their office, or which clerks were capable of doing their job properly.

The overall picture of the way the Victualling Board dealt with misdemeanours against the Crown, its property or its servants, matches the way the Board dealt with other situations. When acute problems were brought to their attention, they took prompt action to resolve the problem and prevent a recurrence, although with one major exception they did neither

81 *6th Report from the Select Committee on Finance (Navy)* (ordered to be printed 23 June 1817); Searle's passing certificate of 2 October 1780 states him to be 'more than 23 years of age': TNA ADM 107/8/76.

82 TNA PC2/204.

83 TNA ADM 111/256, 22 January to 21 February 1822; ADM 109/25, 21 January 1822, Croker to Victualling Board.

without consulting their masters at the Admiralty. But where there were chronic situations which they should have detected by maintaining proper observation of their employees, or ensuring that those employees kept their work up to date and thus detected misdemeanours perpetrated from outside the organisation, they failed to do so, as evidenced by the fact that most of the cases which did come to their attention were as a result of information from outside.

They clearly lacked the ability to see situations which invited staff misbehaviour or actual theft, and their yard visitations demonstrated more concern with leaving the status quo undisturbed than to conduct proper stock-checks. Although they took a high moral tone over misconduct, they had few policies in place to prevent it. It is thus not surprising that although this period did not include any major frauds such as those allegedly committed in the West Indies in the 1780s, the incidence of other misconduct remained fairly constant.

Such action as they did take on discovery of one particular major misfeasance, which was to a large extent of their own creation, was immediately afterwards ignored, and, unless the commissioners themselves were actively involved in this situation (a strong suspicion of which remains), they had failed to notice that the banned practice had continued in one case for eight and in the other for over twenty years.

9

Parliamentary Inquiries

BETWEEN 1788 AND 1807, there were four major parliamentary inquiries which delved into the workings of the Victualling Board and victualling office: the Fees Commission, the Select Committee on Finance, the Commission of Naval Inquiry, and the Board of Revision.[1] The parts of these reports which cover the salary and wages systems for the Victualling Board, its clerical and yard staff and a fraud in the cooperage at Plymouth, have already been discussed; here we are concerned with those parts which cover better management.

Fees commission

After much procrastination, one of the recommendations in the Fees reports, that of splitting the Navy Board into committees, was passed by the Privy Council in 1796, but it was not until 1799 and 1800 that the recommendations to abolish the fee systems in the Navy and Victualling boards were adopted; the new pay system for the Victualling Board was effected by an Order in Council dated 29 January 1800.[2] The other recommendations in the eighth report of the Fees commissioners, those on the head office of the Victualling Board and its yards at home, seem to have been either tacitly ignored or rejected as unworkable. These included splitting the Board into committees, attending to the arrears of accounts, preventing the clerks in the office acting as agents for naval officers and contractors, and preventing fraudulent practices in the yards.[3] The commissioners found no real fault with the accounting systems, but were less than complimentary on the

---

1 See Bibliography for the formal titles of all these inquiries.
2 Breihan, 'William Pitt', pp. 62–3, 66, 72, 74.
3 *Fees 8*, passim.

management abilities of the Victualling commissioners, in particular that their control over the yard at Deptford was 'rather nominal than real'.[4]

Select Committee on Finance

In the intervening years, the inquiry of the Select Committee on Finance had taken place. Its report on the Victualling Board, as had the reports on fees, found little fault with the accounting systems, but did emphasise the need to put the recommendations of those reports into effect.[5] However, as before, little was done in response to this. Appendix M of this report showed the responses of the Victualling Board to the recommendations in the Fees reports; some of the responses are particularly interesting for the way they reveal the mindset of the commissioners: for instance, in response to the recommendation that, because the victualling commissioners could not be expected to have proper experience of the processes of manufacture, they should no longer oversee the manufacturing departments at Deptford, one of them remarked 'it never was understood or intended that an actual clerk-like daily and unremitting attendance with real practical skill or knowledge could or should be expected from them'. And on the suggestion that the Board should be divided into committees, the Victualling commissioners said that they saw no utility in this idea; they also remarked that they felt that during the present war it would not be beneficial to alter the present system.[6] The Board of Revision referred to these in its minutes as 'ill-founded objections'.[7]

Board of Revision

It took the deliberations of the Board of Revision to effect any real changes to the operations and systems of the Victualling Board. This board produced three reports on the victualling operations: the tenth, on the victualling office, which included the duties of the commissioners, the eleventh, on the victualling yards at home, and the twelfth, on the victualling yards abroad. The Board of Revision consisted of five commissioners: Charles Middleton (later Lord Barham and First Lord of the Admiralty), John Fordyce (Surveyor General of the Land Revenue), Admiral Sir Roger Curtis, Admiral William Domett, and Ambrose Serle (one of the commissioners of the Transport Board). However, the work on the different naval boards was shared out

---

4   Ibid., p. 567.
5   *SCF 32*, passim; *Fees 8*, p. 570.
6   *SCF 32*, pp. 104–22; TNA ADM 110/44, ff. 108–16, 9 June 1798.
7   TNA ADM 109/405, 18 December 1806, minutes of the meetings of the BOR.

among those commissioners and most of the work on the Victualling Board was done by Curtis with some assistance from Domett.[8]

The Board of Revision's brief included the requirement to consider the recommendations of the two previous enquiries which had not been put into effect; to consider which of those would be practicable and useful, and to work out how these could be best introduced.[9] Early in the tenth report, they remarked that it was a pity that the commissioners of naval enquiry had only looked into one aspect of victualling (the fraud at Plymouth), as they had found that board's reports on other aspects of naval administration very useful.[10] The crux of the inadequacies in the victualling office was stated as follows:

> though the information, which at different times came before us, tended to impress us with the idea that the amendments necessary to be made in the existing system, would be considerable, yet it was not until we entered minutely into the investigation of the system of management in the Victualling Board, and the several victualling departments, and our information became pretty complete, that we were convinced of the insufficiency of any partial alterations or amendments, and that nothing less than an entire new system would be likely to produce any effectual and permanent good.[11]

As had the Fees commissioners, they believed the system of each victualling commissioner having the supervision of one branch of the business (e. g. the brewhouse, the bakehouse, etc.) had led to mismanagement; this system should be abolished and the board of commissioners formed into two separate committees, possibly adding a third later to deal with all correspondence, conduct the current business and attend to the economy of manual labour in the yards.[12] Of the two committees immediately recommended, one should deal with general business, the other with cash and store accounts.[13]

The general business committee should consist of a civilian chairman, a deputy chairman who should be a naval captain, two more committee members, one of whom should be a civilian and the other who should have served in the navy as a purser, with a secretary, who should be the secretary

---

8 TNA ADM 7/405, 16 January 1805. Both Curtis and Domett had considerable experience of fleet administration, each having served as Captain of the Fleet with several admirals: A F P Lewis, *Captain of the Fleet: A Memoir of Sir William Domett GCB* (London, 1967); *Dictionary of National Biography*, vol XIII (Oxford, 2004), pp. 778–9 (Curtis).

9 *BOR 10*, p. 3.

10 Ibid.

11 Ibid., p. 4.

12 *BOR 10*, pp. 48–9.

13 Ibid., pp. 4–5.

to the main board. It should superintend the secretary's office, the office for keeping a charge on pursers and for stating and adjusting transport accounts, and the office for examining and stating pursers' accounts.[14]

Its duties, as well as dealing with ongoing business and all correspondence, would include ensuring that adequate stocks were maintained in the yards at home and abroad by requiring regular reports of amounts in stock and replenishing them from Deptford or by delivery from contractors, and ensuring that replenishments for the yards at the western ports were sent before the winter set in. They were to arrange contracts for bulk supplies when necessary, first checking market prices. At the ports where the supply was dealt with through a contractor's depot they should require the contractors to send a quarterly statement of their stocks at each place. Finally, this committee was, twice yearly, to compare the wage rates of the yard workmen with those paid in private trade and adjust their wage rates up or down accordingly.[15] They were also to consider whether any of the work could be done more economically by machinery.[16]

The cash and store accounts committee should attend to all receipts and disbursements of money and the speedy recovery of debts, and pass all accounts except those for pursers. It should consist of a 'first' civilian commissioner and two others, one of whom should be a civilian and another who should have served in the navy as a purser, and a dedicated secretary.[17] It should superintend the department of the accountant for cash (comprising the accountant's office, the imprest office and the assigning office), the office of the accountant for stores, the office for examining and stating agents' and storekeepers' accounts and the office of the clerk of the issues.[18]

This committee was to deal with all the accounts of yard accountants, yard storekeepers and agents, whether attached to specific yards or other situations. The state of all such accounts was to be listed by the various offices and put before the committee each quarter, listed separately as those which had not submitted any accounts for over three months, those which had been submitted but not examined (with a reason for this), and those which were in process of examination but not yet completed. When accounts had been examined and were ready to be passed, the committee was to check them against the vouchers to ensure that all entries were properly substantiated; once satisfied, those accountants who owed money should be instructed to pay it, and those to whom money was due were

14 Ibid., p. 34.
15 The 1814 incident with bakers suggests that this was not done.
16 Ibid., pp. 35–8
17 Ibid., pp. 25–6.
18 Ibid., p. 34.

to be paid. This committee was also to examine the office expenses on a quarterly basis.[19]

The two committees were each to meet on four days a week, and on the other two days (Tuesday and Friday) the whole board would meet, although if necessary, the chairman could call main board meetings on other days.[20] These divisions of work were not, however, intended to make the allocated departments the exclusive domain of the relevant committee; other commissioners might enquire into those departments if they wished.[21]

The report then moved on to forbid any sort of fees for any member of staff, required new types of oath to be sworn, and laid down various other new procedures for the office work, including a statement of office hours (10 a.m. to 4 p.m. except when the press of business required longer hours, but then to be unpaid except by special arrangement).[22]

The commissioners of the Board of Revision were, as had been the commissioners of previous enquiries, extremely concerned about the uncollected debts and arrears of accounts. Given that many of those dated back twenty years, and some as much as fifty years, the report was unequivocal about the low level of efficiency in the victualling office, although they did lay the blame on the system rather than the management of the Victualling Board's staff:

> Nothing can, we think, tend more forcibly to show how ineffectual the present system has been, than to give a history of the fruitless attempts which have been made for nearly a century past (during which the present system has existed) to prevent an increasing arrear of unliqui- dated accounts …[23]

This statement is, however, rather undone by another, a few pages later, referring to the outstanding store accounts of foreign and home agents and storekeepers:

> We therefore called upon the commissioner presiding over the store branch of the office,[24] to state to us how many of these two descriptions of accounts had been reported as being ready to be laid before the board for their final decision, and when those reports were to be made to the board; in reply to which he informed us that "although the dates were not specified of the period when each account was ready for the board, yet he trusted that would not be considered a matter of importance." Not,

19   Ibid., pp. 38–41.
20   Ibid., pp. 26–8.
21   Ibid., p. 35.
22   Ibid., pp. 28–30.
23   Ibid., p. 5.
24   This was Towry.

however, viewing the omission in the same light, we called upon the chief clerk in the office … to supply the deficiency …[25]

Nor was the Board of Revision impressed with the delay in dealing with Cuthbert's accounts as agent for the East Indies station; the amount involved was £1,024,526, and there had been suspicion that this included excessive charges which tended 'to shew the existence of enormous abuses in India'. By the time this account had been finalised, twenty-two years had passed. The report remarked

> We cannot think that the examination of any account, however strict it may be, can be at all effectual at such a distance of time; and it is therefore not surprising that the public should not have recovered any part of those sums which a speedy examination would no doubt have shewn they were entitled to: the circumstances which occasioned the expenditures, so far from being fresh in recollection, must be totally lost sight of; neither the necessity nor propriety of disbursements can be judged of; still less can the reasonableness of the charges be ascertained; moreover, as the party himself, in this case, had been dead many years before his accounts were passed, even the chance of obtaining any information from him … was altogether lost.

They went on to mention that the account of the most recent East Indies agent and contractor, Basil Cochrane, was pending; covering the eleven years 1794 to 1805 and totalling £1,418,236; they hoped that this would be dealt with 'without further delay'.[26] As we have seen in Chapter 4, it was not. Interestingly, Cochrane remarks in these pamphlets on Cuthbert's relationship with George Marsh, who was, when Cuthbert returned from India in 1785, the first commissioner of the Navy Board: Cuthbert married his daughter to Marsh's son, and 'gave with his daughter' £40,000. Cochrane attributes the comparative ease with which Cuthbert's accounts were passed to this situation, although he does not specifically state that it was overcharging for victuals which provided this dowry.

To put the seemingly vast sums of these arrears of accounts into perspective, it is worth looking more closely at Cochrane's accounts. The figure of £1,418,236 was not a debt, but the total disbursements which had passed through his accounts for victualling the East Indies fleet over the period 15 October 1794 to 31 December 1805: over eleven years, or an annual average of £126,534 for a fleet of some 6,000 men.[27] It did not include the cost of

---

25   *BOR 10*, pp. 14–15.
26   Ibid., pp. 11–12.
27   This figure is taken from the list books, TNA ADM 8/80, 84. Compare this figure with the estimate for 1798 shown in Appendix B; using the figures given there, the annual cost for 6,000 men elsewhere (without meat but with necessary money and casks etc) would have been £103,971. Thus the costs of storing and transporting

meat, which was sent out from Deptford on East India Company ships, but it did include the cost of all other victuals, victualling stores, their storage and care (including cooperage) and their transportation between delivery ship and warehouse, warehouse and warship, and between warehouses as far apart as Bombay, Calcutta and Prince of Wales Island (now Penang).[28] In order to pay for all this, Cochrane had been writing bills of exchange on the Victualling Board, as was the norm, and the amounts of these had been building up in his imprest account. The problem for the victualling office in such cases was having to go through all the detailed accounts submitted by the agent or contractor (and Cochrane was both, acting as agent for the meat and contractor for everything else) and check each entry against the vouchers of issues and receipts from the fleet; an enormous task because it was the Victualling Board's practice to leave this task until the agency contract had come to an end. It was for this reason that the Board of Revision, whilst recognising this was impracticable for foreign agents, recommended that for agents and storekeepers at home, accounts should be examined and passed quarterly.[29]

As to the reasons for the vast backlog of accounts in arrears, three excuses were given: as the commissioner presiding over the store branch, Towry remarked that he would rather be criticised for delay than for 'falling into errors by precipitation'; while the Victualling Board as a whole pleaded pressure of current business and lack of space. They said they had long wanted a separate room for commissioners to use to work apart from the rest of the board, and that their current offices were so overcrowded that the staff were frequently off sick due to 'the want of proper air and space'.[30]

Although sympathising to a certain extent, and recommending that the victualling office should be given the space in Somerset Place recently vacated by the Sick and Hurt Board, the Board of Revision laid the blame squarely on the victualling commissioners: the lack of space might have impeded the clerks in preparing accounts, but it should not have prevented the Board making decisions on the completed accounts. Nor did they accept the third reason (pressure of daily business) as an adequate excuse, pointing out that after the Admiralty had applied pressure, in the five months from November 1806 to May 1807, the Victualling Board had managed to

provisions within the East Indies station was £22,563, or almost 18 per cent of the whole.

28   The correspondence contains annual letters about sending this meat, for instance NMM ADM C/680, 21 November 1793. Cochrane's contracts are at TNA ADM 112/118, 119.

29   *BOR 10*, p. 18.

30   *BOR 10*, pp. 16–17.

pass accounts totalling almost £1,500,000, whereas in 'the five years which preceded that admonition' they had only passed £45,055.[31]

In order to deal with the existing arrears of cash and store accounts the Board of Revision recommended that a special team should be set up, this consisting of some of the more experienced clerks, these to receive additional payments 'provided their zeal and diligence should entitle them thereto'.[32]

Tenders and contracts

Some minor changes were recommended to the tendering system, and also to the contracts for bulk supplies and those for contractor depots. As far as the tendering system was concerned, very little alteration was suggested: the additional lock for the box in which the tenders were collected, and the requirement for the person tendering, or their agent, to be present when the box was opened and the tenders considered. The existing practices of sometimes accepting spontaneous private tenders or circulating merchants privately instead of advertising for tenders were ratified, but advertising was to be the preferred method.[33]

On the contracts themselves, the report recommended a number of changes. Firstly, on 'the terms being settled between the Victualling Board and the contractor' (this phrase suggests that the requirement for the tenderer or his agent to be present was to allow some last-minute price adjustments) the accepted tender was to be attached to an agreement, duly signed and witnessed to bind the parties until the contract was executed.[34] Substantial penalties were set for non-performance or late delivery. The Victualling Board's approval was required for any transfers of contracts, and in such cases an affidavit was required to the effect that the original contractor was receiving no payment for the transfer.[35]

The three inquiries differ somewhat in their opinions on the situation of buying through a commission agent rather than by contract. The Fees commissioners did not like this approach, citing a recent fraud (not named, but probably the Atkinson case).[36] The Select Committee on Finance were more sanguine, stating that this method of purchase tended to keep prices down.[37] The Board of Revision felt it was not generally desirable, but when

---

31 Ibid., p. 17.
32 Ibid., pp. 41–2.
33 Ibid., pp. 44–5.
34 Ibid., p. 45.
35 Ibid., pp. 46–7.
36 *Fees 8*, pp. 568–9. See also Syrett, 'Christopher Atkinson'.
37 *SCF 32*, pp. 4, 54.

it was necessary to use a commission agent, the Victualling Board must first obtain permission from the Admiralty, and the contract was to stipulate an immediate account of what had been purchased, from where and whom, and at what price, whether the agent himself had any interest in the goods or whether they had been consigned to him for sale, and that he must submit quarterly accounts with affidavits to the truth of the above. The agreed rate of commission was to be the sole remuneration.[38]

The work of the agents victualler and other officers at the yards

The existing basic instructions for agents victualler dealt mostly with cash handling and accounting procedures and the vouchers and other documents to be produced by pursers when collecting and returning victuals, but also included the inspection and care of victuals and the hiring of vessels to deliver victuals to ships. All this seems comparatively straightforward, given that all yards were dealing with the same items and theoretically had to deal with the same paperwork. It transpired that they did not.

Although not seen as a problem by the agents victualler or the Victualling Board, and certainly not by the members of previous inquiries, both from the Board of Revision's eleventh report and the reports of the 1803 inspection of the outports by the Victualling Board commissioners, it is clear that there were major organisational and accounting inadequacies at the yards.

The eleventh report of the Board of Revision tells a rather damning story. Their instructions, they remarked, included taking into 'their particular consideration, all such suggestions as have been made by the different boards of enquiry and select committee on finance and have not yet been adopted'; they had already, in their tenth report suggested various alterations in procedures, and now, as far as the victualling establishments at home and abroad were concerned, thought that 'any partial alterations or amendments would be insufficient; and that nothing less than an entire new system would be likely to produce effectual and permanent good.' Despite the recommendations resulting from the previous enquiries, the business of these establishments was

> conducted in a loose and confused manner, without system, clearness, regularity or method; that with respect to the accounts of stores, they are unnecessarily intricate and voluminous, without providing any sufficient check, being in most cases unsupported by any vouchers; that some of them, intended for the charge and discharge of store accountants, are so erroneous as even to leave the accountant himself completely ignorant of the real quantity of stores in his possession – that various descriptions of

38   BOR 10, pp. 47–8.

publick [sic] stores are received and issued in large quantities, without any accounts thereof being kept or rendered – that the superintending board in town has no means of fully charging and discharging the store-keepers with stores received and issued, other than from the accountant's own statements; that in many important instances the board has no means of forming a judgement of the propriety or impropriety of the expenditure of stores set forth in the accounts submitted for their approval; and, what is not a little extraordinary, no uniformity is observed at the different ports, there being many books and accounts kept and rendered from one establishment not required from another, though the nature of the business transacted is precisely the same; that with respect to the accounts of cash, some of the disbursements are subject to no controul [sic], and the accounts to no check, and a few even to no examination.

They then made haste to state that this was not necessarily the fault of 'the mismanagement of those to whose care the conduct of the victualling service has been entrusted' but more of gradual changes over the last century,

for however well suited the regulations which were established at the beginning of the eighteenth century might have been to the small extent of the victualling service at that time, it was by no means surprising to find them but ill adapted, or rather wholly inadequate to conduct it properly on its present extended scale.[39]

After these general comments, they moved on to specific remarks on the outports, and finally Deptford.

The Outports

At the outports, all the storekeepers and master cooper-storekeepers were responsible for the receipt, issue and accounting of everything that came into or went out of the yards' stores. The clerks of the cheque, as well as mustering the workmen and calculating their wages, witnessed all the receipts and issues of the storekeepers and made up his own separate accounts for them, as did the agent (adding these to his own accounts of cash received and disbursed). The Board of Revision had two wry comments on this: 'The effect of this system, on the present extensive scale of the navy, is such as might be expected.' and 'In consequence of so many officers being concerned in rendering accounts, extraordinary as it may appear, it is a matter of great doubt even at the present time, among the officers themselves, who is considered really responsible for the stores'.

39   *BOR 11*, pp. 3–5.

The officers at Portsmouth, when asked, had said they believed that the designated storekeeper was responsible, under the control of the agent; those at Chatham believed it was the storekeeper alone; while at Plymouth the storekeeper believed he had equal responsibility with the agent but the agent emphatically did not. (Dover was not mentioned.)

All the storekeepers/master cooper-storekeepers, as well as the agents, made up and submitted quarterly accounts, but the Victualling Board considered the agents to be 'the public accountants' and relied on their accounts, despite these being largely produced from information supplied by the storekeepers. However, even this varied from yard to yard: at Portsmouth the agent and the clerk of the cheque each sent a clerk to conjointly take account of all stores received by the storekeeper; at Chatham the agent's clerk checked the receipt of all stores from victualling transports or contractors and issues of fresh beef, wine and spirits, but nothing else; at Plymouth the agent did not send a clerk at all.

The Board of Revision then moved on to outline and finally detail these systems under three heads: details of unnecessary books, accounts and returns kept and submitted which, although expensive and troublesome to produce, mostly served only to complicate the documents and failed to render proper checks; details of the deficiencies of these documents which left the Victualling Board unable to judge the 'propriety' of expenditure and which not only included some fictitious transactions but omitted the receipt and issue of some stores or included 'mere paper statements, formed from probable calculation but not from fact'; and finally the disadvantages of the master cooper acting as his own storekeeper.

The paperwork consisted of unnecessary vouchers related to receipt of stores, returns for information purposes, and accounts which were supposed to form checks. There were three sorts of receipt vouchers: two made out by the two clerks who witnessed the delivery of stores, each in a daily receipt book; a list made by the storekeeper from his clerk's receipt book and passed to the clerk of the cheque who checked it against his own clerk's receipt book before passing it to the agent who made three copies: one on the bill of lading, one which he sent to the victualling office in London, and one which he sent to the port where the cargo originated.[40]

The Board of Revision pointed out that the officers at the originating port posted a copy of each vessel's bill of lading to the receiving agent; all that was necessary was for the storekeeper's clerk to write that he had received the listed items on the back of each copy (or note shortages or surpluses), pass these to the clerk of the cheque who checked and passed them to the agent, who returned one to the vessel's master and kept the other to check against the storekeeper's accounts in due course. This would obviate all

40   Ibid., p. 7.

the duplications of receipts; there was certainly no need to send one to the originating port as the victualling office in London passed the account for payment of the freight, using the copy that came to them. Similarly, the lists of goods received from contractors could be reduced from ten to three. Not only would this reduction in copies save the time of those who made the copies (they did not mention the cost of the extra paper) it would also reduce the risk of copying errors.[41]

Much the same unnecessary duplication applied to the returns of information for the Victualling Board. Most of these were sent to the victualling office on a weekly basis, the main purpose being to provide a sort of running stock-check of what was in the stores and expected to arrive in the next few days, and thus allow timely replenishment. However, no physical check was made, the returns being based on the the previous stock figure and the week's receipts and issues. The storekeeper did this in a multi-phase procedure, copying figures from his original 'entries and issues' book to several other books in date order (one wonders why they were not already in date order) then copying them into another book in a different format, finally producing abstracts of remains before copying these yet again into another book from which a fair copy was made and passed to the clerk of the cheque. These, with similar copies created by the same procedure from the master cooper and the clerk of the brewhouse, having been checked (and copied) were passed to the agent who 'blended' them with other information in yet another format, which was copied into a book which went to London, plus a separate copy of that part which related to the master cooper. The Board of Revision summed up:

> Thus it generally happens, according to the present system, that, before the board receives an account of the quantities of stores remaining in the magazines of an outport, the receipts and issues of stores, which in wartime are very numerous, have been three times transcribed, and two weekly abstracts have been made out therefrom in each of the offices of the storekeeper, the clerk at the brewhouse, and the master cooper; they have also been three times transcribed in the clerk of the cheque's office; and once transcribed, and two weekly accounts or abstracts made up, in the agent's office.

and added another wry comment:

> It is perhaps too obvious to remark, that much of this laborious and tedious process, to come at so simple a piece of information as the quantity of stores in the magazines of an outport, is wholly unnecessary. There is evidently an essential difference between the nature of an examination that a return should undergo, which is intended as a mere matter of

41   Ibid.. pp. 7–8.

information, and that species of check which should be imposed upon an account by which an individual is to be charged with or discharged of specific quantities of stores, and upon the faith of which it is to be ascertained whether any frauds or abuses have been committed ...[42]

All that was really needed, they pointed out, was to keep a single and accurate account, taken from the original daily receipt and issue books, for the purpose of producing the quarterly accounts, from which account a weekly net abstract of all items received and issued could be added to the previous week's remains figure to arrive at the figure of this week's net remains. This would, as well as simplifying this task, prevent the quarterly accounts going into arrears as was the case, since these accounts 'are never begun to be made up until long after the quarter was ended'.[43]

The accounts forming checks were of two types: those relating to the accounts of pursers and other persons to whom provisions were provided for 'public service',[44] and those relating to the store accounts of the victualling yards. When the first set of instructions were issued to the Victualling Board, the 'comptroller of the victualling' (one of the members of the Navy Board) required a monthly statement of all receipts, issues, and returns, the purpose being to estimate future requirements. However, within a few years [not specified] of those instructions, the Victualling Board began using the weekly accounts detailed above for that purpose, but the monthly accounts, although really no longer needed, continued to be produced. One part of these, detailing the stores returned by ships' pursers, was still used, but, says the report, 'it is curious to examine the use to which it is applied, because it will tend to shew [sic] the force of habit in keeping up established forms for benefits altogether imaginary.'[45] But this information was already available in the storekeeper's quarterly accounts and there was no point in duplicating it in a monthly account.

The 'most laborious and troublesome' of all the accounts was the quarterly statement of the issues to each purser. This was a single paper known as a 'purser's charge', which went to the victualling office, where the content was entered into that purser's ledger account, along with details of any items he had returned. But since only the total amount of those charges was posted, and these could be found in the storekeeper's quarterly account, this was a pointless exercise when the main use of the purser's charge was to settle the rare disputes on quantities stated to be issued by the storekeeper and those stated as received by the purser. Or rather, not to settle the disputes, but to trace the date of the issue which would enable the storekeeper to produce

42   Ibid., pp. 8–9.
43   Ibid., pp. 9–10.
44   These would include the officers of ships in ordinary, etc.
45   *BOR 11*, p. 10.

the purser's receipt of the disputed items. Or it would have done, if he had not 'lost or mislaid' those receipts as was often the case. It would be better, said the report, if each purser's quarterly charge was accompanied by all the purser's receipts, numbered progressively, and in separate parcels for each purser. In fact, it concluded, if those were sent there would be no need for the purser's charge sheet to be made out at all.[46]

Turning next to the 'accounts forming checks' (those quarterly accounts for the principal officers at each yard), the report then describes the procedures carried out when these were submitted to the victualling office in London, and here again the story was of much unnecessary duplication of work. The agent of each yard, having made up his own quarterly account (which included material from the three produced by the storekeeper, clerk of the cheque and master cooper) swore to its content and sent all four to London, where each was compared with the certificates of stores delivered by contractors, bills of lading of victualling transports delivering stores despatched from Deptford, and whatever other documentation they held, including the weekly returns. In other words, each yard's quarterly account was examined and checked four times, even though the master version (the agent's) contained the same information as the three others. In all, no less than sixteen sets of documents were produced and examined, each accompanied by a formal certificate signed by three persons (agent, storekeeper and clerk of the cheque) and the whole sworn to by two of these same officers (agent and storekeeper). 'It is difficult,' says the report, 'to perceive what additional validity is given to the account by sixteen certificates signed by the same individuals.'[47]

All the above duplication at the yards was estimated by the Board of Revision not only to involve three times as much labour as was necessary to 'attain the end in view', but also to take at least one third of the work of the clerk of the cheque's office. And moreover, they continued, since it was the duty of the agent 'to superintend every branch of the establishment', which included oversight of the stores, the manufactures, and the workforce, as well as the production of accounts, his work with those accounts should be that of an auditor, not the yard's accountant.[48]

The report concluded its comments under the first head by remarking that although similar duplication and unnecessary work was done on the supply of provisions to ships in ordinary, separate quarterly accounts of the loss of wine by evaporation or leakage, stores issued or returned from transports and 'many others which it is not necessary to enumerate', they felt

46   Ibid., p. 11.
47   Ibid., p. 121.
48   Ibid., p. 14.

they had made their point and did not intend to describe these in detail.[49] Given all this, it is, therefore, hardly surprising that later in the report they state that the outport yard establishments could be reduced by a total of twenty clerks (eight each at Portsmouth and Plymouth, three at Chatham and one at Dover), this being almost one-third of the total number at that time of sixty-four.[50]

On the second head, that relating to the fictitious and generally inaccurate nature of some of the accounts, the Board of Revision restricted themselves to giving only one example of each type of what they called 'defect'. The first of these related to the staves supplied to the master coopers to make casks. The average annual cost of these over the previous three years (1804 to 1806) was £107,353; but although the Victualling Board could tell, by the payments made to the supplying contractors, what quantity went to each master cooper and from his quarterly accounts what number of casks were issued by him, they did not receive any accounts correlating the number of casks made with the quantity of staves used. Nor were the stocks of staves and casks remaining at each quarter's end accurately reported: at one point the master cooper at Plymouth found he had 4,184 tuns of casks in his store more than he thought, while the master cooper at Portsmouth had 1,704 fewer than he thought. A few months after this, when two Victualling commissioners went to these yards to check, they found a surplus of only 23 tuns at Plymouth and a surplus of 3,583 at Portsmouth. This was found to be due to two different forms of faulty accounting; but at the point of the Board of Revision's investigation nothing had been done to rectify either.

It transpires that the fault was in the way the master coopers made their count: they counted the casks according to the amount of liquid they were expected to hold, measured in tuns, so twelve hogsheads (or twenty-four half-hogsheads, four leaguers, six butts, nine puncheons, or eighteen barrels) were all deemed to hold three tuns of liquid and three tuns was the figure used. The same method was used to record staves; using an arbitrary number of staves required to make a certain number of casks (for instance, 156 staves was deemed to make six butts which would hold three tuns liquid measure) they were also recorded as a number of tuns, not of actual staves. However, as the master cooper at Deptford pointed out when consulted:

> any large cylindrical or cubic body occupies much less surface when entire than when broken into several smaller cylinders or cubes; on this principle, … every cooper knows that a tun of butt casks may be made from considerably less than two-thirds of the quantity of wood which would be consumed in making a tun of hogshead casks …

49   Ibid., p. 14.
50   Ibid., p. 26.

In addition, the form in which the suppliers were now sending the staves allowed the coopers, using a new type of saw instead of the old method of an axe or adze, to produce twice as many staves, but they were still being counted to the old format. This, combined with the same method of counting casks returned from ships' pursers, commented the report, not only demonstrated that the officers of the yards (and thus also the victualling office) did not know what quantity of casks and staves they had in their possession, but served to demonstrate how it had been so easy to perpetrate the fraud in the cooperage at Plymouth uncovered in the eighth report of the Commissioners of Naval Enquiry.[51]

Another instance of 'mere paper statements, formed from probable calculation but not from fact' was that of the coals used in the yards; these had cost, over the previous three years, an annual average of £8,082. The actual receipts were entered in the books but no proper record was kept of expenditure at any of the yards, the figure used in the quarterly accounts being a fictitious calculation. Apart from the basic principle involved, the report remarked that since no record was either kept or submitted to the victualling office of the expense of coals, it was not possible to compare this expense between the departments of a yard, or between the yards.[52]

This section of the report closed with three more examples; two of fictitious accounting and one of non-accounting. The first example of fictitious accounting was the way in which pursers' 'remains' were checked when a purser either moved to another ship, when the ship was paid off, or in the event of his death, this being done by survey. It was done under the usual rules of survey, by three pursers from three ships, except when the ship was in a home port when it was done by two clerks from the victualling yard (who received extra pay for this, despite the fact that while they were conducting the survey their own work was neglected), a pointless exercise, says the report, when there were numerous pursers available to do the job. Their principal objection, though, was 'an absurd practice' of creating an imaginary transaction with the port on the occasions when the remains actually stayed with the purser: it was pretended that these remains had been returned to store and then reissued to the purser, the accounting of these pretended returns and issues being included in the storekeeper's quarterly accounts as though they had really happened. Since this was done in the normal way these pretend transactions could not be distinguished from the real ones.[53]

The second example of fictitious accounting was the way in which issues to ships in ordinary were dealt with. Unlike ships in commission,

51   Ibid., pp. 14–18.
52   Ibid., p. 17.
53   Ibid., pp. 17–18.

which were victualled in advance, these ships were victualled one month in arrears, which meant that the issue for, say, September was made on 1 October. But instead of entering this in the accounts for October, they were entered for September. The end result was that the accounts for any given quarter could not be made up from the issue books until those issues to ships in ordinary were made, thus delaying the whole process.[54]

The example of non-accounting relates to the numerous small issues of items such as candles for the office which were just not entered at all. There were over two hundred items which came into this category, and although each one was for a small sum, in the aggregate the cost was large.[55]

On the third and last of the main heads, that of the master cooper being an independent storekeeper for his own department, the Board of Revision based their comments on the division of the master cooper's time into supervision and direction of the artisan workers under him, and his work as a storekeeper-accountant. Other master workmen, they pointed out, like the master brewers, master millers and master bakers, who had fewer workmen to supervise, did not have to act as their own storekeeper. The master cooper, moreover, did not actually do the accountancy work himself but had a staff of clerks to do it: 'he knows nothing more of the accounts than that he has signed them'. He did spend considerable time in issuing and receiving stores from ships, with much of his time spent on the wharves; time which would be better spent in supervising coopers' work. As with all the other situations, unnecessary duplicate sets of books were kept, and since the storekeeper was already keeping accounts, all he would need to do to take over this function would be to add a few columns to his existing accounts. It might be objected, remarks the report, that the master cooper's stores were not in the same place as the other stores, and that this would inconvenience the storekeeper, but this objection would not stand up as the storekeeper already had clerks stationed at the breweries which at Portsmouth and Plymouth were in the same place as the cooperage.[56]

The existing circumstances at the outports was then summed up:

> the useless labour, confusion, perplexity and want of systematic order in the victualling establishments at the outports, are to be ascribed to the following causes; to a multiplicity of business being required to be performed, which is altogether unnecessary, to having a plurality of accountants concerned in rendering of accounts of the same matters ... when the objects of regularity, simplicity, and check, may be better attained by having only one.[57]

54 Ibid., p. 18.
55 Ibid., p. 18.
56 Ibid., pp. 18–22.
57 Ibid., p. 22.

They then outlined the principles of their proposed new system:

> As the duty of the storekeeper is to receive and issue the different spe-
> cies of provisions and stores committed to him, the only business which
> seems necessary to exact of him, in the way of clerkship, should have rela-
> tion to one of these four heads:
>
> 1st. To make out acknowledgements for what he receives, and state-
> ments of what he issues, both to be signed by himself.
>
> 2nd. To obtain acknowledgement from the persons to whom stores are
> delivered, in support of his statement of issues.
>
> 3rd. To give regular information to the superintending board, from time
> to time (usually done every week), of the state of the magazines, that they
> may provide supplies, and
>
> 4th. To prepare periodical accounts (usually every quarter) properly
> digested, of the stores received and issued by him within each period,
> supported by authentic vouchers, distinguishing, in the former cases, the
> sources of receipt, and in the latter, the services for which, and parties to
> whom, the stores are issued.

They also said that these transactions should be checked by the clerk of
the cheque, and that there should be a regular full stock-taking, to which
the yard books should balance; that the clerk of the cheque should have
charge of the public cash and that there should be only one set of cash in
each yard, not several as was then the case. There were also some comments
on the clerk of the cheque's duties relating to wage payment.[58]

All the above, and what follows below relating to the yard at Deptford,
conjures up a picture of offices full of busy people, all working hard at what
they believe to be important tasks. The fact that a high proportion of these
tasks served either no useful purpose (or, one might cynically suggest, only
the purpose of boosting the importance of their immediate superiors) can
hardly be blamed on those clerks; it has to be laid at the feet of the top management, the victualling commissioners, who clearly were not aware of the
detail of the procedures, and/or failed to see the futility of much of the work
or the stupidity of some of the accounting methods. What was worse was
that even when they visited the yards they also failed to see and correct the
scope for embezzlement offered by the continuation of those counting and
accounting methods. This is evident in the reports of the victualling commissioners who visited the outport yards in 1803.[59] Their brief, as well as
inspecting various aspects of yard management was to conduct a survey of
stocks 'as far as practicable' (this in itself a mistaken concept).

The first part of this seems to have been reasonably efficient, although
of course we do not know what they failed to notice and thus to remark

58 Ibid., pp. 22–7.
59 NMM ADM D/45, 17 November 1803.

on. Among other things at Plymouth they arranged for the miller to have a third pair of mill stones, so that he did not have to stop one of the mills for several hours when the stones needed dressing, and recommended a new, less expensive, contract for boat hire; and at the Southdown brewery they recommended moving the tap from its current position near the yard gates to somewhere more central, where the workmen visiting it could be seen and thus not encouraged to loiter and waste their time. But as we have seen, their concept of stock-taking displayed such a level of naïvety that they might just as well have not bothered.[60]

Deptford

The yard at Deptford was on a very different basis from those at the outports. Because it had been, for many years, the only yard (the others being little more than storage depots) it had eight principal and seven inferior officers, these being the superintendant, hoytaker, clerks of the cheque, cutting-house, dry stores and brewhouse, master cooper and clerk of the issues (who was based at Somerset Place rather than at the yard), and master brewer, baker and butcher, principal boatswain of the wharf, principal stevedore, inspector of the works and porter.[61] Because the London yard had originally been in the same premises as the victualling office at Tower Hill, and because each of the departments at the yard was designated the responsibility of a named commissioner, there was no agent victualler. According to his instructions, the superintendant was in charge, but in practice he had no authority over the other principal officers, acting as little more than a postman between them and the Victualling Board. There were three problem areas associated with his position: the first being commissioner-control of departments; the second being the jealousy with which those commissioners defended their responsibilities from what they saw as interference from the other commissioners; the third, and worst, being that the other principal officers did not consider themselves inferior to him and would only take instructions from their own commissioner.[62] And, as the Fees commissioners had remarked, those victualling commissioners were not actually qualified to oversee yard operations:

> … to direct with effect the process of manufacture, requires … practical skill and knowledge with respect to the particular species of manufacture,

---

60   See pages 55–8 above.
61   *BOR 11*, p. 27.
62   *BOR 10*, p. 22; *11th Report*, p. 19.

which few, if any, gentlemen in their habits of life can be expected to possess.[63]

The superintendant's actual duties, then, consisted of passing reports and accounts from the other principal officers to the board and instructions from the board to those officers, having first either consolidated them into one report/account or split them into their component parts, each time making copies; otherwise he created three copies of bills of lading for transport ships taking provisions to other yards, one of which went to the receiving agent and two to the clerk of the issues at Somerset Place; made some small disbursements to the officers of ships in ordinary or pursers of other ships; and superintended the porters and various yard security staff (warders, rounders and watchmen). The report summed up his duties by remarking that most of the accountancy resulted from the excessive numbers of storekeepers, that these accounts were unnecessary and that he should be relieved of them and given duties to perform 'suitable to the important office he holds'.[64]

The first of the principal officers was the clerk of the cheque. His duties were similar to those of the clerks of the cheque at the outports, except that he did not actually check the stores and receipts of the various storekeepers, nor make the wage payments to the yard workers, this being done by clerks from the Treasurer of the Navy; he did, however, attend the payment and he, or his clerks, did muster the workmen three times a day and prepare the pay lists.[65]

The report then outlined the duties of the other officers of the yard: the clerks of the cutting-house, dry stores and brewhouse, and the master cooper, who were partly storekeepers and partly supervisors of manufactories; and the clerk of the issues, who worked at Somerset Place. His function, very like that of the agents at the outports, fell into three areas: calculating the precise amounts to be sent to the other yards, consolidating items issued to warships, army transports or ships in ordinary from the various stores into a single charge for pursers' accounts, and calculating the payments due for lighterage.[66]

Of the two remaining inferior officers, the porter was equally a storekeeper, in charge of janitorial supplies; he also superintended the work of the security staff, had the custody of the gate, and had charge of the tap, which supplied the greater part of his income. The inspector of works, who actually worked for the Inspector General of Naval Works, rather than the

63 Quoted in ibid., p. 19.
64 *BOR 11*, p. 28.
65 Ibid., p. 30.
66 Ibid., pp. 31–9.

Victualling Board, monitored the condition of the buildings in the yard, and certified that tradesmen's bills were reasonable.[67]

In summing up the managerial personnel at Deptford, the Board of Revision remarked that of the eight principal officers (each independent of the others), three were mainly employed in superintendence or checking (superintendant, clerk of the cheque, hoytaker) but that together they did not control even half of the yard business. There were five accountants for cash (superintendant, clerks of the brewhouse, cutting-house and dry stores, and the master cooper) who received imprests from the public purse, disbursed money and produced quarterly accounts, and five accountants for stores (the three clerks as above, master cooper and porter) who received and issued stores and passed regular accounts.[68] The recommendation was that the establishment at Deptford should be changed and modelled on that which had been recommended for the outports; in other words, the yard at Deptford should be put on the same footing as the outports.[69]

This recommendation had already been made by the Fees commissioners, and also discussed by the Select Commission on Finance of 1798; the latter asked the Victualling Board for their opinion, a copy of which was passed to the Board of Revision. That opinion boiled down to two main objections: that the work of accounting, receiving and issuing stores at Deptford would be too much for one storekeeper, and that the 'great variety, perishable nature and large quantity' of stores at Deptford were too much to be in the care of a single storekeeper and his department. These objections were not valid: the Board of Revision had compared the business at Deptford with that at Plymouth for the year of 1806 and found that there were four times as many receipts and issues at Plymouth as at Deptford, and that the number of issues to individual warships, 'which create more trouble than issues of any other description', was ten times greater; since the amount of work could be done by one storekeeper's department at Plymouth, so it could at Deptford. As to the variety of items, this was actually greater at Plymouth than Deptford, and being of the same kind at both places they were equally perishable. It was true that the amounts of stock at Deptford were considerably greater than at Plymouth, and there was therefore some validity to the argument that they might be more exposed to embezzlement or damage from improper stowage. However, since much of it, under the new system, would remain in the care of the master tradesmen, the responsibility would not devolve on the single storekeeper. The stores would remain locked up in guarded warehouses, as currently, and

67   Ibid., pp. 32–3.
68   Ibid., p. 33.
69   Ibid., p. 34.

since it was already in large quantities, larger amounts (e.g. 20,000 bags of biscuit instead of 10,000) would not be any more vulnerable to theft.[70]

However, although Deptford, being so close to the London livestock markets, might be the best place for slaughtering and curing meat,[71] as far as other manufacturing was concerned there was the disadvantage of the higher labour costs so close to London, especially for coopers' work. So, although Deptford was probably still the best place for sending off provisions for fleets abroad, it was not the best place for sending them to the outports. It was also recommended, especially in view of the cost of labour, that the manufacture of biscuit and cooperage stores should be gradually decreased at Deptford and increased at Portsmouth and Plymouth.[72]

There was also a discussion about the wisdom of continuing to brew beer at Deptford. Some of this was for the ships in the Thames but most was sent to Chatham for the ships in ordinary there and at Sheerness. Possibly from the bad water quality at Deptford, or the frequent movement, this beer was condemned in far greater quantities than that brewed elsewhere, which raised the cost of this beer to between £6 and £7 a tun, as against the cost of drinkable beer supplied by contractors at Yarmouth at £4.2.0 per tun (the contractors standing the loss on any that was condemned). Before they decided to continue to brew beer at Deptford, it was suggested that there should be an investigation into the causes of the problem.[73]

When it came to discussing the lack of management control at Deptford, the report condemned the present system: 'so far from any advantage superior to those at the outports … the business is not … so well conducted'. They could say much about the loose method, but would confine themselves to a few examples. Although they repeated throughout this report that it was the system which was at fault rather than the individual officers, it is quite obvious that they were not impressed with those officers' devotion to duty. Their examples included many instances (in fact almost all) where checks were either not made at all or only done in a cursory fashion, and by junior clerks, not the office-holder.

The only situation in which the quality of the stores delivered by contractors was checked properly was that of malt and hops; with the exception of cooperage stores, the examination of receipts for quantities received was done, if at all, by one of the storekeeper's clerks. For the cooperage stores, the count was done by a labourer-tallyman. It was the same with issues: in most cases it was the labourer-foreman or tallyman who counted items out

70 Ibid., pp. 34–5.
71 The report remarked that there had been a suggestion that it might have been more advantageous to abandon this process at Deptford and buy all the salt meat from contractors but this does not seem to have been followed up.
72 Ibid., pp. 35–6. This does not appear to have happened either.
73 Ibid., p. 36.

of the stores and reported the amount to the clerks in the clerk-storekeeper's office. Those clerks made up lists which were passed to the superintendant's office from which the bills of lading were produced; somewhere in what should have been a smooth sequence of events things often went wrong so that

> the cargoes of provisions very frequently disagree with the bills of lading … the error, though it may be discovered on landing the cargo, or afterwards, will never appear on the accounts of the clerk of the [type of item issued], because the board's order or warrant to issue, and not the receipt of the party to whom the stores are delivered, is the voucher looked for as evidence to the account of issue.

So, there was no proper check on the quantities of items received into store or issued from store and 'not the smallest check whatever on the truth of the statements contained in the several store accounts'.[74]

The final example of bad practice was the sale, at prices much below market value, of the offal from the slaughterhouse (in this case the tongues, legs, shins, and marrow-bones which were not required for commissioned officers or the portable soup) to the staff of the victualling office and Deptford, in proportions according to their rank. This practice, says the report, should be abolished and the offal sold by contract for the best price.[75]

To sum up the Board of Revision's staffing recommendations for Deptford: it should be put on the same footing as the other outports with an agent victualler in charge; that instead of the existing five accountants for cash and stores, those functions should be performed by the clerk of the cheque and one storekeeper, both of whom would report to the agent victualler. The other principal officers would then not be needed, nor eleven of the subordinate clerks. What had been eight principal officers and seven subordinate officers with thirty clerks would become three principal officers, eight subordinate officers and nineteen clerks.[76]

The other area of staffing where the Board of Revision felt reductions could be made at Deptford was that of the labourers and coopers. Each of these was 'entered' in a specific branch of the yard (for instance, at the time of the report, there was a grand total of 871 labourers in four separate branches); these men thought of themselves as belonging to their branch and were reluctant to assist in the work of another branch. At Plymouth where 'very nearly an equal number of stores is received and issued' there

---

74 Ibid., pp. 37, 30. This business with the bill of lading is doubly strange, because it indicates that no-one on the ships transporting these items bothered to count them as they were loaded and compare the count with the bill of lading.
75 Ibid., p. 39.
76 Appendix F shows the 'present' and proposed establishments.

were only 400. The Board of Revision thought that if the labourers and coopers at Deptford were entered for 'general purposes', to work in any branch in which they were needed, as was done in the dockyards, the total workforce for the yard could be reduced by 200 to 300 men.[77]

They also remarked that the physical layout of the yard at Deptford showed 'a want of judgement' and they recommended that some appropriate person should be employed to make a survey and recommend improvements to the layout and the use of the buildings. One thing which had come to their attention was the location of the superintendant's house and offices on the wharf, a place which would be better utilised for receiving stores; the reduction in storekeepers and other officers would free up living accomodation elsewhere, into which the chief officer should be moved. Such rearrangements would also allow sufficient space to move the army victualling stores into Deptford, and the premises at St Catherine's could be vacated.[78]

Concluding general remarks

This part of the report concludes with some general remarks on the victualling yards. The first of these was on the desirable frequency of surveys of stores, which they felt had been very much neglected. The fees commissioners had recommended that surveys should be done every three months; these commissioners thought that with the exception of cooperage stores, this was too frequent and, in wartime, impossible, but that it should be done annually. If it needed extra people to be sent to the port being surveyed in order to do it properly, then this should be done.[79]

There was a master miller at Portsmouth, who also had charge of the granary; at Plymouth there was only a labourer in the mill who did not oversee the granary. The Board of Revision recommended appointing a master miller at Plymouth with the same duties and salary as the one at Portsmouth.[80]

They thought that the method of paying for the bavins to fire the bread ovens at Portsmouth, whereby payment was made according to the amount of biscuit baked rather than by the number of bavins delivered (as at the other yards), was better and should be adopted by all the yards. The main advantage was that there would be no need to count bavins received or in stock, but they also mentioned the advantage of no longer having the

77 BOR 11, p. 38. See also Chapter 7 on yard staffing: this does not appear to have been done.
78 Ibid., p. 41–2.
79 Ibid., pp. 40–41.
80 Ibid., p. 41.

trouble of removing the ashes or 'small coals' as this would be done by the supplier.[81] Whether this recommendation was given any thought is not apparent from the minutes, but the contract ledgers show that no change was made.[82]

Unlike the dockyards, where the workers' perquisite of taking home 'chips' had been abolished in 1801 (although replaced by a cash payment) the coopers at Deptford and Portsmouth still had the privilege of taking out several bundles of chips or ends of staves each week, paying 7d a bundle. The master cooper at Deptford said that these bundles would sell for 3s. It was therefore recommended that the privilege should be withdrawn and a cash payment made instead: 4d per day for coopers and sawyers and 3d for labourers; and that all the chips should be sold for the best available price.[83]

Two long-standing practices of which they did not approve were the master brewers having contracts to provide horses for pumping water, and the porter at Deptford and the storekeeper's clerk at the brewery at Portsmouth running the tap. No officer or employee should, they said, hold any contracts 'of any description whatever'; and as far as taps were concerned these were a clear conflict of interest for the officer involved. On the one hand it was profitable to them for the workmen to spend time and money in the tap; on the other it was every officer's duty to prevent the workers 'idling away their time'. The taps, they proposed, should in future be run by someone from outside the yard, operating under strict regulations.[84]

The final point, apart from various recommendations on the pay structures of both clerical and yard staff, was that they thought agents victualler should be naval captains; the Victualling Board was the only civil department of the navy where this was not the case: the dockyards, the naval hospitals and the port offices of the transport service were all headed by naval officers:

> the desired superintendance and controul [sic] would be more complete if vested in an active and zealous Captain … from his rank and previous habits, an officer of this description would be better qualified to cooperate with the commander-in-chief at the port, and the respective captains, in the equipment of … ships; and from his knowledge of the business of shipping, provisions, etc. than can be expected from a clerk officer

---

81 Ibid., p. 41.
82 TNA ADM 112/195–201.
83 *BOR 11*, pp. 41, 45.
84 Ibid., p. 41.

... [everybody concerned] would be more likely to stand in awe of his authority[85]

The last of the Board of Revision's reports which covered the Victualling Board was the twelfth; this covered the yards abroad. It was extremely short, running to only two pages, the gist of which was that the old instructions to agents victualler should be scrapped and replaced with a new version (which was appended to the report, as had been those for the yards at home), and that the agents at those yards should be placed under the supervision of the resident naval commissioner.

These reports were duly approved by the Privy Council and the Victualling Board were instructed by the Admiralty to put all the recommendations into effect.[86] Apart from the situation of the antecedents of the chairman and deputy chairman, and the shifting of manufacturing operations from Deptford to the outports, this instruction was carried out, although it took until May 1809 for everything to settle down. It had taken over twenty years for the reorganisation of this Admiralty department which Middleton had wanted to be put into effect.

85 Ibid., pp. 43–4.
86 NMM ADM C/719, 16 September 1808, Admiralty to Victualling Board, relaying Order in Council of 14 September 1808.

10

Conclusions

T HE BOARD OF REVISION's reports on the Victualling Board are a damning indictment of the whole of the management of the victualling, both
in the victualling office in London and in the yards at home and abroad.
The previous enquiries suggested some improvements but had basically
concluded that the systems at the yards were adequate, conclusions which
the Board of Revision found itself unable to comprehend.[1] They tactfully
remarked several times that it was the system which was at fault rather than
the individuals running it, but they also made several comments which
clearly indicated that they thought the commissioners were not up to the
job: '… a want of judgement', 'unless all the commissioners be men of real
ability, professional knowledge and uninterrupted industry', '[chosen for
no other reason than] their being the fittest men that can be found'.

Before coming to a conclusion on the management competence of the
victualling commissioners who served during the French Revolutionary
and Napoleonic wars (or as close to a decision as one can come, given the
elapsed time and the inherent danger of anachronism), it is perhaps wise to
consider what the term actually means. By any standards, it has to mean the
ability to get the *whole* job done promptly and properly, without allowing
deep-seated problems to develop or remain without remedial action; with
proper attention to detail, understanding of the processes and a willingness to instigate change when necessary. Thus far we can be objective; to
what extent the victualling commissioners did demonstrate this ability is
necessarily subjective. Any judgement on success is dependant on who is
judging it, and here there are, and were, different views on the importance
of the various parts of the task and how well these were achieved.

To the naval seamen and officers of the day, the primary (perhaps the
only important) objective was to get sufficient quantities of good food on to

---

1   BOR 11, pp. 3–4.

the seaman's plate; this was important not only to fuel the fighting machine, but also to maintain the morale which kept that machine enthusiastic. This viewpoint has dominated the historiography of the subject, as written by and for naval historians and as written by and for serving officers. Even here, views differ: historians have until recently tended to report only failures; although some have discussed purchases or manufacture of food, few mention the system which delivered it to warships. Modern serving officers look at the matter differently: they make the assumption that an adequate supply chain can be taken more or less for granted, and emphasise the importance of delivery. According to *US Naval Doctrine Publication No 4*, the 'most important principle of logistics [is] providing the right support, at the right time, in the right place', a doctrine which is repeated or paraphrased in most of the modern books on logistics.[2]

If that was the only criterion, there is little doubt that the Victualling Board did a good job during this period. There were exceptions, documented by complaints from commanders-in-chief, when the delivery system failed; most were caused by events outside the Victualling Board's control, such as unseasonable weather or political events like the embargoes imposed by the American government which affected supply in the West Indies, but a few were caused by a lack of foresight, such as the failure to provide sufficient stocks at Plymouth before the adverse winds of autumn set in; it took the Board of Revision to point this out.

It is relevant to consider the difficulty of this core part of the Victualling Board's task: it was in fact quite easy, as it was based on long-established procedures and the immediacies of 'acute' events. The size of naval manpower was decided once a year (with occasional additions at other times) and that figure drove the purchasing; expeditions and shifts of theatre drove the delivery side; directions from above such as using rum instead of brandy merely had to be acted upon. The magnitude of the cost of all this required high-level supervision but it should not have required the constant attention of seven expensive commissioners. Following the Board of Revision's recommendations, after 1808 these functions were performed by a committee of only four commissioners with no more than oversight by the other three at full board meetings. There is no evidence that these core tasks ran any less smoothly under the new arrangements; the other committee was then able to devote most of its time to dealing with accounts.

Other areas which were well handled were those non-core tasks which were also of an immediate or 'acute' nature: maintenance and replacement of buildings and vessels, the provision of management information to the Treasury and other government bodies; and various ad hoc tasks. On these

---

2   Quoted in T M Hull, *Military Logistics in Strategy and Performance* (London, 2001), p. 5.

tasks, the Board would have been judged by people at the other boards with whom they interacted. The Navy Board and the Treasury would have been satisfied with the prompt arrival of the financial information they needed, and the Admiralty would have considered the prompt way in which the Victualling Board dealt with ad hoc tasks (and complaints from commanders-in-chief) to be a sign of high competence and efficiency.

The Victualling Board would also have been perceived as having done a good job handling the supply problems caused by adverse weather conditions: the severe winters which made movement of cattle impossible and stopped deliveries to ice-bound ships, and the deficient harvests which caused corn shortages. That perception would have been based on the lack of complaints from naval officers, particularly during the corn shortages when the government was receiving pleas for assistance from the civil authorities throughout the country.[3] However bad these situations were in the civil world they do not appear to have caused the Victualling Board any major problems; they had adequate stocks (although the state of the market made it expensive to replace them), they were able to utilise the substitute system and they were also able to reduce the amounts issued to ships in home waters.

They would also have received the government's approbation for their concern over 'alarming the markets' and the steps they took to avoid the associated speculation and concomitant escalation of prices which would lead to public unrest. That the government were right to be concerned about such unrest is demonstrated by the outbreaks of public disorder which occurred during the grain crises.

It was the other tasks, those where directions did not arrive from above to prompt action, and which come into the 'chronic' category, where the performance of the victualling commissioners was woefully inadequate. They allowed the keeping and passing of accounts and the collection of debts, which after the core tasks were the most important part of their function, to fall into horrendous arrears, and they had failed to pass some accounts which had been ready for up to five years. Although a major element of any accounting work is that of identifying fraudulent transactions, they hardly ever detected those without anonymous tips. On their rare visitations to the yards, they seemed naïvely unaware of the necessity to make accurate stock-checks and to properly reconcile physical stock with the book figures proffered by the yard staff, instead happily accepting disingenuous explanations for substantial differences. It is also clear that the commissioners had little idea of exactly what their clerical staff did with their time: quite apart from the time-

---

3   TNA PC1/29/64–73, Privy Council papers, contain many of these pleas for relief during the shortages of 1795.

wasting activities of the clerks at the outports, the misdeeds of the staff at head office went undetected until the arrival of anonymous letters.

It took outsiders, in the form of the commissioners of the various inquiries, to see what was wrong with the subordinate boards, and even when it had been pointed out to them by the first two of these inquiries, the Admiralty managed to evade the issue.[4] It was not until the Board of Naval Enquiry had demonstrated the serious lack of control in the dockyards, and the Board of Revision had exposed the depth of the management failings at the Victualling Board, that the Admiralty was forced to acknowledge that something needed to be done. Other than issuing a reprimand when some major problem was brought to their attention, the Admiralty was either unaware of these inadequacies or unconcerned. It was, to use a modern aphorism, a case of 'if it ain't broke, no need to fix it'. The Admiralty's highest priority was, after all, keeping the government in good odour by winning the war without spending too much money, and the internal affairs of the Victualling Board would have come lower down their list of priorities, certainly below the work of the Navy Board in keeping the fighting fleet at sea. This was reflected in the differential between the salaries of the Navy and Victualling Board commissioners.

The completion of the Board of Revision's reports on the Victualling Board was followed within months by the exposure of the misbehaviour of numerous clerks in the victualling office, and this gave the Admiralty the opportunity to get rid of the chairman and two other seemingly supine victualling commissioners and replace them with some more professional men who fitted the model recommended by the Board of Revision. The fact that it did not force the retirement of Towry, who was by that time aged 74 and who appears to have been the author of much of the procrastination over accounts, can only be due to his connection with the influential Grey family and his son-in-law Lord Ellenborough, who as the Lord Chief Justice was a member of the Cabinet.[5]

It is unfortunate that we lack information on Towry's career between his commission as a lieutenant in 1757 and his joining the Victualling Board twenty-six years later, as this might have given some insights into his character and thus his influence on the other members of the Board. However, even without this, the impression gained from the documents we do have is of a pompous and domineering individual, anxious to keep in with his rich and influential relatives (an expensive business, which might have been the

---

4   Breihan, 'William Pitt', passim; P K Crimmin, 'Admiralty relations with the Treasury, 1783–1806: The preparation of naval estimates and the beginnings of Treasury control', *Mariner's Mirror*, vol. 53 (1967), pp. 63–72.
5   Basil Cochrane, in his publications, believed Ellenborough was influential in this.

reason Towry did not want to be retired on a reduced income and without free accommodation).

To what extent Towry extended the influence of his family connections to other members of staff cannot be known, but it is not unreasonable to suggest that he would have 'returned the favour' when it was his turn to recommend applicants for junior clerkships. Given his own unprofessional attitude to the priorities of his position as head of the stores accounting department, it is difficult to see that he would have prioritised administrative ability in such appointees (although it is only fair to say that he did seem to have had a hand in the career development of Richard Ford, who was undoubtedly extremely competent).

There was one other major sphere of influence obvious during this period: that of Admiral Lord Keith. Not only does he seem to have been influential in the decision to deal with the arrears of pursers' accounts, he must have been the influence behind the appointments of three professionally competent commissioners: Searle, Brown and, later, James Meek.[6] These seem, unfortunately, to have been exceptional appointments.

The level of procrastination and the lack of awareness of office activities which the victualling commissioners displayed, both in the matter of misbehaviour and unnecessary procedures, may have been due to the fact that the commissioners were so busy with the pressure of work which assailed them every day. This situation was one of their major failings, and is neatly summarised by another modern aphorism: that when you are up to your neck in alligators, it is difficult to remember that amongst your objectives is draining the swamp. Until 1809, the Board as a whole entity dealt with everything that came into the office, and did so on the premise that everything, regardless of its importance, had to be dealt with immediately; that this was their standard operating procedure is evident from the minutes of the daily board meetings and the endorsements on the backs of the letters received. In other words, they lacked the ability to set priorities and they failed to set up a system where low-priority matters were automatically passed to lower-level personnel. As with the lack of foresight problem mentioned above, it took the Board of Revision to see through this waste of the commissioners' time and recommend that some of the low-level tasks should be handled by the Board secretary and his staff.[7]

6 Keith's connection to the Prince Regent may well have assisted Searle's efforts to gain the pay rise which appears to have been granted by the Prince Regent. Meek was a commissioner from 1830–32, and had also been Keith's secretary.
7 Over two-thirds of the Victualling Board's in-letters from the Admiralty and other boards and government departments were standard and low-level matters which required no more than to be passed on to the appropriate person. These in-letters are analysed in Macdonald, 'Documentary sources'.

Le Roy Ladurie remarked that historical figures 'cannot be invited to stretch out on the couch of some hypothetical historian-psychoanalyst … one can only note certain obvious traits, that are generally encountered in similar cases'.[8] This is one of the areas where one has to be careful of anachronistic thinking, but even so, there are some traits of human behaviour which do not change. People in comparatively lowly positions who feel they deserve better often resort to ego-boosting mannerisms (such as Searle's constant pushing for salary and status enhancement) and work practices (such as micro-management). The comparatively lowly position of the victualling commissioners is demonstrated by the subservient tone of their letters to the Admiralty and the fact that they neither took decisions on matters that were not within their narrow brief nor suggested that that brief should be expanded to include the various repetitive situations which could, and should, have been dealt with by setting up parameters on how to tackle such requests instead of having to refer all such decisions to the Admiralty.[9]

The victualling commissioners were, in general, reactive rather than proactive; one of their major faults was that they failed to instigate changes to their internal systems and office procedures. This may have been because they had not bothered to find out what those procedures were, or because they did not want to admit to their superiors that they had allowed the unsatisfactory situations to develop on a large scale. They did make some small changes, but these tended to involve minor matters, such as the standard letters which changed from being hand-written in full every time to filling in the blanks in printed pro-formas, or pointing out to the Admiralty that it really was not necessary to issue an Admiralty Order every time a ship came into port to replenish its victuals. But it took Lord Keith's complaint to make them address the matter of dealing with arrears of pursers' accounts; they failed to see and correct the faulty thinking in the way the master coopers calculated their stocks of staves and casks; and they do not seem to have investigated the Board of Revision's comment that it might be better to abandon meat packing at Deptford and buy it all in from Ireland; they certainly did not stop the operation at Deptford.

MacDougall, referring to the period immediately before the abolition of the civil boards in 1832, believes that the commissioners of those boards openly defied the Admiralty, delaying or preventing changes which they saw as undesirable. They felt able to do this as they knew that the frequent alterations in the political make-up of the government were usually

---

8   From Le Roy Ladurie's *The Peasants of Languedoc*, cited by Peter Burke, *The French Historical Revolution; The Annales School* (Stanford, CA, 1990), p. 71.

9   For an example of the subservient tone of their letters, see TNA ADM 110/68, ff. 525–7, 6 June 1814.

followed by similar alterations to the Board of Admiralty, and the removal of the Admiralty lords who had desired those changes.[10]

During the period of this study, there is no indication that the victualling commissioners openly defied the Admiralty, but they certainly abandoned their efforts on the arrears of accounts once the commissioners of the two earlier enquiries had departed, and they appear to have ignored the recommendations of the Board of Revision which covered some work practices in the yards. There were certainly numerous changes at the Admiralty during the period, and as Macdougall remarks, the new appointees to the Admiralty would have been unable to argue with the experienced commissioners of the inferior boards, and thus would not press for implementation of any changes required by their predecessors.[11]

It may seem anachronistic to suggest that the victualling commissioners should have applied cost accounting practices to their operations but although not designated under that term, the concept was not new at that time. It was inherent in the meat-packing question and in the matter of bringing salt meat all the way up the Channel to Deptford then sending it back to Portsmouth and Plymouth; the victualling commissioners' stated reason for doing this was that they were able to use the casks of meat as a bottom layer for mixed loads of provisions, thus preserving the more delicate items such as flour from damage.[12] They did not appear to have considered the differential between the cost of freight on meat all the way up the Channel and the cost of other dunnage as a bottom layer on the way back down to the outports. Samuel Bentham was fully aware of the concept; in his 'Answers to the Comptroller's Objections [to Bentham and Nepean's revision of the fees report relating to the Navy Board]' he made three relevant points: that costs such as repairing or replacing small boats (or these costs at different yards) were not being compared; that costs of any given work were recorded in different books and never brought together; and that no account was taken of the cost of interest when work was delayed or started unnecessarily soon.[13]

And the concept certainly existed in the commercial world: as early as 1770 Josiah Wedgwood applied it to his product range (and in the process discovered that his head clerk had been defrauding him for years).[14] That

---

10   MacDougall, 'Somerset Place', p. 347.
11   Ibid., pp. 347–8.
12   To a large extent this practice seems to have ceased or at least diminished by 1803; the contract ledgers show substantial deliveries of supplies being delivered straight to the outports: see Appendix C. It is unfortunate that we do not have consistent details of quantities of supplies being sent from Deptford to the outports.
13   Quoted in Morriss, *Naval Power*, p. 155.
14   Neil McKendrick, 'Josiah Wedgwood and cost accounting in the Industrial Revolution', *Economic History Review*, 1970, vol. XXII, pp. 45–67.

the victualling commissioners were either not aware of the concept or failed to appreciate its utility is another example of their lack of professionalism.

Whether the Victualling Board's performance improved on a grand scale after 1809 is difficult to ascertain, mainly because it coincided with an escalation in the war effort. The chain of command at Deptford had been altered, the staff numbers at the yards had been adjusted, and at head office they had almost caught up with the arrears of pursers' accounts and had set to work to deal with the other arrears of accounts. But they failed to see the stupidity of using one of their accounting department heads (Richard Ford) as a trouble-shooter for tasks which any competent businessman or vice-consul could have handled, and the events of 1822 demonstrate that they still had no idea of what their staff were up to. And it is clear, from the long drawn-out saga of their failure to bring Basil Cochrane's accounts to a satisfactory close, that the competence of the clerical staff was little improved. This clerical incompetence, according to Cochrane, included more than one incident of documents lost in the office as well as their inability to arrive at a correct balance. Basil Cochrane had no hesitation in laying all this at Towry's door, and since it was Towry's department which was responsible for the work (and probably the attempt to bully him into accepting their figures by instigating legal action) Cochrane was almost certainly right.

It seems, therefore, that certainly before, and probably after, the changes to the system in 1809 brought about by the Board of Revision, the board of victualling commissioners, as the managers of an important and high-spending government department, were only competent when dealing with routine matters which had clearly laid-down parameters, or which arose in a manner which prompted an immediate response.

But is it reasonable to lay the blame for all this entirely on the victualling commissioners as individuals and as a management group? They were, after all, operating in a restricted role (as evidenced above), most of them, certainly before 1809, had no real qualifications for the job, and they were chosen for reasons which rarely included professional suitability. Some seem to have been given the job mainly to provide them with an enhanced income while they performed another job such as private secretary to the first lord of the Admiralty, others were left in place during long periods of physical and mental decline.[15] It is thus hardly surprising that they were not as competent as they should have been.

There was nothing unique about the Victualling Board in this respect. Until similar studies of the other boards have been completed, it is not

---

15 Nicholas Brown remarked to First Lord Melville in 1814 that Edgecumbe's 'necessary attendance on Mr Yorke precluded me almost entirely from the benefit of his useful assistance': Knight, 'Politics', p. 148, n. 42; Sainty (*Admiralty Officials*, p. 65) gives the salary for these private secretaries as £300 p.a., but this only commenced in 1800.

possible to make an informed judgement on their competence but despite Charles Middleton's long struggle to improve Navy Board administration, the Board of Revision found many changes to recommend in their reports on that board. The Sick and Hurt Board had already been deemed incompetent and closed, with its functions handed over to the Transport Board. The Transport Board itself had neither arrears of accounts nor other unfinished business to contend with prior to 1806, and at that point seemed reasonably competent, but as a newly formed organisation it did not carry the burden of a hide-bound organisational culture. Carl H Builder remarks that institutions have personalities of their own which govern much of their behaviour, even though they are composed of frequently changing individuals; although he was discussing modern military institutions, this seems to be equally applicable to the Georgian navy.[16]

Nor have there been deep studies of management competence in other contemporary government departments or large commercial organisations which can be used as comparators. Indeed, there were no non-government organisations of any size equal to the Victualling Board or the Navy Board; and those few commercial organisations which did employ hundreds of people were usually run by their owners.[17] This does not mean they were necessarily more efficient, but it does mean that because there was no significant number of professional large-business managers moving between organisations and no management training for those individuals outside their immediate employment, there had been no general development or promulgation of management theory on which the victualling commissioners could have drawn. Nevertheless, commissioners joining the Board should have taken their new responsibilities sufficiently seriously to have striven to improve matters; prior to Searle's joining, they do not appear to have done so.

The attitudes displayed by the victualling commissioners seem to have been common not only to the naval administration or even to government departments, but part of the general mindset of the time. Crimmin remarks on the lengthy delays in closing the accounts of high public officials such as Treasurers of the Navy, and Cohen points out that the systems of checks and controls in most public offices were faulty and inadequate, commenting that although there was an Audit Office, the commissioners examining the public accounts remarked in their twelfth report that they had 'not been able to discover … any solid advantage derived to the public [by the work of this office]', and recommended closing it. The staff of another major government department, the Exchequer, were so set in their ways that they

---

16 Carl H Builder, *Masks of War: American Military Styles in Strategy and Analysis* (London, 1989), p. 3.
17 MacDougall, 'Somerset Place', pp. 345–6.

insisted that all their business (including accounts) should be conducted in Latin, and continued this practice until 1832, despite several attempts at reform.[18]

Brewer remarks on the inability of the average back-bench Member of Parliament to understand any form of business that did not equate to running a landed estate.[19] It could be argued that this stemmed from the social chasm between gentlefolk and trade; it is notable that naval commissioner Shield and others stigmatised those whom they wished to have dismissed as being 'ungentlemanlike'.

This distaste for trade and the concomitant lack of knowledge of accounting and business practice may have been part of the reason why the victualling commissioners put off tackling large and complex sets of accounts. It might also have been why they were prepared to accept the excuses offered for incorrect stock-counts when they made yard visitations. These examples raise some anomalies of the trust and loyalty between the Board and its staff: they were over-trusting of the agents victualler at home (notably Matthews at Chatham) and generally distrustful of the agents victualler abroad, even when those men had worked blamelessly for many years at the head office at Somerset Place. The real problem with such a lack of trust is that it invites the very situations which it seeks to prevent. These attitudes create resentment, which can often lead to the conclusion that a dog with a bad name might just as well commit a hanging offence if there is a chance of getting away with it.

It also means more work for senior management when there are no layers of staff trusted to perform certain tasks without *all* their work being checked. It is difficult to know if this is what happened at the victualling office, but the indications are that it did. All types of accounts, from major contractor/agents such as Basil Cochrane down to the pursers of the smallest warships are referred to as being 'passed' by the Board. This 'passing', in the case of small accounts, might have consisted of the accountant bringing a batch of accounts to board meetings, stating that he had checked them, and the board accepting his word and 'signing them off' without checking for themselves, but the build-up of arrears (some of which involved only small sums), and the fact that the Board had to get Admiralty approval to write-off equally small debts, suggests that this was not the case.

Modern management techniques usually involve a series of financial authorities at different levels of management (for instance, a junior manager can sign for sums up to £500, a senior manager for up to £1,000, and so on); this stems from the thinking that the time-cost of senior managers might

18   Crimmin, 'Admiralty Relations', p. 68; Cohen, *The Growth of the British Civil Service*, pp. 30–2, 37–8, 50.
19   Brewer, *Sinews*, p. xvi.

be greater than the sums they spend their time signing for. Much the same applies to modern debt-collecting: the amount of time and expense devoted to chasing debts is in direct proportion to the size of the debt and the likelihood of a positive result. This raises the question that if the Victualling Board could see this in 1817 with the old Sick and Hurt Board's debts (and the Admiralty could agree with them), why had no one seen it earlier? Was it perhaps because this tranche of debts was not the fault of the victualling commissioners of the time?

To a large extent all this boils down to the principle of delegation with built-in parameters, and it is not anachronistic to suggest that late Georgian naval administrators should have been aware of the principle. It was, after all, the principle on which warships were run, with the captain delegating part of the job of running the ship to his lieutenants, setting parameters with his 'Captain's Orders' and the proviso that he should be consulted at non-routine events. There were always naval officers on the Admiralty board and a tendency to require the subordinate boards to include captains, and to fill other senior posts at the yards with captains, so the concept would not have been new to the administrators.

Another principle of warship operations was that the junior officers were known, even if it was not expressed in these terms, to be undergoing management training. Midshipmen were expected to become lieutenants, lieutenants to become captains and so on; but with the exception of Moody (who may have been the beneficiary of family influence) none of the commissioners in the 1793–1815 period had come up through the victualling administration. The promotion 'ceiling' in the victualling office seems, with that sole exception, to have been department head (i.e. accountant or secretary).

Although there was a conviction throughout the naval administration that naval captains were the ideal candidates for high-level administration jobs, hindsight suggests that it was not necessarily the case. They would certainly have developed the habit of command (a valuable attribute at a time when subordinates did not normally do other than obey) and to a certain extent would have been accustomed to the need for orderly paperwork, although by the time they had reached post rank they would have been assisted by a dedicated clerk. Relevant questions are whether their command habit was always appropriate when dealing with civilians (e.g. the attitudes of the resident naval commissioners at the Cape and Malta), and whether the administrative requirements of running a single warship were adequate training for a seat on a board. Certainly there were some captains who had administrative genius, but these tended to be those such as the Board of Revision commissioners Curtis and Domett who had assisted an admiral as fleet captain. The final attribute of naval captains was that they were gentlemen, which their contemporaries would have regarded as essential but the modern mind sees as negative when it included the usual disdain for commercial acumen.

While the victualling commissioners were no doubt convinced that they were doing a good job, there were many ways in which they were not. They were generally unprofessional, they seemed content to let things go along as they had always done, and although they responded quickly when events or queries from above prompted a reaction, their lowly position in the naval hierarchy (demonstrated by the way they were firmly in their place by the Admiralty over the oaths for staff) did not encourage them to be proactive.

That even after the Board of Revision report and comments on the need to select commissioners for their professional ability, those commissioners could be appointed for other reasons (e.g. Edgecumbe) and that the one commissioner who should have been replaced for his advanced age, if nothing else (Towry), was left in place, puts much of the onus for this lack of professionalism on the Admiralty and other members of the government who made those appointments. Even so, the most telling example of the inadequacies of the board of victualling commissioners was the situation uncovered in 1822 by Cockburn and Clerk, and this at a time long after the war was over and the pressures of work associated with war had subsided. This situation, publicly discussed in Parliament and the newspapers, must have been part of the ammunition built up by the Whigs in their campaign to reform the Admiralty and its subordinate boards which resulted in the abolition of those subordinate boards in 1832.

We must now return to the last of the principal questions posed in the introduction: did the Victualling Board and its staff perform their jobs as competently as they might? We have seen that the late eighteenth- and early nineteenth-century victualling system was capable of handling vast amounts of routine business and focusing on the core tasks; but in the process it neglected many of the non-core tasks and it is clear that its management lacked the professionalism and expertise to generate internal efficiencies and reforms. Therefore we must conclude that while the Victualling organisation as a whole performed its core task of supplying the navy effectively, it is not unreasonable to say that it achieved this Herculean task despite its managing commissioners rather than because of them, due to the Augean stable of outmoded and inefficient management over which they presided. The Board of Revision reports made this quite clear; its conclusions in that respect may have been prompted by Charles Middleton's frustration, but they also had to be a product of the Burkean thinking of the day, which eventually led to the creation of the permanent civil service. In that context we can conclude that not only was the Victualling Board incompetent in many areas of its task, but that there was contemporary recognition of the fact.

Appendix A

Substitute Provisions[1]

When it may be found necessary to issue any other Species of Provisions or Substitutes for the [usual items], it is to be observed that they are to be furnished in the following proportions, viz.

A pint of Wine, or half a pint of Spirits, is equal to a Gallon of Beer, and when Wine or Spirits are demanded, one fourth part only of the whole proportion is to be issued in Wine.

Four pounds of Flour, or three pounds thereof, with one pound of Raisins, are equal to a four-pound piece of Salt Beef. Half a pound of Currants, or half a pound of Beef Suet, is equal to one pound of Raisins. Four pounds of Fresh Beef, or three pounds of Mutton, are equal to four pounds of Salt Beef; and three pounds of Fresh Beef, or Mutton, to a two-pound piece of Salt Pork, with Pease.

One pint of Calavances, or Doll, is equal to a pint of Pease.

Whenever Rice is issued for Bread, Pease, Oatmeal, or Cheese, one pound of Rice is to be considered as equal to one pound of Bread, a pint of Pease, a quart of Oatmeal, or a pound of Cheese.

A pint of Wheat, or of Pot Barley, is equal to a pint of Oatmeal; five pounds and three-quarters of Molasses are equal to one gallon of Oatmeal.

When Sugar is substituted for Oatmeal, Butter, or Cheese, one pound of Sugar is equal to two quarts of Oatmeal, one pound of Butter, or one pound of Cheese.

A pint of Oil is equal to a pound of Butter, or two pounds of Cheese; and half a pound of Cocoa, or a quarter of a pound of Tea, is equal to one pound of Cheese.

---

1   *R&I*, 14th edition, 1806, p. 288 (shown here verbatim).

Appendix B

An account of the expense of victualling 110,000 men for 13 lunar months[2]

				£	s	d
bread	27,500 cwt	@	£1.0.0 per cwt	27,500	0	0
spirits	182,500 galls	@	£0.4.6 per gall	43,312	10	0
beef	220,000 8lb pieces	@	£0.4.2½ per piece	46,315	15	9¼
pork	220,000 4lb pieces	@	£0.2.3 per piece	24,750	0	0
pease	13,750 bushels	@	£2.0.0 per quarter	3,437	10	0
oatmeal	20,625 bushels	@	£15.0.0 per ton	5,800	15	7½
butter	165,000 lbs	@	£3.15.0 per cwt	5,524	11	¾
cheese	330,000 lbs	@	£2.16.0 per cwt	8,250	0	0
vinegar	27,500 galls	@	£12.12.0 per tun	1,443	15	0
	necessary money and contingencies supplied at 1d per man per day			12,833	6	8
	casks, slops and bags supplied at 1d per man per day			12,833	6	8
				192,001	10	9½
	one month on those articles calculated at the present prices to cover the losses, condemnation and waste in the several stores			11,872	0	1
	expense of extra articles furnished by this office such as sugar for lemon juice, wine for the sick, vegetables etc estimated at 6d per month			2,750	0	0
			sub-total	212,174	9	4½
	Amount for 13 lunar months		Total	2,758,268	1	10½

2   NMM ADM DP/17, 19 October 1797. There is a calculation error in the document (which is shown here verbatim): the calculation of cost of beef should give £46,291.13.4 (not £46,315.15.9¼) on which basis: the first total should be £191,977.8.4½; the second total should be £212,150.6.11¼; the grand total should be £2,757,954.10.2¼.

Appendix C

Victualling Commissioners – biographic details[3]

John Aubin

Commissioner from 3 December 1808 to 20 February 1822 (forcibly retired).

He had been a purser, then secretary to Lord Howe and attended him at the Spithead mutiny in 1797; clerk of the survey at Deptford dockyard, storekeeper at Chatham dockyard (1803 to 1808). He had a total of forty years' service and was one of the commissioners removed in 1822 as a result of the scandal following Sir George Cockburn's investigation. He had by this time suffered an attack of 'the palsy' and was mentally incapacitated. Originally awarded a pension of £200 p.a. (a quarter of his salary) he appealed and this was increased to £300.[4]

William Boscawen

Commissioner from 19 December 1785 to 4 May 1811 (died).

He was the son of General the Hon. George Boscawen (Admiral Edward Boscawen's younger brother). He had attended Eton school, then Exeter College Oxford, and was a Barrister on the Western circuit before joining the Victualling Board. His obituary in the *Naval Chronicle* said that he was 'An excellent scholar, good poet – his translation of Horace esteemed the best English version in point of spirit and accuracy'.[5]

---

3   Most of the dates given here correlate with those given in the Institute of Historical Research's provisional listing compiled by J C Sainty (February 2003); however, Sainty is in error with some of the dates, e.g. the patent rolls TNA C66/3897, which is 1783, not 1784, and C66/4219 which is 1820 not 1821. Sainty is also incorrect in stating that the victualling commissioners received pay rises in 1803; this was actually 1800: TNA ADM 181/12–15.

4   NMM C/720, 19 November 1808; TNA C66/4084, 4085, 4112, 4138, 4184, 4219; TNA ADM 6/22, f. 429; ADM 1/5235, 28 March & 18 May 1822; ADM 7/871, ff. 59–60.

5   TNA ADM C66/3855, 3864, 3895, 3899, 3929, 3951, 3957, 4022, 4038, 4054, 4069, 4084, 4085; *Fees 8*, p. 594; *Naval Chronicle*, vol. XXV, p. 51; D B Smith (ed.) *Letters of Admiral of the Fleet the Earl of St Vincent, whilst First Lord of the Admiralty*, vol. II (London, 1922), pp. 230–1n; Knight, 'Politics', p. 145.

Nicholas Brown

Commissioner from 3 December 1808 to 10 June 1830 (died).

He spent eighteen years as a purser, then as secretary to Admiral Keith (during which time he spent some months as a peripatetic agent victualler to Keith's fleet during the Alexandria campaign). Whilst with Keith, he was one of the people accused by captains Alexander Cochrane and Benjamin Hallowell of overcharging for a purchase of seamen's shoes.[6]

William Budge

Commissioner from 3 May 1805 to 3 December 1808 (forcibly retired, ill-health).

He served as a clerk to the Committee of the Privy Council for Trade and Plantations (predecessor of the Board of Trade) from 25 August 1786 to 10 December 1794 when he resigned and took up the position of clerk in the office of the Secretary of State for War (Henry Dundas, later Lord Melville). He is also shown as a clerk in the Colonial Office from 11 July 1794 to 10 April 1805, then resigning to take up the post as a victualling commissioner (and also as joint private secretary to the Secretary of State for War from 5 July 1797 to 17 March 1801); and as private secretary to the First Lord of The Admiralty (Lord Melville) from 12 July 1804 to 8 May 1805. It is not known whether the seeming overlap of posts in 1794 is an overlap, or whether there is some confusion with someone else of the same name.[7]

6   NMM ADM C/720 18 November 1808; TNA C66/4084, 4085, 4112, 4138, 4184, 4219, 4243, 4257, 4329, 4351; ADM 6/22, f. 322; PROB 11/1772; Christopher Lloyd (ed.) *The Letters and Papers of Admiral Viscount Keith* (London, 1950, 1955), Vol. II, pp. 235, 252, 256, 292–7, 311–13, 326, 412, Vol. III, pp. 12, 113n; see also Sir John Knox Laughton (ed.), *The Barham Papers*, vol. III (London, 1911), pp.185, 257.

7   TNA C66/4038, 4054, 4069; C/706, 9 April 1805; NMM ADM D/51, 6 May 1808 (Victualling Board reporting to Admiralty that Budge needs leave of absence to go to Bath for treatment of a paralytic affliction which had robbed him of the use of his hands and feet); BL Add. MSS 38233, ff. 134, 151; Sainty, *Officials of the Board of Trade* (London, 1974), p. 90; Sainty, *Colonial Office Officials*, p. 38; Sainty, *Admiralty Officials*, p. 113. Knight ('Politics', pp. 143, 145) gives the first position as the Home Office, citing Home Office Officials where Budge does not appear, and gives his dates as private secretary to the First Lord as 15 May 1804 to 2 May 1805, but these are Henry Dundas (Melville)'s dates as First Lord rather than Budge's dates as secretary. *The Naval Chronicle* (Vol XXXV, pp. 1–16) also states that Budge had early naval service, but this may have been as a volunteer since he does not appear in any of the usual naval listings.

George Cherry

Commissioner and Chairman from 1 September 1785 to 5 April 1799 (retired).

He had previously been a purser and then agent victualler for Howe's fleet on the North America station, then employed as agent for army provisions at Cowes.[8]

He was appointed to the Victualling Board by Howe, who was then First Lord of the Admiralty.[9]

Alexander Chorley

Commissioner from 27 July 1767 to 6 March 1794 (died).

He had previously been a clerk in the Navy Office since January 1741.[10]

Charles Cunningham

Commissioner from 4 November 1803 to 30 June 1806, then transferred to be Commissioner of Deptford and Woolwich dockyards until 1823.

He was a commissioned naval officer (Lieutenant 6 November 1782, Commander 28 January 1790, Captain 12 October 1793). Knighted 1832.[11]

Frederick Edgecumbe

Commissioner from 29 June 1811 to 1 June 1832 (died).

He passed as a lieutenant 1790, but was never commissioned; he was a clerk in the Home Office from 19 October 1803 to 29 June 1811, and also served as private secretary to Charles Yorke as Secretary of State Home Office (17 August 1803 to 11 May 1804) and as First Lord (7 May 1810 to [no day given] March 1812), and Richard Ryder as Secretary of State Home Office (1 November 1809 to 5 May 1810).[12]

8   Syrett, *Shipping and the American War*, pp. 143–5, 149, 150.
9   TNA C66/3855, 3864, 3895, 3899, 3929, 3951; *Fees 8*, p. 591; TNA ADM 6/22, p. 378; 110/46, f. 214, 20 June 1800; 110/57, f. 176, 29 March 1808.
10 TNA C66/3855, 3864, 3895; *Fees 8*, p. 593; NMM ADM D/38 7 March 1794 'announcing death yesterday'; Knight gives this second date as 28 March, but this was the date of the patent appointing his replacement; 'Politics', p. 145; Collinge, *Navy Board Officials*, p. 91.
11 TNA C66/4022, 4038; C/700, 11 October 1803; NMM PJ, vol III; Smith, *Letters ... St Vincent*, Vol. II, pp. 210n.
12 TNA C66/4112, 4138, 4184, 4219, 4243, 4257, 4329, 4351; TNA ADM 107/14/25 (passing certificate); Sainty, *Home Office Officials*, p. 50; Sainty, *Admiralty Officials*, pp. 65, 122; TNA ADM 7/871, f. 134; MacDougal states that he was a purser and admiral's secretary, then naval storekeeper from 1796, then Comptroller of the Sixpenny Office to 20 May 1811, but may be confusing him with James Meek who was a victualling commissioner from July 1830 to June 1832 ('Somerset Place', p. 70). Knight gives the dates of his secretaryship to Yorke as 4 May 1810 to 25 March 1812, but these are Yorke's dates as First Lord rather than those of Edgecumbe's dates as secretary.

John Harrison

Commissioner from 27 March 1799 to 22 August 1807 (retired – but his pension paid from 'another naval department'.)

He also served briefly (6 February to 18 March 1806) as private secretary to Lord Spencer when he was Home Secretary.[13]

Sir Francis John Hartwell

Commissioner from 4 December 1793 to 5 July 1796, then transferred to be commissioner at Sheerness dockyard September 1796, ditto at Chatham 1799 to 1801, Navy Board commissioner 21 January 1801 to 3 December 1808, and deputy comptroller 3 December 1808 to 21 August 1814 when he retired.

His previous career was as a commissioned officer (Lieutenant 7 July 1775, Commander 28 January 1790, Captain 12 October 1793). Baronet 26 October 1805. Knighted 1832.[14]

Robert W Hay

Commissioner from 14 June 1813 to 12 August 1825, then appointed one of the under-secretaries of state to the colonies.

He was private secretary to Lord Melville when the latter was First Lord of the Admiralty from 22 June 1812 to 3 April 1823.[15]

Joseph Hunt

Commissioner from 9 December 1790 to 2 October 1798 then transferred to be commissioner of the Transport Board November 1798 to February 1802, then to the Ordnance Board in May 1802, which he left under a cloud in 1810, absconding with Ordnance money and fleeing to Lisbon where he died in 1816.[16]

---

13 TNA C66/3957, 4022, 4038, 4054; NMM C/691 7 March 1799 Admiralty order; TNA ADM 110/57 f. 176, 29/3/08 to NB about pensions; C/717, 25 January 1808; ADM 110/57 f. 176, 28 January 1808, Victualling Board to Navy Board; Knight gives the dates of this secretaryship as 7 February 1800 to 19 February 1801 but Sainty (*Home Office Officials*, p. 52) gives them as 6 February 1806 to 18 March 1806, during the period when Spencer was home secretary.

14 TNA C66/3895, 3929; NMM PJ vol. V; J Collinge, *Navy Board ...*, p. 109, John Marshall (ed.), *The Royal Navy Biography: or Memoirs of the services of all the flag officers, superannuated rear-admirals, retired captains, post captains and commanders*, 12 vols. (London 1823–30), Vol. II, p. 60.

15 TNA C66/4138, 4184, 4219, 4243, 4257; ADM 7/871, f. 133; Sainty, *Admiralty Officials*, pp. 65, 130.

16 Thorne, The History of Parliament (Vol. II, pp. 266–7) gives this as Lisbon, Knight, 'Politics' (p. 139) gives it as France.

He was previously clerk to the surveyors of the navy August 1779 to June 1780, private secretary to Sir Samuel Hood 1781–82, to the 2ⁿᵈ Earl Chatham when he was First Lord of the Admiralty, Receiver of the Sixpenny Office at Greenwich Hospital August 1789 to December 1790, and Director of Greenwich Hospital 1791–1810. Someone of this name was MP for Queenborough 1807 to May 1810. He was thought, but not proven, to be the son of Edward Hunt (surveyor of the navy).[17]

John Marsh

Commissioner from 2 October 1798 to 3 December 1808 (forcibly retired).

He was previously consul at Malaga (1768–77), army commissary at Cork during the American War of Independence, reappointed consul at Malaga 1795, then a commissioner of the Transport Board 8 June 1795. His uncle George had been a commissioner of the Navy Board.[18]

Samuel Marshall

Commissioner from 31 October 1787 to 4 December 1793, then deputy comptroller of Navy Board to 2 October 1795, when he died.

His previous career was as a commissioned naval officer (Lieutenant 11 February 1760, Commander 24 September 1762, Captain 24 January 1771). Knighted circa 1794.[19]

Robert Sadleir Moody

Commissioner from 28 March 1794 to 20 January 1809 (forcibly retired, having suffered a physical decline).

Moody joined the Victualling Board in 1759; by July 1787 he was chief clerk for stating/balancing pursers accounts. He may have been related to Aaron Moody and Richard Vernon Sadleir, the Portsmouth-based contractors, and this was perhaps the influence behind his appointment. [20]

---

17   TNA C66/3864, 3895, 3899, 3929; Collinge, *Navy Board*, p. 114; R G Thorne, *History of Parliament: The House of Commons 1790–1820* (London, 1986), Vol. II, pp 266–7; Knight, 'Politics', pp. 139, 145. It is unlikely that he would have been sitting in both the House of Commons and the Ordnance Board simultaneously, which means there may be some confusion between two people of the same name.

18   TNA C66/3951, 3951, 3957, 4022, 4038, 4054, 4069; NMM ADM C/690 12/9/98; NMM BGR/35; http://www.jjhc.information/ (family history website); Baker, *Government and Contractors*, p. 101.

19   TNA C66/3855, 3864; Collinge, *Navy Board*, p. 121.

20   TNA C66/3899, 3929, 3951, 3957, 4022, 4038, 4054, 4069, 4084; Fees 8, p. 627; *The Times*, 22 March 1809. J Collinge's *Navy Board Officials* shows someone of this name as a temporary clerk to the clerk of the acts from October 1793 to September 1794, then as a clerk at the ticket office; this man died on 14 December 1794. Although

The Hon. John Rodney

Commissioner from 5 July 1796 to 4 November 1803, when he went to Ceylon as chief secretary, without giving notice.

His father was Admiral George Bridges Rodney; John was at the Royal Navy Academy Portsmouth, until discharged by his father's request. (midshipman September 1780, Lieutenant 10 September 1780, Captain 14 October 1780 (notoriously promoted by his father at age 15). He was MP for Launceton 1790–96 but made few appearances in the House.

There are conflicting stories about some of the events of his naval career and his personal life. He may (or may not) have had a leg amputated after a carriage accident, he may (or may not) have been court-martialled and dismissed the service in 1799. All available sources state that he eloped with an heiress and subsequently married her.

He was Equerry to the Duke of Clarence 1789 to 1814, and chief secretary of the government of Ceylon 1803–34. He died 9 April 1847. [21]

John Clarke Searle

Commissioner from 30 June 1806 to 20 February 1822 (forcibly retired). On being 'retired' from the Victualling Board he was put back on the list of retired officers as rear-admiral 8 February 1822. He died 19 December 1824.

His previous career was as a commissioned naval officer (Lieutenant 9 October 1780, Commander 17 March 1795, Captain 13 July 1796). Much of his seagoing career was under Lord Keith, whose influence probably served to get him the Victualling Board position. He was court-martialled but acquitted for the loss of *Ethalion* on the Penmark rocks in December 1799, and captain of Keith's flagship *Monarch* from May 1803 to summer 1806. He was related by marriage through his wife's sister to Major General John Murray. [22]

this is an unusual name, this seems to be a coincidence; www.familysearch.org/English/search/frameset_search.asp?PAGE=ancestorsearchresults.asp (downloaded 5 May 2008) suggests that 'our' Robert Sadleir Moody was the nephew of Richard Vernon Sadleir (brewer and contractor for troops in Nova Scotia during the American War of Independence) and Edward Moody, both of Portsmouth. (Baker, *Government and Contractors*, pp. 37, 45, 144, 224, 247).

21 TNA C66/3929, 3951, 3957; TNA ADM 6/185/237; TNA ADM 110/49, f. 372, 1 January 1803; NMM ADM C/700, 4 October 1803; Thorne, *History of Parliament: House of Commons*, Vol. III, p. 33–4; David Spinney, *Rodney* (London, 1969); W. O'Byrne, *Naval Biography*, Vol. III (London, 1849, 3rd edition 1990), p. 998.

22 TNA C66/4054, 4069, 4084, 4085, 4112, 4138, 4184, 4219; TNA ADM 107/8/76 (passing certificate), C/710 19 June 1806; ADM 1/5351; 1/5235, 8 February 1822; NMM PJ. vol. X; Lloyd (ed.) *The Letters … Keith*, Vol. II, pp. 87, 115–16, 309, 318–19, 411–12; Marshall, *Royal Navy*, Vol. II, p. 727; TNA ADM 1/5351 (Court martial on loss of Ethalion); TNA PROB 1694 (Searle's will); PROB 11/1898 (his wife Euphemia's will).

Francis Stephens

Commissioner from 21 January 1790 to 3 May 1805 (retired).

He had nearly 50 years in His Majesty's service, as purser, secretary to different admirals, and in 'the navy department' as well as the Victualling Board; was (according to the *Naval Chronicle*) 'one of the Vice Presidents of the Society for Encouragement of Arts, Manufactures and Commerce' and a fellow of the Royal Society. [23]

The Hon. Edward Richard Stewart

Commissioner from 20 January 1809 to 14 June 1813; then commissioner of the Navy Board June 1813 to February 1819, commissioner of Customs 1819 to 1821, commissioner of the Audit Board 1821 to 1827, deputy chairman of the Board of Customs circa 1833–46. Previously MP for Wigtown Burghs 1806 to 20 January 1809, he vacated this seat on being appointed to the Victualling Board.

He was the fifth son of the Earl of Galloway, brother of George, Admiral Viscount Garlies. He was a guards officer, first in the 3rd Regiment of Foot, then the 7th Regiment of Dragoon Guards, retiring as brigade major 1807, paymaster of marines 1812 to 1813. Died 1851.[24]

George Phillips Towry

Commissioner from 3 October 1783 to 8 March 1817 (died). (deputy chairman from 1804).

He was briefly a commissioned naval officer (Lieutenant 7 February 1757) but does not appear to have served in the navy for any length of time; his career between that date and his joining the Victualling Board in 1783 is not known. Originally known as George Phillips, he took the additional name Towry, following his brother Captain Henry John Towry who did so to comply with a legacy from his uncle Admiral John Towry. He was related

23   TNA C66/3855, 3864, 3895, 3899, 3929, 3951, 3957, 4022; www.royalsoc.ac.uk.; TNA ADM 6/22 p. 87; *Naval Chronicle*, vol. XVIII, p. 520; despite the statement in the Royal Society website that he was in the 'navy department', he does not appear in Collinge's Navy Board Officials.

24   TNA C66/4085, 4112; C/720 26 December 1808; Thorne, *A History of Parliament*, Vol. III, p. 271; P Collinge, *A List of all the Officers of the Army and Royal Marines on Full and Half-Pay with an Index: and a Succession of Colonels, 1800*, p. 109; ditto 1807, p. 74; TNA WO 12/410 (Regimental Pay Books, 7th Dragoon Guards, 1807.

through his grandmother Mary to the influential Grey family of Howick. His daughter married Lord Ellenborough, the Lord Chief Justice.[25]

Thomas Welsh

Commissioner from 22 August 1807 to 20 February 1822 (probably forcibly retired, but died soon after).

He was mentioned in *The Times* as 'Colonel Welsh', thus may have been the Thomas Welsh described in Hodson's listing of the officers of the Bengal Army.[26]

25 TNA C66/3855, 3864, 3895, 3899, 3929, 3951, 3957, 4022, 4038, 4054, 4069, 4084, 4085, 4112, 4138; Fees 8, p. 591; NMM PJ, vol. XI; Sainty (www.history.ac.uk/office/comms_victual.html) and Knight ('Politics', p. 145) give this incorrectly as 1784 (as evidenced by the first patent Roll (TNA C66/3855), the 8th report of the Fees commissioners (p. 591), and numerous references in the correspondence and minutes). Morriss and Knight also state incorrectly that Towry was Victualling Board secretary; TNA ADM 107/4 (passing certificate); PROB 11/829, will of Admiral John Towry (died 1757); TNA PRO 30/42 (correspondence and family tree of Lady Ellenborough).

26 TNA ADM C66/4069, 4084, 4085, 4112, 4138, 4184, 4219; Knight 'Politics', p. 143; V C P Hodson, *List of the Officers of the Bengal Army 1758–1834: Alphabetically Arranged and Annotated with Biographical and Genealogical Notices* (London, 1947), pp. 427–8.

Appendix D

Staff numbers at Somerset Place[27]

	1788	*1798*	*1815*
Commissioners	7	7	7
Secretary's department.			
Secretary	1	1	1
clerks	3	3	11
extra clerks	3	6	8
temporary supernumerary clerks		2	0
Department of the Accountant for Cash			
Accountant	1	1	1
chief clerks	4	2	2
clerks	8	9	21
extra clerks	11	13	23
temporary supernumerary clerks		11	0
Department of the Accountant for Stores			
Accountant	1	1	1
chief clerks	4	3	4
clerks	7	11	39
extra clerks	14	12	39
temporary supernumerary clerks		6	0
Clerk of the Issues		1	0
clerks	2	1	0
extra clerks	1	1	0
Registrar of Securities	0	0	1
Watchmen/Warders	4	2	1
Messengers	5	9	6
Housekeeper	0	0	1
Total	76	102	166

---

27   Figures are taken from: *Fees 8*, pp. 584–5 (1788); *SCF 32*, pp. 20–31 (1798); TNA ADM 110/70, ff. 363–5, 4 July 1815 (1815).

Appendix E

Head Office staff salaries (£ p.a.)[28]

Position	1800	1807
Secretary	850	1000
Secretary's chief clerk	500	700
Accountant for cash	700	750
Chief clerk of Imprest Office	500	550
Chief clerk of Assigning Office	400	500
Accountant for Stores	700	750
Chief clerk for stating agents' and storekeepers' accounts	400	500
Chief clerk for stating and balancing pursers' accounts	400	500
Chief clerk for keeping a charge on pursers, etc.	500	550
Clerk of the Issues	500	
Secretary's office		
2nd clerk	350	550
3rd clerk	200	500
4th clerk	150	300
5th clerk	120	250
6th clerk	100	200
7th & other clerks	80	160
8th, 9th & 10th clerks		140
11th clerk		120
1st to 6th extra clerks		110
7th & 8th extra clerks		100
Cash Department		
Accountant's office		
1st clerk	400	450
2nd clerk	250	300
3rd clerk	200	280
4th clerk	150	220
5th clerk	120	200
6th clerk	100	200
7th clerk	90	200
8th to 10th clerks	80	200
11th clerk		160
1st to 12th extra clerks		110
13th & 14th extra clerks		100

28   £50 of the secretary's salary was an allowance for coals and candles.

Position	1800	1807
Imprest office		
1st clerk	300	350
2nd clerk	150	200
3rd clerk	100	200
4th and other clerks	80	200
Assigning office		
1st clerk	200	250
2nd clerk	120	200
3rd clerk	100	200
4th and other clerks	80	200
Store Department Accountant's office		
1st clerk	400	450
2nd clerk	250	300
3rd clerk	200	250
4th clerk	150	200
5th clerk	120	200
6th clerk	100	200
7th clerk	90	200
8th & other clerks	80	200
9th to 15th clerks		160
16th to eighteenth clerks		140
19th clerk		120
1st to 5th extra clerks		110
6th to 16th extra clerks		100
Pursers' charge office		
1st clerk	300	350
2nd clerk	100	200
3rd clerk	100	200
4th and other clerks	80	160
6th & 7th clerk		140
8th clerk		120
Pursers' accounts office		
1st clerk	250	300
2nd clerk	150	200
3rd clerk	100	200
4th and other clerks	80	160
5th to 7th clerks		140
Agents' & storekeepers' accounts office		
1st clerk	400	500
2nd clerk	200	250
3rd clerk	100	200

4th and other clerks	80	160
5th clerk		140
Clerk of the issues	300	not shown
1st clerk	150	not shown
2nd clerk	80	not shown
Temporary supernumerary clerks	39s p.w.	not shown

Appendix F

Establishment of Officers and Clerks at the Victualling Yard at Deptford, as proposed by the Board of Revision[29]

Present Establishment			*Proposed Establishment*		
	Numbers borne of			Numbers borne of	
Quality of Officers	Officers	Clerks	Quality of Officers	Officers	Clerks
Principal Officers			Principal Officers		
Superintendant	1	2	Agent Victualler	1	2
Hoytaker	1	3	Clerk of the Cheque	1	8
Clerk of the Cheque	1	6	Storekeeper	1	8
Clerk of the Cutting-house	1	4			
Clerk of the Dry Stores	1	3			
Clerk of the Brewhouse	1	5			
Master Cooper	1	4			
Clerk of the Issues	1	3			
Total	8	30		3	18
Subordinate Officers			Subordinate Officers		
Master Brewer	1		Master Cooper	1	1
Master Baker	1		Master Brewer	1	
Master Butcher	1		Master Baker	1	
Principal Boatswain	1		Principal Boatswain	1	
Principal Stevedore	1		Principal Stevedore	1	
Inspector of Works	1		Inspector of Works	1	
Porter	1		Porter	1	
Total	7		Total	8	1
Grand total	15	30	Grand total	11	19

29   *BOR 11*, p. 40.

Appendix G

Victualling Board purchases of cattle from Smithfield market[30]

Total purchases of cattle as percentages of Smithfield total sales

Year	Total purchased by V B	Total sold at Smithfield	Percentage
1793	8666	116848	7.4%
1794	8928	109448	8.2%
1795	11099	131092	8.5%
1796	18921	117152	16.2%
1797	15535	108377	14.3%
1798	13817	107470	12.9%
1799	20857	122986	17.0%
1800	17172	125073	13.7%
1801	8340	134546	6.2%
1802	4916	126389	3.9%
1803	9779	117551	8.3%
1804	11807	113019	10.4%
1805	11976	125043	9.6%
1806	13857	120250	11.5%
1807	15741	134326	11.7%
1808	18134	144042	12.6%
	209546	1953612	10.7%

30 Figures for Victualling Board purchases are only shown until April 1809 and are thus excluded

Glossary

Bavins — bundles of wood, 6 feet long by 4 feet round, used to fire bread ovens.

By-product — a proportion of original material which is not wanted for the specific purpose, for instance bran as a by-product of wheat when milling it for biscuit flour.

Calavances — chick peas, used as a substitute for the British-grown dried pease.

Commissioned officers — those appointed by a commission from the monarch; those who ran the fighting side of a ship's operations.

The Course — the system by which, at times when money was in short supply, the government settled its debts. All bills of exchange were paid, when money was available (often many months late) in the order in which they had been presented for payment, usually with an amount of interest added.

Discounting bills — the process by which holders of forward dated bills of exchange could obtain immediate money for them on the market. The further from the payment date, the bigger the discount.

Dunnage — material used for packing goods in a ship's hold, often to raise the goods above bilge water level.

Gauger — a professional measurer (often an officer of Customs and Excise) who calculated the volume of bulk goods.

Godown — Indian word for warehouse.

Hoytaker — an official who dealt with the hiring of merchant ships and small craft.

Imprest account — a sort of business overdraft account granted to contractors. Advance payment of officers' and seamen's wages were also dealt with this way.

Malt — grains of barley which have been moistened until they germinate and then dried in a kiln.

Messer	a worker who cuts strips of meat into regular sized 'mess' pieces of two, four, or eight pounds.
Month	in the Royal Navy context, always a lunar month of twenty-eight days.
Offal	any waste or rejected part, including bran from milling and waste wood as well as innards of animals.
Ordinary	in naval parlance, items covered by the ordinary estimate, usually meaning ships out of service but retained with a skeleton crew for maintenance.
Petty warrant provisions	those issued for use whilst a ship was in port; they were of a slightly different type (e.g. fresh meat, loaves of bread) than sea provisions and issued for only a few days at a time.
Pickle	the brine in which meat was preserved, sometimes with sugar and spices.
Pipe	a wine measure of about 105 gallons.
Pollard	a mixture of meal and bran left after extracting flour from grain in the milling process.
Precept	a written order to give information to a Parliamentary or other inquiry.
Promiscuous	correspondence received without invitation, actions performed without a specific order or precedent.
Protections	certificates issued to men to exempt them from naval service.
Purser's necessaries	items which were necessary for the running of the ship but not the responsibility of other warrant officers, e.g. candles.
Purser's remains	unused portion of stores, as counted when the purser left the ship (e.g from death, change of ship, paying off at the end of a commission).
Purveyance	royal prerogative of purchase of provisions or other items required by the Crown.
Ran/run	the act of going absent without leave, deserting.
Rander	a worker who cuts meat into strips.

Salter	a worker who rubbed salt into raw meat and made the brine in which it was stored in the casks.
Sea provisions	those victuals intended for use when at sea, issued in large quantities.
Shake (of casks)	to take apart.
Short allowance money	money paid to seamen to recompense them for provisions which they did not receive.
Start (of liquid)	to pour away.
Survey	an all-purpose word used to cover stock-checks or other formal inspections.
Tap	a place where beer was sold.
Victualling stores	the non-comestible items associated with food and drink (e.g. biscuit bags, casks, coals).
Victuals	a word covering all food and drink.
Warrant	an all-purpose word for official orders issued by the Admiralty, including the appointment of staff.
Warrant officers	those appointed by warrant rather than commission; including the lower ranking officers on board ship, such as pursers, boatswains and masters.

Bibliography

Primary material

The National Archives, Kew, London

ADM 1 series	Board of Admiralty, in-letters from various persons.
ADM 3 series	Admiralty Board rough minutes.
ADM 6/22	Commissions and warrants.
ADM 7/182–44	Navy estimates, salaries of victualling commissioners and office staff, 1771–1818.
ADM 7/401–412	Various papers of Board of Revision – correspondence, minutes, etc.
ADM 7/593, 663–4	Minutes of visitations to dock and victualling yards, 1802, 1813.
ADM 7/644–8	Instructions to the Commissioners of the Victualling, 1684, 1700, 1711, 1715.
ADM 7/869–872	Victualling Board pay and pensions, 1805–21.
ADM 8 series	List Books, showing monthly disposition of ships.
ADM 12 series	Indices of Admiralty in-letters, etc.
ADM 20/225–248, 303–335	Ledgers of the Treasurer of the Navy.
ADM 49/59	Letters of appointment with instructions to agents victualler and other victualling yard officials, 1704–78 .
ADM 68/500	Greenwich Hospital Household accounts.
ADM 106/1718–20	Navy Board in-letters from 'public' boards, including Victualling Board.
ADM 106/2022	Navy Board out-letters, naval commissioner at Gibraltar to Victualling Board.
ADM 106/2350–52	Navy Board out-letters to Victualling Board, 1799–1803.
ADM 107/4	Lieutenant's passing certificate George Phillips (later Towry).
ADM 107/8/76	Lieutenant's passing certificate, John Clarke Searle.
ADM 107/14/25	Lieutenant's passing certificate, Frederick Edgecumbe.
ADM 109/102–110	Victualling Board in-letters from Treasury on army victualling, 1793–1815.

ADM 109/21–25	Victualling Board in-letters from Admiralty, 1816–25.
ADM 110/39–76	Victualling Board out-letters, 1793–1819.
ADM 111/126–288	Victualling Board minutes, 1793–1816.
ADM 112/1–47	Audited accounts of agents victualler and agents victualler afloat at various locations.
ADM 112/84–161	Victualling Board, various information on contracts, and some copy contracts.
ADM 112/162–212	Contract ledgers, 1776–1826.
ADM 112/190–91	Balances of pursers' accounts.
ADM 113 series	Pay lists for various victualling yards at home and abroad.
ADM 114/3–4	Records of arbitration between Basil Cochrane and Victualling Board.
ADM 114/26	Victualling frauds, 1788–1821.
ADM 114/40–4	Correspondence on property at outports.
ADM 114/55	Letter book of Richard Ford, 1804–08.
ADM 114/68–69	Victualling office correspondence with yards at Deptford and Portsmouth, 1809–11.
ADM 114/96	Course of the Exchange, 1795.
ADM 174/294–300	Miscellaneous correspondence and contract information on victualling at Plymouth.
ADM 174/411	Plymouth victualling yard correspondence, mostly internal.
ADM 181/12–16	Ordinary estimates of navy expenditure, 1791–1807.
ADM 224/17–18	Letter books, victualling office to agent victualler at Portsmouth.
ADM 224/60–64	Pay registers for Portsmouth yard, 1770–1822.
ADM 224/71–72	Portsmouth victualling yard internal correspondence.
ADM 224/80–81	Portsmouth yard, register of workers entries and discharges.
B3/1903	Bankruptcy of John Grant.
B3/3906	Bankruptcy of Thomas Pinkerton.
C 66 series	Patent rolls.
PC1 29/64–73; 30/71	Privy Council papers, 1795 on grain crisis.
PC1/3578	Order forbiddng the shaking of casks, 18 July 1803.
PC2/204	Privy Council Register, 1822.
PRO 30/8/246	Treasury minute, additional pay for Victualling Office staff for duties in connection with army victualling.
PRO 30/42	Correspondence and family tree of Lady Ellenborough.
PROB 11/829	Will of Admiral John Towry.
PROB 11/1033	Will of Peter Mellish senior.
PROB 11/1122	Will of Samuel Mellish.
PROB 11/1403	Will of Peter Mellish junior.
PROB 11/1694	Will of John Clarke Searle.
PROB 11/1772	Will of Nicholas Brown.
PROB 11/1831	Will of William Mellish.
PROB 11/1898	Will of Euphemia Searle.
T 52/9 ff. 227–230.	Privy Seal book, appointment of Victualling Board, 1683.
WO 12/410	Regimental Pay Books, 7th Dragoon Guards, 1807.
ZHC 2/13	The Parliamentary Debates (Hansard), Vol. XIII.
ZHC 2/47	The Parliamentary Debates (Hansard), New Series 5 February to 22 April 1822.
ZJ1/89	*The Gazette*, 25 June 1793

National Maritime Museum, Greenwich, London

ADM C/678–748	Victualling Board, in-letters and orders from Board of Admiralty, 1792–1815.
ADM D/37–52	Board of Admiralty, in-letters from Victualling Board, 1792–1808.
ADM DP/1–42	Board of Admiralty, in-letters from Victualling Board (loose papers), 1781–1822.
ADM DP/105	Board of Admiralty, in-letters from Victualling Board (loose papers), 1773.
ADM G/790–798	Victualling Board, abstract of in-letters and orders from Board of Admiralty, 1792–1819.
BGR 35	Journal of John Marsh.
KEI 1/23/24–33	Keith Papers.
SER 107	Sergison Papers.
WAR 73	Warren Papers.
YOR 16a/92–98	Yorke Papers.

The Admiralty Library

MSS 93	Instructions for the Board secretary on the duties of staff.
DA 0128–0132	Plans of victualling premises at Southdown, Plymouth, Weevil (Gosport), Portsmouth and Chatham.

London Metropolitan Archive: Corporation of London Joint Archive Service

CLA/016/FN/01/001	Dues collected at Smithfield Market, 28 March 1777 to 31 December 1817.

British Library

Stowe mss. 152, 130	Report on quantities of provisions condemned.
Add. mss. 34790	Admiral Lord Nelson's order book.

Wellcome Trust Library

Western mss 3667–3681	miscellaneous documents and letters relating to ships under Admiral Lord Nelson's command 1780–1805.

Official Published Documents

Report of the Commissioners of Naval Inquiry, 1803–06.

Regulations and Instructions Relating to His Majesty's Service at Sea, various editions, from 1731.

Instructions and Regulations for the Guidance of the Officers of the Several Victualling Establishments at Home, Proposed by the Commissioners for Revising the Civil Affairs of His Majesty's Navy, in their Twelfth Report, dated 22nd December 1807, and ordered to be carried into execution, by His Majesty's Order In Council of the 14th September 1808. (Copy at TNA ADM 7/216).

Instructions for the Agents of the Victualling Establishments Abroad, Proposed by the Commissioners for Revising the Civil Affairs of His Majesty's Navy, in their Twelfth Report, dated 22nd December 1807, and ordered to be carried into execution, by His Majesty's Order In Council of the 14th September 1808. (Copy at TNA ADM 7/217).

Regulations and Instructions Relating to His Majesty's Service at Sea, 14th edition, 1808.

Additional Instructions to the Flag-Officers, Captains, Commanders, Commanding-Officers and Pursers of His Majesty's Navy. 1813. (Copy at TNA ADM 7/972.)

Regulations and Instructions for the Pursers of His Majesty's Ships and Vessels, 1825.

Eighth and Ninth Reports of the Commissioners appointed to inquire into the fees, gratuities, perquisites and emoluments, which are or have been lately received in the several Public Offices therein mentioned; to examine into any abuses which may exist in the same; and to report such observations as shall occur to them for the better conducting and managing the business transacted in the said offices. 17 April and 1 May 1788.

32nd Report of the Select Committee on Finance, ordered to be printed 26 June 1798.

Eighth Report of the Commissioners appointed to inquire into Irregularities, Frauds and Abuses practiced in the Naval department and in the business of the prize Agency. Ordered to be printed 16 July 1804.

Tenth, Eleventh and Twelfth Reports of the Commissioners for Revising and Digesting the Civil Affairs of His Majesty's Navy. 11 August and 22 December 1807.

Reports of the Committee appointed to consider of the present High Price of Provisions: HC 174 of 1800–1801.

Papers relating to Supplies embarked for services in Portugal and Spain 1808 (victualling office), BPP 1809 (102).

Ninth Report of the Commissioners of Military Inquiry for the more effectual examination of Accounts of Public Expenditure for His Majesty's Forces in the West Indies: HC 141 of 1809.

6th Report from the Select Committee on Finance (Navy) (ordered to be printed 23 June 1817).

Navy and Victualling Contracts: HC 417 of 1823.

Directories, dictionaries and almanacs

Collinge, P. *A List of all the Officers of the Army and Royal Marines on Full and Half-Pay with an Index: and a Succession of Colonels* (location not stated, 1800).

Dictionary of National Biography (Oxford, 2004). (Also at http:/www.oxforddnb.com/articles).

Hodson, V C P, *List of the Officers of the Bengal Army 1758–1834: Alphabetically Arranged and Annotated with Biographical and Genealogical Notices* (London, 1947).

Kent's Directory, 62nd edition, 1794, 69th edition, 1801, 76th edition, 1808.

Lowndes or A London Directory, 33rd edition, 1794.

Marshall, John (ed.), *The Royal Navy Biography: or Memoirs of the services of all the flag officers, superannuated rear-admirals, retired captains, post captains and commanders*, 12 vols (London 1823–30).

O'Byrne, William R, *A Naval Biographical Dictionary: Comprising the life and services of every living officer in Her Majesty's Navy from the rank of Admiral of the Fleet to that of Lieutenant* (London, 1849, 3rd edition 1990).

The Post Office New Annual Directory, 2nd edition, 1801 and 9th edition, 1808.

The Royal Kalendar: or, complete and correct Annual Register for England, Scotland, Ireland and America, for the year xxxx. (London, annually).

Wakefield's Merchants and Tradesman's General Directory, Vol. 94 (1794).

Periodicals

The Glasgow Herald, 28 January 1822.

The Morning Chronicle, 23, 25, 26 & 29 January 1822.

The Morning Post, 24 & 25 January 1822.
The Naval Chronicle, Vols XVIII (1811), XXXV (1816).
The Times, 19 May 1809, 23 to 29 January & 19 March 1822.

Secondary material

Aylmer, G E, 'From office-holding to civil service; The genesis of modern bureaucracy', *Transactions of the Royal Historical Society*, 1980, 5th series, part 30, pp. 91–108.

Baker, Norman, *Government and Contractors: The British Treasury and War Supplies* (London, 1971).

Barnes, Donald Grove, *A History of the English Corn Laws* (New York, 1930, reprinted 1965).

Baugh, Daniel A, *British Naval Administration in the Age of Walpole* (Princeton, NJ, 1965).

—— (ed.), *Naval Administration 1715–1750* (London, 1977).

Beaven, Alfred B, *The Aldermen of the City of London*, vol II (London, 1913).

Benady, Tito, *The Royal Navy at Gibraltar* (Gibraltar, 1992).

—— 'The Role of Gibraltar as a Base during the Campaign against the French and Spanish Fleets 1796–1808' (Unpublished MA dissertation, Greenwich Maritime Institute, 2006).

Beveridge, William Henry (with the collaboration of Liepmann, L; Nicolas, F J; Rayner, M E; Wretts-Smith, M, and others), *Prices & Wages in England, from the Twelfth to the Nineteenth century, Vol. 1, Mercantile Era* (London, 1939, reprinted 1965).

Boot, H M, 'Real incomes of the British middle class, 1760–1850: The experience of clerks at the East India Company', *Economic History Review*, LII, 4 (1999), pp. 638–68.

Bowen, H V, *The Business of Empire: The East India Company and Imperial Britain* (Cambridge, 2006).

Bowler, R Arthur, *Logistics and the Failure of the British Army in America 1775–1783* (London, 1975).

Breihan, J R, 'William Pitt and the Commission on Fees 1785–1801', *The Historical Journal* 27 (1984), pp. 59–81.

Brewer, John, *Sinews of Power: War, Money and the English State* (London, 1989).

Buchet, Christian, *Marine, économie et société. Un example d'interaction: l'avitaillement de la Royal Navy durant la guerre de sept ans* (Paris, 1999) .

Builder, Carl H, *Masks of War: American Military Styles in Strategy and Analysis* (London, 1989).

Burke, Peter, *The French Historical Revolution: The Annales School, 1929–89* (Cambridge, 1990).

Clausewitz, Carl von, *On War*, translated and edited by Michael Howard and Peter Parrel (Princeton, NJ, 1976).

Coats, A, 'Efficiency in dockyard administration 1660–1800: A reassessment', in Tracey, N (ed.) *The Age of Sail*, vol. 2 (London, 2004).

Cobbett's Parliamentary History of England (London).

Cochrane, Basil, *A Narrative of the Transactions of the Hon. Basil Cochrane with the Victualling Board* (London, 1818).

—— *A Statement of the conduct of the Victualling Board to the Hon. Basil Cochrane during his transactions with them in India* (London, 1820).

—— *A Narrative of the Transactions of the Honourable Basil Cochrane, late contractor and agent for victualling His Majesty's Ships and Vessels in the East Indies, with the Honourable Victualling Board* (London, 1821).

——*An Enquiry into the Conduct of the Commissioners for Victualling His Majesty's Navy as it related to the examination and final passing of accounts; showing the delay that took place, etc, etc* (London, 1823).

Cohen, Emmeline, *The Growth of the British Civil Service 1780–1939* (London, 1941).

Collinge, J M, *Navy Board Officials 1660–1832* (London, 1978).

Collinge, P, *A List of all the Officers of the Army and Royal Marines on Full and Half-Pay with an Index: And a Succession of Colonels* (London, 1800 & 1807), p. 74.

Corbett, Julian S (ed.), *The Private Papers of George, 2ⁿᵈ Earl Spencer 1794–1801*, 3 vols. (London, 1913, 1914).

Crimmin, P K, 'Admiralty relations with the treasury, 1783–1806: The preparation of naval estimates and the beginnings of Treasury control', *Mariner's Mirror*, vol. 53, no. 1, 1967, pp. 63–72.

Cross, Anthony, *By the Banks of the Neva: Chapters from the Lives and Careers of the British in Eighteenth Century Russia* (Cambridge, 1997).

Day, John, 'The Role of the Resident Commissioner at the Cape of Good Hope 1809–1813' (Unpublished MA dissertation, University of Exeter, 2007).

Devine, T M, *The Tobacco Lords: A Study of the Tobacco Merchants of Glasgow and their Trading Activities c.1740–90* (Edinburgh, 1975).

Dicey, A V, *Lectures on the Relation between Law and Order and Public Opinion in England during the Nineteenth Century* (London, 1905).

Edlin, A, *A Treatise on the Art of Bread-Making: Wherein, the Mealing Trade, Assize Laws, and every curcumstance [sic] connected with the Art, is particularly examined* (London, 1805, reprint 1992).

Ehrman, John, *The Navy in the War of William III: 1689–1697* (Cambridge, 1953).

Ellis, K, *The Post Office in the Eighteenth Century: A Study in Administrative History* (Oxford, 1958).

Elvin, David, 'The Founding and Development of the Victualling Yard at Deptford in the 1740s' (Unpublished MA dissertation, Greenwich Maritime Institute, 2005).

Ernle, Lord, *English Farming Past and Present*, 6ᵗʰ edition (London, 1961).

Floud, R, Wachter, K, & Gregory, A, *Height, Health and History: Nutritional Status in the United Kingdon 1750–1980* (Cambridge, 1990).

Fussell, G E, 'The London cheesemongers of the eighteenth century', *Economic History*, Vol. 3 (January 1928) pp. 394–8.

Fussell, G E, and Goodwin, C, 'Eighteenth century traffic in milk products', *Economic History*, vol. XII (February 1937), pp. 380–7.

Galpin, W Freedom, *The Grain Supply of England during the Napoleonic period* (London, 1925).

Haas, J M, *A Management Odyssey: The Royal Dockyards, 1714–1914* (London, 1994).

Hall, Christopher D, *Wellington's Navy: Sea Power and the Peninsula War 1807–14* (London, 2004).

Hancock, D, *Citizens of the World: London Merchants and the Integration of the British Atlantic Community 1735–1785* (Cambridge, 1995).

Hans, Nicholas, *New Trends in Education in the Eighteenth Century* (London, 1951).

Hansard's Parliamentary Debates (London).

Hardman, William, *A History of Malta during the Period of the French and British Occupation 1798–1815* (London, 1909).

Harling, Philip, *The Waning of 'Old Corruption': The Politics of Economical Reform in Britain, 1779–1846* (Oxford, 1996).

Hattendorf, John B; Knight, R J B; Pearsall, A W H; Rodger, N A M; & Till, Geoffrey (eds), *British Naval Documents 1204–1960* (London, 1993).

Hodson, C P, *List of the Officers of the Bengal Army 1758–1834: Alphabetically Arranged and Annotated with Biographical and Genealogical Notices* (London, 1947).

Hull, T M, *Military Logistics in Strategy and Performance* (London, 2001).

Jones, E L, *Seasons and Prices: The Role of the Weather in English Agricultural History* (London, 1964).

Jones, L and Mingay G E (eds), *Land, Labour and Population in the Industrial Revolution* (London, 1967).

Knight, R J B, 'The Royal Dockyards in England at the Time of the War of American Independence' (Unpublished Ph.D. thesis, London, 1972).

—— 'Pilfering and theft from the dockyards at the time of the American War of Independence', *Mariner's Mirror*, vol. 61, no. 3, pp. 215–225.

—— 'Politics and trust in victualling the Navy, 1783–1815', *Mariner's Mirror*, vol. 94, no. 2, pp. 133–49.

Knox Laughton, Sir John (ed.), *Letters and Papers of Charles, Lord Barham*, 3 vols (London 1907, 1910, 1911).

Laird, Emma, 'The Victualling of the Channel Fleet in 1800' (Unpublished MA dissertation, Greenwich Maritime Institute, 2001).

Lamb, H H , *Climate, History and the Modern World* (2nd edition, London, 1995).

Lavery, Brian (ed.), *Shipboard Life and Organisation 1731–1815* (London, 1998).

Lewis, A F P, *Captain of the Fleet: A Memoir of Sir William Domett GCB* (London, 1967).

Lewis, Michael, *A Social History of the Navy* (London, 1960).

Lloyd, Christopher and Coulter, Jack L S (General Editor Keevil, J J) *Medicine and the Navy*, Vol. III *1714–1815* (London, 1961).

Macdonald, Janet, 'Victualling the British Mediterranean Fleet, May 1803 to June 1804' (Unpublished MA dissertation, Greenwich Maritime Institute, 2003).

—— *Feeding Nelson's Navy: The true story of food at sea in the Georgian Era* (London, 2004).

—— 'Two years off Provence: The victualling and health of Nelson's fleet in the Mediterranean, 1803 to 1805', *Mariner's Mirror*, vol. 92, no. 4 (November 2006), pp. 453–4.

—— 'The victualling yard at Gibraltar and its role in feeding the Royal Navy in the Mediterranean during the revolutionary and Napoleonic wars', *Transactions of the Naval Dockyards Society*, vol. 2 (December 2006), pp. 55–64.

—— 'Regulations for preservation and repair of buildings', *Newsletter of the Naval Dockyards Society*, December 2008, vol. 13, no. 2, pp. 18–19.

—— 'The introduction of iron water tanks in the Royal Navy', *Mariner's Mirror*, vol. 95, no. 2 (May 2009), pp. 215–19.

—— 'Documentary sources relating to the work of the British Royal Navy's Victualling Board during the French Revolutionary and Napoleonic wars: 1793–1815', *International Journal of Maritime History*, 21.1 (June 2009), pp. 239–62.

—— *The Victualling Board 1793–1815: A study of management competence.* (Unpublished Ph.D. thesis, London, 2009)

—— 'A New Myth of Naval History?: Confusing magnitude with significance in British naval victualling purchases', *International Journal of Maritime History*, 21.2 (December 2009), pp. 159–88.

Martin, L C, 'John Crane (1576–1660) of Loughton, Bucks, Surveyor-General of all Victuals for Ships 1635–42', *Mariner's Mirror*, vol. 70, no. 2, pp. 143–8.

McDonagh, O, 'The nineteenth century revolution in government: A reappraisal', *Historical Journal*, 1 (1958), pp. 52–67.

MacDougall, Philip, 'Somerset Place to Whitehall: Reforming the Civilian Departments of the Navy 1830–34' (Unpublished Ph.D. thesis, Kent, 1995).

McKendrick, Neil, 'Josiah Wedgwood and cost accounting in the Industrial Revolution', *Economic History Review*, XXII (1970), pp. 45–67.

Merriman, R D (ed.), *Documents Concerning the Administration of Queen Anne's Navy* (London, 1961).

Morriss, R A, 'Labour relations in the Royal Dockyards, 1801–1805', *Mariner's Mirror*, vol. 62, no. 4, 1976, pp. 337–46.

——(ed.), *The Royal Dockyards during the Revolutionary and Napoleonic Wars* (Leicester, 1983).

——*Naval Power and British Culture, 1760–1850* (London, 2004).

——'The supply of casks and staves to the Royal Navy, 1770–1815', *Mariner's Mirror*, Vol 93, No 1 (February 2007), pp. 43–50.

——'*Corruption' in the Management of the Royal Navy: The Internal Evidence of Fraud, 1770–1820* (Unpublished paper).

Naish, G B P (ed.), *Nelson's Letters to his Wife* (London, 1958).

Nauticus Junior [sic], *The Naval Atlantis; or a display of the characters of postcaptains who served during the late war*, Part II (London, 1789).

Nelson, R R, *The Home Office 1782–1800* (Durham NC, 1969).

Nicolas, Sir Nicholas Harris, *The Dispatches and Letters of Lord Nelson,7 vols.* (London, 1844, repr. 1997–98).

O'Donovan, J, *The Economic History of Livestock in Ireland* (Dublin, 1940).

Olson, Mancur, jnr, *The Economics of the Wartime Shortage: A History of British Food Supplies in the Napoleonic War and World Wars I and II* (Durham N. Carolina, 1963).

O'Sullivan, William, *The Economic History of Cork City From the Earliest Times to the Act of Union* (Cork, 1937).

Parris, H, 'The nineteenth century revolution in government: A reappraisal reappraised', *Historical Journal*, vol. 3 (1960).

——*Constitutional Bureaucracy: The Development of the British Central Administration since the Eighteenth Century* (London, 1969).

Perrin, W G (ed.), *The Letters and Papers of Admiral Viscount Keith*, vol. 1 (see Lloyd, Christopher for Vols 2 & 3) (London, 1950, 1955).

Pool, Bernard, *Navy Board Contracts 1660–1832* (London, 1966).

Price, Jacob M, 'Directions for the conduct of a merchant's counting house, 1766', *Business History*, vol. 28 (1986), pp. 134–50.

Ragatz, Lowell Joseph, *The Fall of the Planter Classes in the British Caribbean 1763–1833* (New York, 1963).

Reader, W J, *Professional Men: The Rise of the Professional Classes in Nineteenth Century England* (London, 1966).

Robinson, William, *Jack Nastyface: Memoirs of an English Seaman* (London 1836 as *Nautical Economy*, reprinted 1973).

Rodger, N A M, *The Wooden World: An Anatomy of the Georgian Navy* (London, 1996).

——*The Command of the Ocean: A naval history of Britain, Volume Two 1649–1815* (London, 2004).

Roseveare, H, *The Treasury, 1660–1870, The Foundations of Control* (London, 1973).

Sainty J C, *Officials of the Board of Trade* (London, 1974).

——*Admiralty Officials 1660–1870* (London, 1975).

——*Home Office Officials* (London, 1975).

——*Colonial Office Officials* (London, 1976).

Schwarz, L D, *London in the Age of Industrialisation: Entrepreneurs, Labour Force and Living Conditions, 1700–1850* (Cambridge, 1992).

Sheldon, Matthew, 'A tale of two cities: The facilities, work and impact of the Victualling Office in Portsmouth, 1793–1815', *Transactions of the Naval Dockyards Society*, vol. I (July 2006), pp. 35–45.

Smith, D B (ed.), *Letters of Admiral of the Fleet the Earl of St Vincent, whilst First Lord of the Admiralty*, vol. II (London, 1922).

Spinney, David, *Rodney* (London, 1969).

Sugden, John, *Nelson: A Dream of Glory* (London, 2004).

Sutherland, Gillian (ed.), *Studies in the Growth of Nineteenth Century Government* (London, 1972).

Syrett, David, *Shipping and the American War 1775–1783: A Study of British Transport Organization* (London, 1970).

——'Christopher Atkinson and the Victualling Board, 1775–1782', *Historical Research* (1996), pp. 129–42.

Tanner, J R (ed.), *Catalogue of the Pepysian Manuscripts, Vol. 1* (London, 1903).

Taylor, Henry, *The Statesman* (London, 1955, originally 1836).

Taylor, Stephen, *Storm and Conquest: The Battle for the Indian Ocean, 1809* (London, 2007).

Thorne R G, *History of Parliament: the House of Commons 1790–1820*, 3 Vols. (London, 1986).

Thorne, Stuart, *The History of Food Preservation* (Kirkby Lonsdale, Cumbria, 1986).

Tooke, Thomas, *History of Prices and Circulation from 1793 to the Present Day*, Vol. 1 (London, 1838).

Vale, Brian, *The Audacious Admiral* (London, 2004).

Watson, Paula K, 'The Commission for Victualling the Navy, the Commission for Sick and Wounded Seamen and Prisoners of War and the Commission for Transport 1702–1714' (Unpublished Ph.D., London, 1965).

Westerfield, R B, *Middlemen in English Business: Particularly between 1660–1760* (London, 1915).

Wren, Daniel A, *The History of Management Thought* (Hoboken, NJ, 2005).

Young, D Murray, *The Colonial Office in the early nineteenth century* (London, 1961).

Web sites

www.familysearch.org/English/search/frameset_search.asp?PAGE=ancestorsearchresults. asp [downloaded 5 May 2008].

www.history.ac.uk/office/comms_victual.html [downloaded 28 May 2008].

www.jjhc.info/ (Marsh family history website) [downloaded 15 June 2007].

www.jmr.nmm.ac.uk [downloaded 5 February 2003].

www.oxforddnb.com/articles/1616142-article.html [downloaded 19 March 2007].

www.royalsoc.ac.uk. [downloaded 20 May 2007].

www.stalbansobserver.co.uk/misc/print.php?artid=66497 [downloaded 22 November 2005].

Index

accountant for cash 43, 71, 121, 125, 171, 172 n.36, 176
accountant for stores 120–1
accountant/accounts 80–93
'A Contractor' 171–2
ad hoc tasks 99–102
advertisements 29
'A Friend to the Cause' 176
agents, purchasing 28, 29, 34, 35, 36, 64
agents victualler 16, 46–85, 121, 135–59, 195, 209
agriculture 24, 38
Alder, Lieutenant William 137–8
aldermen 35
ale 101
Alexandria 27, 74
Alldridge, Thomas 74
American War of Independence 4, 33, 35, 36, 66
anachronism 213, 218
Anholt Island 20, 65
anonymous letters 172, 216
Antigua 65, 66, 165–6
anti-scorbutics 98
Appert, Nicholas 101
army 1, 16, 20, 41, 64, 78, 82
arrack 22
arrears of accounts 77, 86–90, 114, 191, 193, 215, 218
artisans 145, 155
Atkins French & Canning, Messrs 37
Atkinson, Christopher 2, 28, 119, 194
Atlantic, East 77
Atlantic, North-west 78

Aubin, John 115–16, 176, 184–5, 227
Audit Office 221

Bahamas 20
bakehouse, the 120
bakeries 11, 26, 34
bakers 149, 153–4, 155 n.76, 161 n.3
Balfour & Baker, Messrs 79
Balfour, James 79
Ball, Sir Alexander 74
Baltic 21, 42, 45, 68
bankruptcy 44
Banks, Sir Joseph 101
Barbados 164
Barcelona 72
barge 121
barge crew 134
Barham (see Middleton, Charles)
Baring, Francis 127 n.63
barley 12, 27
Barons, Denham 171–5
bavins 22, 100, 210
Bay of Bengal 79
beans 25
beef, fresh 11, 23, 27, 28, 34, 42, 44, 46, 49, 51, 82, 83
beef, salt/Irish 16, 18, 19, 20, 24, 28, 32, 34, 37, 44, 49, 73, 79, 85
beer 16, 18, 21, 22, 42, 49, 51, 56
Belcher & Brymer, Messrs 78, 85
Belcher, Andrew 78, 84, 85
Bell, Adam 180 n.60
Bell, John Robertson 179, 180
Bell, Thomas 32, 36

Benamor, Lieutenant 158–9
Bentham, Jeremy 7
Bentham, Samuel 6, 7, 50, 53, 61, 97–8, 219
Bermuda 20, 78, 84, 85
Bertie, Vice-Admiral Albemarle 147–8
bills of exchange 28, 163
bills of lading 197
biscuit 16, 18, 31, 34, 39, 46, 57, 67, 70, 99
biscuit bags 21, 43, 49, 51, 56, 149
biscuit meal 35, 46
Bishop, William 168
Blackburn, Mr 164
Blackburn, Quintin 43, 44
Black Sea 73
Blane, Dr 100
blockade 11
Board of Agriculture 25
Board of Revision passim
Board of Trade and Plantations 1, 180
boatswain 136
boatswain of the wharf 137, 149, 158
Bogle French, Messrs 32, 33
Bombay 79, 193
Bonaparte, Napoleon 24, 179
book-keeping 110
Booth, Richard 75
Bornholm 75
Boscawen, William 115–16, 227
Bowring, Anthony 182
Bowring, Robert 138
Brady, Mr 164
brandy 22, 23, 67
bread 17, 20, 25, 46, 75
bread ovens 22, 57, 61, 62, 67, 70
Brereton, Thomas 11
Brest 11, 46, 53
breweries 11, 22
brewers 149
brewhouse, the 120
brewing 121, 150
Brickwood & Inglis, Messrs 105
Brickwood, J 106
Briggs, Mr 178, 181
Bristol 78
Brixham 45, 53, 97, 136
broad arrow, the 161
Broad Mr 101
brokerage fees 173
Brown, Nicholas 74, 115–16, 176, 178, 181, 217–18, 220 n.15, 228

Bryan, Arthur 167
Brymer, John 78, 85
Budge, William 114–15, 176, 178–9, 181, 228
building maintenance 145
building workers 149, 155
bulk suppplies 16, 29, 38, 41, 46, 190
Bull, Mrs 134
bullocks, see oxen
Burgoyne, Maurice 118–19
Burke, Edmund 73
butchers 138
butter 18, 20, 24, 27, 28, 35, 36, 48, 67, 179
buying agents 64

Cadiz 74
Caffa 73
calavances 70
Calcutta 71, 193
Callaghan, Mr 57
Canada 20, 68, 78, 85
candles 22, 46, 203
canned meat 101
Canton 79
Cape of Good Hope 4, 7, 10, 22, 65, 66, 71, 143–5, 155–6
captain's orders 223
career progression for agents victualler 141
career progression for clerks 123, 141
Caribbean 20
cask marks 32, 50, 170
casks 21, 43, 46, 71
casks, embezzlement of 170
cats 101
cattle 11, 69, 71, 72, 75
Cawsand Bay 46
chairman of Victualling Board 109, 111–14, 116, 120, 122, 189
Channel fleet 53
Channel Islands 44 n.10
Channel service 47, 48
Channel, The 24, 40, 44, 54, 219
Chatham 11, 31, 44, 57, 97, 136–7, 142, 168–70, 189, 197, 226
cheese 18, 19, 23, 27–8, 35–6, 48, 56, 101, 149, 179
Cherry, George 81, 115–16, 229
Cheshire 23
chestnuts 25

China 103
Chingford 34
chips 211
Chorley, Alexander 115–16, 229
City, the 38
Civil Architect and Engineer, the 97, 111
civilians 102–3
Civita Vecchia 71
Clarence, Duke of 232
Clark, Thomas 167
clerk of the brewhouse 137
clerk of the cheque 137, 140–1, 145, 204
clerk of the cutting house 137–8
clerk of the dry stores 137
Clerk, Sir George, Bt 157, 177, 181–2, 185, 224
clerks at Somerset Place 122–4
clerks at the yards 135–59
climate 68
coal 21, 46, 167
Cochrane, Sir Alexander 81, 84, 181, 227
Cochrane, the Hon. Basil 79–81, 85, 90, 116, 119, 192–3, 216 n.5, 220, 222
Cochrane, Captain Lord Thomas 81
Cockburn, Sir George 157, 177, 181–2, 185, 224
cocoa 22, 28
Coffin, Sir Isaac 100
collective responsibility 120
Collier, Benjamin 141
Colonial office 132
Colquitt, Captain 163
Combination Act 153
combinations 29
commissaries 17
commission, payment by 28
commissioners of the Victualling Board 112–21
commissioners, duties of 188–91
committee for cash and store accounts 121–2, 189–90
committee for general business 122, 189
complaints 14, 62
contract ledgers 43, 60, 80
contractor depots 16, 17, 41, 42, 65, 190
contractors 16, 19, 30, 33, 34, 46, 82
contracts 12, 31, 190, 194
convicts 1, 17
convoy 83–4
cooperage 120

coopers 31, 51, 136, 149, 150, 155, 161 n.3, 209
Corbet, Captain Robert 147
Cork 24, 45, 54, 57, 58, 84, 136
corn exchanges 35
corn laws 25
corn shortages 21, 215 n.3
Corsica 70
Corunna 71, 75
cost accounting 219
Coulthred, John 156–7
Course, the 13
cow beef 32
Crees, William 141 n.15
Croker, J W 183
Cruden, J 78, 82
Cunningham, Charles 115–16, 229
Curtis, Sir Roger, 159, 188–9, 223
Curtis, Sir William 35, 36
Customs 29, 54, 105
Customs officers 162, 168
Cutforth, James 71, 96, 145
Cuthbert, Arthur 88, 120, 192
cutting house, the 60, 120–1, 138, 150
Cyprus 74

Dalrymple, Sir John 99
Dantzig 75
Dawson, John 73
de Horne, Abraham 35
Deal 50
Dearman, John 36
debt collecting 87, 215
delegation 223
delivery notes 33
Denmark 78
depot ships 68, 95, 167
Deptford 205–10 & passim
deputy chairman 121, 189
Derbyshire 23
Desborough, George 66, 89, 141 n.15, 166
description books 135
Dick, Sir John 127 n.63
Dickinson, Robert 102
discounting bills 173, 175
distilling 25
Dixen, Henry 152
dockyards 5, 160
Domett, William 188–9, 223
Donaldson, Alexander 43, 44, 78, 83, 172–3

Donkin & Hall, Messrs 101
Dornick, Baron von 102 n.62
Douglas, Robert 117–18
Dover 11, 38, 44, 50, 136, 142, 149, 154
Downs, The 44, 50, 103, 167
dredger 97
Druce, Thomas 165
drunken sailors 52, 53
Duncan, Admiral Adam 103
Dundas, Henry, Lord Melville 220 n.15, 228, 230
Dunkin, Christopher 35
dunnage 24, 40, 219
Dunsterville, John 57, 58, 141 n.15
Durham, Bishop of 100
Dutch crews 103
duties of yard officers 139–41, 143–6

East India Company 22, 26, 79, 132, 193
East Indies 22, 78–81
Eastlake, Mr 171
Eckhardt, Mr 100
economies of scale 36
Edgecumbe, Frederick 115–16, 224, 220, 229
Elba 70
Ellenborough, Lord 81, 116, 119, 216, 234
Elliott, William junior 173
Elliott, William senior 171 n.34, 173–6
Elphinstone, George, Admiral Lord Keith 74, 77, 81, 88, 117, 181, 217–18, 232
Elphinstone, Miss Mercer 88 n.3
Elwin, Michael 129
embargoes 39, 83
embezzlement 166–71
embezzlement officer 161–2
English produce 21
epidemic diseases 68, 83
estimates 19
Eton, William 72
Everett, James 162
Exchequer 221
Excise 22, 23, 54, 168
extra petty warrant 49

Factory Acts 3
Falmouth 46
Faversham 34
fees 32, 54, 124, 126
fees, abolition of 172

Fees commissioners 60, 87, 127, 133–4, 141–3, 187–9, 191
Fenn, Nicholas 9
Fernandez, Angel Garcia & Francisco 76
Ferrol 75
fictitious accounts 201–2
Finance, Select Committee on 188,194
fiscal military state 13
fishing 18
Fitzgerald, William 75–6, 93 n.19
flour 12, 17, 20, 25, 27, 35, 70, 74, 75, 82, 161 n.4
Flower, Charles 35, 36, 37, 177, 179
Flower, Matthew & Co 179
Flushing 71
food marketing 38, 39
Ford, Richard 70–1, 74, 76, 124, 141, 178, 183–4, 217, 220
Fordyce, John 188
foreign service 47, 48
foreman of the flesh store 149
Forrester & Yeames, Messrs 73
Fraser, Percy 148
fraud 64, 66, 163
freemasons 37
freight, cost of 219
fruit 71, 80
Fry, J & Co 22

Galloway, Earl of 233
Gambold, purser 118
Garlies, George 233
Garrett, Captain Henry 97, 137
gaugers/gauging 54, 55, 110
Gaynor, Edward 71
Gazette, The 29 n.59
Geoghegan, John 70, 141
George, Grace 136
Gibert, J B 72
Gibraltar 20, 65–8, 71, 82, 96, 143–5, 148, 156
gifts required 171
gin 22
Glasspoole, Mr 132, 183
Glenny, George 83, 172–3
Gloucestershire 23
Goate, Arthur 164
Gosling, John 178, 181, 183
Gosling, Lucy 120
Gosling, William 120, 178, 181, 183

Gosport 45
government departments 13, 40
graffiti 157
grain prices 25, 27
granary 55
Grant, John 43, 44, 78
Graves, General 70
Graves, Vice-Admiral 51
Green, J 36, 37
Grenada 164
Grenville, Thomas 117
Grey, Charles, Lord Howick 119
Grey family 114, 119, 216
guard ships 49
Guyer, John 173–5

Haddock, Sir Richard 9
hair powder 25
Halifax 84–5
Halloran, Mr 156–7
Hallowell, Captain Benjamin 181, 227
Harman, Richard Hawes 37, 172 n.34,
    174–5
Harrison, John 99, 115–16, 122 n.45, 230
Hartshorne brewery 9
Hartwell, Sir Francis John 115–16, 230
harvests 24, 25
Haslar hospital 118
Hawkesbury, Lord, see Jenkinson
Hay, Robert W 115–16, 230
Hay, William 11
Heard, Gilbert 171
Heatley, David 65, 69–72
Heligoland 20, 65, 69, 82, 95
hemp 21
Henry VIII 8
Hicks, Lieutenant William 163–4
Higgins, Joseph Blake 165–6
Holland 101
Holmes, Richard 93 n.19
Holt, Henry 156, 178, 183
Hood, Captain Sir Samuel 74
hoops 21,51
hops 28
horses 9, 89, 211
House of Commons 19
Howick, Viscount, see Grey
hoys 51
hoytaker 59, 120–1, 137
Hughes, John 34

Hulke, Manley 141, 172 n.34, 173–5
Hume, Joseph 177–8
Hunt, Joseph 115–16, 230
Hunter, Samuel 9
hurricanes 66, 83, 85

identification of property 161
Idle, Christopher 180
imprest accounts 28
India 143
inferior officers 135–7, 205, 209, 210
Inglis, Ellice, Messrs 82
Inglis, James 82, 106
injuries at work 155
Inkpen, Mr 101
innovations 99
inspector of the cutting house 121, 159
inspector of works 136
instructions to Commissioners 9, 10, 86
instructions to victualling agents 67
invoices 33
Ireland 24
iron water tanks 21, 102
Isle of Dogs 34
Italian book-keeping 110
Italy 65, 70

Jamaica 66, 68, 83, 143, 164, 166
Java 79
Jenkinson, Robert Banks, Lord
    Hawkesbury 58
Jervis, Admiral John, Earl of St Vincent 5,
    31, 37, 53, 57, 65, 70, 73, 78, 80, 101,
    113–14, 119, 151,162
Jones, Valentine 82
Jordaine & Shaw, Messrs 33, 35, 37

Keith, Lord, see Elphinstone
King, Thomas 147
Knight, Edward 35

labourers 145, 149–51, 161 n.3, 209
Lane, Walter 57, 58
Langton, W A 159
Lee, Henry 9
Leeward Islands 89, 143
Leghorn 70, 177
lemon juice 98, 112
lemons 71, 72, 74
Lisbon 20, 65, 69, 70, 103, 141, 143

Littledale, Joseph 70
Liverpool 43, 163
lobsters 99
Lord Mayor 35, 179

MacNeil, Archibald 72
Madalena Islands 71
Madeira 20, 82
Madras 79
Maidstone assizes 167
malaria 61
Mallard, Edward 156
malt 28, 35, 46, 55, 57
Malta 65–8, 70,73–4,144,155
management competence, definition of 213
management training 223
manual workers 135, 149–56
manufacturing 16, 121
marines 17 n.4
Marmaris 74
Marr, John 165
Marsden, William 163
Marsh family 120
Marsh, George 192
Marsh, John 113–16, 120, 176
Marshall, Samuel 115–16
Martin, Henry, MP 113
Martinique 82, 84
Mason, Mr 181
master baker 136
master brewer 136
master butcher 121, 136–8
master cooper 21, 136–7
master miller 136
Matthews, John 169
Matthews, Joseph 57,141 n.15 168–70, 222
Maude, Mr 146 n.38
Maudsley, Henry102
Mauritius 147
McCartney, Lord 103
meat processing 11
meat, fresh, see beef, fresh
meat, salt, see beef, salt
medical supplies 98–9
Mediterranean 24, 26–7, 64, 67–8, 70–1, 77, 81, 141
Medway, River 49
Meek, James 181, 217, 229 n.12
Meheux, Francis 109 n.1

Mellish, Peter junior 34, 37
Mellish, Peter senior 34
Mellish, Samuel 134
Mellish, William 28, 29, 34–7, 138, 172–3, 183 n.74
Melville, Lord, see Dundas
Members of Parliament 10, 110, 116
men of business 5
messengers 134
messers 149
Messina 69
micro-management 122
middlemen 30, 36
Middleton, Charles, Lord Barham 2, 7, 128, 188, 212, 221, 224
Middleton, Lambert 167
Military Inquiry, Commission of 82
milk 26, 27
Millar, Andrew 146
Miller, Thomas 170–1
millers 149, 150
Millman, George 172, 174 n.39, 175
mills 46
Minorca 82
misfeasance 171–85
Mobbs, Mr 174
molasses 6, 28
Molleson, William 127 n.63
money brokers 13
Montague, John, Lord Sandwich 2, 104
Moody, Aaron 35
Moody, Edward 232 n.20
Moody, Robert Sadleir 35 n.87, 57, 114–16, 123, 169, 176, 232 n.20
moonlighting 176
Morning Post, The 180
Morocco 69
Moss, Charles 172 n.34, 173, 174
Mulgrave, Lord 114, 179
Munton, Anthony 165
Murray, Major-General John 232
muster books 91

Naples 70
Naval Inquiry, Commission of 113, 170, 187, 216
Navy Bills 13
Navy Board 93–6, 100, 111, 128, 152, 165, 181, 216, 221
necessary money 71

Nelson, Horatio 67, 70, 71, 73, 75, 77, 92
Nepean, Evan 174, 219
neutral vessels 105
New Brunswick 20
New Orleans 85
New South Wales 1, 16, 17, 20, 105
Newcastle 43
Newfoundland 20, 65, 69
Newman, William 35 n.85
newspapers 29
nitre 99
Nore, The 42, 44, 95, 103, 168
no smoking rule 155
North Africa 64, 69
North America 20, 45, 71, 72, 77, 83
North Sea 44, 78
Northcote, Samuel 163
Nova Scotia 20

oaths 172, 183, 224
oatmeal 35, 44
oats 12, 49
Odessa 72
offal 37, 139, 209
office hours 140, 191
Old Bailey 167
'Old corruption' 4
'Old Pratt' 133
onions 72, 74
Orders in Council 119, 126–7, 129, 172, 174
Ordinary, ships in 49, 203
Ordnance Board 96, 106
Orkney 103
Otway, William 73
outports 17, 23, 44, 196–205
overcharging for purchases 163, 165
oxen 24, 28, 32, 35, 60, 71, 74, 82, 100

Palermo 71
Pallister, Henry 146
Papillon, Thomas 10
Papps, Henry 89
Park, Henry 173
Parker, Hyde, Vice-Admiral 66, 83, 84
Parsons, John 9
patronage 125, 158
Patton, William 34
Payne, Mr 167–8
Peace of Amiens 19, 31, 65–6

pease 18, 25, 26, 28, 31, 35, 49, 73–4
Peck, Lieutenant George 163
Pelham, Henry 104
Pellew, Admiral Edward, 75
penalties in contracts 33
Peninsula, the 17, 45, 71
Penrose, Captain Thomas 8
pensions 94, 131–2, 152, 154–5
Pepys, Samuel 8, 9
Perigal, Henry 178, 181–2
personnel files 108
perpetual oven 100
perquisites 125
Phillips, George, see Towry, George
piece-work 9, 153
Pinkerton, Thomas 43, 44, 78, 82, 84–5
Piombino 70
pithing 100
Pitt, William (the younger) 127
Place Act 11, 113
plums 17
Plymouth passim
Pole, Sir Charles, 113
Pole, Wellesley 114
Pope, the 70
pork, salt/Irish 18, 19, 24, 32, 34, 37, 44, 79
port 139
Port Mahon 65–6
portable soup 61, 98, 112
porters 134, 136 ,149, 155, 162
Portsea Island Water Works Company 50
Portsmouth passim
Portugal 20
potatoes 25, 26
Potter, Christopher 36
Pratt, Sir John 133
precedence of commissioners 120
presents 172–5
Pridham, Joseph 170–1
Prince Regent 117, 217 n.6
Prince of Wales Island 79, 193
prison ships 49
Privy Council 126, 130, 185, 212
professional men 5, 113, 213
property management 96–8
protections 21
public finance 13
pudding bags 49
Puget, Peter 79
pumps 50, 97

punishment for theft 161
pursers passim
pursers' accounts 88–9
pursers' eighth 104–5

quarantine 68, 74
Quebec 82, 85
Quiberon Bay 103
quorum 114, 120, 122

raisins 74
randers 149
Ratcliffe Cross 61, 98, 112
ration, the 17, 18
rats 101
Ravensbourne River Water Company 50
Read, Mr 172, 176
recruitment of staff 109, 110, 124
Red House Estate 11
Reeks, William 141
Regulations & Instructions, the 91–2, 145
Regulations ... Pursers 91
Regulations ...Home 139, 140
Regulations ... Abroad 67, 155
reservoirs 50
resident naval commissioner 144–5, 212
Responsibility, individual/collective 6, 7
returns of unused provisions 50, 51
Revell, Thomas 11
Revision, Board of, 188–212 & passim
rice 20, 26, 27, 28, 40, 70, 74
Richardson, Thomas 172, 174 n.39, 175
Rickards, John 131 n.80
Riely/Reilly 178, 182
Rigden, John 34
Rimington, Henry 168
Rio de Janeiro 65–6, 141
Robertson, William 116–18
Robertson, Mr 146 n.38
Rochester 8, 169
Rodney, Admiral George Bridges, 119, 232
Rodney, Hon. John 115–16, 119–20, 232
Rome 70
Rosas 71
Rose, George 133, 150 n.52
Rosia Bay 96
rotation of stock 50
Rotherhithe 61, 167
Rowcroft, Thomas 35 n.85, 37

Royal Clarence Yard 45
Royal William Yard 46
rum 22, 23, 40, 44, 82, 85
Russia 21, 73, 85
Russian navy 101
Ryder, Richard 229

Sadleir, Richard Vernon 232 n.20
salaries 109, 117, 124, 127–30, 139, 140, 142, 216
sale of offices 127
sale of old stock 50
salt 24, 29
salters 149
Sandwich, Lord, see Montague
Sardinia 69–71
savings of provisions 88
sawyers 149–50
Scott, Claude 26, 106
Scott Idle & Co 177, 179, 180 n.59
sea provisions 43, 48, 49
seamen, numbers of 19, 39, 214
Searle, John Clarke 57, 58, 114–17, 123, 138, 153, 177, 182, 184–5, 217–18, 221, 232
seasonal workers 150–1
Secretary of State for Home Affairs 229
Secretary of State for War 110, 228
secret services 122
Select Committee on Finance 3, 24, 63, 139, 143–4, 184, 188, 193
Serle, Ambrose 188
settlements, British 1
Seven Years' War 12, 35, 36, 178, 179 n.54
Shadwell Dock 34
shaking casks 51
Shaw, Sir James 35 n.85, 37
sheep 11, 69
Sheerness 95, 103
Shelburne, Lord 133
Sherlock, Thomas 99
Shetland Islands 1, 103
Shield, William 146–7, 156
ship owning 37
ships' boats 51
Shirley, Mr 164
shoes 177
shortages 83
short allowance money 27
Sicily 27, 71

Sick and Hurt Board 61, 90, 98, 111–12, 165, 193, 221, 223
sinecures 125
slaughter houses 11, 34, 52, 138
slaves 155
Smith, John Arthur 171 n.34, 174 n.39, 175
Smithfield Market 24, 39
smuggling 48
soap 101
soldiers 20
solicitor 164
Solly & Gibson, Messrs 75, 177–8
Solly, Isaac 21
Somerset Place 11, 96, 98, 121, 128, 135–6, 140, 156–7, 193, 205, 222
sourdough bread 100
Southdown Brewery 170–1
Spanish Main 20
specie 64, 145
spelling 110
Spenser, Lord George 99, 130
spirits 17, 22, 48
Spithead 45, 84, 104
spruce beer 101
St Catherine's 16, 58, 136, 150
St Jean d'Acre 74
St John's 69
St Kitt's 164
St Petersburg 73
St Vincent, see Jervis
staff recruitment 109
'Stale Bread Act' 25
standing contracts 42
starch 25
staves 21, 102, 161 n.4, 180
Stephens, Francis 115–16, 121, 233
Stephens, J 168, 170
stevedores 136, 149
Stewart, Hon. Edward 115–16, 176, 230
stock-checks 54–7, 215
stock-fish 17
Stokes, Henry 169
Stokoe, A 181
storekeeper 137–8, 140, 150
strikes 143–4
Sturt, Anthony 9
subsistence pay 12, 164
substitutes 11, 18
suet 27, 29, 34, 79
sugar 17, 28, 74, 161 n.4

superannuation 131
superintendant at Deptford 121, 135, 206
superintendant of the wharf 138
superior officers 135, 205, 209, 210
sureties 30, 31, 87, 89
surveys 32, 49
syndicates 37
Syria 74

tallow 101
Tamar Brewery 170–1
tap, the 210
tea 19, 22, 28
tendering system 29, 30, 39, 46
tenders 194
Tetuan 74
Thames, the 11, 49, 50, 137
theft 75, 155–6, 161–2
Thomson, Alexander 78
Tilghman, Abraham 9
Times, The 180
tobacco 11, 22, 80
Todd, William 172, 174 n.39, 175
tongues 29, 104
Tonkin, Digory 141 n.15
Torbay 44, 45, 77
Toulon 12, 65, 70
Tower Hill 58, 136
Towry, George Phillips 57 n.58, 80–1, 113–20, 123, 154, 164, 168–9, 184, 191 n.24, 193, 215–16, 220, 224
Towry, Captain Henry John 233
Towry, John 233–4
trade guilds 35
Transport Board 59, 61, 90, 98, 111–12, 121, 137, 145, 197–201, 221
transports 48, 54, 67
Treasury 20, 22–3
Trevithick, Richard 85, 133
Trincomalee 79
Trinidad 82
Trinity House 167
Triscott, Samuel 170
Tucker, Benjamin 68
turnips 12, 25, 26
Tynemouth 12, 43
typhoid 8

Udney, John 70, 78 n.52
unnecessary paperwork 195, 197–200

vegetables, fresh 11, 42, 49, 71 ,80
'Veritas' 178–181
victualling books 93
victualling stores 21
victualling warrants 47, 49
vinegar 18
Virginia 165
visitations to yards 54–7, 151, 204–5
volcanic eruptions 25

wages 139, 140, 152–4, 190
Ward, William 164–5
warders 134, 149
Warren, Sir John Borlase, 73
Warwickshire 23
watchmen 149, 150, 155, 162
water 21, 42, 97, 101
Waterford 24
Watson, Ralph 172 n.34, 173–5
Watts, John 105, 126–7, 131
Watts, Thomas 167
weather 24, 39, 41, 64, 69, 83, 215
Wedgwood, Josiah 219
Weevil yard 45, 97, 158
weevils 99
Wellesley, Lord Richard 101
Wellesley, Lt General Sir Arthur 71, 82
Wellington, see Wellesley, Arthur
wells 97
Welsh, Thomas 115–16, 184–5, 234
West Africa 20
West Indies 12, 20, 22, 48, 66, 68, 77, 78, 82, 83, 164

wheat 12, 25, 26, 27, 28, 40, 46, 48, 55, 57, 73
whippings 161
White & Son 105
White, John 170
Whitehead, William 165
Whitshed, Admiral 57
Whitstable 34
Wickey, William Henry 144, 178, 181–2
widows 154
Wilkie, Patrick 67, 148
Wilkins, chief clerk 118
Wilkinson, William 138, 165–6
Wills, William 74
Wilson, John 57
Windham, William, MP 114
wine 22–3, 37, 67, 71–2, 145, 182
Wingo Sound 69
women's ration 17
Woodford 34
Woolwich 59
workers' wives 161
Worswell, Alexander 82
wort cake 99

Yarmouth 34, 43–5, 70, 77–8, 103, 136
Yeames, Henry Lavage 73
yeastless bread 99
yellow fever 68
Yorke, Charles 116, 220 n.15, 229
Yule, Captain J 99